THE VANKE WAY

THE VANKE WAY

Lessons on
Driving Turbulent Change
from a
Global Real Estate Giant

WANG SHI

New York Chicago San Francisco Athens London
Madrid Mexico City Milan New Delhi
Singapore Sydney Toronto

1 2 3 4 5 6 7 8 9 0   LCR   21 20 19 18 17 16

ISBN 978-1-259-64307-1
MHID 1-259-64307-7

e-ISBN 978-1-259-64308-8
e-MHID 1-259-64308-5

Translated from the Chinese by Martha Avery.

McGraw-Hill Education books are available at special quantity discounts to use as premiums and sales promotions, or for use in corporate training programs. To contact a representative, please visit the Contact Us page at www.mhprofessional.com.

CONTENTS

FOREWORD

BY NING GAONING*

Many praise Wang Shi these days, as well as Vanke, the company founded by him in 1984. Looking back, however, one can see that this company started as a very ordinary and immature enterprise. It made all possible mistakes, yet it is one of the fortunate few to survive. The real estate industry in China has been around for only 20 years or so, but Vanke has already become one of its old-timers. Wang Shi woke up in time to take action before mistakes swept him under, and therefore he has a story to tell. It is the story of a hero and also that of an ordinary man. In my opinion, it is well worth retrospection.

This past 20 years has been an epoch of condensed and ferocious change. Chinese enterprises that survived, and their entrepreneurs, have been put through challenges posed by the transition of politics and economy. They have become pioneers and precedents; those who follow are now able to look at the future from a wholly new perspective.

Opportunistic ventures, transaction driven, were the primary modus operandi when businesses were being set up in China 20-some years ago. Wang Shi began with the business of flipping things for a profit, or *dao-mai*.† He did not look very far into the future, certainly not to today. Recognize an opportunity, use the prevailing government policy, and make a pile of money was the game. Vanke played this game well: the chicken-feed story would not have become a Vanke legend otherwise. Wang Shi has said that if he persevered in that business, he would be China's King of Chicken Feed today. That may be true, but I dare say back then he had nothing like the breadth of vision he has now. His abilities had not matured in terms of selection of business lines, sophistication of business management, and evaluation of industry structures. If he had continued with a simplistic trading model, he would long since have joined the myriad of Shenzhen companies that disappeared.

---

*Ning Gaoning is chairman of the Sinochem Group as of early 2016, a company that is in the process of buying Syngenta for around $48 billion. Known in English as Frank Ning, he received an MBA in the United States in 1987. He headed China Resources for many years, one of Vanke's main shareholders.

†Reselling at a profit: China began a two-track system of pricing in 1981; the system ended about 1998–1999. During this period, it was possible for those with access to lower-priced goods to resell those goods at a higher market price and keep the profit. This was known as *dao-mai*, which means flipping something, or reselling. Lower prices applied to materials allocated by the state plan; higher prices applied to materials available through the market.

Instead, Wang Shi learned how to change. This is what distinguishes his story. He planted a seed that had the genes of an oak tree in it, not a blade of grass. He constantly evaluated his environment, explored alternatives, and forced himself upward. I believe that studying Vanke's ability to change is more important than studying the company's successes. Recognizing the company's confidence and belief in itself is more important than merely looking at its business devices.

Vanke was ambitious from the beginning. In the early days, the business environment was seductive, and Vanke was not able to withstand temptations: Wang Shi took the company into highly diverse operations. He felt that it could do anything and everything, not because he had an unwarranted sense of confidence but because he lacked an understanding of strategic planning and the competitive environment. Problems of over-diversification are some of the most intractable issues in China. Vanke also went through this phase.

Today, Vanke is a specialized professional real estate company. Getting to this point has been less a matter of buying land, building buildings, or excelling in financing methods than it has been a matter of faith in its ability to transform itself. After recognizing that its core business was real estate, Wang Shi began a program of divesting assets. This took courage. It required firm stewardship, since opposition from many people could easily have derailed the process. If Wang Shi leaves any trace on China's corporate history in the future, it will be because he was able to restructure his company in a smooth, stable manner, even as he continued to do business and to grow at a fast rate.

In the years that I have known Wang Shi, I have seen him divest Vanke of a distilled water company, a retail chain, a film production company, an advertising company, and a company that makes commercial gifts. I have seen him pour investment into land, real estate, and real estate companies. Vanke's balance sheet shows the results. It is impressive. In the years since China Resources* became the largest shareholder in Vanke, China Resources has not only seen its investment rise at a respectable rate but it has seen this company raise the level of professionalism of the entire industry.

Relative to 20-some years ago, we are all more professional. Essentially all levels of management in China have been through a baptism of fire. Wang Shi and Vanke are rightly praised for being in the forefront of the real estate industry, but at the same time they have won people's respect as they transformed themselves. We can all benefit from reflecting upon their example.

---

*Ning Gaoning was the head of China Resources when it bought control shares of Vanke. This state-owned company was originally set up in 1948. China Resources remains one of the largest and most powerful state-owned enterprises in China. It includes a handful of publicly traded companies under its banner, which constitute more than half of the group. Control shares of these are held by China Resources, but financing is international.

My name comes from the surnames of my father and mother: Wang (King), and Shi (Rock). I am glad that the combination suggests mountains. My mother's real name was once much longer due to her Manchu heritage as a member of the Xibo tribe. My mother and her nomadic heritage have been a major influence in my life—my love of mountains has been one result. It is a theme throughout this book since the analogy of mountain climbing is apropos to the challenges of modern China.

My life has traversed an extraordinary period in China's history. When friends encouraged me to write this book, they asked me to put my story in the context of what happened over the past 30-some years. As chairman of the board of a very large urban housing developer, I can say that I have ridden the crest of a wave that has lasted for more than three decades. I have seen changes beyond belief. I cannot claim to see into the future, but some of what I have learned may be helpful to those who face accelerating change as we go forward.

Mountain climbing requires a firm decision, then focus, discipline, and all the things that one might expect of any extreme physical effort. Above all, mountain climbing requires the ability to meet the unexpected with equanimity and a willingness to adapt and change. My cardinal message in this book is that we must be able to change. We must clearly evaluate where we are, globally, nationally, individually, and be prepared for the toughness and versatility that will be required to meet what is ahead.

In these chapters, I set down my own record. Where possible, I draw lessons that seem to have served me well. I note that these are different from the Machiavellian notions in the business books now found in such profusion in our bookstores. My approach to doing business and my approach to people are similar: be open, remain aboveboard, and "let the sunshine in." I believe that this approach is effective and also necessary whether one is building a stable business or considering long-term solutions to global problems.

I have taken inspiration from many people in my life. There are notable individuals I could mention, but the most encouraging people have been a group of blind children I came to know in Tibet. They cannot see, but they can hear and they have minds to think. They feel one's face with their hands, and their openness and humanity is palpable. Their great gift, to themselves and others, is self-confidence and a sense of hope. Whatever our limitations or our capacities, we can always move out and move upward. In some small measure, I hope that this book will encourage others to feel the same way.

ACKNOWLEDGMENTS

My profound thanks to my mother, Shi Lei; my father, Wang Hui; and my publisher CITIC Press Group. In addition, I would like to express my immense gratitude to Martha Avery, to McGraw-Hill, and, of course, to my readers.

CHAPTER ONE

Scarlet and Black,
1983–1987

A Wild Spirit

I was born into a military tradition. My father was in the army and then worked in the Railroad Bureau in Zhengzhou, in central China. My mother descends from the Xibo tribe, a nomadic and martial group of people.* Historically based in the northeast, the heartland of the Manchu empire, one branch of the Xibo trekked from Liaoning to the Ili River Basin in the far west during the Qing dynasty. They stayed there to protect the western border for the Manchu rulers. I have always liked to think that I carry on that wild spirit and that deep appreciation of life's journey.

I began to climb mountains when I was small. In my first year of grade school, when I was still in Beijing, I remember being taken by our teacher on an outing with classmates to the nearby mountains. Three teams competed to reach the top of a mountain first. Competitive from the beginning, I carried the banner for my team and planted it on the summit before anyone else. This was the first time I had achieved "glory" outside the family circle, and from that time I began to love mountain climbing.†

As children, my siblings and I were sent to my maternal grandmother's home every summer in the mountainous part of Liaoning Province. Traveling there required two train changes, and after we reached a small station in western Liaoning, we still had to walk through the mountains for miles. We were living at the time in Zhengzhou, in central China, and our mother took us to the first train station, but the rest was up to us.

Being competitive had its problems. Once I joined the local mountain children in stealing melons. When the man watching over the melons fell asleep, we

---

*Xibo: The name is a Manchu word, alternately spelled *Xibe* and *Sibe* in English transliteration. Remaining members of the tribe around Ili use a modified Manchu script. The Qianlong emperor of the Manchu Empire conquered Xinjiang, then known as Eastern Turkestan, and garrisoned part of the Xibo tribe there in 1764 to defend the new frontier. Some scholars assert that the Russians named Siberia after the Sibe/Xibe.

†As a passionate mountaineer, Wang Shi climbed Mount Everest from the North and South faces in 2003 and 2010, respectively. He is the eleventh person in the world to accomplish "7 + 2"—reaching the seven summits (the highest peaks in the seven continents) in 2004 and the North and South Poles in 2005.

crept into his patch and began to take the fruit. The others fled when he woke up and saw what was happening. I hid where I was, and when the guard eventually went back to sleep I took off my shirt, filled it as full as I could with ripe melons and took them back to the others. From that point on, I was considered chief of the local gang. I was mediocre as a student, however, in all subjects except math. I often played hooky.

The Cultural Revolution broke out in 1966, before I had graduated from middle school. Two years later, at the age of 17, I was recruited into the Third Military Convoy Team of the air force, as a truck driver. After six months of training, I was assigned to the Ninth Vehicle Brigade of the air force, stationed in the far western province of Xinjiang. I was responsible for hauling equipment and provisions from north to south in this vast province. Even in Xinjiang, I took the chance to climb hills whenever possible. Once, on a job in southern Xinjiang, I stayed at a military post at the foot of some mountains. Early the next morning, I headed out to climb a peak alone, without telling anyone, thinking that I could get back by dinnertime. Night came on and I couldn't feel my way down. Hungry, freezing, exhausted, I finally made it back in the early hours of dawn. To my surprise, the troop had mobilized forces to search for me, since two convicts from a nearby labor camp were on the loose and fellow troop members thought I might have been killed.

The discipline required for solo climbing and the group discipline required by the army were quite different. In both respects, life on the frontier trained my willpower. Sandstorms, freezing winters, and scorching summers were the least of it. The worst was the monotony. To deal with this, I asked my older sister to mail books to me that I read under my bedding after the lights of the troop had gone out. I taught myself a certain amount of math, biology, and chemistry, and it was during this period that I read Stendhal's *Le Rouge et le Noir*, Pushkin's *The Captain's Daughter*, Cao Xueqin's *Dream of the Red Chamber,* and other classics.

I was demobilized and sent back to Zhengzhou in 1973. I began repairing boilers in a factory that belonged to the railroad system: from this position one had the slight possibility of being sent to university. One year later, I was indeed sent to study, albeit in the Drainage Department of the Lanzhou Railroad Institute. Since I was not actually fond of the subject of drainage, I spent my spare time studying English and political economy. By the time I graduated, I could read things like Dickens's *David Copperfield* in the original.

After graduating in 1977, I was assigned to be a technician in Guangzhou at the Fifth Section of the Railroad Bureau. This was the start of a whole new chapter in life, and also a new chapter in the story of China's economic ascent.

The province of Guangdong was changing dramatically just at that time. Mao Zedong had died in 1976, the Gang of Four had been deposed, and a new political will was changing the contours of China's economic system. The first place to feel the new policy was Guangdong. Considered a backward place, it was selected to be the start of an experiment, an opening, due to its proximity to Hong Kong. A new era was beginning, changing the destinies of countless people, some sooner, some later. People in Guangdong became thoroughly immersed in a tremendous wave of change, and I was in the earliest group of people there to feel its effect.

Life in the South

The fuzz of local cottonwoods had already blown free of the trees by April 1978.

Instead of spring breezes, what one noticed were the dead pigs tossed by the roadside, crawling with flies. The stench of animal excrement and rotting corpses was ubiquitous at my first job in the south China coastal area known as Shenzhen.

My task was to supervise the drainage project of a quarantine disinfecting station. China supplied the densely populated city of Hong Kong with all live animals. Any animals that entered Hong Kong from China had to be shipped first to Shenzhen. There they were funneled into the "North Station" at a place called Sungang. In addition to rotten produce, any livestock that were sick or had died were removed here before the rest were shipped in railroad cars into Hong Kong territory. The train passed over what was soon to become a famous bridge called Luohu Bridge. Part of the quarantine process involved disinfecting the empty cars on their return.

In 1978, Shenzhen was still a restricted region. Few could get into this part of China's border defense; I had been assigned here because of my expertise in drainage. After graduating from the Railroad Institute in Lanzhou, Gansu Province, in western China, I was first assigned to work in the Railroad Bureau's Fifth Section (Company). My salary at the time was RMB 42 (about USD [U.S. dollars] 24.70)* per month. Our group was responsible for various construction projects along the railroad section from Pingshi in the north, at the border between Guangdong and Hunan, to Luohu Bridge in the south, at Shenzhen. Several projects might be underway at any given time in this section. In 1978, we were given the task of overseeing the disinfecting at Sungang. Since Shenzhen was still strictly controlled, not just anybody could get in.

One time I went briefly to Shatoujiao town in the east of Shenzhen. I walked along a winding path paved in stones until I came to a large and forbidding stone monument that marked the border with the territories of Hong Kong. One was strictly forbidden to go beyond this point. Another time, I received permission through someone I knew to visit the inspection station beside Luohu Bridge. Among restricted border areas, Luohu Bridge was the most forbidden of all. Trains that were to cross the bridge were inspected several times. Armed soldiers would go up and down, poking long poles under every car. The poles had mirrors on the end of them, to catch people clinging to the underside. While railroad cars were being inspected for dead animals at Sungang, people would

---

*USD 1 was approximately RMB 1.7 in 1978. In this book, all local currencies are converted to USD according to the exchange rate at the time the amount is specified.

sneak into the spaces between axles and the bottom of the chassis. They hoped to escape detection and make their way to Hong Kong, there to seek their dreams in a totally different world. They risked their lives doing this. Some did get through, but most were intercepted and some were knocked off their perch by the train's vibration and killed.

Directly on the other side of Luohu Bridge lay Hong Kong. Beyond the river, a seductive landscape shimmered in the distance.

Those familiar with history will remember that Hong Kong was ceded to Great Britain by the Qing dynasty government in three stages. The first was after the Opium War of 1842, when the Qing government signed the Treaty of Nanjing with England under which Hong Kong Island was ceded. The second was in 1860, when the British and French Allied Army occupied Beijing and the Qing government signed the Beijing Treaty, under which the southern part of Kowloon Peninsula was ceded. The third was in 1898 under the Sino-British special accord delineating the Hong Kong boundary, when the Qing government leased the northern part of Kowloon Peninsula as well as Lantau and other islands and coastal regions to England. The term of this lease was 99 years, and it ended on June 30, 1997.

Work conditions at the North Station of Sungang were primitive. Temporary quarters were erected beside the railroad. More than 30 people crowded into living quarters in bamboo-mat huts. I chose an upper bunk among rows of iron bunk beds, and crawled in to write time schedules for our work, to read, and to sleep. The mosquitos of this southern region are notorious. Bites would swell into huge sores and itch unbearably. Ants invaded everything. Flies covered the clotheslines strung up in the tent and the string pulls to the lights, giving us gooseflesh.

After dinner, the men would gather before a 19-inch TV set. I generally retreated under my mosquito net to read, but sometimes I would be tempted out and find to my amazement that my colleagues were watching Hong Kong stations. We saw a world of sexy ads and vivacious faces. We would furtively watch for five minutes at a time, then switch the channel back to Guangdong. After two minutes we'd switch again to Hong Kong, back and forth. A regulation in this restricted region of the border absolutely forbade anyone to watch capitalist, corrupt, decadent, fallen-lifestyle Hong Kong television.

The biggest headache for those of us who had to supervise the workers was not that they watched Hong Kong television, but that they constantly disappeared. Every morning, a bunk or two would be empty—its occupant had escaped to the other side of the river. I always wondered as I looked at the empty bunks, had they gone in search of a better job? Gone for freedom and the ability to watch Hong Kong television? Many left families behind, though some managed to take them. If caught, they were returned and sometimes lost their lives. Was it worth it?

One Sunday morning, a sturdy farmer rode his heavy-duty bicycle up to our huts. He put me on behind, and pedaled me to a place 6 kilometers (3.73 miles) north of our station at Sungang. He took me to a village called Huanggang. During the Socialist Education Movement, my father-in-law had stayed in this village doing what in the parlance back then was called "living at the grassroots level in order to guide work." His host at the time was this very same farmer who now came to fetch me. The farmer's name was Zhuang Shunfu, but everyone called him Cowboy. By now, he was the mayor of Huanggang.

Cowboy invited me into his home. The furnishings were sparse. A blackened wok sat on top of a wood-burning stove. A bellows stood beside it, and on the wall was a palm-bark rain cape. Cowboy did not talk much and his Mandarin was hard to understand. When his mother, who managed the household, and his wife, who worked in the fields, came in, I found their dialect even harder to comprehend. We ate dinner together, and the two women kept adding food to my bowl. Even without the aid of language to communicate, they made me feel that, in this Hakka home,* I was welcome.

Cowboy took me home after dinner, riding fast down the road. He explained that he was simultaneously troop chief of the local militia, so he had to dash back to be on duty. Huanggang was right on the border, beside the river, and was therefore a favorite spot for illegals to escape. The town itself was in a privileged position: for historical reasons, half of its fields lay on the far side of the river. Villagers were authorized to cross over to tend their fields, and so could go freely back and forth. In fact, most of them went only in one direction. Cowboy said that he was the only one of his age left in Huanggang of all of his middle school classmates.

As our project continued, I looked forward to its early conclusion. I wanted to get away from this place called Shenzhen, even though it was only a river away from Hong Kong.

Things were soon to change. In the summer of 1979, the western part of Shenzhen, called Shekou, "snakemouth" in English, due to its geography, was granted approval to be developed. This was done under the management of the Hong Kong Merchants Bureau.†[1] Bulldozers were soon pushing earth here and there. Mountains were moved, and the most energetic people in all of China swarmed to Shekou. In just over one year, a new coastal city sprang up. It pulsed with vitality, was connected to convenient transportation, and looked modern. It happened so fast that it seemed like a mirage.

Deng Xiaoping was later to say, "Shekou was fast because people were given a few rights." This small portion of "rights" was enough to propel the start of

---

*Hakka people are a cohesive group who immigrated into southern China centuries ago but retained their language and identity. Sun Yat-sen was Hakka, as have been many other notable people in China.

†See the end note for a description of the China Merchants Bureau. A man named Yuan Geng, who Wang Shi mentions later in this book, was made deputy head of this historic organization and given a patch of land to develop a new economic model. That model, at Shekou, was not far from Shenzhen. It was successful, and Shenzhen was then given the green light to "open" to the outside world.

a whole new set of management concepts and methods, what people were soon to begin calling the Shekou model.

The principles of the Shekou model sound commonplace today. They included reducing multiple levels of authority; simplifying organizations; appointing people for actual work and not just to positions; establishing jobs that fit the needs, not forcing jobs into a structured hierarchy; and allowing the enterprise itself to determine jobs, costs, and profits. People were hired for a given task and would be rehired only if there was a need and if the person was capable. All ranks of "cadres" were not allowed to be classified by their previous standing. Instead, they were given a vote of confidence once a year or were either voted in or voted out. Mobility of staff and personnel in general was permitted: factories could fire workers, and workers were allowed to leave their jobs. These were "rights" that existed in just one tiny corner of China at the time. At the time, they represented earth-shattering change to most people.

Chosen by Fate

When the Shenzhen project ended, I continued to shuttle back and forth along the main railroad line, although I was not very keen on the work. A romantic, I was more inclined to the richer palette of idealism. I dreamed of becoming all kinds of unattainable things. Perhaps a traveling doctor? A sailor on the wide ocean? Maybe an engineer working in wireless communications?

In fact, I was chosen by fate to live in the real world. At the age of 17, as a soldier, I yearned to be a wireless operator but instead was assigned to five years of trucking in a desolate place. Demobilized in 1973, at the age of 22, I desperately wanted to go to college and study medicine or law. Instead, I was given two choices: I could rivet boilers, or I could continue to be a driver. I chose the boilers. I received a coupon for 24.5 kilograms (54 pounds) of rice every month for my work, and I worked on boilers for one year.

At the time, driver was a privileged occupation. Instead, I chose hard labor. This was the price I paid for the chance to be on a list of names of those who might conceivably be allowed to go to college. I got on the list, but the school to which I was assigned was not what I wanted, and the subject of drainage was even less appealing. After graduating I was assigned to southern China, to Guangzhou. I liked the scenery and I liked the modern feel of Guangzhou with its new ties to the outside world, but the job of cleaning up after dead pigs was again not my first choice.

Still, what would I have done if given my own choice? The dreams of my youth had long since faded. I was approaching my thirties, when one should be able to stand on one's own, as the Confucian saying has it. I was clear about only one thing: before any possible opportunity came by, I had to study. I had to seize every moment and study. I had to lay in knowledge for future use, no matter what it might be, so that I could catch the chance of the future when it came. Otherwise, I might miss it.

I always took a book along when I traveled the railroad. After dinner I read, and I took notes on what I read.

I focused on the English language in particular. In the course of studying foreign languages, I came to know professor Zeng Zhaoke in the Foreign Languages Department of Jinan University. Professor Zeng had been senior superintendent in the Hong Kong–British government police department, and he was well versed in Hong Kong politics, economics, and social conditions. Studying with him opened a door to understanding the life of Hong Kong.

One weekend, there was a concert at the Guangzhou Friendship Theater. The Hong Kong violinist Liu Yuansheng played a concerto with the Guangzhou Orchestra. I went backstage afterwards to congratulate the soloist. Mr. Liu immediately gave me a record of his performance of the piece and this became the start of an enduring friendship. Mr. Liu was to become one of our business partners in Shenzhen Vanke. After the company went public, he was one of its major shareholders.

Time passed quickly as extraordinary events began to unfold in China. On August 26, 1980, Ye Jianying, head of the Party Committee of the National People's Congress of China, presided over the historic occasion of the Fifteenth Session of the Fifth National People's Congress.* This Congress passed a resolution officially establishing the Shenzhen Special Economic Zone. August 26, 1980, was the day Shenzhen was born.

As a result of these changes, I was finally able to leave the railroad system that same year. I was hired to join the Foreign Trade Commission of Guangdong province, with the invigorating task of attracting in foreign trade and investment. My life changed overnight. I was now allowed to enter previously forbidden fancy hotels. I participated in the Canton Trade Fair every spring and autumn. The sun was new every day; everything was fresh and exciting. I got up early, went home late, and worked hard, trying to make up for the precious time I had lost. In 1981, Japanese 125cc motorcycles made their appearance in Guangzhou. Our division bought two of them, one of which was assigned to me. With a safety helmet on my head, I drove this red machine in circles around the city, nearly exploding with joy.

Problems began to crop up just as I was happiest.

They came during the spring fair of 1982, at the Dongfang Hotel. I accompanied my boss as he entertained an important foreign manufacturer. One of the links in the process of courting foreign investment was to introduce the guest to the chairman of the Foreign Economic Commission at a banquet. To lighten the atmosphere of the occasion, I spoke volubly on light subjects and helped create a happy mood among the guests. At the end of the dinner, the foreigners praised my abilities, which undeniably stoked my vanity.

After the guests left, my boss took me aside and criticized me savagely:

---

*Ye Jianying was born into a wealthy Hakka family in Guangdong. As the most powerful man in the province after the fall of the Gang of Four, he was instrumental in taking Shenzhen and then Guangzhou into the modern world.

"Who do you think you are to take over the role of host? Remember, the gun shoots the bird that takes off first!"

I was speechless. This rigidly traditional approach to people's rank effectively killed my enthusiasm. From then on, I came to work and left promptly on time. My papers were organized and ready before it was time to leave. I put 10 percent of my energy into work and 90 percent into ever-wilder motorcycle rides, Ping-Pong, and chess.

At the end of the year, I was astonished to hear the leaders say in my evaluation that I had made a very satisfactory change. They praised my maturity, my stability: "This is the very sort of person we want to bring along, for promotion in the future." Hard work was criticized; slacking off was praised. This was too ironic. I began to think of leaving, but where to go? Try to study overseas, or maybe accept an offer to become a sailor with a shipping company?

Just at this time, the pioneer Yuan Geng was espousing a new slogan at a place called Shekou, 130 kilometers (81 miles) away from Guangzhou and next to Shenzhen:* "Time is money; efficiency is life." Suddenly, Shenzhen now became the biggest construction site in the world. The People's Liberation Army sent 20,000 soldiers there to engage in a mighty construction "battle" under the orders of the State Council and the Central Military Commission. They worked night and day to build a new city.

In the blink of an eye, it was springtime 1983. Mr. and Mrs. Cowboy arrived in Guangzhou to pay a call on my wife's father and mother. They brought fresh shrimp that they had caught themselves and a basketful of California apples. Cowboy wore a jacket made in Taiwan. He had lost a lot of hair, but his wife's hair was the more remarkable because it was permed into tight curls. When we asked where she had accomplished this, she just put her head down and blushed. In the space of three years, major changes had been taking place in Shenzhen.

Cowboy happily told us that the two mountains flanking the Luohu District had been leveled. The dirt had been bulldozed into low-lying areas. Many young people from Hong Kong had come back, driving eight-ton dump trucks for moving dirt. They were making a fortune, more than they could ever make in Hong Kong.

What interested me most was Cowboy's description of the needs of a troop of soldiers who were garrisoned near Huanggang, assigned to work on the construction. Not only did they need water, electricity, and housing, but Cowboy recognized they needed a food supply. The local produce was insufficient, so he found a northerner to partner with and soon was able to import fresh vegetables from over the border in Hong Kong territories. He also began to import equipment for construction.

Five years of abysmal army life suddenly floated before my eyes. Determination

---

*See endnote on page 263.

came over me and I felt my spirits rise: I would go to Shenzhen. I would begin to test my worth as an individual.

I was 33 years old. I had been a soldier and a laborer. I had spent three years in a government office. I had experience and considerable self-confidence. Like the main character in my beloved *Le Rouge et le Noir*, I was not willing to be mediocre. I was ambitious and I wanted to fight with my own individual strength.

I knew at that moment that my future lay in Shenzhen.* There I would realize my dreams.

The Building of the Shenzhen Special Economic Zone

On May 7, 1983, I took the train into Shenzhen. Cowboy was at the station to meet me. A dilapidated Japanese car had replaced his heavy-duty bicycle.

This car bounced along the bumpy road to Huanggang with its engine sputtering, as though it might die any minute. Through its windows, I saw a forest of construction cranes. Workers in helmets crawled everywhere; diesel engines roared as dump trucks went by in a continuous stream. Clouds of exhaust turned daytime into a brown haze, and my nose and throat were soon coated with dust. Feelings of crazy joy and terror passed over me, and I found myself sweating.

After three years, everything at Huanggang had changed. The northern part of the village was now a warren of temporary housing—metal shacks. A mountain of old tires was piled on the side of Main Street. The surrounding rice fields had been excavated and turned into fishponds on which floated white bits of plastic and empty Coca-Cola cans. The bamboo groves were gray, covered with soot. An enormous dump truck was parked at a crossroads, and a young man covered with axle grease was lying underneath trying to fix it. Cowboy told me that he was one of the young men who had gone to Hong Kong to work three years ago and who had returned this year, driving this truck.

I wondered if transport had become Huanggang's main source of income. It turned out Cowboy bought the tires and discarded construction materials in Hong Kong, then sold them up in northern China; the business was lucrative. He encouraged me to join in the trade.

I was not inclined to deal in trash, but I could see a wealth of business opportunities. I politely declined Cowboy's invitation. That night, I stayed in a five-story building on the east side of Shenzhen. Floors 2 to 5 were let out to guests. The first floor was a small workshop making semi-transistor radios. It hired around 30 employees and was run by a small-time investor from Hong Kong.

---

*Shenzhen opened to the "outside" in 1982–1983, when the central government allowed the zone to import consumer goods. Deng Xiaoping visited the zone on January 24, 1984, and declared, "We were correct in our policy of setting up Special Economic Zones." This statement confirmed that it was now permissible to do business, and it had the effect of catapulting not just the development of Shenzhen but also the economy of China in general.

Before visiting Shenzhen, I had already made up my mind what to do. The most influential company in Shenzhen at the time was the Shenzhen Special Economic Zone Development Company, generally abbreviated to Special Development (SD). I had already decided to approach this unique organization. Its parentage was of key importance, since it was an offshoot of the party committee that managed the zone. In the early days of the Special Zone, most projects were negotiated and contracts signed by this "management committee." It also served as the zone's acting government. After the Special Zone's government was officially established in its own right, the committee was dissolved, but the same people were phased into becoming the heads of SD. SD had the right to control imports and exports in the Special Zone. The only difference from before was that its official stamp for approving imports and exports had a No. 2 on it, to distinguish it from the government's No. 1 stamp. One can imagine the power of a company that was given the right to approve all imports into China and all exports out of China.

With a letter of introduction in hand that was from the provincial Foreign Economic Commission, I looked up a Mr. Sun Kaifeng, the man at the helm of this company called SD. Mr. Sun came from Jiangsu. He was rather chubby. His face was ruddy and gleaming, and he looked prosperous. He had been the party secretary in charge of what now would be called the Sports Bureau of Guangdong province before coming to Shenzhen.

Our talk went well. It was agreed that I would be the local representative sent by the Foreign Economic Commission of Guangdong Province to work with SD on business development. SD would provide me with permits to carry on certain businesses, and it would assign me a bank account number. It would not invest in any potential business, however. It would take no risk. Any and all profits were to be split 50/50 between SD and the Foreign Economic Commission.

The next day, I reported in to the trade department of SD. A professional military man named Zhang Xifu* reported in on that same day. Prior to the Cultural Revolution, this person had been assigned to the air force, to learn to be a pilot. During the Cultural Revolution, however, he was made to work as a common laborer due to being tainted by the "background" of his father. Once the father was rehabilitated, Zhang Xifu went back into a military uniform and was now in a second career. Like me, he was quite happy to seek his fortune in the Special Economic Zone.

The person who received the two of us was a Mr. Lu Runling, general manager of the Trade Department of SD. A thin Hakka man, he had been editor in chief of a newspaper and had long been involved in propaganda work. He explained the situation succinctly: "The Trade Division has no money. Instead, it has three kinds of rights. It can grant permits, issue documents—that is a paper right. It can grant land—that is a location right. And it has bragging

---

*The given name is pronounced "she-foo." In Chinese transliteration, the letter x is pronounced "sh." Zhang Xifu figures prominently later in Wang Shi's story.

right—it is supposed to talk up the benefits of the Special Zone and reform. If you want to follow the straight and proper road, first, you do not do things that are against the law. Second, you make sure to stand near a big tree, which means you rely on the protection and resources of ministries in Beijing. Third, you get close and stay close to major sums of money. Our purpose is to draw international funding into the Special Zone. To summarize: walk the upright road, rely on a big tree, get close to the god of wealth."

Zhang Xifu and I were assigned to the Trade Department's First Division. The head of the division was a woman from Beijing named Shan Xuan. There was a professional staff member named Qiu Qihao whom everyone called by the nickname Qiu Gong—"worker Qiu"—since he was senior to us in having an education. Then there was a local person, Cai Zuoxing, and a person who had just graduated from the Guangzhou Foreign Language Institute, named Chen Chao.

Everyone in the division did his own business, relying on his connections and vying for deals that came through the door. Ms. Shan, from the Pharmaceutical Bureau in Beijing, went back and forth from Beijing importing medical equipment. Worker Qiu, who originally came from the Seventh Machinery Department, busied himself with supplying that department with imported central processing units for computers. Little Cai, who was tall and thin, imported spare parts, while Zhang Xifu immediately began to make phone calls to a construction group that was part of a steel factory in Guangzhou, hoping to get business from them.

I had no idea what I should do.

After making calls on a number of import and export companies in Shenzhen, I found that the best-selling imports were a Japanese flavoring called Ajinomoto and Taiwanese folding umbrellas. If you had a permit to import half a ton of Ajiimoto your life was easy, since the demand for this product would quickly take it off your hands. The same was true with umbrellas. I rejected both of these opportunities, however. I figured that by the time I had the goods in hand, the demand would have been met by others.

Instead, I went into chicken feed. The reason was simple: I saw the opportunity to add considerable value. One day, I took a minibus to Shekou. At an intersection, I saw a tall white metal-sided silo. Curious, I inquired about it and learned that this was a corn granary, for feed for the livestock industry. Three parties jointly invested in this granary: the Chia Tai Group of Thailand, an American grain company, and a Shenzhen-based chicken-raising company. It was a joint venture for producing feed that was called the Conti Chia Tai Group.* A major company in Singapore called the Singapore Far East Organization relied on a mill at the port of Shekou for processing its flour as well as feed; the company that carried out this business was the Shekou Far East Gold Coin Flour and Feedmill Company.

---

*Chia Tai is also known as Charoen Pokphand Group. It is the leading agro-industrial and food conglomerate in Asia, and is one of the largest food companies in the world.

"What about corn?," I asked. Guangdong does not grow corn, after all. "Where does the corn come from?"

"From Hong Kong," a worker at Shekou told me.

"But surely Hong Kong does not grow corn either."

On further inquiry, I learned that the corn comes from the United States, Thailand, and the northeastern part of China.

"Why don't the buyers get their feed directly from China's northeast?"

To learn more, I went to see Conti Chia Tai Group. A tall man in glasses with a Chaozhou accent,* whose name was Lu Damin, received me. He told me that indeed the company would prefer to buy directly from China's northeast, to lower the cost of its raw materials, but that he could not resolve the problem of direct shipping.†

Freight was something I knew about. "I can handle that for you," I said. "Rail freight, ocean freight—no problem. Would you buy our corn if we handled all those shipping issues?"

"We certainly would," he responded. "We could sign a contract immediately. We are just in the process of arranging transshipment. Our feed mills can handle 300,000 tons per year, 70 percent of which is corn. Each month we need around 170,000 tons."

This was going to be big business from the start. I asked with some trepidation if Conti Chia Tai Group could open a letter of credit to the seller. That would mean I could endorse it on the back and give it on over to the real seller without having to put up any money myself. This was known in Chinese as "catching a white wolf with bare hands."‡

"As soon as we sign a contract, I'll open that letter of credit," Mr. Lu said happily.

"And you pay in foreign exchange?"

"Renminbi and foreign currency are all the same to us."

I told him that since the product would be supplied by a foreign trade organization, what I needed was foreign exchange.

"Okay."

I was not in fact familiar with transport between Northeast China and Shenzhen, but a large business opportunity encouraged me to learn fast.

---

*Many overseas Chinese in Thailand are of Chaozhou ancestry and speak the Chaozhou dialect.

†Shipping required Chinese government approval and being included in "the plan." As a foreign company, Chia Tai was not in a position to talk to the right people.

‡Also known as the "empty-handed way," since it required no capital investment. This was possible because there was an assured buyer, given the extreme scarcity of goods in the early 1980s. As China began opening up, the demand for goods greatly exceeded supply. The government imposed import restrictions on items and doled out authority, or "quota," for imports. Anyone with such quota could make money simply by selling the right to import an item. One way to build up capital therefore was to obtain quota from a government agency and resell it to importers. Since it required no capital investment, it was known as the empty-handed way. Meanwhile, importers often bought on terms that allowed them to resell the items before they ever needed to put up money. This too was an example of the empty-handed way.

First, I looked up the Port of Chiwan and asked about shipping between Dalian, the biggest port of China's corn-growing northeast area, and the Chiwan port. The manager told me that this newly established port could only accommodate bulk fertilizer from northern Europe. It had not yet established relations with all shipping lines.

I asked, "How large a bulk commodity freighter can you accommodate?"

"Ten thousand tons, no problem," the manager of the port told me.

I then looked up the Guangzhou Far East Shipping Company to see if there was any possibility of shipping between Dalian and the Port of Chiwan. The answer was that authority over shipping from nearby places was under the jurisdiction of the Guangzhou Ocean Shipping Co., Ltd.

I found out that the headquarters of this bureau was in Shameen, a sandbank island in southwest Guangzhou, so that was my next stop. I learned that so long as I had a commodity source, this company could open up a new shipping route at any time. They asked how much I intended to ship.

"Twenty thousand tons at a minimum, every month," I said with a certain authority in my voice. I already had a well-thought-out plan: 10,000 tons for Conti Chia Tai and 10,000 for Far East Gold Coin.

That is how the corn business began.

With permission from Mr. Lu, the thin Hakka man, we set up the Feedstuff Trade Team, which was independent of the trade department's first division. I was the head of the team, and our accounts were separate from the division. My problem now was that I needed someone to come help me do the business.

I remembered the assembly workshop owned and operated by a Hong Kong businessperson on the first floor of that little guesthouse in Shenzhen. Every day an acrid smell would waft up and down the halls of the building. I went back there, found the guard on duty, and asked if he could recommend a person to be a worker for me. The fellow swiveled his head in the direction of a man who was welding tin together: "Would he do?"

I saw that the object in question was puny, so small that he seemed a child worker. I held back a feeling of dismay. Nevertheless, my lips said, "Yes, he's fine."

He was 18 years old. That is how Deng Yiquan became my first employee. Together, we went into the business of corn.

How Can a Sparrow Know the Vision of a Swan?

Our first piece of business was for 30 tons of corn. This corn was packed into a railway car and sold to the Shenzhen-based chicken-raising company.*

Trucks carried off that 30 tons of corn, and I then went to the chicken-raising company to collect the money. I rode my bicycle. I had tied two bags on the

---

*Author's note: This company was the precursor of one that later went public and became highly successful, called Shenzhen Kondarl (Group) Co., Ltd.

back of the bike to carry the cash. As I rode along, I thought about how danger-ous it might be to carry all that money on a bicycle, and I resolved to be careful.

When I got to the chicken-raising company on Hongling Road, I found Manager Yuan of the company, and pointed to my bags. "The goods have all been taken away," I said. "I've come for the money."

Manager Yuan kept smoking a cigarette as he looked me over. "Invoice?" is all he said.

Invoice? I had worked at the Foreign Economic Commission of Guangdong province for three years and I was familiar with contracts, letters of credit, and so on, but I had never heard of an invoice. I was too embarrassed to ask. I guessed it must be a document like a receipt. "Ah, you want an invoice," I said. "I'll get it for you."

Biking back to SD, I went to the finance department and asked them to write me out a receipt, a "proof." The accountant had just graduated from Jinan University's Accounting Course. Her name was Zhang Min.

"Zhang, write me up a proof of receiving funds, please."

"What kind of proof?," this tiny lady asked me, doubtfully.

"Just write: 'Sold 30 tons of corn to Shenzhen Chicken-Raising Company, each ton 1,300 RMB [USD 660], total 39,000 RMB [USD 19,797]. This is proof of the fact.' Stamp it, and that should do it."

"I've never written that kind of proof before."

"Just write it up. The customer has requested it."

Zhang gave me the requested proof and sealed it with the stamp of the finance department. Back I went on my bike to the chicken-raising company, still with the bags clipped on back. I passed the proof over to Manager Yuan. "Here you are," I said, "the invoice."

Manager Yuan looked over this "proof" and his eyebrows rose. Then he let out a snort of pleasure. "Come along, Wang," he chuckled. "Come along with me."

He took me into his own finance department and drew an invoice from a drawer. "This has the seal of the National Tax Bureau on it," he explained. "This is printed specially. A proof cannot serve as an invoice that has been passed by the tax authorities. Go back and tell your finance department that you want an invoice. Your accountant will know what to do."

Zhang Min laughed when she saw me again. She had already prepared the necessary invoice, knowing I would be back. When I delivered it to the finance department of the chicken-raising company, they gave me a bank transfer docu-ment with duplicate copies.

I knocked yet again at the office of Manager Yuan. "How is it I get this paper and no money?," I asked. I was completely confused.

"Wang," he said with gentle pleasure, "you take these back and give them to your finance department. One copy goes to the bank. When the bank sees it, they transfer funds from our account to the SD account."

Part of me did not believe him. I went back to the company and handed the transfer documents to Zhang Min. "Is this supposed to be money?," I said.

"If the bank rejects the bill, it means the chicken-raising company has no money in its account. But that rarely happens. There shouldn't be any problem."

I began to relax after her patient explanation.

These two round-trips made me realize how little I knew about business, especially the financial side. I was out of my depth, so I set up a schedule: every evening after work, no matter what, I studied finance for two hours. Through self-study, I began to understand balance sheets, assets and liabilities. I also practiced with daily accounts. I studied how every day's transactions, payments, and income were recorded. At the beginning of each month, together with Zhang Min, I did a cross-check. Within three months, I was adept at reading financial statements.

With the money I made from this transaction, I bought a 1.5-ton Toyota truck. I now had several jobs: head of the team, marketing, transport manager, chicken-feed salesman, and driver. I was too busy to think. Working 20-hour days, I couldn't keep up.

Business was expanding, and even with three heads and six arms, we couldn't catch our breath. Since one assistant wasn't enough, I hired another, a local person named Huang Shihao, who taught in a private school. Gradually, through recruiting people and also through introductions from SD, our Feedstuff Trade Team grew to be seven people.

Although Deng Yiquan was small, he turned out to be super-energetic and willing, and he became a vital member of our team. What's more, every Friday he would wash "Manager Wang's" dirty clothes (he never called me "Team Leader Wang.") He had a grade-school education, wrote with strange and rudimentary handwriting, and was no good at math at all. Except for Huang Shihao, who had taught school, the verbal and writing skills of everyone in the village were on a par with Cowboy's. I therefore decided to start a class in culture for the young people. We met every Wednesday evening, for an hour. I taught math and language every other week. After teaching them, I would do my own studies in finance. Then, before sleeping, I would listen to half an hour of music, on tape, often Vivaldi's *The Four Seasons* or Dvorak's *From the New World*.

The business went ahead full steam. Once the shipping line was opened, the business with Conti Chia Tai Group and Far East Gold Coin Feedmill Company went smoothly. Money poured into the Feedstuff Team's line item account within SD's overall account. The word began to get around: the system that Wang set up by himself has made huge amounts of money but it has taken advantage of the reputation of SD. Anonymous letters came in thick and fast to the office of the general manager of SD.

The head of this office, Li Shoufen, was a man who had formerly been director of the General Office of the government of Bao'an County. He was short and stocky, with graying hair, and his voice was raspy, probably due to smoking. Whenever I went to get quota for feed imports approved at the SD office, I would generally nod politely if I happened to see him. It was just common courtesy. One time, however, Li Shoufen called me in to his office. He pulled out a sheaf of envelopes that had been opened. "You are doing a great job," he said. "The office is quite aware of this. I therefore don't feel I need to tell you what these letters have to say."

As I was leaving, this local person, born and bred there, patted me on the shoulder and said, "You go out there and fight. Don't you worry about not having us guard your back." The support of this old cadre warmed my heart.

Several people in the finance department generally handled communications with SD, but sometimes a business secretary named Zeng Guohua, a man with whom I particularly enjoyed talking, went with me.He had graduated from the Bao-an No. 1 High School. He liked to think about things. As we traveled along to the office of the general manager, he would start in on the subject of how to change the system of a socialist country in particular. For example, Hungary—he felt that an economist named Kornai in that country had ideas that were worth studying. In the midst of all the rumors and uncertainty about what was going to happen, it was a joy to meet a colleague with whom I could really converse.

The arrival of a new shipment of corn at the Sungang North Station was always exciting in these days. I would take Deng Yiquan with me, and we would hire some local boys to help package the corn into bags. It was like being a general on the field except that I generally joined in with the work crew. Young and strong then, I could easily hoist a 75-kilogram (165-pound) bag onto my shoulder and carry it, and keep that up for a dozen trips or more. During a rest break, one of the locals said to me, "It's not right for a city guy like you to be doing our work, hauling gunnysacks!" I laughed with him, but inside I was thinking, *How can a sparrow know the vision of a swan?*

A Two-Pack Cigarette Bribe

We kept selling corn to feed mills, but at the same time we began to expand our business. We sold feed for pigs and also for chickens, and our customers were soon distributed throughout the Pearl River delta area, as well as Hunan, Jiangxi, Guangxi, and other southern provinces. Our feedstuff products were well appreciated by companies that raised various animals, and marketing companies would line up with cash in order to get the goods. Bags with the brand name of Conti Chia Tai would roll out of the ovens, full of fragrant feed, ready to be shipped. Transport became a bottleneck to sales. From a cost standpoint, it was more rational to ship by rail for any distance over 200 kilometers (125 miles). The feedstuff products of the Special Economic Zone had not yet been incorporated into the railway freight traffic plan of the Ministry of Railway, however. At that time, if you wanted to use the railroads to ship your products you either had to be in the plan or you had to apply for an external or extra quota to get included in the plan. After making inquiries, I found out that it was in fact hard to get this application through proper channels.

I learned that the freight director of the Sungang North Station was a man named Yao. I also discovered that he liked to smoke cigarettes, and I found out where he lived. I gave Deng Yiquan RMB 20 (USD 10.10) and asked him to buy two packs of "555" cigarettes. I told him to take them over to Yao and just put them down, not saying anything: "Just leave them there and then come back." In 1983, "555" cigarettes cost RMB 10 (USD 5.05) for one pack.

Two hours later, Deng Yiquan was back, along with the cigarettes. "Director, Director!" he cried. "Yao won't take them."

"You mean I can't even give away two packs of cigarettes? If I can't make money, at least I ought to be able to spend it!" I decided to go see him myself. Riding my bicycle, I arrived at his residence. I knocked on the door and went in, then put the two packs on the table. All of this was done in a most unnatural fashion. It was the first time I had "sent presents" in order to get commercial benefit in return.

"You want railroad wagons?" asked the very practiced freight director. He smiled at me.

I was taken aback by this direct approach. To say yes seemed too abrupt. To say no was silly, for what was I doing there anyway? I asked if he could perhaps extend permission to use two railroad cars from the out-of-plan quota for shipping things by rail.

Director Yao picked up the two packs and handed them back to me. "Here, take these home," he said. "Tomorrow, either you or that small fellow of yours should meet me in my office. Come directly to the freight office. Two wagons are nothing. I'd even give you ten."

I was speechless.

"I noticed you long ago. You didn't know? I often saw this city boy working together with the locals out there, packing corn. It didn't seem to be punishment for some crime, and you also didn't seem to be hired labor. I thought to myself: this kid wants to get things done. All right, I thought, I'll help him. What can I do? I'm in the business of shipping freight by rail. What I can do is provide some out-of-plan railroad wagons. I had no idea you'd come knocking on my door. Do you know how much you should pay in a 'red-packet' (that is, a bribe) for getting one railroad wagon?"

I was suddenly drenched in sweat.

Director Yao extended two stubby fingers: "The red-packet for just one wagon is RMB 100 [USD 50.50]. Two packs of cigarettes, or RMB 20, are only one-fifth of the prevailing 'red-packet.' "

I carried the two packs of cigarettes back to my guesthouse. I lay down on my bed as Director Yao's face floated in my mind. Did he resent the fact that two packs were too little, or did he truly want to help me? I couldn't decide, and I spent a sleepless night tossing and turning.

The next day, permission came through smoothly for two out-of-plan railroad wagons.

This experience taught me an important principle: even in the business world, money does not buy everything. Money cannot buy respect and honor, which is what the director wanted from me. His needs were simple. He wanted to show appreciation of a certain work ethic and of my willingness to work together with local boys. He wanted to extend a helping hand and gain satisfaction from right behavior.

People have needs at two levels, material and spiritual. The former can be satisfied by money, but the latter cannot. Relations between people are also of two kinds, one that is nakedly materialistic and one that involves respect and honor. Since people have two sides, why not use your own behavior to create a resonance in someone's non-materialistic side? I blushed with shame as I thought of my motivation in taking cigarettes to Director Yao.

Having thought this through, I became clear about the bottom line in how I did business. I would not take or give bribes.

In some Southeast Asian countries, extending bribes has become the unwritten rule. If an enterprise does not engage in the practice, it finds it hard to survive. Unhealthy practices, including bribes, now also exist in China as the country experiments with market reform. Will China continue to follow this well-trodden path? If so, will it mean that clean companies cannot survive? I have no way to predict the future orientation of Chinese society, but I can only assume that China in its reform will not follow the wrong path. If this assumption proves to be incorrect, I would rather be a failure than dirty myself with the others.

On the Brink of Bankruptcy: When Cornered, Fight Back

In August 1983, newspapers in Hong Kong reported that cancer-causing elements had been discovered in chicken feed.

Within the space of one night, Hong Kong people stopped eating chicken. Instead, they ate pigeon. Nobody who raised chicken for the Hong Kong market could sell his products. The feedlots stopped buying any feed, and the feed factories stopped production. The sight at Conti Chia Tai was shocking: chicks that were just hatching were being shoveled into furnaces and burned. In the past, one had only read about these things in books—things like milk being poured into the ocean and newborn calves being slaughtered. Now this was happening for real. Tragedy and waste were there right before our eyes.

There's an old saying about collateral damage: "When the gates to the city catch fire, the fish in the moat suffer." Recently irresistible, the corn of the Wang Shi Feedstuff Team now became unsalable.

Within a month, feedstuff that had been on their way to Shenzhen in railroad cars began to pile up at the Sungang North Station. Warehouses were stuffed full of corn. Platforms were piled high with corn. Railroad cars loaded with corn kept arriving and there was nowhere to put it. Temporarily, it was poured out beside the tracks. Notices for arrival of cars full of corn began to increase beyond reason, and I began to feel that something was wrong. I got hold of packing slips and compared them to order slips and realized that we had already received four times the amount of corn that was to have come that month. We already had 4,000 tons!

A few calls to people who had shipped the goods told the story. Corn that had originally been ordered by others was redirected to Wang Shi. This was because the Hong Kong buyers did not open their letters of credit as required, or they sent word that their ordering plans had changed. The goods were simply sent to Wang Shi. Without the cancer-causing incident, this would have been great—the more corn, the better. Under current conditions, it was enough to make a person weep.

By now, the entire North Station at Sungang was covered with enormous piles of corn. Another 20 tons waited nearby, still in railroad cars.

A few days later a typhoon raked Shenzhen. After it had passed, I went to look over the stocks and found white bubbles frothing out of rips in the canvas that had been used to cover the corn. It was like the spittle produced by hairy crabs. The corn had sprouted. It had also begun to produce gas in the muggy weather. The air was full of the smell of fermentation. We were not just making fermented corn here, we were in the process of making corn alcohol! I quickly mobilized everyone in the company, and we hired 20 workers to open out the canvas sheets. We ripped open the hemp bags. We tried to spread out and dry the moist corn. We tried to get rid of any corn that had already molded beyond use.

Cutting open the seams of the hemp bags, spreading out 75 kilograms (165 pounds) of corn, lifting up the corn, spreading it out . . . suddenly I discovered that the hemp bags were covered in blood. Looking at my hands, I realized that all 10 fingers were dripping in blood and I had not felt a thing.

We dried corn every morning. Every afternoon, we loaded up a small truck and tried to sell corn in a 150-kilometer (93-mile) radius around the Pearl River delta. We combed through all of the top production brigades' feeding facilities with a fine-tooth comb. When Hong Kong people were not eating chicken, however, nobody had any interest in raising chicken. When business was good, buyers would order 30 tons at a time. Now, any order at all was welcome.

Via telephone, we made contact with a feedlot in Huiyang. After cajoling the manager for some time, we finally worked the order up from 30 tons to 150 tons. The condition was that he could pay 45 days after delivery. He wanted to pick it up after four or five days, but we declared that we would be delivering it tomorrow.

"We haven't got the warehouse here ready to handle it," he replied.

"Here's the deal: tomorrow at 4 p.m. we will deliver 200 tons," I said.

"One hundred fifty tons it was—how's it adding up to 200 now?," he asked.

"You get the extra tons for free."

After putting down the phone, I drove the truck to Huanggang. Cowboy was in Hong Kong and I couldn't find his son, "Calfboy." On inquiring, I found that all of the dump trucks of the town were in Shenzhen, delivering sand. I found Calfboy there in his truck, amidst clouds of dust. I honked at him. "Hey!

Calfboy! Mobilize your troops. I need every dump truck in town to help me deliver corn tomorrow from Sungang to Huiyang."

"Can't do it. We have to work here for the whole week."

"Start again day after tomorrow."

"Can't do it. I'd be fined."

"I'll pay twice the transport rate. Will you do it?"

"How many trucks do you need?"

"The more, the better."

"What's that mean?"

"All of them!"

The next day, with Calfboy in the lead, 38 trucks arrived at Sungang North Station, among which were 21 eight-ton dump trucks. We piled seven tons of corn on trucks that could legally carry five tons. We piled 11 or 12 on trucks that could carry eight. In all, we packed in 360 tons.

As the head of the Feedstuff Team, I led the convoy in my little Toyota truck. Thirty-eight trucks full of corn came behind. At four-thirty in the afternoon we arrived at the company in Huiyang. Manager Huo flipped when he saw us. I comforted him: "What you don't want, we can consider mine. Just park it here for a while."

We were going to put it in Huiyang, come what may. The transportation cost was going to be less than the fines for keeping it piled in the warehouse at the train station. Demurrage at the station was RMB 0.3 (USD 0.15) per ton for the first three days, then 0.6 (USD 0.30) for the three days after that. The next three days went to 1.2 (USD 0.61), then 2.4 (USD 1.21), then 4.8 (USD 2.42), then 9.6 (USD 4.85), then 19.2 (USD 9.70), and so on. The value of the goods was less than the cost of storage for a month.

Thin little manager Huo did his best to show me this wasn't going to work, but goods that I had hauled over were not going to be hauled back again. Next to the chicken-raising company was a grade school. We got in touch with the right people and were allowed to use three of the classrooms as temporary storage.

On the way back to Shenzhen, I put on the Dvorak's *From the New World* and felt nerves that had been stretched to the limit for days begin to relax.

An even bigger challenge was waiting for an exhausted Wang Shi, however.

It was dark by the time we got back to Shenzhen. With a worried expression, Deng now handed me a notification. The Municipal Government Transportation Department was accusing me of looking down on them disrespectfully if I did not remove the rest of the corn immediately. Not only would there be a large fine, but all the goods would be confiscated. I had no intention of looking down on anyone; I simply needed storage space! As I tried to think of what to do, I quietly nursed my grievance.

Soon I had tracked down the home address of the director of the Transportation Department. With a watermelon under my arm, I went in the middle of the night to knock on his door. Although I was finally allowed in, Director Jiao was incensed. "We've been trying to figure out who the owner is of all these goods. Why's he so special? He's taken up all the space, and nothing else can be unloaded! Coal! Rice! Flour! Within three days you have to get this corn cleared out of here. Otherwise there's going to be a major fine."

"Give me a week," I replied.

"No room to maneuver," he said. "Three days is it. Any later, and you will bear all consequences."

Emerging from Director Jiao's house, I drove to Huanggang. It was dark and the only sound was the barking of a few dogs. I knocked on the door of Cowboy's house. He came sleepily to the door and asked if it couldn't wait till tomorrow. I told him it was a business opportunity, and he said that one still has to sleep, even if one is making money. I explained the matter, from start to finish. Cowboy thought this over and then asked what he could possibly do.

I had come up with the idea of selling corn to the Huanggang fish farmers. It seemed to me that fish could eat corn as well as anything else. I explained to Cowboy that Director Jiao had taken this thing to the higher level of principle. I had become the chief culprit in destroying the peaceful life of Special Economic Zone citizens. I told Cowboy that if I didn't get the corn cleared out in three days, they might well be locking me up.

He snorted. "You would have been better off selling old tires, as I told you. Easy work, easy money, no risk." But he looked with some sympathy on his exhausted friend.

Then he agreed to my plan. We decided to hold an auction of the corn the next morning, and we would invite all local fish farmers in to bid. Cowboy was to start notifying his friends immediately, and they were to start notifying others.

Next morning at ten o'clock, I stood on a mountainous pile of corn surrounded by more than 20 fish-farm managers and their deputies. Raising my voice, I called out, "This pile is around 30 tons. You can see that some of it got wet and is a little moldy, but most of it is fine. And the moldy part can be fed to the fish anyway. The cost to me was RMB 40,000 [USD 20,202]. Starting price here: 20,000 [USD 10,101]. Any takers?" No response. "Eighteen thousand [USD 9,091]?"

"Three thousand [USD 1,515]," came a voice from among the crowd.

"You mean U.S. dollars, right?" Everyone laughed.

"Seventeen thousand [USD 8,586]," I said, trying hard to stay calm. I felt as though I had been stabbed with a knife.

"Okay, 16,000 [USD 8,081]." I still stubbornly called out each price as I went down by RMB 1,000 (USD 505) increments.

"Five thousand! [USD 2,525]" Somebody finally responded. From then on, people began to bid. The 30 tons was eventually sold for 12,000 RMB (about USD 6,061), or roughly RMB 400 (about USD 200) per ton. Then we went on to the next pile. And then the third, the fourth, and so on.

In the afternoon we kept at it, pile by pile. The auction went on until the evening rays dyed Sungang a deep red. In one day, we had auctioned 400 tons, and on the next day we would continue the bloodletting. No matter what, we had to have the place cleared out by the day after tomorrow.

That same evening, several unfamiliar guests came to the Dongmen lodging house. They announced themselves as being from the Shenzhen Huaqiao Everbright Farm. They had heard that a large amount of corn was being let go, cheaply. The head of the guests explained their own situation. The farm raised milk cows. It supplied fresh milk to Hong Kong's Vitasoy company. At a reasonable price, they could order unlimited quantities. They hoped that they could set up a long-term cooperative relationship. "Each ton, RMB 700 [USD 354]. We take it all and sweep it clean. What about it, Manager Wang?"

I told them it was equivalent to selling my corn for the price of the hemp bags alone. "You are taking advantage of the fire to plunder the goods," I said, putting on a very dissatisfied look. Internally, I calculated that I would be making RMB 300 (USD 151.51) more off each ton than I could get from the fish bosses. This one deal would lessen my loss by RMB 1 million (about USD 505,050). The problem was that I had never done business with the Everbright Farm before, and I didn't know if they were reliable.

"Okay!' I made my decision, put out my hand, and told them that I accepted their price.

The next day, when the fish bosses gathered at the Sungang North Station and learned that all the corn was sold, they ground their teeth in frustration.

When Hong Kong people stopped eating chicken, I was the one who took the fall. The loss of this entire debacle came to RMB 1.1 million (USD 555,556). After starting the company with nothing, we had made RMB 400,000 (USD 202,020) in profits. We were still responsible for a debt of RMB 700,000 (USD 353,535). If our suppliers insisted on their money right away, I would be bankrupt. Something had to be done.

I slept for an entire 24 hours. When I got up, I threw together some clothes and caught the train north. From Guangzhou I caught a flight to Dalian. I found my way to the Dalian Cereals and Oils Import and Export Corporation. I asked them there how much corn they had left in their warehouses.

They had 15,000 tons.

"I'll buy it all. I'll dispatch the freighter and take delivery at the port. As for payment terms, I'll pay 100 days after the goods reach Shekou, in Shenzhen." I knew that I could demand stringent terms, since the foreign trade authorities were eager to dispose of overstocked inventories. My second stop was Tianjin and my third was Qingdao. I bought the entire stock of corn in the foreign trade warehouses of those three places, a total of over 30,000 tons.

I did not believe that from this day forward Hong Kong people would never eat chicken again. When they wanted to eat chicken, there would have to be people raising chicken. Those chickens would be consuming a large amount of corn, and only I would have the corn in my hands. Right now, the market price was extremely low. The key question was time. If my timing was off and Hong Kong failed to revive its enthusiasm for chicken, I would have to admit total defeat.

The first cargo ship loaded up 7,000 tons of corn at Dalian and headed for the South China Sea, going through Bohai Bay and across the Yellow Sea. As it came closer and closer to Shenzhen, I began to get worried. Every day I would fix my eyes on the media and pray: "Hong Kong people, eat chicken! Eat chicken!"

The summer of 1983 saw an unusual number of typhoons, but my 7,000 tons of rice did not encounter any problems. It reached the South Sea region right on time and began to enter the mouth of the Pearl River.

There was still no news from Hong Kong about people liking chicken again. I added my own prayers to Mozart's as I listened to his sublime music: *Typhoons! Winds of the South Seas, blow ye seas, blow! Stop that ship! Best of all, sink it to the bottom!* The contract allowed for insurance in the event of natural disaster.

In just two days, the 7,000 tons would be docking at the Port of Chiwan. With only two days to go, newspapers in Hong Kong published an item: previous reporting had been mistaken. Chicken feed did not in fact contain any cancer-causing agent. This news was like spring rain! Hong Kong people immediately began to order up their tender white chicken again.

First to Huanggang. I found Calfboy, and ordered the services of 28 eight-ton dump trucks to load up the 7,000 tons of corn.

Then to the Port of Chiwan. I stood on a high terrace and watched as the contents of the massive 10,000-ton ship were unloaded. The corn went crane load by crane load into trucks. The crane would lift each scoopful of 8 tons in a net and slide it over till it stopped above the truck's position, then open out the net. Over 100 of these scoopfuls cascaded into the dump trucks. As each truck was filled, it moved off and another took its place. The trucks went straight to Conti Chia Tai, to Far East Gold Coin, dust rising behind them. With my hands on my hips, I looked up to the heavens. The heavens were so blue. The clouds were so very white.

During this second campaign, I not only made back the loss but earned another RMB 3 million (about USD 1.52 million) for good measure.

Corn became like golden nuggets. Representatives from Shenzhen companies dashed up to the north to try to buy it. Corn now began to pour into Shenzhen and the Pearl River delta, and by November corn was truly in oversupply. One day, I was called in to the SD offices where the former propaganda man, Mr. Lu, shoved a newspaper editorial into my hands. This criticized SD by name for allowing zone companies to blindly import corn and create a wasteful situation. I had fortunately been alerted to this editorial before our meeting.

Mr. Lu barked out a question, demanding to know what it was all about. I blandly asked what he meant. "There's a huge oversupply," he raged, "and I am being blamed and asked to write a report to my superiors to explain!"

"Oh?," I said mildly. "I didn't know."

He railed against my pretending to be innocent. He insisted that I accompany him to the docks. We sped down to Shekou in his official car.

Corn was everywhere. Little tender sprouts were already stubbornly working their way through cracks in the bags. Pointing at them, this man who had been a little revolutionary soldier in the Dongjiang Column during the anti-Japanese war days erupted in anger. "How do you explain this?"

I quietly said, "This isn't mine." In my heart was a tremendous gladness.

I explained that we had stopped buying corn some time ago. We now served as a middleman for Conti Chia Tai, taking the company's buyers around to existing supplies in the Pearl River delta. We made less profit but we also took less risk. Mr. Lu wanted to know why Conti Chia Tai didn't buy on its own. I explained that they trusted Wang Shi. There was little Mr. Lu could say to that.

By that time, I had already drawn away from navigating the rapids of this turbulent business. I did not think that the feed industry would have a great future, so I decided to pull out. My interest turned in the direction of scientific instrumentation, and I began helping Zhang Xifu import computers and copiers.

Five years after I stepped back from the feedstuff industry, in 1989, two brothers in Sichuan, named Liu Yongxing and Liu Yonghao, decided to enter it. By the mid-1990s, their Hope Group had become second only to the Thai company Chia Tai in producing feedstuff. It had also become one of China's largest private enterprises.

I once joked with these two brothers, saying that if I had kept at it I might be China's King of Feedstuff today. Actually, I not only felt that the future was not good for this industry, I saw that its risk was too great for the slim margins one could make. It was a tough business. The reason the Liu brothers were so successful was that they moved into the more secure business of setting up factories and doing actual production. Based on this real industry, they became one of the outstanding private enterprises in the 1990s.

The Year that Deng Xiaoping Visited Shenzhen

January 24, 1984.

I was biking out the east gate of SD's headquarters when I noticed crowds of policemen and bystanders in front of Shenzhen's International Trading Building. Pushing my way through, I spotted a tall figure I knew, the deputy general manager of SD, Mr. Gao Lin.

"What's going on?"

After pulling me to one side, he said in a low voice, "Comrade Deng Xiaoping is in Shenzhen. The Municipal Party Committee asked us to clear the way, so that he could come to the top of the Shenzhen International Trade Center and get an overall view of the Special Economic Zone. I am checking out the security arrangements with the Public Security Bureau. Wang, don't tell anyone, okay?"

"Okay." I turned back toward the east gate on my bike.

Several days later, headlines announced that Comrade Deng had indeed come to Shenzhen, accompanied by leaders from central government such as Wang Zhen and Yang Shangkun. As a result of his visit, he had issued a document with a vital comment written on it: "The experience of Shenzhen proves that we were correct in our policy of setting up Special Economic Zones."

This was both a green light to Shenzhen's further development and a confirmation of what had already been done. In a few short years, Shenzhen had gone from being a sleepy village to being a medium-sized new-style city of 400,000 people.

Its economy was spiraling upward. The leadership of SD made invaluable contributions to this process, including both Gao Lin and Sun Kaifeng. The zone now had new roads, a major highway to Shekou, gas stations along the roads, the Port of Chiwan at Shekou, a golf course, the Shuibei Industrial District, and various holiday resorts. Other companies under the jurisdiction of the municipality were active in building the zone too, including Shenzhen Import & Export Trading Group, Shenzhen Trade Services Group, Shenzhen Friendship Group, Shenzhen Duty-Free Group, and Shenzhen Materials Company.

The Shenzhen Special Economic Zone enjoyed preferential trade policies with respect to importing from the outside world. Policies said that foreign products that had been imported into the zone could not be sold outside the zone. There was no restriction, however, on customers from outside the zone coming in and purchasing goods and then shipping them into China. As a result of this favorable circumstance, a new company under SD was born. It was called the Shenzhen Modern Scientific Education Instruments Exhibition Center.

Preparations of this Exhibition Center began in May of 1984. The site was at 1 Construction Road, where we would be exhibiting imported office equipment and video equipment. Chen Lu was manager and Cai Zuoxing was deputy manager. Ms. Chen Lu had been a college student prior to the Cultural Revolution; she then moved from Shaoguan to Shenzhen together with her husband. She was extremely capable in the area of foreign trade but she had an unyielding character. The two of us had an argument not one month after the preparations for the company began. Neither of us would give way. As we confronted one another, she finally stood up from her manager's chair, flung the keys on the desk, and declared, "I will not be manager!," whereupon she pushed open the door and stormed out.

The next day, Zhang Xifu came to me and stretched out his two hands in supplication as he said, "She has completely abdicated. What are we supposed to do? I've talked it over with Manager Lu and we think you should be legal representative."

"I belong to the Foreign Economic Commission of Guangdong Province," I replied. "I'm under their jurisdiction. It's not a problem for me to work on the planning stages of this company, but serving as manager at the same time begins to get tricky. It gets into the matter of how to split income."

"The split of profits with the Feed Department would not change in the slightest. And the Foreign Commission of Guangdong province does not need to invest a penny. The percentages could be three to seven, but any losses would also be shared in that same proportion. What do you say?"

"That is very reasonable. I will report this proposal to the provincial authorities right away and see if it flies."

As it turned out, the leadership of the provincial Foreign Economic Commission had other ideas. They did not want to bear the risk of any loss, and they wanted to close down the feed business. They wanted me to come back and work for them in Guangzhou as soon as possible. I now had two options: either close down the feed business and go back to my old bosses, or disengage from the Foreign Economic Commission of Guangdong Province altogether and stay with the SD company.

I had no intention of going back along a road I had already traveled. My only real choice was to wrap up the feedstuff business and move on.

In wrapping up the feedstuff business, there had to be a final reckoning. The question was how to allocate the Feed Department profits between SD and the commission for that last incomplete year. I did not want to wait for year-end—it had to be done now in order for me to extricate myself and start a new business. I therefore suggested coming up with an estimated year-end figure of RMB 2 million (about USD 1.01 million), and splitting profits on that basis. SD would take half of that amount and members of the commission would allocate the rest, whatever the end-of-the-year profits turned out to be. Mr. Lu initially nodded his head in happy agreement, but by the next day he had changed his mind. There had been dissenting voices. The commission equivocated, saying an audit was needed. In the meantime, it began its own independent investigation. Before long, I was informed that dividing on the basis of RMB 2 million would be fine—the commission had learned that our year-end results would far surpass that figure. Indeed, in the end, the amount that we earned came to more than RMB 3 million (about USD 1.52 million), although what went into the commission's official account was based on the RMB 2 million.

After a check for RMB 850,000 (USD 429,293) had been written and given to a specified account at the Foreign Economic Commission of Guangdong province (1 million less 15 percent income tax), I felt as though a heavy weight had been lifted from my chest. I had finished playing the awkward role of one servant with two bosses. I immediately assumed the position of manager of the new so-called Exhibition Center.

Ending the Role of Being the Servant of Two Masters

Our Exhibition Center formally opened on September 21, 1984. Zhang Xifu invited the standing deputy mayor, Zhou Ding, which was all the "face" we needed. Mr. Liu Yuansheng of Hong Kong's Renda Company attended, as well as Mr. Zhang Gongtai of Hong Kong's Guandu Company. These two companies had already become suppliers in the preparatory period. After the opening ceremony, Zhang Xifu brought out a very special bottle of Moutai liquor, and the guests all took a sip to congratulate the birth of the Shenzhen Modern Scientific Education Instruments Exhibition Center.

The center occupied the entire second floor of a tall building on Construction Road in the Luohu District. A large neon sign with the characters of our name shone in bright colors from the top of the building. The building faced directly toward the elevated railroad tracks, so all those riding into the city at night could see the ad.

In fact, we had nothing to do with educational instruments. We imported such things as cameras, video equipment, copiers, and other office equipment. From the name, one might think otherwise—people from the procurement departments of Beijing Normal University and Peking Union Medical College came to see our offerings, and only then did I realize that the name was misleading. Nevertheless, the name had already been registered and there was nothing we could do but use it and not think about it.

The business model of the exhibition center was different from the empty-handed way of the corn business. It depended first and foremost on our ability to get foreign exchange quota. With quota for foreign exchange in hand, we could exchange renminbi (yuan) for foreign currency and import foreign-supplied goods.

First, we took an order from a customer and at the same time got a 25 percent deposit of the price of the goods from him. The order was then placed in Hong Kong and the same percentage was paid to the Hong Kong merchant. When the goods arrived in Shenzhen, the buyer paid the balance of 75 percent before receiving the goods, and we then paid the supplier. Key to this process was that the buyer in China paid us in renminbi, while we paid the Hong Kong supplier in foreign currency. On average, we exchanged 5 million Hong Kong dollars (HKD)(USD 640,000) per month in our first few months in business.

Converting foreign exchange at the time in Shenzhen's trading companies was as follows. If a company wanted to conduct business with a foreign firm and do a transaction in foreign currency, it first needed authorization, that is, a permit to import goods. Then it also needed to have ties to a unit within China that had a quota of foreign exchange that had been derived from exporting. Foreign exchange was strictly controlled at the time in China.

When we first started out, we had less than a dozen people. By the end of the year, we had 120 employees who were 25 years old on average.

We had several categories of employees. One group came over from SD or were introduced to us by that company. They included Cai Zuoxing, Yang Yanfei, Huang Shengquan, Zhao Xiaofeng, Wang Xiaoling, Che Weiqing, Zhang Xiaomei, Cai Wenbo, and Zhong Yilin. People like Zhou Shiping, Li Yaohui, Huang Tao, and Liao Dexian came from the Information Center of the Provincial Planning Commission of Guangzhou. Then we also recruited some students who had graduated in electronics from the Guangzhou Professional School. We also opened our doors enthusiastically to people who had been in the arts and sports. We had three volleyball players. In the arts, we had the pianist named Liu Xiaowei, a dancer named Fu Lan, a painter named Zhai Yashen, and several others in traditional arts. Our staff constituted a creative crew, and our parties were lively.

Less than 30 percent of staff members had graduated from anything higher than a vocational-technical school, however. Because of this, the company hired an elderly "intellectual" named Professor Cheng Zhiliang to be responsible for employee education. He made it possible for those who had a middle-school education to carry on with adult education and to graduate from high school.

Deng Yiquan, the slender fellow who had been in the Feed Department, was transferred over to the Exhibition Center to be in charge of customs applications, and he too went on to get a higher degree. From the day I came to Shenzhen, I felt that if I were to handle an enterprise properly I had to give young people an opportunity to put their intelligence and talents to use. Unlike the way my own choices had been distorted to fit the mold, I wanted to respect their choices, give them equal opportunity, and in particular respect their private lives. Chinese people in a country that has reformed and opened up should have a work environment that respects them and that allows them to pursue their ideals.

To a large degree, China's traditional culture suppresses individuality. An individual is required to subjugate himself or herself to group objectives. China's slogans in the recent past reflected this: we were encouraged to be like nails that allowed themselves to be hammered into wherever the nails needed to go. This denial of self-direction extended to personal lives. One's spouse was often introduced by one's "working unit" (employer, that is), and divorce was absolutely forbidden. Work had to submit to revolutionary needs and to the allocation requirements of the unit. One could not even decide about dying: suicide was regarded as severing oneself from the party and the People. From birth to death, an individual basically had no rights. During the Cultural Revolution, one slogan demanded that we resolutely struggle against any glimmer of an *I* in our deepest souls. Living like this meant that individuals were like goldfish in a glass bowl, constantly under the judgmental gaze of the masses. When I set up the company, my fundamental bottom line was that individuals should enjoy respect, should have the right to choose, and should have full control over their own private matters.

Not long after we started the company, a female employee got married. Two months later, she came to me and said that she wanted to get divorced. She asked my opinion, and naturally I said that it was up to her. In the traditional setting, she would have been subjected to staff meetings and consultations with the Communist Youth League, the Women's Association, and others. All these organizations would have tried to persuade her not to get divorced. Even though not getting involved seemed a cold way of handling the matter, it expressed the company's respect for the principle that individuals should make their own choices in life.

The Case of the 40 Million U.S. Dollars

The autumn of 1984 was a prosperous time for the Special Economic Zone. One evening, two of my colleagues, Zhang Xifu and Wang Xiangning, recommended that I meet with a certain visitor from Beijing. His name was Wang Chuntang and he represented something called the New Age Company. Wang Xiangning had a strong Beijing accent. She got straight to the point: the New Age Company had USD 30 million (RMB 111 million) in foreign currency that it could sell me, at a conversion rate of USD 1 to RMB 3.7.

Despite the fact that Wang Chuntang was tall, sat straight in his chair, was amiable and looked trustworthy, this whole scenario seemed dubious. I wondered how the company could have the money to start with, and the favorable exchange rate was simply unimaginable. The official rate at the time was USD 1 to RMB 2.8, but the market rate was 1 to 4.2. By selling to me at 3.7, Mr. Wang would be losing a potential RMB 0.5 (about USD 0.08) on each dollar, or a total loss of RMB 15 million (about USD 4 million). It was unlikely that such delicious pancakes simply fell from heaven.

Wang Xiangning went on to explain that "Mr. Wang Chuntang has already signed an agreement with the general manager of SD, Sun Kaifeng. If the Exhibition Center also wants some foreign exchange, we could allocate you a portion of the total."

I just laughed. Extremes always come back on themselves, I thought. This guy also seems a little over the top.

Twenty days later, I got a call from Zhang Xifu, saying that the foreign exchange had arrived. It was in SD's account. He asked how much I wanted. My reactions were slow since I had forgotten the offer.

"What foreign exchange?"

"The 30 million U.S. dollars from New Age. It is in SD's account in Shenzhen. How much do you want?"

I thought for a moment. At a cost of 3.7 × 10 million, that would be RMB 37 million.

"Can you give me 10 million?"

"Fine. No problem. We'll give another 10 to Li Jingquan, who has had his eye on it." Li Jingquan was head of the International Trade and Commerce Mall. He had previously been Sun Kaifeng's secretary, and his business was going well.

The Exhibition Center then easily borrowed RMB 20 million (USD 5.4 million) from the Bank of China. Together with cash already in our account we soon handed over the RMB 37 million to New Age. The bank promptly credited USD 10 million worth of foreign exchange quota to our account. With this infusion of funds, our business suddenly soared to new heights.

At this point, our core team had been put in place. Zhang Min had replaced Zhong Yilin as head of the finance department—he had been recruited over from SD. Zhan Hongxiang was head of the business department; Liang Yi was head of warehousing and transport. Li Yaohui was responsible for technology and repairs, Su Cheng headed the advertising department, and Zhao Xiaofeng was responsible for administration and processing of imported materials.

The company now began to import large quantities of video recorders, copy machines, and computers. Hong Kong's Renda Company and Guandu Company were doing their best just to keep up with supplying all of our orders.

Ten million U.S. dollars was spent very quickly. We now wondered if we might be able to get another 10. We approached Beijing's New Age Company directly and, after getting a positive response, I sent a man named Huang Shengquan to Beijing with full authority to do the transaction.

By this time, our center had set up business rep offices in Guangzhou and Beijing. Zhou Shiping was in charge of the business in Guangzhou, while Cai Shuncheng and Zheng Xiaowen were responsible for Beijing. Since the center was selling a continuous stream of office equipment north to Beijing, however, this was noticed by others. A trading company from Beijing now came down to the Pearl River delta and, like a proverbial thief in the night, began to steal our sources. What's more, it leased a military cargo plan to ship things back to Beijing. It was becoming a formidable competitor based on its advantage in shipping time alone. The full name of that company was the Beijing Huayuan Trading Company. It was under the jurisdiction of Beijing's Xicheng District government. Its legal representative was Dai Xiaoming. The "assassin" it sent to do the business in the Pearl River delta was someone who later became the number-two man at Beijing Huayuan, namely Ren Zhiqiang.

Our center still focused on building up its initial capital through trade, but several large groups in the zone had begun to look at the prospects for building high-rise buildings in the Luohu District. A cacophony of pile driving soon began, resulting in some of the huge buildings that are now well known in Shenzhen.

Starting in 1985, the market for imported electronics stopped moving at "Shenzhen speed" and began to soften. Our business began to focus on national ministries, departments, and institutions in Beijing that dealt with education as well as the equipment departments of provincial broadcasting stations, and procurement centers of the Ministry of Education in the south. The business model was called "three points and one line": headquarters in Shenzhen handled the foreign exchange and the importing of goods; Guangzhou handled warehousing and shipping; and sales and marketing were done in Beijing.

The business of all the major groups in the zone was also cooling off, however, with the turn in markets. As a result, foreign exchange controls now became extremely tight and the Public Security Bureau began to investigate cases that involved violation of foreign exchange rules. People were interrogated, criminal cases were launched, and jail terms became common.

Given this, our center was soon rolled into the case that became known as the "40 million dollar foreign exchange case." To this day, the case is regarded as one of the largest in the country for circumventing proper foreign exchange procedures. The case related to the activities of a tall genial gentleman named Wang Chuntang.

Shirking the rules? We did everything by the book. We put the money through a bank, spent the foreign exchange quota according to our import licenses, paid according to contracts, and so on. What did we do wrong? To call us on it seemed strange.

Beijing sent two investigation teams to Shenzhen. One came from the Central Disciplinary Commission and one from the Military Disciplinary Commission. Since the Beijing New Age Company was under the jurisdiction of the Party Work Committee of the Ministry of Defense, it was under the army-administered plan and the military was involved—that is why there had to be two teams.

Of the USD 40 million (RMB 148 million), our Exhibition Center knew where 30 million had gone. It had enjoyed the use of 10 million itself, and it had participated in the allocating and sole use of the second 10 million. The Special Zone's Investigation Court therefore worked together with the two teams in investigating and sealing the accounts and contracts of the center that related to this business.

Meanwhile, those who were interrogated at the center included me, Huang Shengquan, and Zhang Min.

During my interrogation, I vehemently protested that it was incomprehensible to me how we could be accused of obtaining foreign exchange without state authorization

The young woman from the Central Disciplinary Commission person said outright, "The New Age Company used improper procedures with regard to its reserve of foreign exchange quota."

"In that case," I said, "how could the bank have agreed to transfer U.S. dollars to the zone?"

The young woman from the Military Disciplinary Commission explained, "When Premier Zhao Ziyang came to the Defense Ministry to hear a report on foreign exchange, he agreed that the foreign exchange reserve held by the Defense Ministry's subordinate companies could and should be used in a more flexible manner. This was in order to liven up the economy. The New Age Company proceeded according to the spirit of the premier's remarks. It's just that the State Council did not give formal approval in writing."

I was interested at the subtle difference in attitude between the two investigation groups.

As the investigation deepened, the critical issue focused in on whether or not there had been any giving or taking of bribes in the course of signing contracts for the two allocations of foreign exchange (that is, USD 30 million and USD 10 million).

The transaction relating to the Exhibition Center's second USD 10 million was clear-cut: I had Huang Shengquan handle this matter, and there was absolutely no gift of any kind involved. The matter of the USD 30 million transaction of SD was more uncertain. I was originally invited to partake in the deal, but I did not believe that such pancakes fell from heaven for nothing, and I took myself outside of the process. I placed myself on the outside, but nonetheless I was eventually one of the recipients of the funds.

It turned out the people directly involved in signing the contracts for that first 30 million had also participated in a transaction relating to a quantity of television sets. If these had been gifts, then they constituted a bribe. If the transaction was more like a sale through an agency, then they did not. The former turned out to be the case. The people involved became subject to criminal proceedings.

Just at this time, theoretical circles in the north were debating the issue of whether the Shenzhen Special Economic Zone should be called "capitalist" or called "socialist." Moving toward a market-oriented economy became far less certain. For the first time, I began to appreciate how closely individual lives and fates in the Special Economic Zone were tied to the fate of the zone itself. I began to understand how dependent we were on the attitude of Beijing decision makers.

According to knowledgeable sources, the investigation groups from Beijing asked the Shenzhen authorities to detain Zhang Xifu in order to question him. A motion was put forward to the standing committee of Shenzhen's Municipal Party Committee. The party secretary and mayor Liang Xiang determined that evidence was insufficient. He opposed the arrest. Liang's refusal to arrest Zhang Xifu thereby protected a group of reformers who were vital to the growth and success of Shenzhen.

As time went by, the furor surrounding the case subsided.

"Your Warehouse Is My Warehouse"

In the fall of 1984, the Third Plenary Session of the Twelfth Central Committee passed the Decision Regarding Reform of Economic Structure. For the first time, the term *commodity economy* was written into a document that had the force of the central government's party line behind it. The central government was now officially supporting the struggle to remove the shackles of the old economic system. With this document, the great wave of a commodity economy* came crashing against China's shores with a force that could no longer be held back.

Our Exhibition Center was packed with customers every day. My office, the office of the general manager, was separated from the main hall by a glass partition so that I could take in the situation at a glance.

One day, I saw a man quietly standing to one side of the line of people, as

---

*The term *commodity* as used here implies goods that are produced for sale on a market, as opposed to goods produced for satisfying quota targets in the plan. China was still allergic to using the term *market economy* at this point.

though he were not remotely connected to those who had to wait in line. He wore a mink hat, tied under his chin with a ribbon. He looked like some actor who had just walked off a movie set.

I asked my secretary to bring that young man wearing the fur hat into my office.

"What is your honorable purpose in visiting us?," I asked politely.

"I would like to meet the general manager," he replied.

"That's me. May I help you?"

"I would like to buy video equipment."

"Ah. And the fur hat?"

"To get your attention. With so many people waiting in line, my turn was going to take a long time."

This was my first encounter with Chen Yuguang. We were to have many business dealings in the future. I had a secretary do what was necessary to supply his list of goods, and we then began to talk. It turned out Chen's family included two little brothers, Chen Yu'an and Chen Yujian, and the three of them had a business selling woolen shirts in Chengdu before they switched to electronic appliances.

Chen Yuguang soon began to come weekly from Sichuan to buy goods. He would bring a check for some hundreds of thousands of yuan (RMB). Once the shipping list had been drawn up, he would immediately go to the warehouse in Guangzhou to pick up the goods.

One day he appeared just at closing time with his head in a bandage that was still oozing blood. I was shocked to learn that he had been in a car accident in which his taxi flipped over. Nevertheless, once he was stitched up in the hospital, he rented another taxi and came straight to the Exhibition Center.

"You are playing with your life," I told him. "Slow down. Make money once you have rested a bit."

"To tell you the truth," he now confided, "I do 'empty-handed' business. The money in my hands is customers' money. I tell people I'll give them the goods as soon as I get paid, but then I rush here to you to get the shipping invoice and I rush to Guangzhou to get the goods. If I don't get things done in that window of time, I'll be exposed."

"I understand. I'll have the secretary get things done right away."

One week later, Chen Yuguang came again and by now he had a bandage over the cut on his forehead. I invited him to a meal, and at the meal I asked, "Since the goods are actually in my warehouse, how do you get your customers to hand over a check?"

He let out a crafty smile. "Oh, that's easy. Your warehouse is my warehouse."

Come again?

"I take customers on a visit to the warehouse of the Exhibition Center," he went on to explain. "You have two young women there who handle the picking up of the goods. I got to know them by giving them two packages of Sichuan peanuts. Then I praised the way they use makeup and said they looked like models. They couldn't resist the flattery. Please don't blame them. I asked them to call me Boss Chen when I bring in customers and to ask something like, 'When are you coming to pick up your goods?'"

All I could do was laugh at the sly old fox.

One early morning in the springtime of 1985, I heard a knock on the door. There was Chen Yuguang, with briefcase and bag in hand. I asked him in but noted that my wife and daughter were sleeping and we should be quiet. He put the leather briefcase down on my glass table and opened it. I saw that it was absolutely full of 10 RMB [USD 3.57] notes. "With the help of your esteemed company," he said, "I made 300,000 [USD 107,143] this year. I only mean to express my appreciation with this."

"Do you know anything about me?"

"I know that you don't care about money. Since I was afraid you'd misunderstand me, I brought it only after the business of the year was done. It's not a bribe to do anything, just an expression of my thanks."

I smiled. "I am a man with very large aspirations. How can this box of cash even come close to satisfying my hopes and dreams?"

It was an awkward moment. By Chen Yuguang's logic, sending gifts in the course of business was a necessary thing to do. Could it be that I felt the money was too little?

"Don't misunderstand me," I went on. "I want to do things. State-run companies have their rules, and ours is a state-run company. Gifts are bribes. That's it. If I had wanted money I would long since have started a private enterprise. I don't cooperate with you so that I can get private benefit in secret. I work with you because you help sell our goods. In this coming year, we'll continue to work together. What impressed me most about you is that you think the trust of your customers is most important. This is most important to me too. A promise is worth a thousand pieces of gold."

It was now his turn to smile. "Can I leave the Sichuan peanuts with you?" He held out the plastic bag.

"Take the cordyceps sinensis. Leave me the peanuts. That should keep you from buying our guards at the warehouse again."

The Shareholding System and the Failure of "Parachuted Forces"

In 1986, the Exhibition Center moved from 1 Construction Road in Shenzhen to 50 Peace Road. This building was formerly a dormitory for single people working in the customs department. The Exhibition Center took a five-year lease on it and rebuilt it into an office building. All that was required was to sheath the outside in mirrored glass so that it looked more modern and stylish. When clouds rolled by in the sky above, it looked as though the building itself was slowly moving.

Another company moved into this building, a newly established Sino-foreign joint venture called the Shenzhen International Management Services Company

(Guo Qi). The general manager was Huang Shengquan. Prior to this, it had been a joint venture with Beijing's Peking Union Medical College, with Liang Jian as general manager.

The business of Guo Qi focused on exhibitions. The company created exhibition halls out of the first and second floors of the building. Our Exhibition Center held 75 percent of the shares of this company, and Hong Kong's Guandu Company held 25 percent. Anyone who knows the rules can see at a glance that 25 percent is the minimum shareholding for gaining the preferential policy treatment that is accorded to Sino-foreign joint ventures. The boss of the Guandu Company was Zhang Gongtai. He had graduated from the Peking Union Medical College and then emigrated to Hong Kong in the early 1980s. His father-in-law was a famous Thai named Yi Meihou.

Guo Qi's first piece of business was to hold an exhibition jointly sponsored by the organization department and the propaganda department of the Shenzhen Municipal Party Committee. Exhibitions followed one after another, but a young group of people within this company aimed for better business and so shifted the focus of Guo Qi to the more challenging business of advertising. The company soon became the most creative advertising company in all of the Special Economic Zone. A well-known professor from the Xi'an Academy of Fine Arts also joined the company once he came to Shenzhen. A number of famous logos and corporate identities in Shenzhen came out of Guo Qi, including those for cigarettes, alcohol, and various medicines.

In May 1986, Liang Xiang retired from his position as party secretary of the Shenzhen Municipal Party Committee, and Li Hao was appointed in his place. On October 15, 1986, the Shenzhen municipal government announced provisional regulations aimed at turning large state-owned enterprises in Shenzhen into shareholding companies. This was a pilot program, in preparation for extending the experiment nationwide. The regulations encouraged enterprises to carry out reform of their ownership systems.

At a forum held to discuss this matter, the newly appointed municipal party secretary declared that he believed the only way for state-owned enterprises to carry on was to make them into shareholding entities. He felt that this was particularly necessary for large state-owned enterprises.

But none of the large entities under the jurisdiction of the Special Economic Zone government was enthusiastic. (These included the Shenzhen Special Economic Zone Development Company, the Trade Import and Export Company, the Trade Development Company, and the Materials Company.) They were not interested, since their management was getting along quite well under the existing modus operandi.

In contrast, I regarded these new regulations as a very fortuitous opportunity—indeed, a heaven-sent gift. They would allow me to begin to move out from under the onus of SD, which still controlled my operations. The regulations included 62 items in seven chapters that clearly laid out all procedures. Items included explanations of general principles, shareholders' rights, organizational structure of shareholding companies, human resource management, taxation, division of income, and so on.

Going into 1987, our company was administratively separated from SD by two layers due to name changes and organizational changes, but the firewall between us was still inadequate. In theory, at any time, I could be transferred away by just one command, one signature on a piece of paper. This administratively determined risk was far greater than any business risk we faced. I felt that the new shareholding system would be the best way to deal with this problem. Our management team quickly came to a consensus. We decided to adopt the provisional reforms.

I was not totally clear on how to do this, however, nor was I certain we would be successful.

Not long after, the Structural Reform Office of the Shenzhen municipal government co-hosted a forum together with Sun Hung Kai Securities.* The Sun Hung Kai representative, a woman named Qiu Xiaofei, explained in detail how to restructure a company into a shareholding entity, and how to list on the Hong Kong market, and I began to see the light. I carried the explanations home as if they were made of gold, and we began to prepare for "shareholder reform" with the aim of eventually listing.

The first thing we needed to do was standardize all procedures. In order to be trusted by people at large, our company had to have transparent finances and a legitimate business that could stand up to annual audits by an independent accounting firm. I therefore approached the Shekou accounting firm. Accompanied by Zhang Min, I met with its very clear-thinking director, Zhu Qiheng. We asked for an independent audit, which at the time was unheard of for a state-owned enterprise. Our willingness to take this initiative voluntarily raised all kinds of doubts in Zhu Qiheng's mind. He felt there must be problems that we wanted him to cover up. At the time, regulations said that the financial bureau of the government was responsible for annual reviews of state-owned enterprises in Shenzhen. Accounting firms were only responsible for auditing what were called "foreign-invested enterprises"—namely, those in which foreign entities invested. These foreign-invested companies generally had less than clear-cut finances, so they were not in favor of being audited. For a state-run company to voluntarily propose an independent audit was unique.

Nevertheless, Director Zhu was finally persuaded to receive this commission. It took another year of getting more familiar with one another before Director Zhu's subordinates explained what he had been worried about.

The direction of shareholding reform was now clear, and we began to follow

---

*In Mandarin, Xinhongji. Sun Hung Kai was founded in 1969. Sun Hung Kai Securities Limited was listed in Hong Kong in 1975, and Sun Hung Kai & Co. Limited was listed on The Stock Exchange of Hong Kong Limited in 1983. In 1988, the company was appointed as advisor to the Shenzhen government for developing the Shenzhen stock market. It was also one of the first approved B-share brokers in both the Shanghai and Shenzhen exchanges. It continues to be involved in both real estate development and share trading.

the internal procedures necessary to be a company that was attractive to investors on the Hong Kong market. At the same time, cracks began to appear in our senior management.

A person named Cai Zuoxing had left the company to start his own trading firm dealing in cashmere and video equipment. He was a local Shenzhen person, very honest and conscientious, and an excellent businessman. He was not, however, good at making small talk and connecting with customers. After a year as my deputy, he resigned, due to the pressure of handling the fast-paced Exhibition Center. To take his place, I promoted a person who had recently joined the company, named Du Xiaoteng. I appointed another person who had come into the company at the same time as manager of marketing and sales. These two were Guangdong people, formerly with the Guangdong Commercial Bureau's warehousing and transport company. They were Vanke's first professional employees to be hired from regular commercial companies.

Vanke's original management team, including me, had little experience in managing a commercial venture. We came from government organizations, schools, the army, publishers, and so on. Our business looked red hot, but its management was haphazard, particularly at warehousing and inventory control. We had no written procedures for entering data on what was coming in and going out of the warehouse. We had no way to cross-reference and figure out what needed restocking. The system urgently needed to be improved. The two men that I now put in these positions were not under anyone's scrutiny but mine—they did not rely on the opinions of others. They were highly professional, clear and logical in how they managed things, and they soon got sales channels set in place for solid expansion. Strengthening management in this way meant that customary ways of doing things had to be revised, or even jettisoned. When such things created conflict with the older employees, I stood firmly on the side of these two professionals.

Between the two, Liu Shanle was better at communicating with people and moderating conflict. Du Xiaoteng was tall, thin, and had the sharp hooked nose of a raptor. He spoke quickly and precisely and did not try to hide his opinions and his intelligence. It was inevitable that he would offend the older managers. The cracks appeared as work proceeded. The manager in charge of warehousing and transport was a man named Zhou Shiping. He was one of those people who works like mad yet is meticulous about his clothing. He might have to work all night, but he made sure that his shoes were shiny enough to reflect shadows. Such a punctilious man was naturally not going to let things slide over lightly. Open conflict was bound to develop between Du Xiaoteng and Zhou Shiping.

One afternoon, after work, Zhou Shiping came to me with a recommendation: "Call a rectification meeting. Let the leaders hear our opinions so they can advise us on how to improve work methods. Otherwise, we will begin to damage what has always been a first-line company." Obviously, presenting opinions to leaders was a way to attack Du Xiaoteng, to put him on stage in a defensive posture.

As head of the company, I canvassed others in the management team and to my surprise learned that essentially all of the old-timers supported Mr. Zhou. The reform faction was isolated.

I then approached Du Xiaoteng to exchange views and see if there could be any compromise. The pressure had my stomach in knots as I tried to find ways to communicate the problem to him.

Then I met again with Zhou Shiping. I asked, "Are you all conspiring to gang up on Xiaoteng and chase him out?"

"Not at all," Mr. Zhou replied. "I came up with the idea of giving opinions to leaders on my own. I was in the dark about the others until you said they support me. I will be happy to submit to Xiaoteng's leadership if he changes his ways a little." That put my mind at ease somewhat.

On the way back to Shenzhen from Guangzhou, I sat in a car together with Du Xiaoteng. My own hope was that this matter would resolve itself if Xiaoteng took a more humble and willing attitude. Du Xiaoteng was the first to speak: "There is nothing wrong with having the older employees collectively oppose new ways. That means my reforms are reaching their real target. However, I cannot have someone like Zhou Shiping in the center. With him, I simply can't do the work. If he stays there, I'm out. If I stay, he goes."

I had not anticipated this uncompromising attitude, and I spent a sleepless night.

The next day, I asked Du Xiaoteng to have dinner with me. I told him that it was unavoidable for there to be conflict between older and newer employees, but that his exclusionist attitude was something I could not accept. Even though older employees were resisting change and even though Zhou Shiping brought the contradiction to a head, I noted that "he did not do this in order to force you out." I told him that if he gave up this idea that it had to be one or the other, there would be a way to find some solution.

"I won't play," he said, disappointed with my attitude.

On the third day, both Du Xiaoteng and Liu Shanle resigned.

This first instance of bringing in professional staff had resulted in total failure. After Du Xiaoteng left his position, I promoted the manager of the Beijing company to be my assistant, a man named Cai Shuncheng. I learned an important lesson from this whole experience. In the process of reforming a management team, bringing in "parachuted forces" (that is, appointing a manager or director by transferring staffs from the highest authorities) carries with it considerable risk. It is more important to get new and old team members to agree on values and approaches than it is to tinker with the technological side of things. Of foremost importance in a management team is a sense of common values. If there is a discrepancy in core values, then the resulting conflict will be impossible to mend.

People living in Shenzhen, a city of immigrants, have a much stronger sense of shared values than anywhere else. In June 1987, the Shenzhen spirit was broadly characterized by the government as "opening up, creating, contributing." The party secretary and deputy party secretary of the committee applauded this description. They felt that since people come to Shenzhen from all over China, they need the encouragement of recognizing they are pioneers. To be in step with the beat of the modern age, it is appropriate to have a Shenzhen spirit that is aligned with the growth of the zone.

By now, quite a few of the enterprises founded in Shenzhen have done well and are major corporations. They include Huawei, ZTE, Ping'an Insurance, China Merchants Bank, Overseas Chinese Town Group, Zhongji China International Marine Containers Group, and others. These companies are unlike the many privately owned enterprises in the Pearl River delta that lasted three to five years and then disappeared. I feel that one of the important reasons for this was Shenzhen's open culture and openness in terms of fewer controls. Vanke benefited greatly from this open culture as the company developed.

CHAPTER TWO

The Sound and the Fury, 1988–1994

Foundations of the Real Estate Industry in China

At the end of 1987, something happened in Shenzhen that I didn't think much about at the time but that was critical to the future of Vanke and also to the urbanization of China. It took place on December 1, in the Shenzhen City Hall. Fifty-year usage rights to a piece of land that measured 8,588 square meters (9,393 square yards) were auctioned. The auctioneer was a man who later became the head of the National Land Planning Bureau of Shenzhen, Liu Jiasheng.

The auction started promptly at 4:30 p.m. Forty-four enterprises lifted their boards in the bidding. Liu Jiasheng opened up with a starting price of RMB 2 million (USD 540,540), and the rivalry officially began. As the auctioneer called out the bids, dozens of placards immediately went up and some of the bidders shouted out their prices as well. Seventeen minutes later, it was all over. Luo Jingxing, the boss of the Shenzhen Special Economic Zone Real Estate Company, raised his board one last time.

"RMB 5.25 million [USD 1.42 million], going once!" The auctioneer stood on his dais with his wooden gavel in the air. He looked out over a sea of rapt observers below him, some 80 percent of whom were journalists from Beijing, Hong Kong, and Shenzhen.

"5.25 million, going twice!" There was still no sound. Even the birds outside went quiet.

"5.25 million, going three times!" The gavel came down, and Luo Jingxing, a short thin man, became the star of the zone that day.

The media reported it as follows: "In an earth-shattering move, this auction separated the 'ownership' of land from the 'usage rights' of land in China. It was a breakthrough in the management of state-owned land. Member of the central politburo of the Chinese Communist Party and director of the State Commission for Restructuring, Li Tieying, stood at hand, observing the action."

The Shenzhen municipal deputy party secretary, Wang Ju, expressed his satisfaction to reporters at the auction: "The price was much higher than what the government had hoped for. Since the July 1 policy decision came down about reform of the municipal government's management of land, we have already used three different forms to handle the transfer of three pieces of land. The open auction on December 1 was one of them. We have received usage fees of RMB 23.3688 million [USD 3.51 million] just since July of this year. Before this, for all of 1985, and 1986, all of Shenzhen's Special Economic Zone only got some RMB 23 million [about USD 6.75 million]."

On December 29, 1987, twenty-eight days after this auction, the standing committee of the People's Congress of Guangdong Province passed new regulations: Regulations on Managing Land in the Shenzhen Special Economic Zone. These went the additional step of stipulating that usage rights to land could be sold to others for compensation. Cities throughout China observed what was happening in Shenzhen. They too began to implement systems of selling and transferring land-usage rights for compensation.

On April 12, 1988, the First Session of the Seventh National People's Congress passed a Draft Amendment to the Constitution of the People's Republic of China. This deleted the word *lease* from the phrase that said it was forbidden to lease out land. Instead, the provision now read: "usage rights for land can be transferred to others in accordance with legally defined regulations."

This then set in place the foundations, the critical cornerstone, for urban real estate development in China.

During this same period, we changed the name of the Shenzhen Modern Scientific Equipment Center. The name had been in use just one year. We now named it the Shenzhen Modern Enterprise Limited (MEC).

Others were beginning to move as well. On March 1, 1988, the Shenzhen government issued a "red-headlined document" (that is, an official document) stating that six large state-owned enterprises were implementing share-ownership systems. These included the Shen Electronics Group, the Urban Construction and Development Group, the Materials Company, the Shenzhen Petrochemical Company. We put all our forces into doing the same.

We formed a preparatory group to shepherd the process and hired three stellar talents: Sun Lu, a young professor from Tsinghua University; Li Jie, a young cadre from Wuhan; and Feng Jia, a graduate student from Southwestern University of Finance and Economics. Sun Lu was responsible for drafting papers and publicity, Li Jie was responsible for communications and coordination work among all departments, and Feng Jia played the role of "brain trust" and pulling in investment.

Older employees began to resist the momentum. They naturally were unaccustomed to seeing these fresh young faces around them all the time. The manager of the sales department, Zhan Hongxiang, publicly expressed his disdain: "They look busy all the time, but if you want to make money you still have to depend on the sales department." He made it clear he thought that the three depended on his department for their salaries, that they merely wagged their tongues while others did the work. Some older employees got together to debate the matter and began calling the three new recruits "grandpas who depend on the boss." They felt that they themselves were already doing everything necessary: getting financing, processing products, and marketing products. Why was there any need for these "grandpas"? Attitudes against a share-ownership system gradually crystallized into opposition as the process drew nearer.

The crux of the problem was that employees of the state were not willing to abandon the privileges they had been enjoying. These included not just the security of the proverbial Iron Rice Bowl (that is, an occupation with guaranteed job security), but also the benefits of a successful enterprise. They feared for their futures. They assumed that once the reform was accomplished, they would no longer be working in a system of lifetime employment. Even though our enterprise was established in the Special Economic Zone, it still was a state-run company. "Do you want to put us on the street to beg?" was the plaintive lament.

The older employees chose two men, Zhan Hongxiang and Gao Jianming, to serve as their representatives in presenting their case to me. "Once the company undergoes shareholding reform," Mr. Zhan and Mr. Gao said, "we suddenly will no longer have a patron. It would be best, frankly, to just split up the money we've already made over these years. After that, you all can do what you want." The idea was that these older employees did not want to share earnings accumulated earlier with upstarts who came later. Once the older employees got what was due to them, then whatever Wang Shi and his young recruits wanted to do was fine.

After that, the call went around among older employees that we should "first privatize housing before we carry out shareholding reform."

The Shekou China Accounting Office conducted an audit of the company that listed assets up to October 1988. Its net assets were RMB 13 million (USD 3.51 million) at the time. Housing assets represented RMB 5 million (USD 1.35 million) of that total. If this portion were separated out for the older employees, the company's assets would be reduced by nearly one-half, and this was not conducive to increasing the value of shares. Naturally, I would not make that compromise.

After considerable discussion and various forms of persuasion, some of the older employees still balked at share reform, but most were ready for the company to proceed with it. We then began to write and rewrite a prospectus, under the guidance of consultants from Sun Hung Kai, the Hong Kong securities firm. Seventeen drafts were necessary before the thing was finally done.

One major sticking point was the language about standardized procedures, transparent dealings, and observance of the law. It aroused a heated controversy. Most people felt that the great majority of our competitors did not abide by upright and proper standards of behavior, so it would hobble us to commit to such standards ourselves. They felt we should not bookishly subscribe to what patently was not in our interests. As part of the minority faction, I disagreed. I maintained that we had to distance ourselves from the past and begin to walk down a new path. It might not go through for us, but in the future the market would definitely be standardized; if our path did go through, we would be striding out ahead of all the rest.

"At the outset, we had to rely on trade to get the company going," I said.

"What's more, as we all know, it was often necessary to have good connections to do business when Shenzhen was just starting to be liberated. We had to get permits, define policies in ways that favored us, move through loopholes in the law. But if the company is to develop and really do something, it cannot keep walking the old path. From now on, it has to standardize and do things properly. Regulated proper business is imperative if China is to move into a market economy. As much as possible, we must seek to operate in line with international conventions. After undergoing shareholding reform, we must put our core efforts into being a 'standard' company. Indeed, we intend to be the most standard enterprise in all of China."

The meeting in which we debated this matter went on until 2 a.m. I suddenly asked Sun Lu, "Hey, Sun Lu, think of it. If what you are working so hard on today still carries on after 10 years, 20 years, won't that be pretty amazing?"

When I realized the full significance of what we were aiming to do, a great weight seemed to fall from my tired body. A banner waved in my mind, on which was the emblem of a company that was leading the way, guiding others along the broad boulevard of innovation and reform. Wave on! I thought. Oh, wave on!

After that, the next steps were to hand over our reform report to the Shenzhen Municipal Office of the Reform Commission. Once we put our application in, two other companies in Shenzhen also handed over their plan for shareholding reform, namely Jintian and Yuanye.

The reform commission was extremely excited by this positive response of a state-owned enterprise to the call for shareholding reform.

"Jumping Out of the Palm of Buddha"

Our application for shareholding reform began to make its way through the approval process. First, the director of the Infrastructure Reform Office, Xu Jing'an, led his staff to our headquarters at 50 Peace Road to look over the situation in person. The most sensitive part of our application was our proposal that the RMB 13 million (USD 3.51 million) in net assets be split 50/50: fifty for the state and fifty for the employees of the enterprise.

This issue then arrived on the desk of the deputy mayor of Shenzhen, the man directly responsible for reform of enterprise structures, Zhu Yuening.

This deputy mayor had previously wielded his pen in the Research Office of the State Economic Commission. Sitting across from Zhu Yuening, I got in the first word: "From a legal perspective the company has a license from the state, and the state is supposed to carry the risk. In point of fact, the state has not put in one cent of investment. The company's assets were built up entirely by me and my staff, barehanded. It is therefore not quite right to say that the entire company belongs to the state, because, after all, the funding came from us. Since that's the case, half and half. What do you say?"

Deputy Mayor Zhu looked with appreciative eyes at this company founder who so eagerly wanted to carry on with reform. "Fifty-fifty won't do,'" he said. "Forty-sixty."

"You take 40; we take 60?"

"Ha ha! How can the state hold the minority! Naturally the government takes 60 and you take 40."

"Well, okay, then. A gentleman's word is his honor—no taking it back." I tried to hide my joy. I was thinking to myself, 40/60, 20/80, 10/90 would be fine! Any clear division of assets would mean that we could move forward.

As I was leaving his office, Deputy Mayor Zhu asked, as though it were an afterthought, "Have you reported this to your parent company?"

"Yes," I replied. "We sent them a copy of the same application we made to the reform commission."

"That's good. Tomorrow the office of the municipal government will issue the permit that approves your application to undertake share reform."

The next day we were eagerly awaiting the all-important red-headlined document when a telephone call came from the municipal office. A representative from SD, our parent company, was at the municipal office submitting a strongly worded petition. This demanded that the municipal office retract permission for us to go forward. Its reason: we were interfering with "normal internal management procedures" by going around SD. We were bypassing our immediate authority and appealing to a higher level.

I called Xu Jing'an, head of the Infrastructure Reform Commission. Nobody answered. I called Deputy Mayor Zhu: his secretary told me that he had a bad stomachache and would be in the hospital for an indefinite length of time.

In light of SD's strong opposition, the municipal office temporarily suspended its permission for the Modern Enterprise Company (MEC) to undertake shareholding reform by implementing a shareholding plan. We were told to work this out with our immediate superior authority before proceeding to send the document on for examination and approval.

This news was like being hit with a pail of cold water. Our prospectus was ready to be announced in the *Shenzhen News*, and the first shareholder meeting was planned to the last detail. I met with our internal shareholding reform committee to discuss countermeasures. It was clear that we had no alternative. We had to grit our teeth and have a face-to-face meeting with a parent company that fiercely opposed our independence.

Sun Kaifeng had already left his position at SD Group and been succeeded by a man named Yuan Taoren. He was formerly head of the computer department at the Ministry of Electronics in Beijing.

Scene: the conference room at the headquarters of the SD Group. Yuan Taoren heard my explanation while his face remained impassive. When I was done, he let loose: "You, Wang Shi, have thought you were a stallion striding through the heavens, going wherever you wished to go. You are only now beginning to realize that you can go as far as you like, but you will never be able to jump out of the palm of Buddha."

This phrase from the ancient Chinese classic *Journey to the West* was quoted to indicate that I would not be able to escape the clutches of SD control.

Li Jingquan, deputy manager of SD and the man who had submitted the petition opposing our independence, was sitting next to Yuan. He now spoke: "One of our other companies, Guoshang, is also applying for share-ownership reform. Their application, which we support, has also been put to the Infrastructure Reform Commission. In fact, it went through us, but for some reason yours, which went around proper channels, got red-headlined treatment, whereas Guoshang has not had any reply. If enterprises under the authority of SD are going to mess with authority like yours, Wang Shi, things will get totally out of control."

My heart was pounding. I said to myself, "All right, mister. We'll see. You, Yuan Taoren, have just been transferred from central, from 'inside,' so you can play big official—you squash little people all you like. There is no way I am going to let Guoshang be first. We will accomplish our share reform before you do, if it kills me."

How was I going to do that? We couldn't sit there and wait for the final bullet. I began to explore alternative channels.

Someone from the New Age Company, Wang Xiaomin, came from Changchun and was in close contact with cadres in the government who had Changchun backgrounds. He recommended that, under my own name, I invite members of the Municipal Party Committee and executive secretaries of the municipal government to a gathering to discuss difficulties encountered in implementing share-ownership reform. He recommended that we also invite the media and bring the issue before the public.

With Wang Xiaomin as our liaison person, we sent out 20 letters of invitation. I expected one-third of the people to respond. To my surprise, every single person came. We presented a kind of instruction course on share-ownership reform to these executive secretaries.

My next step was to request a meeting with the party secretary of the Shenzhen municipality. This was at the recommendation of an emergency plan of our shareholding preparatory group. Party Secretary Li Hao had served concurrently as mayor. My interaction with him had been limited to public forums and conferences in the past. I had never met him or requested a meeting, but he agreed to see me.

His office turned out to be tiny. He sat behind a small table in front of which were placed two stools. I sat on one of these; my colleague Zhang Xifu sat on the other. We watched as he practiced calligraphy throughout the course of my presentation. As I spoke, I kept thinking that the least he could do was put down his brush and pay attention. Nonetheless, I soldiered on.

When my report was finished, Mayor Li finally set aside his brush and looked up at us. "Young people should keep calm, be steady," he said. "Naturally, reform is going to face opposition. Otherwise it would not be called 'reform.' First, we have systems we must follow in our government administration. Government cannot handle your company directly. Instead, we manage ministries, commissions, bureaus. Each of these in turn manages the companies under its jurisdiction. If we were to give you an opinion directly on this matter, the layers in between would not be happy and management would be in a mess. Second, you are correct in moving toward share-ownership reform. However, you should not be in too much of a hurry. The system has to operate according to its normal ways of functioning. You should be aware that Yuan Taoren can be quite rigid, and he is a man with Beijing connections. From now on, if you want to communicate with us, you can contact my executive secretary, Tang Huozhao, directly. However, you must not be seen meeting in public. Be careful in the methods you choose and your tactics."

This was a considerable advance. I soon learned that we were not alone in our predicament. Two other companies, Jintian and Yuanye, had also met with the same kind of opposition. The companies that had jurisdiction over them also refused to allow them to become shareholding companies. We three commiserated on our common ailment. Mayor Li's secretary, Tang Huozhao, met with each of us separately and kept us apprised of progress. This arrangement went outside of all normal channels, so it had the clandestine feeling of being "underground work."

One week later, I walked into the office of Qin Wenjun, deputy secretary of the Municipal Committee. This dyed-in-the-wool scholar had previously been Chairman of the Policy Research Office of the Party Committee of Guangdong Province. He made it quite clear that he was an active supporter of shareholding structural reform of enterprises at the grassroots level. Deputy Secretary Qin's refreshing attitude made me think that we had some hope.

The next day, Deputy Secretary Qin saddled up his horse and paid a personal call on SD. He was there to "comb out" the thinking of Yuan Taoren.

Soon, there was nothing for Yuan Taoren to do but turn his boat around and go in the direction of the flow. Did he really have connections with senior people in Beijing? Some say he did, but it was never proven.

A Communist Party Newspaper Takes a Brave Step

The name of our company kept changing along the way. By 1988 it was Shenzhen Modern Enterprise Limited, a name I rather liked: simple, easy to remember, and capable of being rolled off the tongue. But in the process of handling the procedures to become a shareholding company, we became aware that this name had not taken international registration into account. Our company has the same Chinese pronunciation as the famous Hyundai Group of South Korea, both being "*xiandai.*"

We had to change names again, and this time we were more careful.

To come up with a name, some senior managers as well as a group of employees took a boat ride together. We motored around the waters off the mouth of the Pearl River. As we were sequestered on the boat, the only thing we could do was gaze at the wide ocean and think of names. Back in Shenzhen, we put all of the names people had thought of on a blackboard and began to compare them. In English, the name of our company was Shenzhen Modern Enterprise Company (MEC). In the end, the discussion came around to how to extend a new name from this abbreviation, since that would give the new name more continuity with the old one. Some people said we should just use MEC and not worry about it. However, this was very similar to Japan's NEC. Moreover, the sound of the name in Chinese was a little too similar to a popular idol at the time. Did we want to have people think of an actor instead of us every time they heard the name? At that point, somebody thought we should change the company name to Mai-ke, but in Cantonese this meant something "black," or mafia related. People would think we were a particularly nasty company.

A young graduate of Shenzhen University who had majored in English, Pan Yiyong, finally thought of the name Wan-ke, which means "ten thousand *ke*"—*ke* meaning a branch of study or knowledge. Marlboro cigarettes in Chinese also used this word *wan*, or "ten thousand," so why couldn't we? The name stuck. The company formally changed its name to the Shenzhen Wan-ke Co., Ltd. [In English, *Wan-ke* was then changed to *Vanke*.]

The *Shenzhen Special Zone Daily* had an acute understanding of the significance of Vanke's shareholding reform. The five editors responsible for the front page threw themselves into editing the story. It was rare for five editors from this newspaper to work simultaneously on one topic. During this period, I met frequently with the group, together with Sun Lu and Feng Jia from Vanke. We talked through the night on policies related to the media and propaganda, and we all had an extremely stimulating time.

On November 21, 1988, the Shenzhen municipal government approved the share-ownership reform plan of the company. The Shenzhen branch of the People's Bank of China agreed to underwrite Vanke's shares. The name of the company was confirmed as the Shenzhen Vanke Enterprise Co., Ltd. The net assets of RMB 13.24 million (USD 3.58 million) that had originally belonged to the Modern Enterprise Company would be converted into 13.24 million shares. The state would hold 60 percent; employees would hold 40 percent. Our public offering was for RMB 28 million (USD 7.52 million). Of this amount, RMB 10 million (USD 3.72 million) was to be "special RMB shares," bought by investors outside the country's borders. SD changed from being the authority with direct jurisdiction over Vanke to becoming the company's largest shareholder, with 30 percent of its shares.

We sent a lengthy prospectus to the advertising department of the *Shenzhen Special Zone Daily*. By law, we had to announce the public offering in an open manner in a newspaper.

The head of this advertising department read through our document and painstakingly cross-checked it—it filled two entire spreads in the paper. He then asked the deputy editor-in-chief of the paper to read and check it as well. Apparently too timid to make any decisions, this man in turn handed the matter over to the editor in chief. The editor in chief replied to us in writing: it was not appropriate for a Communist Party organ to advertise the stock offering of a corporation. It was one thing to publicize the party's support of share ownership reform in general. It was quite another to allow advertisements for the share offering of a specific company. He would not publish the announcement of the public offering.

This was a serious snag. The prospectus came back to us.

According to Hong Kong regulations for public offerings, we had to put the news of our offering in a public newspaper. Otherwise it could be presumed that this was a private offering, the meaning of which was not the same. What to do? Our thoughts again turned to the man in charge of reform of the economic structure, Deputy Secretary of the Municipal Party Committee Qin Wenjun.

Again, we strode into his office. He heard us out. He thought quietly for a moment before removing the cap from his fountain pen. Directly on the prospectus lying on the table before him, he wrote four words: "New procedures. Support this."

These four words were the magic spell. The editor in chief was now happy to publish our prospectus. He not only approved the listing, he asked his deputies to publish the entire text for free.

We held our first shareholder meeting on December 6, 1988. This was in the third-floor conference room at 50 Peace Road in Shenzhen. We passed the company bylaws and a set of important resolutions.

On December 22, the Shenzhen branch of the People's Bank of China gave its official written approval for us to issue Vanke shares. On the same day, Vanke and the Shenzhen Special Economic Zone Securities Company signed an agreement on dealing with shares and a contract to serve as sole agent in selling Vanke shares.

On the morning of December 24, the second meeting of Vanke shareholders unanimously elected me to be Vanke's legal representative. This again was in the third-floor conference room at 50 Peace Road.

On December 25, Vanke signed a contract for retail sale of its shares with the Shenzhen International Trust Consulting Company of the Bank of China. On December 27, our prospectus was listed in the *Shenzhen Special Zone Daily* in its entirety. It was the very first prospectus written according to international practices ever to be published in a newspaper in China. It may also be the last time a prospectus has been placed in a Chinese paper for free.

Selling Shares and Giving Up Shareholding Rights

Vanke shares began to be offered for sale to the public on December 28, 1988.

The Shenzhen Securities Company and the Trust Company of the Bank of China were the sole agents and underwriters of the stock. Each took 6 million shares. In the late 1980s, people in Shenzhen were all immigrants, and this immigrant society was quite familiar with the expanses of yellow earth that they had come from, as well as the dollar amount implicit in every import license. They also knew the commercial value of land, but they were complete innocents when it came to shares.

One year earlier, on December 2, 1987, six rural credit cooperatives in the zone had pooled their resources and founded the Shenzhen Special Economic Zone Development Bank. They sold shares through private placement. To support share-ownership reform initiatives, the mayor-cum-party secretary Li Hao called on his colleagues to buy shares, and he led the way in spending years of his own savings to get these pieces of paper. It is one thing to wave a flag, and another to get people to take real money out of their own pockets. The response to his initiative was lukewarm. Five years later, in 1992, Deng Xiaoping made his southern tour, and the value of the few shares then in existence in China shot upward. Shares in such financial institutions as Shenzhen Development were particularly desirable, and Mayor Li's investment increased to multiples of the original price. Financial stocks such as the Shenzhen Development Bank multiplied in value. Mayor Li's shares, purchased way back when, appreciated to prices that ran to tens of millions to hundreds of millions. But that is another story.

In December 1988, Vanke had been allowed to issue a public offering of shares, and the newspaper had trumpeted its virtues, but nobody bought. Nobody was interested. It was up to us to beat the bushes and find supporters. In order to promote the stock, my colleague Sun Lu set what he called a "Dragon-Year Plan," and I was made its commander in chief.

With a slender rod in hand, I went around lecturing to groups of people, trying to educate them about the benefits of the share-ownership system and the virtues of Vanke shares in particular. I talked to banks and I talked to companies. I combed through Shenzhen businesses with a fine-tooth comb. Remembering it later, Sun Lu said, "We almost climbed into fishing boats and asked the fishermen to buy our stock."

Sun Lu led a second charge himself. He headed out the door every day with a sheaf of shares and receipt forms under his arm. We judged his success by how fat his bundle was when he returned. Normal people might buy 300 to 500 yuan's (RMB) worth, and he might be able to sell 4,000 to 5,000 shares in a day. Once he lectured to a group of private entrepreneurs, through the introduction of the Business and Commerce Management Bureau, which got in touch with the Association of Commerce and Industry. This association pulled together some people involved in business. Sun Lu had on his usual broad-rimmed eyeglasses. After he had talked for no more than three minutes, a cry came from the audience: "No more talk! Just give us a number: how much?"*

---

*The term originally used here, *tanpai*, refers to charges and denotions. It literally means "allocation of costs." In other words, the members of the association were willing to pay up, not to invest, but to do their duty by their bosses. They assumed this was like a normal fee required to keep doing business.

As the cut-off day for the issue approached, however, some 7 million shares had still not been sold. Flogging the shares was much harder than we had expected. One night we ended a sales analysis meeting at 1 a.m. "Where shall we go for a midnight snack?," Sun Lu asked. I said I wasn't hungry but I would take everyone to a place I knew.

The cavernous room was cold and empty in the middle of the night. My colleagues looked in and were amazed to see that I had brought them to an ice-skating rink. We all put on skates and headed out, slipping and falling, bruising knees and shins, but laughing and having a good time. In an hour, our bottled-up emotions had relaxed. Still, as I took off my skates, my head was full of that statement by Yuan Taoren: "A Sun Wukong like you may jump 18,000 *li* [about 30 million feet] in one bound, but you can't jump out of the palm of Buddha." In the end, was that going to be true?

One good piece of news finally came through. The company Huawei was receptive to our promotion team. Ren Zhengfei, its boss, had signed up to buy 200,000 shares. He had questioned our staff in detail about the stock system and how it worked, and in the end had said he just regretted not being able to buy more, due to his limited amount of liquid capital. Back then, Huawei was neither famous nor successful. It was mired in the hardships of setting up a company. Ren Zhengfei was already displaying his prowess, however—his alert attitude toward new things, his decisive behavior, attributes that would take Huawei to the remarkable heights that it enjoys today.

On the final day, we still had 3.5 million shares that had not been sold, and it looked as though the placement would not be a success. People can do all in their power, as the saying goes, but the final call rests with heaven.

With just an hour and a half left to go before the end of work that final day, a telephone call came through. The caller announced himself as being Wang Yuelong, General Controller of the Finance Department of the Beijing China Founders Company. "Wang Jianguo in Shekou told me Vanke is selling shares," he said. "I came as fast as I could from Beijing, but it was already midnight when I got here last night. I studied your prospectus today. I then asked for instructions from our general manager, Zhang Xiaobing. We would like to sub-scribe to 4 million shares. Is that okay?"

"Yes!" Whoever this Wang Jianguo of Shekou was, we truly thanked him.

On March 8 of 1989, the Shekou China Accounting Office officially pub-lished its audit of the Shenzhen Vanke Co., Ltd. Our assets came to a grand total of RMB 41,246,680.17 (USD 11 million). This included the original RMB 13,246,680.17 (USD 3,532,500) of the Modern Enterprise Company as of October 31, 1988. We now added RMB 28 million (USD 5.33 million) in cash from the issue of shares.

At 9 a.m. on March 28, the Vanke Shareholding Company, Ltd. held its first shareholder meeting. There were no empty seats. A question-and-answer session followed the business meeting. One man stood up and wielded the microphone: "A question for Wang Shi: How many shares did you personally buy yourself?"

I pulled my share certificates from my trouser pocket and replied, "I personally have savings of RMB 25,000 [about USD 6,650], of which I have put 20,000 [about USD 5,350] into buying Vanke shares." Thunderous applause erupted from the audience below.

Vanke employees received 5 million among 41 million shares. According to share reform regulations, no more than 10 percent of this could be granted as shares under the names of individuals. The rest had to be held as a group. I thought this through and decided to give up the portion that was to come to me and to place it under the group category as a benefit to all employees.

My reasons for this stemmed from three factors. First, Chinese people have a deep-seated dislike of others who have more than they do. The prevailing sentiment is "inequality rather than want is the cause of trouble." An individual who suddenly has money puts himself in an unfavorable position. If, like me, he enjoys an unrestrained way of life and playing a public role in trumpeting reform, he is especially liable to attract jealousy and discontent. I would rather achieve a cause with clear hands than silently make a pile of money.

Secondly, I myself dislike the image of the nouveau riche. When I was young, I read enough admirable authors to turn me against ostentation. Whenever I discover that I am projecting that image, I try to change it.

Third, my family background never seemed to have had a gene for managing wealth. My father's forebears come from Anhui. (I have never been back there myself.) During the process of shareholding reform, I was sent a copy of my family genealogy by my cousin, which I found went back 20 generations. Among all these generations of farmers, not one became a landlord and not one seemed to show any capacity for handling money. After all, when traditional farmers made money, what did they do with it? Built ancestral halls, took mistresses, and gambled.

The shares that I gave up were put into a fund together with other employee shares. The income can be used only for the benefit of Vanke employees. The fund is managed by a committee composed of employee representatives. The emphasis is on employees who entered the company before 1988; the rest is to be used to give back to society, on public works.

A Prenup Before Getting Married

Vanke's business grew dramatically as the share reform became a success.

In 1988 alone, the Vanke joint venture with the Renda Company of Hong Kong set up a number of processing ventures, manufacturing facilities to carry on value-added processing. We went into manufacturing color television sets. We set up a joint venture with an Italian jewelry maker to make karat gold jewelry. We set up a company with the Franklin Mint that made model cars. Together with the China Equipment Import and Export Company, we worked with Sony to set up a Sony service center in Shenzhen. We jointly set up a processing company with a Hong Kong company called Vanke Houli Limited.

With England, we set up an X10 systems company to make the remote control switches for electric heaters. We set up a facility to manufacture parts for video recorders.

All of these different forms of cooperation and joint ventures involved processing materials within China that came from outside China. Among them, the most significant project was that with the Franklin Mint in the United States. This was to make high-end model cars and other gift items. Manufacturing was done at a six-story factory building at Shenzhen's Shuibei industrial park, a building that was also Vanke's procurement facility.

We learned a tremendous amount from this project. We had advertised in various American magazines in an attempt to attract investment for our projects. The Franklin Mint saw one ad and contacted us. Many others had responded, but I saw that this company had a depth of professionalism that others lacked. I felt this was a golden opportunity that we should grab onto. The first person that the Franklin Mint sent over was from Hong Kong. Two weeks later, he was succeeded by an American of German descent. One month later, yet another person took over, this time a Japanese-American. Later, an American Jewish lawyer wrote the contract, and only when it was time to sign that contract did the boss appear, an Irish-American.

The German-American left the deepest impression on me, as we negotiated the contract. He had served his military service as a helicopter pilot in Vietnam in 1968, at a time when I was doing my own military duty as a convoy driver. Our truck brigade was at one point being prepared to go to Vietnam. Instead, another troop was sent and we were transferred to Xinjiang. The German-American and I were almost mortal enemies in war, yet here we were working together as partners in Shenzhen.

At the beginning, I didn't pay too much attention to the constantly changing personnel. As we entered serious negotiations, however, I began to understand the logic of this approach. The Hong Kong man knew the situation on the mainland and could evaluate us accurately. The German-American knew the technical aspects, while the Japanese was a master at controlling production costs. The Jewish lawyer focused mostly on how to get out of the contract with us once it was finished. In this regard, every detail was negotiated, down to what would happen to the glass partitions between offices. It was like making sure you had a divorce negotiated and signed off on before you got married.

I was not accustomed to this protracted and detailed style of negotiating, but I discovered that there was actually room to maneuver in terms of price. You could get a better price, but you had to explain your reasoning and answer the question *Why?*

During negotiation for the space that Franklin would lease in our building, Franklin first wanted just two floors and we eventually gave them the fifth and sixth floors, which they were happy about. They thought the view was better and the air was probably fresher than at lower floors. Later, they wanted another floor and we added the fourth, at roughly the same price as the fifth and sixth floors. Nearing the end of the negotiations, they wanted still another floor, however, and said they wanted it to be the second floor. We had planned to keep that for ourselves, so we hiked the price by 50 percent.

"Why?," they asked.

I had not expected to have to give a reason, so I made an off-the-cuff response: "The second floor is more convenient. You don't have to use the elevator, and when the electricity goes out, employees can get up and down more quickly." In Shenzhen's industrial districts, you often had electric outages, but this explanation was somewhat forced, particularly as Franklin Mint planned to set up their own electric generator on the first floor.

I covered myself with a little laugh, and they laughed too . . . and then they accepted my price. They thought this was, after all, a reasonable explanation.

When we finally signed the contract, it was thicker than a prospectus. The law firm responsible for drawing up the agreement was an U.S. firm based in Hong Kong, and the legal costs alone came to HKD 3 million (USD 385,000), paid by Franklin. I kept thinking, *If only they would give us that money, what we couldn't do with it!*

In cooperating with Franklin, we learned about the professionalism of American business. Making money was still important, but even more important were things like methodology, the makeup of qualified personnel, a rigorous approach to work, an emphasis on efficiency, a respect for the law, and a professional spirit. All of this was invaluable for us in the years ahead.

Contracts that Vanke signed with its partners now became much thicker than before. This bothered many of our partners, especially worrying about the "divorce terms"—ways to part ways even before you've begun to cooperate. I, too, worried with Franklin that the Vanke team might not be able to perform and that we would then come up against their strict conditions. In fact, the worries were ungrounded. Our team performed way above expectations, and, when it came right down to it, the Franklin Mint was fairly flexible in how they implemented the terms of the contract.

The process of cooperating with Franklin was a major step forward in Vanke's learning how to internationalize. Many have said that Vanke's success has been a result of its early westernization and resulting professionalism. The Franklin Mint should take some credit in that.

An Expensive Ticket to Get into the Real Estate Business

In 1988, the threshold for entry into the real estate business in Shenzhen was high. Any non-construction-type company first had to get a piece of land by bidding for it at auction. Only after it had the land could it apply for a one-time single permit to develop that land.

In November, Vanke participated in a land auction for what was to become the Weideng Villa development.

By this time, phase one of Vanke's share reform had been completed. The talented Feng Jia had joined the planning team for real estate. The head of this team, Yang Haisheng, was the son of an army family. He was tough and could take hard work, but he was also stubborn. He had his father's personality, a man who had been head of a tank division in a field army. The deputy head of the group was Zhang Yu, who came from Wuhan and was gentle and suave; he used to be a secretary.

The scene: the Shenzhen Municipal Hall. The auctioneer: again Liu Jiasheng.

On my left sat Feng Jia. On my right was Yang Haisheng, the army man's son, who wielded the auction paddle with our number on it.

The bidding began and the price went straight up. Eventually only two bidders remained, Vanke and another contender taking the price higher in each round. Neither would give in as the bidding went into a white heat. If the bidder did not voluntarily raise his paddle and call out a price, the auctioneer kept going up in increments of RMB 500,000 (USD 75,115). Vanke was determined to win. But what if the other side was too? I cringed internally as the bidding continued. The other side raised the paddle one more time, and the auctioneer called out a price. Once . . . twice . . . why didn't Yang Haisheng lift his paddle?

The auctioneer raised his gavel.

I instinctively grabbed the paddle out of Yang Haisheng's hands and held it aloft, shouting out a higher price as I did so.

The auctioneer announced the new price. Once . . . twice . . . three times he called the price, and then the gavel came down.

The price that Vanke paid for this piece of empty land was high. You could have bought the surrounding buildings, torn them down, and rebuilt something else on the land and still paid a lower price. When I went up on the dais to confirm my final price and sign the transfer, Liu Jiasheng just looked at me and said, "You're crazy. Nevertheless . . . I congratulate you."

We had taken the necessary first step to entering the real estate business. And it was true that the first step was expensive. Who had pushed us into this position? We found out that the other bidder was a privately owned and managed company with a boss from Hunan. The name was the Shenzhen Zhenghua Business Company. He had brought his own "army" of local Hunan people with him to Shenzhen, to set up in business. He came from poverty and was now moving strongly into industrial real estate as well as entertainment. No wonder he had fought so hard. When he finally let go at the end, he too must have thought he had met up with a madman.

Our first pressing task was to deal with reporters. What would we say tomorrow in response to their questions? Back to 50 Peace Road. I asked my secretary to buy up any books he could find in street stalls that dealt with feng shui. When he got back with a stack of books, I spent all night reading. The next day, in the face of questions from reporters, I spoke in lofty terms about the dragon-spine of that piece of land: "You've all seen how the reeds flourish there? Look at it in terms of feng shui: that land has flowing water, and water, as we all know, is wealth. There's a green dragon on the left and a white tiger on the right, vermilion hawk in front and black . . ." I went on in this vein.

When we began construction work on the property, digging out the foundation, in fact we did encounter water exactly where the reeds grew. Since we couldn't stop it, we built a well there after the villas were built, in commemoration of the feng shui story.

For a sky-high price of RMB 20 million (USD 5.4 million), we had bought an entry ticket into the real estate market in Shenzhen. For a while, the thinking among our Vanke management team was that this nettle was too prickly and we should let go of it. We should renege on the contract. Nonperformance would result in a fine, but that would be better than carrying a heavy debt load. I felt differently. Not only would I not renege on the contract, I wanted to buy a second patch of land.

One month later, the Tianjing piece of land came up for auction. Vanke again bid, and again we won the bidding. The Shenzhen real estate community no longer looked down on us—we might be a newborn calf, but we were strangely unafraid of tigers.

We now established a real estatement department within the company. I served as director, Yao Mumin was deputy director. Liu Peng was head of the engineering department. Lin Hanbin was head of finance; Feng Jia was in charge of project development. Guo Zhaobin was in charge of sales, while Zhang Yu managed the office. Che Weiqing, who later became the manager of the Shenzhen Real Estate Company, served as just one of the salespeople at that time. A 12-person team comprised the Real Estate Department of the company. Other than I myself, who once was a drainage engineer, none had ever been involved in real estate development or construction. Everyone learned as he went along.

Being an outsider to the business had its advantages. The company had no rules and regulations. Instead, we searched out people we could learn from, which meant we delighted in hiring young people who were courageous and innovative. Gao Feng and Fu Zhiqiang now came into Vanke's line of vision, two young designers who had graduated from Tongji University. These two won the competition to design the Tianjing project after we had reviewed various plans from a number of design firms.

The funds that we could devote to project development were tight once we had bought these two pieces of land one right after another. The RMB 1 million (about USD 270,000) needed to build a model for the Tianjing Garden project came from an emergency loan that Lin Hanbin was able to get from a branch bank of the railroad bank system. The portion of money needed to actually develop the project came from a friend that Feng Jia had met at a tea shop, from the Yueyin company. Liu Peng broke records in getting the model built for that project. When the electricity went out—a not uncommon occurrence—he would keep working by the headlights of his motorcycle. Meanwhile, Che Weiqing sold rooms in the project as fast as he could, even bringing his children to the salesroom model on Sundays.

Once the Tianjing Garden project began, we pushed forward with the Weideng Villa project at the same time, but we deliberated on every cost as we went along since the price of its underlying land had been so high.

In order to become more professional in the real estate area, we began to bring in people who were expert in different fields, including Xia Nan, Huang Ruigang, and Lou Yingping. A person who later became the boss of Vanke's building management department came in at this time who formerly had been an electrical engineer.

Even as our real estate business moved forward, Vanke now began to diversify. The company set up a movie studio and began to produce films, with the film director Zheng Kainan as general manager. We set up a company to supply electric power, in order for small industrial areas to have an assured source of electricity. Tu Guoqing was its general manager. We had bought an expensive ticket to get into the real estate business, but we were reluctant to let go of other opportunities and the security they provided. It was a busy year.

A Piece of Gold in Each Footprint

In May 1989, Shenzhen was being pummeled by sheets of rain. The Luohu District had become a marsh, and in places I had to plow through knee-high water to reach 50 Peace Road. It was Sunday and our main offices in the three-story headquarters building were empty.

A film crew from Columbia Broadcasting in the United States was making a special trip from Beijing to Guangzhou, and then on to Shenzhen, to interview me. During this honeymoon period in Sino-U.S. relations, American media was looking with great interest on market-economy reforms in China. The production team was coming at the suggestion of the American consulate's commercial section, who told them that "Shenzhen has a company that has already implemented share ownership reform, and the company founder is one of the Chinese Mainland's most successful entrepreneurs."

Li Jie was in charge of the arrangements, with my secretary, Wen Xiangdong, serving as interpreter. She had graduated with a master's in English from Sun Yat-sen University.

Our conference room became a mini studio: lights, cameras, the host on one side, the atmosphere tense and serious.

> HOST: *May I ask Mr. Wang Shi, what is your personal wealth right now?*
> WANG SHI: *I have no personal wealth.*
> HOST: *It's awkward to talk about it?*
> WANG SHI: *No, nothing like that. When we did the share-ownership reform, I had RMB 25,000 in savings. I put 20,000 of that into buying Vanke shares. When we finished the reform, the company assets were divided 40/60, with employees' shares held as a group holding. I did not take a single share.*
> HOST: *Why?*

This was hard for me to explain. In America, a successful entrepreneur is judged by how much money he has. How can someone be considered an entrepreneur in China if he doesn't have any money? The host would quite naturally feel that I was definitely not one of the mainland's most successful entrepreneurs.

During the course of this interview, Wen Xiangdong and the host of the show established a rapport, perhaps because both were women. Not long after, Wen was invited to the United States, and the host, an avid women's rights activist, served as guarantor. She went through all the hoops required to study for a PhD in the history of women's rights in the United States. Li Jie accompanied her on that first trip, as an adjunct student. During this trip, they struck a spark that turned into real love.

Between spring and summer of 1989, a political storm raged in China.* Due to personal reasons, I left Shenzhen on June 12 and did not return for a year. Cai Shuncheng served as acting general manager of the company during that period. Feng Jia and Zhou Shiping also temporarily left the company.

China's economy weakened during this period. Value-added processing of imported materials became our main source of profit, although the real estate sector also performed fairly well.

The next time I returned to Shenzhen, it was already May 13, 1990. At this time, Vanke shares on the Shenzhen exchange fluctuated between 0.88 and 0.92. Other shares listed on the exchange, such as the Development Bank and Jintian, were doing far better than Vanke's.

On the day I returned to Shenzhen, Vanke shares surged upward and kept on going. Rumors were going around among the speculators: Wang Shi was on the road back to Shenzhen, and there was a piece of gold in every one of his footsteps. Looking back on it, the price rise was nothing more than a fluke of timing, for other shares on the exchange rose briskly at the same time.

Back in Vanke, Cai told me a story.

In 1990, Vanke shareholders held their annual shareholders' meeting. Vanke's shares had already fallen below the issuing price. Concerned that shareholders would make trouble, to the extent that the situation might get out of control, the company had prepared an emergency exit plan for the board, just in case. During the meeting, when Cai asked for comments from the floor, a man stood up and approached the microphone. He was middle-aged and short, and he had a dark complexion. "This year," he began, "the management team of Vanke has done well, and I am quite satisfied. The fact that the share price is below the issue price is due to overall trends. Management is not at fault, and I don't think we should be overly concerned. I can see that Vanke's future is excellent. As its stock price comes down, I continue to buy. In contrast, some of you larger investors who are sitting up there on stage are casting off your shares. I don't name any names, but I want to emphasize one thing: as you sell, I am happy to buy." People clapped loudly at this speech, and the shareholders' meeting adjourned smoothly.

---

*The Tiananmen Incident occurred on June 4, 1989. Prior to that, inflation and economic uncertainty were already creating a climate of social unrest.

"Where does this gentleman come from, this Zhu Huanliang?"

"Hakka man. Army. He was a professional soldier, drove vehicles. After getting out he came to the zone to resell government bonds. He is quite influential among small private investors."

"This is a man I want to meet."

After meeting with Zhu Huanliang, I asked him to be on the Vanke board of directors as our representative for small investors. We were to have many and varied adventures together in the future.

One other situation developed during the time I was gone, and came to a head on my return. In 1990, SD, our major shareholder, completed the construction of its own building in Shenzhen. This Development Center Building was an impressive combination of technology and design. SD had spent a fortune on it, however, and wanted to recoup its investment as fast as possible. The company asked Vanke if we would take over the sales effort for finding tenants, since we had been quite successful in selling our own Tianjing Garden. Cai agreed. To handle this, he organized a special team, which conducted a detailed investigation on how best to proceed. The team rented a helicopter from the Jingdezhen military aircraft plant in Jiangxi, and the film director Zheng Kainan had his team of camera operators shoot aerial shots from all angles. The sales prospectus was soon complete. Everything was ready except for the final sales effort.

According to Vanke's projections, the sale of the Development Center Building would bring in close to RMB 13 million (about USD 3.5 million) in profit for Vanke as its commission.

The day before Vanke's ad was to be placed in the paper, SD suddenly withdrew its authorization to Vanke to sell the building and decided to sell it themselves. All we could do was urgently retract that ad copy from the newspaper and replace it with a corporate image piece.

This abrupt change by SD sparked my competitive instincts. So SD wanted to sell the building itself? Fine. We would help them. We would buy it, the whole thing.

SD was stunned. The boss of the company at this time was Wang Xinmin, formerly from the National Economic Commission. He had not been in SD for long and was not familiar with its procedures. The previous boss, Yuan Taoren, had done the sensible thing by exiting the company before things got too hot. He had not been careful enough about trifling economic matters, and this gave people who were opposed to him an opportunity. The person responsible for selling the building, therefore, was an assistant to the general manager named Yuan Chunxi. He had previously been secretary to Mayor Li Hao.

Vanke's ability to put up its own money was limited. We phoned several companies to see if they would participate. These included two firms in Hong Kong: Sun Hung Kai Securities and Tian An China. Sun Hung Kai had been Vanke's advisor during its securitization process. Tian An China was one of Vanke's underwriters. Meanwhile, we were very familiar with Thailand's Chia Tai Group from the time we did feedstuff business together.

The first two companies said they each would take 25 percent. That left

Chia Tai—an indication of interest on the part of this group remained to be seen.

I arranged to meet the key person at Chia Tai, Xie Guomin, at the Shenzhen Golf Club. After hearing me out, Mr. Xie came straight to the point. "Mr. Wang," he said, "just tell me how many shares you want us to take and how much you want us to invest. We trust you."

This was highly encouraging. The reason this affair was handled so smoothly was that our previous dealings had been smooth. I was yet again made aware of the fact that trust is priceless.

With Vanke leading the way, the four companies joined hands and officially issued a notice to SD that they wanted to buy the building. But a competitor now appeared—a finance group in Hong Kong.

SD began to equivocate. Their original conditions stiffened, and they began to raise the stakes. Yuan Chunxi clearly was leaning toward the Hong Kong group. The feeling we got was that SD would rather give it for free to friends than sell it to us. The result was to be expected: 90 percent of the building's assets were sold to the Hong Kong finance group, while SD retained 10 percent that it planned to use for its own new headquarters.

Our move to buy the Development Building had failed. Nevertheless, Vanke's newly launched retail business was going well as Vanke now purchased the fourth floor of the Luohu Commercial Building to serve as its commercial center. The company began to work closely with the Xiangyun Group of Beijing in the development of retail chain stores.

Most importantly, this new line of business led to a man named Yu Liang. In the early 1990s, Vanke's personnel policies welcomed people from Peking University or Tsinghua University—the company took such graduates without worrying about what they had majored in. One day, a visitor arrived in my office, the office of the chairman of the board of Vanke. He was a young man with a very bookish look. He placed his résumé on the table before him, together with a copy of his proposal for a chainstore retail sales model. He was looking for a job, and his name was Yu Liang. He had graduated from Peking University with a major in international economics, and had previously worked in Shenzhen's Foreign Trade Group. He was responding to Vanke's recruitment ad for someone who wanted to work in this area.*

On November 26, 1990, the Shenzhen municipality held a reception in the Xiangmihu Hall, and congratulated the Shenzhen Economic Zone on its tenth anniversary. Jiang Zemin, the Communist Party secretary general, attended, in addition to more than 500 guests from both China and overseas.

Shenzhen entered a new decade. One of the first and most important steps in the new decade was to establish a new stock exchange. The Shenzhen Stock

---

*Yu Liang has been CEO of Vanke since 2001.

Exchange was inaugurated on December 1, 1990, when shares began to be traded on this exchange and trade on the old board was stopped.

Vanke shares were officially listed on the new exchange on January 29, 1991. The registered number of our stock was 0002. We had weathered the vicissitudes of 1989–1990. Together with Shenzhen, we faced the promise of new times.

The Dream of Becoming a *Zaibatsu*

In early 1991, Vanke's annual strategic meeting formally initiated the concept of becoming a "comprehensive commercial association," formerly called a *zaibatsu* in Japan.

This term indicates a super-large trading company that also undertakes a variety of businesses, including financial, manufacturing, shipping, and so on. This proposal was not unrelated to the fact that Vanke had relied primarily on trade in the past, but it was also due to my concerns about the current state of commerce in China.

For some time, I had been aware that the underdeveloped state of China's commerce was closely related to the backwardness of China's contemporary society. China's traditional approach was to emphasize farming and not commerce, while its modern approach has been to emphasize heavy industry and not commerce. The order has always been agriculture—industry—commerce. In contrast, Japan's path of development clearly recognized the importance of trade as a way to build up the country. That country has actively promoted mercantilism as an ideology.

Since the establishment of the People's Republic of China, in 1949, the government has promoted a series of five-year plans that are centered on industrial development. These plans have enabled the formation of well-rounded industrial systems. China has excelled at producing 10,000-ton ships and huge hydraulic generators. We can smoothly detonate atom bombs, launch satellites, and so on. In contrast, our commercial systems have been held back and have remained primitive.

One could see this as an opportunity. Held back over a long period of time, commerce is precisely the area that now has the most potential for growth.

To capitalize on this opportunity, the question then became how Vanke could realize its goal of becoming a comprehensive commercial association, a *zaibatsu*.

Large Japanese trading companies or holding companies use finance as the glue that links all parts of the system.* Subsidiary enterprises have cross-holdings in each other, with financial strings that tie the upper and lower streams of business together to form a mutually beneficial group.

---

*The literal meaning of *zaibatsu* is "financial clique."

The reality in contemporary China is quite different from that of Japan, however. In China, certainly in 1991, finance was still tightly controlled, with no prospect of its being relaxed in the near future. What Vanke could pioneer in developing was the whole sphere of materials distribution. My own experience in the area of trade in the past few years had told me that the system governing import and export licenses and export quotas was already being monopolized by powerful interest groups. As a result, Vanke was restricted to a narrow band of possible action. The one thing that we could expand upon and that might serve as a larger platform in the future was retail distribution. I began to feel that copying the mature model of retail franchising in other countries was the best choice for Vanke.

Second, despite the tremendous growth possibilities in retail, we needed to rely on leveraging capital since our own self-generated savings were not enough. We would have to use the leverage of financial tools, carry out mergers and acquisitions, and participate in cross-shareholdings as well as control shares in other companies. Not only would this help us restructure and enable us to scale up, but it also would promise high rates of return from share investments, given China's newly emerging stock markets.

Another thing—China's state-owned enterprises held dominant control over the resources required for the country's economic development. Private enterprises would never grow on their own without working together with these state-owned entities. Only if both prospered would the market be healthy. Private entities would have to take the initiative in helping state-owned enterprises carry out reform of their systems and become shareholding entities, so that both could grow together.

The new blueprint for Vanke therefore divided the company's four main pillars into 10 specific industries. The four main pillars were trade, industry, real estate, and cultural affairs. The 10 industries were importing and exporting, retail, real estate, investment (including in shares), film, advertising, beverages, printing, machine processing, and electrical engineering.

After this strategic meeting, enthused by this idea that creating comprehensive commercial associations along the lines of Japan's *zaibatsu* would help, I asked key managers in the company to read a small volume on Japanese comprehensive commercial associations. It was around 200 pages long. I have no idea whether anyone actually read this book. When I recommended it to others, I at least had not actually read it.

One year later, on a flight back to Beijing, I had the opportunity to peruse it at some length. I began to break out in a cold sweat. In Japan, only nine companies could at the time be called comprehensive commercial associations, or *zaibatsu*. The smallest among them had revenues of USD 46.6 billion (RMB 247.91 billion) in 1991, roughly 16 times the GDP of Shenzhen in that year. Itochu was ranked number one, with revenues of USD 167 billion (about RMB 888 billion). This was more than the import and export trade of all of China. I realized the truth of that phrase about how the ignorant plunge ahead.

Getting off the plane, the first thing I did was to call the editor in chief of Vanke's weekly magazine. I made sure that he deleted the words *comprehensive commercial association* from our vocabulary, and I hoped that this whole line of thought could quietly be put to rest.

Snatching a Piece of Land in Shanghai, and Pulling Back from Beibu Gulf

The Jintian Company was located at 56 Peace Road, in the Taishan Building, which was just five minutes walking distance from Vanke. Originally in the garment business, Jintian followed shortly after Vanke in reforming its structure and becoming a shareholding company. It went into real estate in the same year as Vanke, and its registration number on the Shenzhen Stock Exchange was 0003. In the market, people always said we were two of a kind.

The founder of Jintian was Huang Hanqing. A Chaozhou man, he spoke with a rough voice, but he had a magnetic personality. He was slightly younger than I, and so he would always call me "elder brother" when we met. When it came to getting hold of land, however, this so-called little brother was many times more powerful than Vanke. Our ability to get hold of land could be rated at 10 to 1. That is, for every 10 patches Jintian got, Vanke got 1. The operating methods that Vanke insisted on using meant that our land reserves were always going to be less.

Once, when both of us were attending a study session on shareholding reform, Huang Hanqing and I began to discuss the real estate market in the Special Economic Zone during a break. Huang Hanqing pulled a list of figures from his pocket and bragged, "Look at how many projects we have. We'll never finish them all—we could give Vanke a couple if you're interested."

Clearly, we were not going to beat out Jintian in Shenzhen and there was little point in hanging around feeling badly about it. Vanke began to look for properties in which to invest that were outside of Shenzhen.

In August 1991, we heard that the Shanghai Land and Resources Bureau would be inviting tenders from international bidders for Lot No. 24 at a place in Shanghai known as Gubei New Area. Together with Super Ocean Group of Hong Kong, we participated in the bidding, and won. We paid USD 15 million (about RMB 80 million) for usage rights of an area of 50,000 square meters (164,042 square feet). The land-use category of this lot allowed it to be developed as what are known as villas in China, individual houses with some yard around them.

Yao Mumin was in charge of the team for this project, which included such people as Fu Zhiqiang and Huang Ruigang. The group settled down in a guesthouse in the western suburbs of Shanghai and began to put together the design plans for the parts that construction companies would bid on. Since this was a cross-jurisdictional project, he lacked administrative help and asked if headquarters could spare someone to come in.

"What kind of person?" I asked.

"Anyone, so long as they are enthusiastic about real estate and aren't needed somewhere else," Mr. Yao said.

I could meet those conditions easily.

The 88 villas designed for this No. 24 plot of land were still at the drafting stage when customers purchased every single one in advance. The market response was beyond belief.

In April of the next year, Shanghai Vanke again put up its hand and obtained the land-usage rights to another piece of land in Gubei New Area, this one authorized to build high-rises. We built the Vanke Plaza there. The first person I sent over to work with Big Yao (Yao Mumin) was Wen Mingsheng. He had originally been deputy manager of the Vanke Beijing Trading Company and had just arrived in Shenzhen when I sent him on to Shanghai to be general manager. He got things done with the proverbial vigor of a thunderbolt and the power of lightning. Always extremely neat and particular, he proved to be a tremendous help to Big Yao.

In the summer of 1992, the party secretary of the Beihai Municipality,* Wang Jilu, and the mayor, Shuai Liguo, came to Shenzhen to look for business partners and invited us to participate in their Beihai Real Estate Development. But by the time I took the mayor up on the invitation to look it over, he spread his hands in a gesture of dismay. "You're too late!," he said. "The ground is already taken!" After further inquiries, he was able to secure two small patches of land for us near the railway station, but this was not enough to satisfy our appetite at the time. Beihai has a small range of mountains and includes some beautiful scenery. I climbed to the top of one hill to enjoy the view down to the bay, and wondered if that ground had been taken as well. "So sorry," said Shuai Liguo, "it has already been taken by Wang Jun of CITIC."

At the dinner table that evening, after I had described Vanke's activities in Shanghai to the mayor, he thought for a moment, and said, "How about this? There is a piece of land that is 40 square kilometers (25 square miles) in size. If you pay just a token, some symbolic amount, we will give that to Vanke to develop."

I was amazed and excited by this proposal. It looked as though the grand blueprint that we could not realize in Shenzhen might be possible here in Beihai. Back in Shenzhen, I held a meeting with our staff to research all considerations, and I was glad to find I was unfazed by the hugeness of the project. Nonetheless, to be fully informed, I invited the economist Tang Xueyi and the urban planning expert from Singapore, Meng Daqiang, to come to Beihai with me to look into specifics.

Mayor Shuai asked the two of them to give a lecture to the Construction Commission of the Beihai Municipality.

Tang Xueyi spoke from the perspective of basic infrastructure. "Up to now,"

---

*Beihai is a port city in Guangxi, in southwestern China.

he began, "Shenzhen has developed an area of 70 square kilometers [43 square miles]. Each square kilometer [0.62 square mile] has cost RMB 200 to 300 million [about USD 30 million to USD 45 million] to develop, so the 70 kilometers has cost close to RMB 20 billion [about USD 300 million]. That amount went into infrastructure alone—even before starting to build any buildings. Looking at the Beihai situation, this proposed 40 square kilometers [25 square miles] is raw land. Labor and materials costs will be lower than Shenzhen, but each square kilometer of land will still require between RMB 150 and 200 million [about USD 22.5 million to USD 30 million]. Forty square kilometers [25 square miles] will need an investment of something between RMB 6 billion and RMB 8 billion [USD 900.24 million and USD 1.2 billion]. Add to that the cost of power plants, water supply, and public transport . . . at the very least, you'll need a total of 14 billion to 16 billion [USD 2.1 billion to USD 2.4 billion]. Then there is the problem of who will buy into this development. Right now, the population of Beihai is less than 150,000. I wonder about that. With such a small population, who is going to be willing to finance such a large-scale project?"

Listening to Professor Tang's lecture, sweat began to trickle down my back. I leaned over to whisper in Meng Daqiang's ear, "This is quite a wake-up call. We certainly do not want that 40 square kilometers!"

We had thought that these experts would educate government officials. Instead, they educated that hot-headed Wang Shi. This was fortunate, for otherwise Vanke might blindly have plunged ahead with results that can only be imagined.

Vanke City Garden: Shouting Over the Noise of Airplanes

From January 19 to 23, 1992, eighty-eight–year-old Deng Xiaoping came with his family to pay a second visit to Shenzhen. Most people learned only later, and then only from the newspapers, that he had visited the train station, the port, the Shenzhen International Trade Center, a few companies, and a botanical park where he planted a banyan tree.

This visit by China's legendary reformer was later described as an "East Wind blowing in a new springtime." The phrase was first used in the *Shenzhen Special Zone Daily* on March 26, 1992. It was then published throughout China by the Xinhua News Agency. It confirmed that the central government supported business, and a new wave of reform and opening up swept across the country. A copy of the March 26 issue of the *Shenzhen Special Zone Daily* was put in China's Revolutionary History Museum, in Tiananmen Square, as an important historical document.

Twelve years later, in October 2004, I happened to be visiting the Normandy region of the coast of France. I went to see the Peace Museum there, which commemorates the allied landing on Normandy at the end of World War II. It also looks back over the course of all the wars in the twentieth century and expresses humankind's fervent hopes for long-lasting peace. Its exhibition is divided into four parts: World War I, World War II, the U.S.-Soviet conflict after World War II, and the multilateral world after the fall of the Berlin Wall. The fourth part includes a section on China. A copy of this very same March 26 issue of the Shenzhen newspaper is exhibited in France! As one who had been through the tumult of those times, I felt tremendously proud to see the words in these surroundings: "An East Wind blows in a new springtime." I myself had been an active participant in that springtime.

In August 1992, Vanke's Shanghai company was offered three pieces of land that were approved for building housing. Each measured 500 *mu*.*

I looked them over, accompanied by the manager of Shanghai Vanke, Wen Mingsheng. They were not ideal. Either they were not close to transportation, or too many houses would have to be torn down and too many people moved, or they were right up against an industrial district. Just before this, however, Jintian had recently obtained a 500-*mu* (82 acres) tract of housing land next to Wuzhong Road of Qibao Town. Our chief competitor from Shenzhen was therefore moving into Shanghai, and I was beginning to feel worried.

I set up an appointment with the head of the Qibao Town in Shanghai to see if he could come up with some other prospects.

Zhang Guilong, the town mayor, turned out to have big eyes and thick eyebrows that rose on his forehead as he listened to me. "I can see that you, Wang Shi, are a man who gets things done," he said. "All right, I will pull out a patch of land that I have had in reserve. It is a precious patch, and the price is fairly steep. The location is excellent, for it is diagonally across from Jintian. Huang Hanqing and I are good friends, and he's often told me that you are his Big Brother."

We dashed off in a car to look at this precious patch, the one with such good feng shui.

Blue sky, white clouds, and rice fields as far as the eye could see—the setting was lovely. Standing by one of these rice fields, not two minutes had gone by when I heard the roar of an airplane overhead. It came low over our heads, and 10 minutes later came another. I now understood: this land had remained undeveloped because it was in the flight path of the nearby airport. Nobody had grabbed this opportunity because it was not suited to being a residential district.

I stood in those rice fields for a long time. Two hours went by as I remained motionless while plane after plane flew over my head.

Back at Qibao Town, I told Mayor Zhang, "Vanke wants it. First, though, we have to see the inspection report on decibel levels."

Back in Shenzhen two days later, I got a call from Wen Minsheng. The general gist of his message was that Big Yao was criticizing Vanke's company in Shanghai for not "guarding the pass," and it should not have let Chairman

---

* One *mu* = 0.1647 acres, so 500 *mu* = slightly over 82 acres.

Wang Shi go look at that land at Qibao. Never mind that we might be fined—we had to get rid of it.

"You realize why I stood there so long," I told him. "I knew full well how tough this project was going to be. Why else would Vanke be the only one to get the chance to develop it? I thought through the considerations. This place has clear advantages. There is no other place in all of Shanghai where you can find a clean piece of 500 *mu* of land. Most land requires moving people out who are already living on it, and that can take two months or it can take years. In an industry in which time is money, the uncertainty is fatal. This land allows us to control the time element ourselves. We could come to market fast—have you thought of that? Given the airplane noise, the consumer has just two choices: to buy or not to buy. If he doesn't buy, we are out of luck. But if he does, we are the only one with the property. Don't worry. I'll handle Yao Mumin myself."

The Shanghai Vanke City Garden was the first comprehensive residential housing development that Vanke ever did. It combined residential areas, shops, and educational and recreational facilities in one large community. It was a project that was to become nationally famous and that launched us into celebrity status as a creative urban housing developer. At the time, Vanke had no experience whatsoever with this kind of large residential community. We wondered if we might learn from other developers in Shenzhen who had done similar projects, and we thought of the Overseas Chinese Town (OCT).* I admired the urban planning that had gone into this, and found that it had been the work of the urban planner in Singapore, Meng Daqiang.

Meng Daqiang was from a Beijing family that had moved to Taiwan when he was a young man. From Taiwan, he went to college in Holland, where he stayed on to work. He spent years in Europe, working in urban planning, before contributing his insights to the rebuilding of Singapore. He had a husky voice and was a man of few words—he gestured in large motions when he talked about design. Since business was not his field or his interest, wherever he went he would take along finance people to take care of the business side of things for him.

Mr. Meng embraced the idea of openness in his plans. He felt that the entire district in any given plan should be open. This represented a revolt against the traditional mode of Chinese living, since in China the ideal was to live behind walls. Openness was, however, suited to modern urban living. Meng Daqiang also emphasized creating a balance, a harmony, between the human being and his natural environment.

Once the design was completed, the next step was to hire a construction team. All construction teams in Shanghai were fully booked at this time, since the basic infrastructure of the city was being built and demand was enormous. We therefore brought in construction workers from Sichuan. Around 10,000

---

*Founded in 1985, OCT is a large-scale state-owned enterprise group engaged in tourism, real estate, hotel, and electronics.

workers moved to Shanghai with their families. We imported not only the families but often their livestock as well—we had chickens and pigs living near the construction site. To maintain order and security at the site, we had our Sichuan construction partner send a public security force as well.

Red flags flew over the construction site, and lights lit it up at night. Our 10,000-man "army" worked 24 hours a day, in two shifts. Each shift worked a 10-hour period, with two hours in between for the transition. We were racing to be first in putting Shanghai City Garden on the market.

Our market positioning was simple: we targeted young people who had gone to Japan to study and were now coming back to Shanghai to work. According to our statistics, in 1992 there were a total of 80,000 Chinese students studying in Japan. Every year, 7,000 of these were returning to Shanghai to start their own businesses. That is to say, five of our city gardens would not have been able to satisfy the demand. We therefore designed the community using a look that was modern and similar to the style of Japanese residential communities. The surroundings would include dry cleaners, libraries, coffee houses, convenience stores, beauty parlors, doctor's offices, and exercise facilities. What's more, all of this had to be executed with perfection.

Within two weeks, the light-steel structures were going up. Within another two weeks, a variety of model homes were finished, behind the construction-site fencing. One week after that, these models were to be opened for public viewing. As I surveyed the bare dirt around these structures, I wished out loud for a carpet of green grass to set off the architecture.

Big Yao, in charge of the project, instantly said, "Boss, no worries. I guarantee that on the day we start receiving visitors there will be a bed of green grass." I wondered what kind of paint he was planning to use. When I came to the site one week later, a bed of soft green was growing all around even though this was November. It turned out a few gunnysacks of winter wheat seed had done the trick.

The public response to our Vanke City Garden was explosive. Visitors who wanted to see it had to line up. The glass of the sales office windows was broken twice from the pressure of bodies. Banks sent people with steel cases to deliver the cash that was being paid to us by customers. The weight of these was so heavy that in one place it cracked the marble floor. We took in more than RMB 200 million (about USD 30 million) in cash for advance deposits.

As they say, one stone can stir up thousand of ripples, and news of this place went coursing through the market: Vanke had built an urban residential area by the airport. "But it's under the flight path!," some cried. These Shanghai residents found it hard to believe.

It cannot be denied that the noise of the airplanes at City Garden is a drawback to living there to this day. In 2004, ten years after building it, Vanke asked a company to do a poll on the noise pollution and its effect on home purchasers. Some 73 percent of home buyers felt that the noise did in fact affect them, but 84 percent of inhabitants were willing to stay on a long-term basis, and only 2 percent wished to leave.

What prompted so many people to disregard the noise and choose to live in the Vanke City Garden? I believe it was a combination of the company's brand and its excellent property management.

Looked at purely from the standpoint of urban planning, Vanke's City Garden is unique in having an open-style community. For several square kilometers around, all of the buildings one sees are of a closed-in type. The building design of Vanke's City Garden is different. It draws one in to the feeling of a community—people have dates here, they get together for meals, to buy things, and not just to sleep. Since local shops and businesses were so successful, the original plans had to be revised. Sheds originally planned as bicycle storage were turned into shops. By now, there are more than 60 restaurants alone.

We Will Not Do Business That Makes More Than a 25 Percent Profit Margin

At the end of 1992, the Shenzhen Land and Resources Bureau held what it called its first "real estate salon." As the representative for Vanke, I declared to those in the audience, "Vanke will not do business that makes more than a 25 percent profit." This statement instantly caused an uproar.

I explained: "In the long run, the market is fair. It takes back what it gives. In general, if you want to be in business for the long run, you will have to give back the money that you have made from explosive profits. What's more, you will generally have to cough up more than you gulped in. Right now, for example, to make money in real estate all you need is a piece of land in your hands. If you don't develop it for six months, the value of the land still goes up by 100 percent. This phenomenon has led to a saying among most developers: 'We will not do business that has less than a 40 percent profit.'

"Is that normal? Vanke started out in trade. In the 1980s, when it traded in video equipment, we too were enjoying 200 percent and 300 percent profit margins. Since that was exorbitant, many companies got into the business. Supply exceeded demand, and the price dropped. The marginal profit on sales then also dropped to the point that profits turned negative. This year, I asked our accountant to make a record of Vanke's trading profits between 1984 and 1992. I said, 'Use black for when we made money, and red for when we lost money.' The results were easy to see. The sum of the two types of figures was a red number. In the end, after all those years of trading, losses exceeded profits. What that says is that the market is fair.

"Right now, the real estate market is so explosive that it is like the 1980s and trade. If it carries on like this, once it turns and profit margins narrow, what are we going to do then?"

There is no such thing as a developer who doesn't want to make as much money as he can. Nobody attending the meeting really understood or wanted to accept what I was trying to say. That included officials of the state land bureau, developers, and also the journalists.

Some called out, "You're just trying to be lofty minded, to take a high moral stance."

Others said, "If you can't make at least 25 percent, you're simply a lousy businessman."

Fast-forward to 1993, first quarter. The price of land continued to rise, and steel, cement, and lumber prices doubled.

We stopped work at the three construction sites that we had underway, since the building contractors asked for an increase in materials fees. Their negotiator was quite clear: if we did not increase fees to them, they would lose money. If we fined them for breaking contracts and stopping work, that would come to the same thing. We had sold space in the buildings already, which meant that if we did not hand over properties on time, we would lose credibility. We had no way out. All we could do was rewrite the contracts with the builders, increase fees to them, and carry on.

In 1993, second quarter, the cost of building materials continued to rise.

Contractors again stopped work, demanding an increase in building installation fees. There was nothing to do but bear the extra cost. Vanke was already losing money—it seemed so unfair since we were doing the best we could.

Just as we were dancing around like ants on a hot griddle, the central government instituted regulatory controls to tighten money supply, because of the bubble forming in both the stock market and real estate market.

Prices for the three main building materials responded immediately by falling. Real estate prices then swiftly fell as well. Developers began to gnash their teeth as the selling prices of their projects plummeted.

Hearing of the macro controls of the government, I raised my hands in jubilation. I supported the policies. I called for an immediate stop to construction at our three projects. Since the prices of materials were falling, I wanted to readjust our sales prices downward accordingly.

Many developers went belly-up in the market correction of 1993. We, in contrast, rode through the bubble easily and continued to grow at an average annual rate of 70 percent. By 1998, I suddenly discovered that Vanke ranked first among publicly listed real estate companies on the Shenzhen and Shanghai markets.

My fundamental belief is that long-term success comes from adhering to ethical principles and sound business practices. At a research forum, I summed up four things that I believe have been the foundation of Vanke's success.

First, from the start, Vanke participated in auctions in order to buy land. It entered the market by paying high prices in order to break through the barriers to entry in this business. Since high land prices meant high development costs, we had to obey the law of high in, high out: we built high-class buildings, sold them for high prices, and thereby turned a profit. Doing so helped drive a newly developing industry in the direction of higher quality. Moreover, it allowed the company to launch other businesses, given the support of its real estate business. The key issue for Vanke after it undertook shareholding reform was whether or not our real estate business would develop as expected. There was only one option—namely, to be successful. At the same time, we hoped to project the image of Vanke as a company that provided quality goods and services. We made a contribution to society by creating excellent living space for people.

Second, by seizing opportunities, Vanke led the way in developing large real estate projects that were in other parts of the country. We moved into a cross-regional strategy. Although it had started relatively late in Shenzhen, the company was able to make up for lost time in entering new markets elsewhere. Before we came to be considered one of the orthodox developers in Shenzhen, we were already having a sizeable influence in other large cities nationwide.

Third, Vanke's real estate started with single-unit housing and small-district development and progressed to large-scale development very quickly. In the early period of Vanke's real estate development, our scope of operations was limited to Shenzhen and to building residential areas like the Tianjing Garden and Weideng Villa, both of which covered a small area. Vanke's influence as a developer was limited by this. As we expanded, however, the projects under way or soon to be under way covered several hundred thousand square meters. Shanghai City Garden is an example—this project occupied a footprint of 300,000 square meters (984,252 square feet) on the ground, but the building area came to 420,000 square meters (1,377,953 square feet). Total investment was more than RMB 800 million (USD 138.88 million). The project was expected to take between two and one-half to three years to complete, and revenues came to around RMB 300 million (about USD 52 million) per year. In 1992, Vanke's total revenues came to just RMB 400 to 450 million (USD 72.6 million to USD 81.67 million), so clearly the real estate operations were having an exponential impact on our growth. They became decisive in terms of total revenues of the Vanke Group as well as return on investment.

Fourth, Vanke set out to promote and to market a new kind of lifestyle. This has dramatically differentiated Vanke's real estate business from that of other companies. Vanke does not consider profit to be its sole criteria in a project, nor do we purely want to provide housing for people. We aim to satisfy the desires of people for comfort, convenience, and aesthetic surroundings as part of a total lifestyle package. We also try to provide customers with excellent ongoing service; we are not in the business of putting up a building and then going away. We make sure every customer feels respected and is living in a place that is elegant, quiet, clean, safe, and convenient. This also requires the participation of residents, so that both Vanke and the community work together to create a comfortable living environment.

For these reasons, we recognize that responsibility for the social fabric of a place is part of our mission. We have formed business principles that, as we say, "combine idealism and realism." The idea of promoting a new lifestyle is only part of this. We also feel the responsibility of creating a new urban culture, and we feel that our housing developments should become part of an ideal cityscape. We have a responsibility to the city and to later generations, and making money is only part of the equation. Naturally, making money is and should be the consequence of gaining the approval of a satisfied public. Relatively speaking, however, making money is secondary.

A Wake-Up Call in the Stock Market on August 10, 1992

On the evening of August 10, 1992, an incident occurred in Shenzhen that was of considerable importance to the development of a legitimate stock market in China. Near evening on that day, thousands of people began a march along what is called the Shennan Road. They demanded a meeting with the mayor. Police cars as well as regular cars were smashed and burned, and confrontations broke out with public security personnel. Police were forced to use high-pressure water hoses and tear-gas canisters.

It is no exaggeration to say that the causes of this incident led to the establishment of China's stock-market regulatory agencies.

The stock market in Shenzhen in 1992 was like an open-sesame fairytale. Everybody played the market, from common people to corporate managers. I was made aware of this by returning unexpectedly from a trip one day and finding all my staff glued to stock quotations on their screens. Gambling on the market had long since found its way into Vanke, it seemed: if our headquarters was like this, one could imagine our offices in other cities.

I had a gut feeling that this gambling on the market was being done with company money. I was not mistaken. The temptations were so very great that only severe measures could deal with them. The day after I learned of the depth of the problems, I called a meeting of our managers and laid down the law. Anyone found trading shares during office hours would be expelled from the company. Anyone found watching computer screens that showed market quotations would be given a warning the first time, have his monitor confiscated the second time, and be expelled the third time. "Zero tolerance!"

Someone raised a suggestion that was then adopted: employees who wanted to invest in stocks could pool their money and have a group of professionals manage it. I could foresee many personal tragedies if it were any other way. Two of our employees in a subsidiary company were already deep into the market and left before the company could take action. One among them was later to become quite a famous speculator.

Another famous speculator came into my office one day, a man who was known as a "rainmaker" by now. This was the very same Zhu Huanliang, the Hakka army man who had bolstered our board in 1990 with his firm declaration of support. Zhu still had that worried wrinkled look on his face, but he now had real power. It was said that at any moment he could move RMB 20 to 30 million RMB (USD 3.63 to 5.44 million). He was smiling as he proposed a new project to me, namely jointly investing with Vanke in real estate projects outside of Shenzhen.

"Oh?," I said. "Don't you want to make your money faster on the stock market?"

It seemed he was getting out of the market. He felt it would be safer to do some business with me. When we came to terms, he sold 70 percent of his total share holdings, and we began to invest in properties.

Just as Zhu Huanliang was letting go of shares, the rest of China was plunging wildly into buying more. Emotions were feverish, and the heat wave reached its zenith in August 1992.

On August 6, it was learned that Shenzhen would be putting five million new shares out for sale.* Names of people who could subscribe to the new issues were to be chosen by lottery drawings at specific sites in the city. The next day, public notices were put up regarding the practices to be used in the subscription. Those who wanted to subscribe were required to show ID cards, and each ID card would be allowed to get one ticket in the lottery. At most, each person could buy 10 tickets at a time, using 10 ID cards. In a one-time drawing, authorities would draw 500,000 valid tickets. Each ticket drawn then allowed a person to buy 1,000 shares of the companies going public.

A frenzy of collecting ID cards now began. For several days running, telephone lines in Shenzhen were clogged with long-distance calls, and the number of telephone lines at that time was very limited. People were calling friends and relatives, asking them to send their ID cards by mail. Post offices were soon jammed with express packages. According to public notices, 300 specific points around Shenzhen were listed as lottery points, and people started lining up days in advance. It was soon impossible to buy a train ticket from Guangzhou to Shenzhen.

On August 8, early in the morning, long lines of people were sleeping on wicker mats stretched out behind the lottery-ticket sales points. By August 9, the streets and alleys of Shenzhen were seething with people. The lines at sales points were now six abreast. People continued to flood in despite a thunderstorm that seemed imminent and that rolled heavy waves of humidity over the tired bodies.

By now, Shenzhen was awash in people with fistfuls of ID cards and currency notes, and with wild looks in their eyes. According to incomplete statistics, more than one million people were lined up at sales points on the night before the lottery. The municipal government held an emergency meeting and decided to print an additional allocation of tickets, to satisfy market demand.

Order soon broke down as the ticket sales began. At some outlets, tickets were sold out two hours after opening. It later turned out that many of the tickets had been sold "through the back door" to insiders. Those who had been waiting for days and nights were now unwilling to leave. Some in the crowds began to shout in anger.

Near evening, the march began that resulted in the violence. Investigations later came up with evidence of illegal sales and corrupt means. This August 10 incident then triggered a sell-off in the overall market. Prices tumbled and a long

---

*New issues were tightly controlled, so any new issue was bound to rise in price due to limited supply. Therefore the ability to buy new issues was doled out through lotteries.

bear market descended. The method of distributing shares by limiting subscribers through lotteries was stopped not long after it had been started.

As this incident rocked the country, not one person among the Vanke Group participated. We had stopped the gambling early enough to prevent disaster. Zhu Huanliang, too, had changed his approach in time to dodge the bullet. This did not mean that we did not invest in corporations as a company. In 1992, the Vanke Group purchased major shares in 12 enterprises that included such disparate businesses as beverages, chemicals, transport, textile printing and dying, and electronic products. These enterprises were based all over China, from Turpan in Xinjiang and Shenyang in the northeast to Shantou in the south.

In 1993, we invested in a further 13 companies. We added telecommunications equipment, car manufacturing, aquatic products, and other things on to our portfolio, again in investments that covered the length and breadth of China. Our investments adhered to a principle of taking no more than 16 percent of a company's shares, however, due to our double 40 percent rule. Vanke and its co-investors would invest in no more than 40 percent of the asset value of a company. Vanke itself would put in no more than 40 percent of the investment of the group in the company. This was in part because of our own limited capital and in part because of the ability to attract cross-investing by others in regional investments. All of these investments had a common denominator: they were in companies that had undertaken share-ownership reform, and they were in companies that included real estate as a part of their holdings. We were highly debt-leveraged, but we dodged and survived the chaotic gambling in the market of 1992.

Slowly Deciding to Issue B Shares*

We were now into 1993. Vanke had picked up the pace of investing in cross-regional development projects, so the company's need for capital picked up too.

At this time, the Shenzhen stock market was under the jurisdiction of the Shenzhen Branch of the People's Bank of China[†] in 1992. The head of this Shenzhen branch, Wang Xiyi, was from China's far northeast. He had come to Shenzhen from headquarters of the People's Bank of China in Beijing. He was a hearty person but also experienced and canny.

Vanke's first intent had been to issue transferrable bonds. It applied to do

---

*B shares: In 1993, China began a system of allowing the sale of a different class of shares to overseas investors. The shares were called "B shares" to distinguish them from "A shares," traded in RMB. Vanke was one of the first to issue B shares. The Shenzhen stock market was under the jurisdiction of the Shenzhen Branch of the People's Bank of China at the time. (The People's Bank of China is the central bank of China.) The head of this Shenzhen Branch first initiated the issuing of B shares, then left the PBOC and set up his own securities company, called Jun'an Securities, as described in the text that follows.

[†]The People's Bank of China is the central bank of China.

this at the same time as did another company, the Bao'an Securities Company, Limited.

Shenzhen had a quota on the number of bonds it could issue, and that quota came to RMB 2 billion (USD 347.22 million). Bao'an had excellent relations in both Beijing and Shenzhen, and it asked for half of this quantity in just one application.

I set up an appointment to see the head of the bank, Mr. Wang, to see if Vanke could also get an allocation. I hadn't opened my mouth when he got in the first word: "Bonds are out of the question," he said. "Issue B shares. It's a new thing. We designed this system of B shares specifically to attract funds from foreign investors. We only allow foreign funds in this market. Go back and give it some thought."

The words of the head of a bank carry considerable weight. The moment this new investment vehicle was out, it would attract strong attention from Hong Kong investors. The market prospects were unknown and uncertain, but no Hong Kong investor was going to miss the chance to catch the first train.

A particular young man now came to the attention of Vanke. He was deputy managing director of Standard Chartered (Asia) at the time and his name was Ning Zhixiang. He had previously worked at the Salomon Brothers Investment Bank, and his expertise was in the newly emerging stock markets on the Mainland. Originally from Kunming, after graduating from college he studied abroad in Europe and North America before beginning to work in investment banking. He was extremely courteous and enthusiastic, and he quickly won my trust and admiration.

When I talked through Vanke's various operations and its ideas for funding with him, Ning Zhixiang expressed doubts about Vanke's primary business. He described his thoughts about Vanke's trade and real estate business: "At the outset, Vanke grew by dealing in trade, but today it is facing a new situation. Its operations are diversifying, and it is not able to scale up since it lacks stable long-term customers. Its real estate business has reached a certain size, but it has not been coordinated into a unified whole."

All this was true. Profit margins for all of our various businesses other than real estate were declining. Our import/export business constituted 70 percent of total revenue but contributed only some 25 percent of profits. In 1992, the trading business only supplied 16 percent of profits. In clear contrast to this, our first real estate project in Shanghai, the Western Suburbs Villa, brought in 5 percent of total 1992 revenue but 20 percent of profits.

Ning Zhixiang soon led his entire team from Standard Chartered over to Vanke to advise us. In addition to this team, we benefited from the expertise of the accounting and law firms that the Standard Chartered team used. The international accounting firm Peat Marwick became responsible for our audits, and the law firm Linklaters LLP handled legal issues. The Chesterton Petty Group did the appraisal of our assets. When these people arrived, they produced lists of questions. Answering these questions exposed just how primitive Vanke's legal documentation and certificates were, spread out over the company's operations in many different cities. In the process of assembling documents, Vanke also exposed a variety of fundamental management issues. It was not uncommon to find that documents had gone missing and procedures were not being fully followed.

The central task that had to be done before issuing B shares was the preparation of a prospectus. Between October 1992 and March 1993, we produced 10 drafts of this document. As each was finished, Standard Chartered would hand it on over to a host of accountants, lawyers, and analysts. Their suggestions would then be incorporated, so that behind the 110-page prospectus was in fact more than 5,000 pages of faxed documentation. The professionalism and the spirit of Standard Chartered made a deep impression on Vanke. It made us resolve to address aspects of our current performance that were unsatisfactory.

The preliminary work of issuing B shares was nearing completion, under the overall guidance of Ning Zhixiang and his team at Standard Charter, and our team with Vanke. Now, however, a new variable appeared with respect to the role of the primary underwriter of the shares.

The August 10, 1992, stock market incident had aroused the fury of Beijing. Because of it, Mayor Zheng Liangyu was transferred away from the Shenzhen Special Economic Zone. The person now directly in charge of handling the securities business was Zhang Guoqing, who also began to consider leaving the People's Bank of China as a result of the pressure. As he dealt with emotional pressures and criticism for being responsible for the problems, he began to organize a securities firm himself.

One day, at the Finance Section of the People's Bank of China, Zhang Guoqing candidly told me, "I am leaving this bank in another month. I'll be running a securities firm. I'll be selling the issues of both Vanke's B shares and Jintian's B shares."

This was more of a statement than a question. Faced with the man holding total life-and-death power over the issuing of B shares, how could I say no?

The company that Zhang Guoqing registered was Jun'an Securities. As described later in this book, this company was to become Vanke's nemesis when it did everything in its power to execute a hostile takeover of us.

The composition of the underwriters of Vanke B shares was as follows. The primary underwriter was Jun'an Securities. Second was Standard Chartered (Asia) Company, Ltd. Distributors included the CLSA Asia-Pacific Markets, Sun Hung Kai Investment Services Company Ltd., and Yamaichi International (Hong Kong) Company.

Jun'an profited from the work of the others without putting a great deal of effort in itself.

In a transaction like this, the profit for the underwriters comes from the fees and is calculated as a percentage of the funds that are raised. The percentage depends on the size of the issue, competition with others in the business, and the riskiness of the issue. Vanke was aiming to raise HKD 450 million (USD

58,012,497). For this, it would be paying fees of 5 percent, including fees of 2 percent and commissions of 3 percent. Totalling over USD 3 million, this was on the high side.

As events were to prove, however, it was a mistake to think that Jun'an didn't earn its money in the end.

By the close of the subscription period, a fair percentage of the shares had not been spoken for, since the market did not yet understand or believe in B shares. Once the underwriting agreement was signed, though, Vanke was due the money whether or not the shares sold. We lost face if the shares did not sell out completely, but we transferred the risk onto the shoulders of the underwriters. In theory, no matter what, Vanke should receive HKD 450 million (about USD 50 million) at the contracted time.

Nonetheless, Vanke's senior management was worried about Jun'an. We were not confident that it could carry off the underwriting of our issue and that of Jintian at the same time, given its limited capital. Intuition told me that Jun'an would be unable to pay out such a large amount of money in such a short time. In the end, however, both issues for Vanke and Jintian went through, on time, and both companies received their full allotment of funds.

In May 1993, B shares of Vanke skidded down to below what the price had been for the initial issue. Underwriters of B shares found they had to hold the paper in their own hands, and because of this Jun'an unwittingly became the largest shareholder in our company. Two months later, the general manager of Jun'an Securities came to me and asked me to give Jun'an some "fees" in order to resolve their short-term problem in paying back loans. Clearly, moving money gained from a stock issuance to the underwriter was irregular. It violated all principles behind issuing B shares.

I refused.

On May 28, 1993, Vanke B shares began to be traded officially, with the price listed on the Hong Kong exchange. On August 26, 1993, at the promotion event at the Hong Kong B-shares stock market, I said candidly that we in China had become ignorant of how a market economy works, after 40 years of practicing a planned economy. The process of issuing B shares had helped discipline us and prepare us for facing a market economy. Those of us who had emerged from planned-economy backgrounds needed to recognize and come to terms with what was holding us back. We had been working in ossified structures, constrained and antiquated institutions. I felt that the whole process of issuing B shares brought benefits that were as much conceptual as merely financial.

After the process was over, we continued to undergo regular audits according to international standards. We regularly published midterm and annual notices in all major Hong Kong publications, in both Chinese and English, in order to improve transparency and to promote the standardization of our business. We also maintained very close ties to securities firms, funds, and other professional organizations in Hong Kong, to alert them to the latest news on the company and solicit their opinions and recommendations on how to grow the company.

With the successful issue of 45 million shares, Vanke now received HKD 451.35 million (USD 57.7 million). This sum helped us considerably, as China was going through macro-economic adjustments, which limited everyone else's access to capital. We had clarified the fact that real estate should be the dominant industry in our five-part structure. The funding gave us sufficient capital with which to move forward in implementing our cross-regional strategy.

Since the market price of Vanke's B shares went below the issuing price, Jun'an was forced to hold its shares for a long time. The sequel to this story was still to come, however.

March 30, 1994: The Opening Battle in the Jun-Van Conflict

Vanke successfully issued its B shares on May 28, 1993. By June, the winds of macro adjustments were swirling throughout China.[*]

With funds in hand, Vanke was now able to take over considerable territory. The company's real estate projects sprang up like proverbial mushrooms after a spring rain. The first group of tenants moved into the Shanghai Vanke City Garden. A shopping mall in Shanghai and a building in Shenzhen were completed. In Qingdao, presales of the Yindu Garden surpassed all expectations. In Beijing, customers thronged the Vanke City Garden. In Tianjin, the Vanke Center sold out without any problems. The Anshan Dongyuan Building was completed, the Shenyang City Garden project began construction, the Shenzhen Haishen Building broke ground, and so on.

All of this was done as we tried to find balance in the midst of uncertainty. It represented a search for order in the midst of disorder, a kind of opportunism in which choices still had to be made. Meanwhile, the company's real estate projects and the percent it invested in real estate continued to climb at a stable rate.

On March 29, 1994, between 2 p.m. and 5 p.m., Vanke held a meeting of the board of directors at the Fulin Restaurant in Shenzhen.

Routine proposals that were put forward passed smoothly. Board members Zhang Xifu and Wang Yuelong had authorized Wu Dasheng to represent them, and Wu did not make any motions. All seemed quiet, peaceful, and normal.

As we entered 1994, unbeknownst to us however, barbarians were lurking just outside our gates.[†] The term *barbarians at the gate* had recently become a metaphor for venture capitalists who attempt to take control of a publicly listed company, as epitomized in the book about a famous M&A case in the late-1980s in Wall Street. Vanke's board of directors remained oblivious to this impending attack.

---

[*] That is, the government was clamping down on economic overheating via various macroeconomic measures.

[†] *Barbarians at the Gate: The Fall of RJR Nabisco*, Bryan Burrough and John Helyar, 1989.

At ten-thirty on the morning of March 30, the general manager of Jun'an Securities, Zhang Guoqing, and his deputy, Zhang Hansheng, strode into my office. They had made the appointment the previous day.

Zhang Guoqing came straight to the point as soon as the two men sat down: "Jun'an Securities is planning to express some views about Vanke's senior management."

Did the top two people in a company need to see me so formally just to express opinions? Something was up.

"Jun'an is planning to hold a press conference this afternoon," he continued. "We will officially express our views at that time. Please do not misunderstand. Since Jun'an represents the small and medium shareholders, we are doing this in your best interests. Our ideas about Vanke's operations and strategies may well be good for the company's long-term growth. It will have even more obvious advantages for the development of China's securities markets."

I began to smell gunpowder in the room.

I held back my anger as I asked my first question: "May I participate in the press conference this afternoon?"

Zhang Hansheng responded with great delicacy that it would be best if I did not attend.

I responded, "If you are presenting views on Vanke, why is it that the chairman of the board of Vanke cannot attend?" I was feeling increasingly less friendly toward my guests.

"If you want to attend, that's not a problem," replied Zhang Guoqing. "We will be presenting our views in the form of a 'Letter to All Vanke Shareholders.' This will also be published in tomorrow's *Shenzhen Special Zone Daily*. It will recommend a reorganization of the board of directors. This approach may seem a little extreme to you, but it is for the good of Vanke. After the reorganization of the board of directors, you will still hold the position of CEO." As Zhang Guoqing was saying this last part, he was standing and already taking his leave.

The visit took five minutes, from start to finish.

We had two and one-half hours to prepare our counterattack.

I immediately called each of the directors on our board, told them about the objection meeting, and asked for their opinions on how to deal with it.

I reached all 13 directors in places as far away as America, Canada, Beijing, Qingdao, and Haikou, as well as Shenzhen. I was astonished to learn that three of them not only knew about this attack, but were co-conspirators. Those three were representatives of our first major shareholder, New Age, as well as Zhongchuang and Hainan Securities. They had helped initiate the objection meeting.

I was almost shouting as I talked to Zhang Xifu of New Age. I told him that New Age absolutely could not attend the press conference that afternoon: "Jun'an gave no indication of this in advance. It is a guerrilla attack, and they are even saying in the newspaper that it is for Vanke's own good! You cannot attend. Do you understand?'

The representative of Zhongchuang was Wu Dasheng. I wondered why he had gone against Vanke by joining the alliance to oppose the Vanke board of directors. Mr. Wu's answer to me came down the telephone line, saying that shareholders have a right to hold opinions and that they also have the right to choose whatever form they wish to present those opinions, so long as it is not against the law. I heard not just discontent with the board in his words, but also a degree of unfriendliness.

Going over his head, I then dialed Wang Yuelong, the head of Zhongchuang in Beijing. "Headquarters is not aware of this," Wang assured me. " 'First, we do not agree that Wu Dasheng should raise issues with Vanke in this fashion, and second, he is not allowed to attend the press conference.'

This support allowed me to catch my breath. I then dialed the number of Wen Zhe, of Hainan Securities Company, and I could hear the amazement in his voice. Mr. Wen said to me, "One month ago, Zhang Guoqing called me. He told me, 'The market isn't very good, so we need to have a news topic to stir it up, lift share prices. Attacking Vanke could be one approach. What's more, Vanke can withstand all this political pressure—it is transparent and healthy. Jintian, on the other hand, can't take too much attention.' I realized that was true so I agreed with him. But I had no idea Zhang Guoqing was going to put on this kind of press conference."

"Does that mean you are going to rescind your part in this, not be a co-petitioner?"

He waffled: "I did not sign the authorization to launch the action. I just gave my verbal approval. Both of you are my friends. How about this? Jun'an cannot make announcements under the name of Hainan Securities, but I too won't make any declaration that embarrasses Zhang Guoqing."

I see. I am in a life-and-death situation and you equivocate, plastering things over.

At that moment, it was obvious to me that I had neglected a cardinal rule: stay in close communication with your board of directors. I had been oblivious to something that I should have seen coming. Other than the above three, all of the other members of the board agreed to stand on my side.

The Jun-Van Confict: Round One

Jun'an Securities held its press conference at 3 p.m. on March 30, 1994, in a small conference room at the Sunshine Hotel. The room was jammed with reporters.

The director of the general office, He Wei, hosted the meeting. He announced that four authorized representatives of shareholders of Jun'an were bringing a petition against Vanke. The four were the New Age Company of Shenzhen, Hainan Securities, Hong Kong's Junshan Investment Company, and the Chuangyi Investment Company. These four held a total of 10.73 percent of Vanke shares.

The petition first gave an overall summary of Vanke's business, including its corporate structure, its shareholding structure, and recent movements of the share price. It analyzed five main aspects of Vanke's business: real estate, shareholding investments, manufacturing, trade, and arts and culture.

It went on in a similar vein, analyzing what it saw as problems in Vanke's operations and management. These included lack of transparency, poor results of a company it had invested in called Shenhua, lackluster performance on the real estate side, unstable returns on shareholding investments, and so on. It declared that Vanke's business was too fragmented, leading to overly dispersed resources and lack of focus on the part of senior management. This made the company uncompetitive in current markets. Because of this situation, it proposed a reorganization of Vanke's business structure as well as its senior management. That involved reducing its trade, commercial, and manufacturing businesses, spinning off the Anhua Company and the shareholding investment company as independent businesses, and focusing on developing the real estate business. At the same time, it recommended that eight to ten alternative candidates be appointed to the board of directors. It recommended that an "Authorization Committee" be set up within the board of directors to provide regulatory oversight on all major policy decisions. That was to prevent the degree to which projects were currently being decided upon in an arbitrary and blind manner.

This lengthy document took a full hour to read.

Listening to the very detailed information in this document, I realized it was the work of considerable expertise and lengthy preparation. It was not the work of just one or two weeks. The conclusion of the document was given a romantic spin, and with it the gunpowder was fully ignited. In the style in which this was done, I could see the hand of Ning Zhixiang, the deputy director of Hong Kong's Standard Chartered. What was he up to, and what role was he playing in the action?

I raised my hand and asked permission to speak.

The chair of the meeting, He Wei, explicitly denied my request. Clearly, this had been agreed upon in advance.

A clamor of voices now rose from the journalists, demanding that Boss Wang be allowed to have his say: "If people are accusing Vanke of things, the chairman of Vanke should be allowed to speak!" "Let Wang go up and respond!"

Embarrassed by the public outcry, Zhang Guoqing, the head of Jun'an, was forced to allow me to speak.

I calmed myself as I strode up to the podium. "I welcome the opinions that our new and old shareholders have raised," I said. "I applaud the professionalism of what has been presented. More than 80 percent of the suggestions just read out were already approved by and in accordance with the results of the board meeting that Vanke held yesterday, the 29th. I want to address points that form the focus of Jun'an's criticisms of this management. First is Vanke's diversification. Over 95 percent of Shenzhen companies are highly diversified, which is both a weakness and what could be called a unique feature of such companies. Vanke's diversification is a result of its corporate history. Simply cutting businesses out is not a matter of just getting rid of them. Jun'an singles out our investment in other companies' shares for particular censure, our venture capital business. Most of the companies in which we have invested are beginning to show good returns on investments and should not be spun off lightly—their value should be evaluated in terms of their actual performance."

I came down more strongly on Jun'an's criticism of senior management: 'When Jun'an says that Vanke's management is not transparent enough, or that its business is not transparent, there is another side to this that should be taken into account. The industry itself has a certain lack of clarity about it. Vanke's corporate practices and the practices of the industry are two different things. You can't talk about them as though they were the same."

As journalists now fired questions at me, I simply responded, "Tomorrow afternoon, at 2 p.m., Vanke will hold a press conference. At that time, it will provide a formal response to this accusation."

I appeared to be confident, but I knew that Vanke was in fact facing mortal danger.

Jun'an's motivation was clear. The company owned 10 million Vanke B shares at a cost of RMB 12 (USD 1.39) per share. The price now stood at RMB 9 (USD 1.04) per share. At the market price, it therefore had an unrealized paper loss of RMB 30 million (USD 3.48 million). Jun'an wanted to get rid of these shares without incurring such a loss. How to do this? Create the impression that Vanke was going to be purchased. The price would rise. At the same time, Jun'an could control the board of directors and more easily manipulate the stock price. Meanwhile, Jun'an could be seen as protecting small investors and could thereby improve its own rather poor reputation in the market.

Vanke was definitely in Jun'an's sights; it was going in for the kill.

This was not an uncommon trick in those days of depressed markets. Manufacturing "material," a story for the public, was often just the right medicine for stimulating a rise in share price. Such a rise was the common voice of the market, but the story was the sole fabrication of Jun'an. The problem was that Jun'an would sell out its own shares the day the price rose, and the price would then fall. Small-time investors, those who blindly followed the trend, would be the ones to suffer the loss. Using their money, Jun'an would get its money out.

There were two things we could do. One was to undermine the alliance that was seeking to reorganize the board. That step was necessary to defeat the motion to hold a special shareholders' meeting. The other was to wage a publicity campaign that educated the small investors and prevented them from blindly buying into our shares and then taking a loss. Both of these things took time.

My first action was to empower my deputy, Yu Liang, to apply for a cessation of trading in Vanke shares on March 31.

Then I analyzed the structure of the Jun'an alliance that held 10.73 percent of shares. Key to its success was New Age, which held 6.2 percent of our shares. Hainan Securities held 1.1 percent. Junshan and Chuangyi together held 3.43

percent, but these were long-term shareholdings and not as important. If New Age pulled out, the alliance would crumble.

At 5 p.m. that same day, I asked Zhao Xiaofeng and Xu Gang to go to New Age and invite Zhang Xifu to Vanke's headquarters in Shuibei. At the same time, I tasked our legal department with finding a law firm that was familiar in corporate law. The head of this department, He Zhengda, recommended Zeng Yijun, a partner with the Guangzhou office of JunHe Law Firm. Ten years earlier, she had been our very first legal advisor. Since then, she had studied corporate law in England and returned to join a private law firm.

Scene: the small conference room on the third floor of Vanke's headquarters. I sat opposite from Zhang Xifu. No matter what, Zhang Xifu was one of us—surely we could resolve things by talking things over. "What I can't understand," I said, "was how you could know about things and yet not say a word at our board meeting yesterday!"

Zhang Xifu explained: "One month ago, four major shareholders signed a secret agreement with Jun'an, regarding bringing this case against Vanke. No single party was allowed to reveal anything about it."

"What was the purpose of such secrecy?"

"'Ah,' Zhang Guoqing said. 'We will have much better results if we keep things quiet.' He also said, 'Wang Shi generally doesn't respond to other people's opinions. He only responds to shock treatment, and this will be for his own good.' I signed the agreement since I thought it might indeed be for your own good."

"I understand. Well, now that it's come this far," I told Zhang Xifu, "surely you can see Jun'an's intent. Publish a retraction." I handed over a declaration that had been drafted in advance, taking New Age out of the alliance. I pulled the cap off a pen. Zhang Xifu read it over carefully. He did not say he wouldn't sign, but he also did not reach for the pen. He simply looked terribly sad. The two of us sat there, refusing to budge.

I understood the bind that this elder before me was in.

During the Cultural Revolution, Zhang Xifu's father was declared a capitalist-roader. Zhang had to leave the prestigious air force academy and do manual labor. In the course of this, he made friends that he trusted as brothers, with whom he went through extremely hard times. Later, some of these people came to Shenzhen to do business and Zhang Xifu worked beside them, helping them, extending his trust. When they owed money, he was the "elder brother" who served as guarantor. He was not much good at business himself.

In a certain sense, as the "elder," Zhang Xifu did his best to carry a burden that became ever harder to bear. Fortunately, he had a number of very capable people around him who were adept at fighting in close quarters. Those included the "old soldiers" in New Age—Ding Xiaoming, Chen Chao, Qiu Qihao, and Huang Xiaomin—and they also included Vanke's Wang Shi. In 1988, during Vanke's shareholding reform, the portion of shares that was to be owned by the state was entrusted to the management of New Age. Each year, dividends from these state-owned shares would be entered into the accounts of New Age.

As I scrambled to start the company, struggling up, being forced down, picking myself up, Zhang Xifu served as a kind of protective shield for me at the next higher level of administration. One could say that we had a symbiotic relationship. By all rights, it should have been easy to see at a glance who counted for more to New Age—Vanke or Jun'an. Now the equation seemed to have changed, however. Why was New Age now being so ambivalent? The only explanation could be that the interests of one of the parties had changed.

Several months earlier, New Age held 9 percent of Vanke shares. It now had only 6.2 percent. The other 2.8 percent had been entrusted to Jun'an to sell. The handling fee for this transaction was set at 50 percent. This was outrageously high. One has to understand that legal-person shares can only be sold after getting approval from the Securities Regulatory Office. I felt that Jun'an's controller had a relationship with the head of this office that was not exactly aboveboard and normal. The fee for this piece of business came to around RMB 55 million (about USD 6.38 million).

This background had a great deal to do with Zhang Xifu's anguished silence as he sat before me.

At 8 p.m., Zhang Xifu and I were still holed up in the conference room. The electricity suddenly went out, and we were plunged into darkness.

We lit candles. The flames flickered, casting black shadows on the wall, and another two full hours went by. Finally, Zhang Xifu looked up at me and smiled. It was a smile that put my mind at ease. A true brother! Zhang Guoqing, see what you can do now!

At 10:30 p.m., my colleague Zhao Xiaofeng accompanied me to the Jun'an headquarters in the Shenzhen Development Center Building.

Zhang Guoqing was there waiting for us, at the agreed-upon time.

The tall building was pitch black, since the electricity was out there as well. I passed over a document signed by Zhang Xifu, that withdrew New Age from the petition and that also cancelled any authorization for Jun'an to include New Age among the petitioners.

Zhang Guoqing glanced briefly at this high-tonnage bomb in his hands. In response, he handed me a document that Zhang Xifu had signed earlier. This was the authorization for Jun'an to act on behalf of New Age as financial advisor with respect to the petition. It clearly stipulated that the authorization was good for six months and could not be withdrawn. The authorization carried the name of the legal advisor, the CITIC Law Firm.

I again had to calm my pounding heart. Xifu, ah, Xifu, I silently lamented. At your most confused, you were never as confused as you are now. From a legal standpoint, the retraction that I held in my hand was a worthless piece of paper.

"So far as Jun'an goes, Zhang Xifu's personal attitude is irrelevant," Zhang Guoqing said. He acted as though everything was already fully under his control.

"We'll read the script as we ride along," I said. I made it clear that I was not going to take this lying down.

The Jun-Van Conflict: Round Two

It was midnight by the time I got back to my office in Shuibei. The lawyer Zeng Yijun had reached the office before me and was going through documents and clearly planning to spend much of the night. I invited her in to my office.

"I am very sorry," I said. "I've just hired you, but I am going to have to let you go."

I briefly described the results of my meeting with Zhang Guoqing, head of Jun'an: "They were more prepared for more contingencies than I had expected. Their choice of CITIC as its law firm means that the case has gone beyond being purely a legal dispute. If it really comes to court, the contest will be decided more by what happens outside the court than what goes on inside. You alone are powerless to go up against CITIC. Do you have any recommendation for a law firm that can handle this kind of thing?"

Zeng Yijun was bewildered by the sudden way in which I seemed to hire and fire law firms.

I continued to talk to her, but I had already made up my mind about who might be the right option for dealing with CITIC. The head of Vanke's legal department was sitting next to me, a man named He Zhengda, and I now asked him if he knew a lawyer named Fu Rui. "Within an hour, no matter what, I want you to find out which law firm Fu Rui is working for," I said. "Find him."

By that time it was already two in the morning.

We worked through the night, researching options.

"Will you still publish Zhang Xifu's statement?," He Zhengda asked me.

"Why not?"

"Legally . . ."

"What is legal is beside the point. The publicity will be extremely unfavorable to Jun'an. You wait and see."

In analyzing the weak points of our opponent, I made two assumptions. Given the style of the petition, I had a strong feeling it was drafted by Ning Zhixiang. Assumption one: he knew the inside story. If so, and he was working in his own self-interest, what would he do? Obviously he would try to grab hold of Vanke shares right away and buy them before the petition was published and shares rose. And if he did so, he would be breaking the law. Assumption two: Ning Zhixiang was working in concert with Jun'an to infringe the rights and interests of the great mass of shareholders.

I believed that my colleagues at Vanke and I were a management team that respected the law. I also knew that people of similar minds were in a minority.

I asked Yu Liang to look into what changes there had been in the last two months among Vanke's shareholders, and who any new shareholding accounts belonged to.

The contest of wills between Vanke and Jun'an, and between Wang Shi and Zhang Guoqing, had now truly begun.

Early on the morning of March 31, lawyer He Zhengda took the red-eye flight to Shanghai, to talk to Professor Gu Gengyun, of the East China University of Political Science and Law.

The *Shenzhen Special Zone Daily* published the "Shareholders' Action against Vanke" in its entirety. The same issue published Zhang Xifu's declaration, stating that New Age was withdrawing from that action.

Morning came. Scene: Vanke's headquarters on the third floor of the Shuibei Building. Vanke's front-line managers were assembled, brought with lightning speed to headquarters from 13 cities in China.

I briefly described Jun'an's actions of the day before and the situation the company was now facing.

The atmosphere in the conference room became extremely grave. The manager of Vanke in Shenyang, Lu Dongyong, broke the heavy silence: "We are fighting on the front lines, but our backside has caught fire." He couldn't keep from choking up as he said, "I suddenly have no idea what my future holds." Even as they were putting up beautiful houses for people, Vanke people now felt they were standing on shifting sands.

Two foreign lawyers from the Linklaters LLP in Hong Kong now hastened to Shuibei.

The lawyer from the Fu Rui Law Firm was already on the flight from Beijing to Shenzhen.

Scene: headquarters of the Shenzhen Special Economic Zone Development Company [SD], in the Development Building. I was there to meet the CEO, Wang Xinmin. The moment he saw me, this gentleman in thick-rimmed glasses reassured me, "Zhang Xifu is muddled," he said. "How in the world could he have done that?"

During this meeting, this CEO of SD authorized me to be in charge of any shareholding decisions to do with the 6.2 percent of legal-person shares held by Vanke.

Next stop: Shenzhen office of the Securities Regulatory Commission. The attitude of the person in charge there, Wang Lin, was decidedly unfriendly, as was I. If a securities firm wanted to place an article in a newspaper criticizing a listed company, it first had to report to this man's office and get authorization. Why, then, had this office not alerted Vanke to the fact that JunHe had put in such a request, and why had the office authorized it? I asked Director Wang if he could kindly explain.

Wang Lin just laughed. "Shareholders criticize their boards all the time," was his response.

Facing his thin, pinched face, I had to keep myself from exploding. You are abusing your authority to get back at me for a personal grievance, I was thinking.

Three years earlier, when Wang Lin was still working in the National Reform Commission, I challenged him on an issue regarding share ownership. It related to the question of who should have jurisdiction over employee shares. He had just been promoted to deputy chair of the Reform Commission. I remember pounding the desk as I said, "You know better than anyone about Vanke's share reform. Now that you've been promoted, you're not willing to acknowledge what was decided?" At that point, he simply stood up, pulled on his cuffs a little, and said to his assistant, "We've leaving." Clearly, in this new battle, the head of Shenzhen's Securities Regulatory Office was settling a score with Wang Shi.

Whether it was intuitive or done consciously, Zhang Guoqing had gathered together considerable anti–Wang Shi feeling as he assembled his forces.

Scene: Shuibei headquarters. The company temporarily fitted a tape recorder to a telephone. I called Ning Zhixiang. I provoked him. I criticized him for having broken faith with me, like some kind of rat attacking in the dark: "I could see at a glance that the piece was written in your style!" Ning Zhixiang was silent for a moment before confessing that he had been the author. The recorder got it all on tape as our talk proceeded.

Meanwhile information came in that showed that blocks of shares had been bought in by new accounts. Over the past two months, two new companies had opened accounts with Jun'an Securities. One was registered out of Dandong, the other out of Taiyuan. Both were registered under the name of Ning Zhixiang. Together, the accounts had purchased a sum of RMB 20 million (USD 2.32 million) worth of Vanke shares. I said to myself, "Mr. Ning, your pigtail is going to be very easy to pull."

Based on this evidence, the Shenzhen exchange agreed to stop trading Vanke shares for a day in order to protect the interests of small shareholders. Vanke had won a full day's reprieve.

Afternoon, two o'clock. Scene: the conference room on the third floor of our Shuibei offices. Journalists packed the room as well as the adjoining hallway.

I appeared on stage accompanied by Deputy General Manager Chen Zuwang, and Yu Liang.

I described the situation briefly, before launching our counterattack: "Vanke has a number of doubts about the methods that Jun'an has used to publish the "Shareholders Petition" and "Reform Proposal" in several newspapers. On the thirtieth, New Age had already withdrawn from the alliance, and on the thirty-first it again published a notice that it was abrogating its authorization to Jun'an to represent it in financial matters. The Hainan Securities has never had any formal written agreement that authorizes Jun'an to serve as financial consultant and undertake this kind of action. Vanke's board of directors has only 14 members, yet the proposal is recommending the election of 8 to 10 new members—clearly this move is aiming to take Vanke over at the least possible expense.

"Jun'an's proposal is highly professional in terms of its layout and methodology. In terms of specific content, however, quite a few places are not in accord with reality. For example, with regard to the plans for the Vanke City Gardens the proposal merely reiterates one employee's opinion. As a professional financial report, this analysis bases its argument purely on the opinion of one employee and, from the standpoint of employee ethics and professionalism, it doesn't stand up to scrutiny.

"Real estate development is Vanke's primary business. In 1993, that business reached its highest levels ever, in completed as well as initiated projects. For the next five years, real estate will continue to be Vanke's primary industry. In the venture investments side of Vanke, the company invested a total of somewhat over RMB 131 million [USD 15.2 million]. To date it has put more than RMB 95.4 million [USD 11.06 million] back in the coffers, so only 40 million [USD 4.64 million] is still outstanding.

"Of the 27 companies in which Vanke has invested, 9 have already been listed on the Shanghai and Shenzhen exchanges. Dividends to Vanke from the 12 holding companies came to RMB 4.52 million [USD 784,722] in cash 1993 dividends." I went on to give various details.

Chen Zuwang then gave a financial report as required of a publicly listed company by the Shenzhen Securities Exchange. This showed that Vanke had exceeded its profit targets over the previous year, despite the macro adjustments underway in the country. Its total assets grew from a low of RMB 960 million (USD 174.23 million) in 1992 to the current figure of RMB 2.1 billion (USD 243.62 million). Both net assets and shareholder interests more than doubled in value.

Finally, at this press conference, Vanke made it clear that it had already submitted a request to the Shenzhen Stock Exchange to extend the order to suspend trading.

Afternoon, three o'clock. Scene: the Sunshine Hotel, where the New Age company now held its own press conference.

I sat next to Zhang Xifu.

Xifu's written statement explained how New Age had at first authorized Jun'an to serve as financial consultant and then had withdrawn that authorization. He described the whole thing from start to finish. After that, he stated that he had authorized Wang Shi to represent New Age at this press conference, as its spokesperson.

Zhang Xifu also noted prior to leaving the press conference that, on March 28, New Age had authorized the Jun'an Securities to serve as its financial consultant since it did not have sufficiently knowledgeable people within the company—that was the reason for the authorization. The term of authorization was from March until September.

Shenzhen reporters were both titillated and perplexed. What exactly was going on here? What was the problem between Jun'an and Vanke? How in fact had Jun'an's "proposal" been put together? Yesterday's declaration of the intent to restructure Vanke was from an alliance that had the name of New Age listed as one of the petitioning shareholders. Yet today New Age was authorizing Wang Shi and pulling out of the alliance? What in the world was this all about?

I knew exactly what was going on, and I knew that Jun'an still held the "mace of an assassin" in its hands. The 6.2 percent of New Age voting rights that had been entrusted to Jun'an were gone. There was no way we could get around that. But Zhongchuang Company had already withdrawn from the alliance. The shares that Jun'an held of its own, plus those of New Age, came to less than 10 percent. The critical piece now was Hainan Securities, with its 1.1 percent of shares. If Jun'an continued to control those as well, Jun'an did indeed have the power to call a special shareholders' meeting under the law. Meanwhile, the Shenzhen municipal government's Investment Management Company held another 2 percent of shares, and these had now surfaced and were in play. Both sides were now contending for those shares as well. Zhang Guoqing and I were both very clear about which card the other side would play. Only the journalists were in a fog of confusion.

The Jun-Van Conflict: Round Three

April 1, a Friday.

Yu Liang flew to Hainan Island. He was seeking the support of the head of Hainan Securities, a man named Wen Zhe, and his 1.1 percent of shares. On the same plane was the deputy general manager of Jun'an, Zhang Hansheng. He too was bent on this life-or-death matter of 1.1 percent.

Wen Zhe, head of Hainan, was a master at handling personal relations. Not wanting to offend either side, he had neither given written authorization to Jun'an nor declared that he had no relationship with Jun'an. Under the persuasive powers of Yu Liang, however, Wen Zhe now confirmed in explicit terms: Jun'an could not use the name of Hainan Securities in opposing Vanke.

Meanwhile, Vanke repeatedly asked the Shenzhen Stock Exchange to continue to stop share trading on Saturday, when the Shenzhen exchange is open for half a day. The day after that would be Sunday, when the exchange would be closed. I hoped the news that might spike our shares would have subsided by then.

The Shenzhen exchange turned us down. Its president, Xia Bin, was off on business in the United States, yet he ordered Vanke to start trading again on Saturday.

I was able to get through to Xia Bin in America on the phone. It was the middle of the night there. I explained to him the reasons for continuing the halt to trading: "There is strong evidence of 'Rat Trading,'"* I said. "If we reopen trading and there is strange spike in the market, and it turns out someone is trying to hoodwink small shareholders who suffer undue losses as a result, who is going to be held responsible?"

Xia Bin held his ground. Vanke would reopen on April 2. No more discussion.

I put down the telephone. I immediately called Yu Liang on Hainan Island and asked him to fly to Beijing to talk directly to the head of the China Securities Regulatory Commission.

---

*The misuse of private trading accounts by mutual fund managers is a practice that is common enough to have been given a colorful nickname in Chinese: "rat trading."

That same day in the afternoon, I called on the president of the Shenzhen Municipal Investment Management Company. We met in his spacious office, and I sought his support with regard to the 2 percent of Vanke government shares they owned.

The head of this company, Xia Deming, explained his position to me: "Jun'an's Zhang Guoqing went to talk to De Cheng.* He wanted his support for some institutional innovations in the stock market. You, Wang Shi, are also now coming, looking for support. We can't figure out what the relationship is. We don't support either of you, nor do we oppose either one of you. We abstain." I was told that Chairman Li Decheng also refused to exercise any influence in the matter. Mr. Li was a leader whom I had high regard for, and I felt that his abstention was in fact a form of support for Vanke.

Shortly before I left my office that night, Yu Liang called to say that the China Securities Regulatory Commission in Beijing had agreed to stop the trading of Vanke shares on the next day. "They will send the official document ordering the stop to the Shenzhen Exchange tomorrow first thing in the morning," he said, "but they have already told the exchange over the phone." Marvelous! After several days of interacting with officials, I found that only this commission firmly upheld the right and proper path.

Evening. Scene: reception room of the headquarters of the Bao'an Securities Company. I was looking for moral support from another publicly traded company. President Chen Zhengli and I traded views on this Jun-Van conflict and possible strategies.

President Chen was pessimistic. He felt that Vanke could not escape this grab for control. He said, "At least they went after Vanke. If it had been Jintian, they would have folded in a day."

"Not necessarily. Vanke adores a civilized way, but Huang Hanqing at Jintian would do anything he wants."

"Who do you think Jun'an's next target will be?"

Shenzhen's listed companies watched the progression of Jun'an's attack on Vanke with complex emotions. Not only were they pessimistic, but they felt a sense of dread.

April 2. Trading in Vanke shares remained on hold. This had not been anticipated in Jun'an's plan of attack. If shares were not traded, that company could not manipulate the market. Four days of no trading, plus Sunday made a fifth day. I hoped and believed that the market would have digested the information on the Jun-Van conflict by then.

In its declaration in the newspaper, Jun'an repeatedly included Hainan Securities as one of the initiators of the proposal to oust Vanke management. Yu Liang gave a photocopy of Jun'an's statement to Hainan Securities. Wen Zhe, head of the Hainan company, now made a public announcement authorizing

---

*Li Decheng was chairman of the board of this institution at the time.

Vanke to represent the company: "Hainan Securities has never authorized Jun'an to represent its voting rights. If Jun'an again uses its name falsely, Hainan reserves the right to take the matter up in court."

Jun'an was stymied.

April 4. Monday. Scene: the Shenzhen Exchange as the morning trading session began. Vanke's shares traded slightly upward and I felt my pulse quicken: *peng . . . peng . . . peng.* The trend soon stopped, and Vanke shares remained quiet the rest of the morning.

I asked Yu Liang to organize a press conference that afternoon at the headquarters in Shuibei to announce that the war was over.

At that press conference, journalists asked, "If Jun'an continues to collect the voting rights of small shareholders, what will Vanke do then?"

"You mean a protracted war?," I asked. "Vanke was established 10 years ago. It has a seasoned and mature management team. Jun'an was set up only one year ago. Its business expanded quickly, and its management team is inexperienced. If we fight a protracted war, Jun'an will lose." Inside, I was glowing. *Ah, dear reporters,* I was thinking. *I am definitely pulling the pigtails of Jun'an. I have the righteous support of the Beijing Securities Regulatory Commission behind me. Zhang Guoqing does not have the power to start another attack.*

But what was Zhang Guoqing thinking?

Jun'an held a forum for securities companies, and He Wei was again at work. He announced that if it had not been for one small shareholder, Jun'an could have done this, and then done that, and so on.

Vanke paid no attention.

One week later, the head of the Investigation Department of the China Securities Regulatory Commission came to Shenzhen to investigate the matter, which was now being called the 3.30 incident. His name was Zhang Ziping.

We met in his room in a certain hotel, just the two of us, Director Zhang and the chairman of the board of Vanke, Wang Shi.

He said, "Chairman [of the China Securities Regulatory Commission] Liu Hongru has already approved our report. We plan to deal with this severely. I am just here to handle the matter. At the same time, Ning Zhixiang was my classmate at Wudaokou.* I can't bring myself to wield the guillotine. In coming to Shenzhen I will certainly investigate, but you should know that this investigation is like a boat that has left the dock. The destination of the boat is clear, we want to get across the river and up on the bank. But when the boat gets in the middle of the river, all kinds of things are going to affect it, wind and water. These may force it to change course. Do you understand what I am saying?"

I nodded my head.

"I would like to ask your opinion on how to conduct this investigation."

---

*Wudaokou is the location of the graduation school of the People's Bank of China, which is the Central Bank of China.

"Hold good will toward people."

"I'm glad to hear that. I'll handle Zhang Guoqing."

Scene: two hours later, the same room. In attendence: Zhang Ziping; He Weixiang, deputy manager of the Shenzhen Stock Exchange and acting manager in Xia Bin's absence; Zhang Guoqing; and Wang Shi.

Zhang Ziping issued a statement on behalf of the head of the commission: Jun'an was not to solicit authorizations from small shareholders. He noted that the chairman of the Securities Regulatory Commission in Beijing was the one sending this message.

Zhang Guoqing, head of Jun'an, responded: "Since the boss has made that decision, I will swallow what I have to swallow, even if it is a plateful of stinking dog shit."

Zhang Guoqing was someone we were eventually going to have to contend with. Looking at his suppressed anger, I thought of an old Chinese saying: "Ten years is not too late for a gentleman to get his revenge." This old soldier at Jun'an was not in fact going to swallow anything. The battle with Jun'an was not over yet. The noose was going to stay hanging on the beam for some time in the future.

No matter what, Jun'an remained an influential securities firm. What's more, it still held 3.43 percent of Vanke's shares, so the best defense would be to keep a close eye on the company. Vanke's senior management invited a representative from Jun'an to join Vanke's board of directors, and then the deputy CEO of Jun'an, Gong Hua, was elected onto the board.

The Vanguard Contretemps

After the Jun-Van conflict, one key change in Vanke's business in 1994 was a reorganization of the company's trading business.

Xu Gang took over management of the Shenzhen Vanke Union Company, Ltd., in 1989, which had not been well managed previously. He had a very strong and open management style. The company's first incarnation was the Modern Medical Equipment Communications Center. Xu Gang's ability to organize marketing soon became apparent. After becoming responsible for trading business, he gradually reduced the number of sales outlets, keeping a sales network in just four places: Shenzhen, Guangzhou, Hainan, and Hangzhou. He decided that the company should grow through more professional operations.

I then asked Xu Gang to take over Shenzhen Vanguard Retail Chainstore Limited, the retail business, at a faster pace by using the resources of these trade outlets.

Xu Gang asked if he could appoint Ding Fuyuan to replace Wu Zhengbo as chairman of the board of Vanguard, and I agreed.

As for Vanguard, its previous incarnation was a company set up in 1991, called the Shenzhen Vanke Retail Chainstore, Ltd. This later was changed to the Shenzhen Vanguard Retail Chainstore Limited. It was organized and set up by Liu Luming, who had returned from New Zealand. After that, we asked Wu Zhengbo to come in to serve as head of operations—he had been deputy director of the department store building in Wuhan.

Doing a retail chainstore business was a part of the whole concept of turning Vanke into a kind of *zaibatsu*, a diversified holding company.

By 1993, Vanke had decided to focus on real estate as its primary business. My first thought was to turn Vanguard into a shareholding company and then sell it to others for ongoing management. However, once several shareholders became aware of this plan, they made it absolutely clear that they opposed it. They had only agreed to buy into Vanguard because of Vanke's shareholding reform and their own prospects for gain. If Vanke left the fold, they were no longer interested.

Vanke therefore continued as before to be the major shareholder in Vanguard Retail, with 35 percent of shares. The Guangdong provincial Nuclear Power Investment Company ("Nuclear Investment") held 25 percent, Huaxi Construction held 20 percent, Tian An held 12.58 percent, and employees held 7.42 percent.

On July 17, 1994, Vanguard Retail opened a warehouse-style retail sales plaza on the first floor of the Hualianfa Building. It contained 5,000 square meters (16,400 square feet) of floor space. It combined a warehouse type of presentation with breakeven pricing. This stirred up an absolute revolution among retailers in Shenzhen and was highly appreciated by consumers as well as the government. Other firms in the business now tried to figure out how to compete with Vanguard by using the same approach. The media made a great deal of this, and Vanguard Retail was frequently in the news. Throngs of people crowded around Huaqiang North Road, which soon became a kind of golden shopping area. The Vanguard phenomenon was all the rage.

As Vanguard's cash flow increased dramatically, shareholders took note and soon expressed a strong interest in moving some of that cash out. Vanke, responsible for the operations of this company, opposed the proposal to siphon off cash flow. This caused a conflict of interest among the shareholders.

Three shareholders in particular formed an alliance to try to change the chairman of the board, and this became a guided missile aimed in the direction of Vanke. After Liu Luming had resigned, Wu Zhengbo was in total control of management and was concurrently chairman of the board. In the course of checking Vanguard's sales promotion activities, the financial department at headquarters discovered that sales volume had indeed increased, but a large number of fake sales-promotion vouchers had also begun to appear. Clearly, there were some loopholes in the management of Vanguard.

Problems would multiply if this kind of thing were allowed to go on. Vanke therefore decided to separate out operating authority from overall management authority at the company. It recommended that Ding Fuyuan become chairman of the board, a man who was Vanke's first chairman of its supervisory committee. Wu Zhengbo would then become CEO.

I called all of the various shareholders and expressed my concerns about Vanguard's management and my ideas for how to improve things. I confirmed that all shareholders were in accord with this way of doing things. We then called a meeting of the board of directors in order to execute the procedures for changing the chairman of the board.

The day before this board meeting was to occur, I was eating in a particular restaurant. I happened to notice that all the Vanguard board members, with the exception of the board member sent by Vanke, were having a meal together at the same place. My thinking was that this situation was rather strange: *We are having the meeting tomorrow, so why should they all be getting together today?* This did not bode well for things to come.

I placed a phone call to Wu Zhengbo and could not reach him.

I then phoned Wu Zhengbo's deputy, Wu Chong, but also could not reach him.

Things looked ominous. I called Li Dahai, an "old soldier" in the Huaxi Company, one of our shareholding entities.

Li Dahai did not beat around the bush: "Wu Zhengbo has alerted several of us shareholders to the idea that he should be squeezed out. We think that Vanke's treatment of him is unfair. How in the world can Ding Fuyuan be chairman of the board?" The moment I heard this, I realized we were facing a palace revolt. Shareholders were joining together with Vanguard senior management, which meant that Vanke was facing a situation that was unfavorable to our overall plan to transfer authority. So far as Vanke was concerned, the plan to divest itself of Vanguard had long been in the works. However, usurping Vanke's management authority without actually buying Vanke's shares was not acceptable. Naturally, I could not agree.

At this time, however, Vanke was already in the minority. It would therefore be put in a vulnerable position in the meeting the next day. I realized I had to find some way to resolve the issue right away. The third largest shareholder was Huaxi Construction. Huaxi was a company that was cooperating on a number of projects with Vanke and, added together, Huaxi and Vanke shares came to 55 percent. We had to persuade Huaxi to stand on our side in this matter.

Unexpectedly, Li Dahai turned out to have other ideas. The three allies planned to wash Vanke out of the picture, so to speak.

The situation was therefore clear. If we did hold a board meeting, Vanke would lose control over Vanguard.

Why should Wu Chong stand on the side of Wu Zhengbo? This situation again had a personal grievance behind it.

When we were issuing B shares, Wu Chong was deputy office manager of Vanke. He was on good personal terms with Ning Zhixiang, the renegade who tried to take over the company. During the Jun-Van conflict, Wu Chong was kept from knowing all the details about decisions so he felt excluded and distrusted. By now, as someone who knew all the ins and outs of Vanke's head-quarters, he had gravitated to being part of the opposition. This fight was not going to be an easy one.

Friendship Never Extends Beyond the Next Horizon

The following day, I went to see Li Dahai. He put me off, saying that he had a visitor, and I was left to wait outside his office. I knew, however, that so long as I did not leave, he could not leave either. The board meeting could not go forward.

I sat by myself in the conference room next to his office, with a cup of tea to keep me company. Nobody so much as glanced at me as the morning wore on.

At noon, I made it clear that I did not plan to leave.

Li Dahai finally came in and said, with an awkward sort of smile, "The other board members are all there at the Haiyan Building, waiting for the meeting to begin."

"The atmosphere is not conducive to holding a board meeting right now," I said. "I recommend that we change it to a shareholders' discussion."

Li Dahai said he would solicit the opinions of the others, specifically Nuclear Investment and Tian An.

After 15 minutes, he reappeared and nodded his head. The "discussion" was scheduled for four o'clock that afternoon.

Four o'clock. All of the shareholders were assembled. Wu Zhengbo and Wu Chong, who had previously disappeared, were suddenly there. Wu Zhengbo looked nervous and did not say anything to me.

In contrast, Wu Chong was quite candid: "I don't agree with the decision to switch Wu Zhengbo out as chairman of the board. After discussions with the three main shareholders, we put forward a motion that Huaxi's Li Dahai be the new chairman of the board." He seemed to have become spokesman for the alliance.

I patiently explained the thinking behind switching out Wu Zhengbo. Toward the end, I said, "Vanke does not agree with your methods. Since we now have a divergence of opinion, either Vanke buys out your shares or you all buy out Vanke's shares."

The reason the three shareholders had joined hands was to gain control shares in Vanguard. This also would then turn a complex personal dispute into a simple matter of buying and selling shareholding rights. My move, however, was something none of them had anticipated, including Wu Chong. They were silent for a moment before Wu Chong said that the three had to discuss this by themselves.

After 20 minutes, they returned to the conference room. Wu Chong declared, "So long as the price is right, the three shareholders are willing to sell their shares back to Vanke."

"Name your price."

"It isn't low," a woman named Li Binlan tossed in. She was the representative of Nuclear Investment.

"How much?"

"RMB 2.8 per share [USD 0.32]." Li Binlan smiled a little as she said this figure. She had reason to be happy—10 months earlier, she had purchased those same shares for RMB 1 (USD 0.17) per share.

"I accept the price of RMB 2.8 per share," I said. "Now it is time for dinner. After dinner, we will sign the purchase and sale agreement—sound okay?"

This amicable acceptance of their price left everyone stunned. They looked around at one another, a gleam coming into their eyes.

"Mr. Wang, you are awfully magnanimous. This is quite a pile of money." Ms. Li's cheeks were flushed with excitement.

"I won't be attending the signing ceremony this evening," I now added.

What? Doubts now flickered through the room as eyes focused on the chairman of the board of Vanke.

"My father-in-law went into the hospital yesterday morning for an operation. I have to get back to Guangzhou. I've been held here in Shenzhen long enough, just so you all could make some money. But rest easy, I am authorizing Xu Gang to represent me in signing the contract."

"Xu Gang has to have a formal written letter of authorization. Otherwise, the agreement will not be valid," Wu Chong blurted out.

In front of the three shareholders, I signed a written authorization and, as per Wu Chong's request, noted that Vanke was purchasing at a price of RMB 2.8 per share.

Before leaving, I had a few words privately with Xu Gang.

On the way back to Guangzhou, I could not keep from smiling as I thought of the scene that was going to take place with these shareholders later this evening.

Eight o'clock. Immersed in the glow of victory, the three allied shareholders hurried back to the conference room.

The meeting continued. Xu Gang handed over an agreement that had been prepared in advance, as he solemnly announced, "As the authorized representative of the chairman of the board, Vanke has decided to buy shares at a price of RMB 2.8 per share. However, among you three, Vanke has decided to purchase the shares of only one. It is up to you to decide who that will be. You can discuss it among yourselves. If the three of you feel this is not acceptable, then Vanke is willing to sell its shares at a price of RMB 2 [USD 0.30]."

The fat was in the fire.

Vanke had won itself time to catch its breath.

The next day, Li Dahai telephoned my secretary to say that they were holding a board meeting that afternoon and they were asking Ding Fuyuan to call the meeting and to preside over it.

Vanke did not send anyone to attend this meeting.

During the proceedings, the three shareholders elected Li Dahai to serve as the new chairman of the board. After the meeting, the newly elected slate, together with security personnel, went to the offices of Vanguard to take control. For a while, the bodyguards of the old guard and the new guard were at a stalemate outside the Vanguard Building.

In the corridor outside the operating room of the provincial People's Hospital, I was using a mobile phone to get reports on progress in Shenzhen. I told Xu Gang, "It worked. We provoked the other side quite effectively. The chairman of the board of Vanke was not present at the board meeting they called, so any decisions made at that meeting are invalid. This stalemate is advantageous for Vanke. What we need is time."

Since Vanke did not recognize the legality of Li Dahai's election, other shareholders wondered if this meant that Ding Fuyuan as chairman of the board had been confirmed, or was Wu Zhengbo still the chairman? Vanguard's unauthorized board meeting had resulted in a situation in which three people were simultaneously chairman of the board. So long as no substantive decisions were taken, Vanke had the ways and means to break the alliance. The reason? The market does not allow for eternal friendship—the only thing it recognizes is eternal interests. What Vanke needed was time for this law to take effect.

My fear was that Wu Chong, who had worked at my side for many years, would not completely come to his senses.

On the third day, the three-sided shareholder alliance delivered a document to Ding Fuyuan, calling for a special shareholders' meeting.

This document also called for two things: recognizing Ding Fuyuan as chairman of the board, and announcing that the appointment of Li Dahai as chairman of the board was invalid.

Clearly, our opponents had changed their tactics. The real power to control Vanguard was in the hands of Vanke, which meant that any delays were against the interests of the alliance. According to the bylaws, any alliance holding more than 10 percent of shares had the right to apply to hold a special shareholders' meeting for special motions. After receiving such a request, the board of directors had one month within which it had to call such a meeting.

Vanke now had a window of one month within which to maneuver.

It was precisely at this juncture that I had planned to accompany a delegation to Melbourne, Australia, to host an international conference on urban development. Should I go or not? Steeling my nerves, I boarded the plane. I was not going to give the other side the impression that Vanke was overly concerned about this matter.

As soon as I reached Australia, however, I made sure to have two cellphones always at the ready, since one would not have been enough.

After being gone 10 days, I returned to Shenzhen. Our strategy remained to focus our main forces on Huaxi's 20 percent of shares. If we could buy those in, Vanke would have 55 percent of shares and absolute control. However, I noticed that whenever Huaxi Construction had any private discussions with us, the other two in the alliance immediately knew what we had talked about. In contrast, when we talked to Li Binlan at Nuclear Investment, the other two did not know what we talked about. Clearly, Li Binlan was intentionally concealing her dealings with Vanke from the others. This meant that Li Binlan was thinking of selling out Nuclear Investment's shares on its own—the alliance was merely a chip she was using to get a good price. The issue was now much simpler, since it had boiled down to a matter of price.

We soon came to an agreement with Li Binlan on price. The other two share-holders were left in the dark.

One week later, the agreement was signed and sealed. Vanke's share holdings in Vanguard now came to 60 percent. Li Binlan spearheaded a move to have a group of employees leave Vanguard and set up a retail enterprise called A. Best, with investment from the China Nuclear Power Group.

Not long after, Ding Fuyuan retired with honors and went back to head-quarters. Xu Gang was formally voted in as chairman of the board of Vanguard. As time went on, the Huaxi Group also sold the shares it owned in Vanguard to Vanke. The contretemps with Vanguard was over. Nevertheless, sooner or later Vanke was going to have to divest itself of the company, since it was not a part of Vanke's strategic plans.

Vanke's First Round of Expansion

Vanke's first round of expansion refers to its business in the years between 1988 and 1993. In 1991, we decided to adopt the business model of becoming a comprehensive commercial association. The company then grew swiftly through a process of diversification and cross-regional operations.

As Vanke went into different industries, the company became more aware of the importance of its real estate business. The real estate industry was going to become one of the hot spots in the national economy.

China's real estate industry can be traced back to the country's housing reform policy. In April 1982, the four cities of Changzhou, Zhengzhou, Shashi, and Siping implemented an experimental reform called "sale of housing allowances to employees." The response was extremely positive. In October 1984, the State Council gave permission to extend this pilot project to other parts of the country. It signed off on a report that called for expansion of the pilot project to allow for subsidized sale of public housing in cities. This meant that public housing could be sold to individuals, using subsidies, as a way to turn housing into something that was bought and sold, as opposed to being granted to state employees. This was a very important step in overall reform of China's housing system.

By the end of 1985, one hundred sixty cities in the country as well as 300 county seats were implementing policies that called for subsidized sale of housing. In January 1986, the State Council set up the Leading Group on Reform of the Housing System. Under the direct leadership of the State Council, it quickly began work on reforming China's housing system in towns and cities.

In September 1988, the Third Plenary Session of the Thirteenth Central Committee of the Communist Party of China declared that an important part of the "control and rectification" process,* and of overall deepening of reform, was "speeding up the sale of public housing and realizing a situation in which housing could be privatized." Meanwhile, the old concept of housing as a way to distribute welfare benefits remained very tenacious. Given that reality, at the end of 1989, the government implemented what it called "incremental reform." This meant changing the *increment* but not the *base*. New policies allowed the sale and leasing of new housing construction, but they did not force people to buy who were already in older buildings. That arrangement thereby reduced opposition to reform. Given this favorable policy environment, China's real estate business began to emerge and to grow in earnest.

Shenzhen led the rest of the country in building new housing. One reason was Shenzhen's unique funding model. Another was that older housing did not exist and there were fewer obstacles—no people to move out, no buildings to tear down. Shenzhen more readily accepted the concept of a commodified housing market. The pace of construction was unbelievable. When reform and opening up was just beginning, the Shenzhen International Trade Center was put up at a rate of one floor every three days. This pace became known as "Shenzhen speed," and this particular building became just a footnote to what was to happen later. By 1987, the Shenzhen municipal government was already implementing the new policy of land auctions.

The central government's clear policy orientation with regard to the privatization of housing undoubtedly contributed to the speed of new housing development. Shenzhen was soon covered with construction projects. In order to get into this new line of business, Vanke paid top dollar for the patch of land called H201–3, classified as "housing-use land." This was in November 1988. For RMB 20 million (USD 5.4 million), it bought an entry ticket into the real estate market game.

The first great expansion of Vanke's real estate business had a great deal to do with its issuing of A and B shares in 1993, and therefore with its increased amount of capital.

Vanke issued A shares in 1988 and raised RMB 28 million (USD 7.57 million) in a public offering. This led to a swift expansion in both assets and operations. In 1989, raising capital through floating shares was complete, and the funds were put toward investment in three sectors: manufacturing, import and export trade, and real estate development. The real estate company was set up in 1989, called the Shenzhen Vanke Real Estate Company, Ltd. In the same year, however, smuggling activity cut deeply into Vanke's video sales, reducing the trade part of overall business. In contrast, manufacturing and real estate

---

*Inflation soared in 1988, leading to government policies that clamped down on bank loans and price hikes. This was known as "control and rectification." Panic buying and inflation continued into 1989.

continued to do well and became the primary source of profits for the company. In 1990, Vanke set up the initial framework structure for four main lines of business: commerce and trade, manufacturing, real estate, and cultural undertakings, including movies.

In early 1991, the company decided to consolidate its various lines into one comprehensive entity or holding company, as a growth model. This brought together information, trade transactions, finance, and manufacturing into one entity. To serve the needs of business expansion, in June 1991 the company carried out a recapitalization by issuing shares. The total number of shares was increased to 77.96 million. Funds raised from this share expansion were mainly invested in real estate development, manufacturing, import and export trade, and the chainstore [franchise] business, as well as movies and TV.

Nineteen ninety-two was described at Vanke as "the year we let the flowers bloom," as the company began operations in different parts of the country. That is, we began operating across different administrative jurisdictions. On the trade side, the company set up a headquarters for trade operations, with Wanli opening malls in Wuhan and Urumqi. It also added companies in Dalian, Zhuhai, Wuhan, Xinjiang, and Beihai. On the real estate side, a number of companies and subsidiaries were set up, including the Hong Kong Yindu, the Qingdao Yindu Garden, the Tianjin Wanxing, and the Wanhua, the Shanghai Vanke Real Estate Company, and the Beihai Wanda Real Estate Company. The company called Vanke Cultural Communications, Ltd., produced and distributed movies, advertisements, and karaoke videos.

In the course of cross-regional development, we opted for joint financing with local partners. By 1992, some 13 companies inside China had coinvested with us in shares in businesses throughout China, as well as a real estate company in Hong Kong. Our policy remained what we called a "0.4 investment practice," meaning that we would not take more than 40 percent of a group investment in a company's shares and the direct investment of the group in the company would not surpass 40 percent of the total investment. The rest would be covered by money derived from advance sales and by credit from banks. The double-40 rule meant that our own direct investment would constitute no more than 16 percent of a company's shares. The practical effect of this was that we were highly leveraged. We operated with a high debt to asset ratio.

Deng Xiaoping made his famous tour of the south in 1992, which had the effect of catapulting China in the direction of a market economy. That fall, on November 4, the State Council promulgated a document called "Notification on Various Issues Regarding Developing China's Real Estate Industry." This made it clear that real estate as an industry was going to be supported and promoted by the central government.

Under the impetus of this document, China now witnessed a nationwide explosion in real estate development. Approvals for the leasing and developing of land increased, the number of companies involved in real estate development soared, and the numbers and prices of buildings for sale also soared.

Vanke had been fortunate to get in on the ground floor. It had grabbed its chances and it now accelerated its cross-regional strategy. It invested in projects in the Yangtze delta area, the Shandong peninsula, the Tianjin area, and the Liaodong peninsula. All of this was helped by the ability of the company to issue B shares and have a base of stable financing. Many other companies were not so lucky. Soon the growing bubble in both shares and real estate burst.

On April 1, 1993, the central government sounded the alarm. The words "guard against economic overheating" were part of a report on economic conditions that came out that day. The overspeculation in finance and real estate sectors had triggered concern. These referred to chaotic fund raising, chaotic tearing down of buildings, and chaotic setting up of financial institutions, propelled by the real estate fever and the development fever.

Starting in May, the People's Bank of China started raising interest rates and also launching inquiries into the balance sheets of banks, which was called "clearing up and rectifying order in the financial industry."

On June 24, 1993, the central government issued a document that became known as Central Document No. 6. Its longer title was "Opinions on the Current Economic Situation and on Strengthening Macro Controls." This was approved by the Central Politburo of the Communist Party of China and the State Council. Fiscal and monetary policies were tightened, the financial system underwent a rectification, and the size of investment was now strictly limited. Enhanced price controls, investigations of distribution links, and import controls all contributed to the tightening.

The measures prescribed by Central Document No. 6 put a severe brake on economic activity. Between July and September of 1993, the rate of industrial growth declined nationwide. Investment was brought under control, and new construction projects were sharply curtailed.

The real estate industry suddenly found it was taking a very cold bath.

Using monetary policy, administrative controls, and any other means possible, the government put a stop to rampant loan making and overinvestment. By this time, Vanke had already expanded—it had 55 subsidiaries and affiliated companies, and it was spread over 12 major cities. Its business was set out in five main categories. It was also feeling the pressures of inadequate capital.

Fortunately, in April 1993 Vanke had successfully issued B shares, raising HKD 450 million (USD 57.7 million). This proved to be vital in weathering the economic tightening. Many people in the industry feel that both Vanke and Wang Shi were very lucky. I admit we are lucky, but if Vanke people had not worked hard to make things come about, luck would not have helped us at all.

The issue of B shares not only enabled the company to get financing, it enabled Vanke to take a hard look at its business structure and evaluate whether or not it was rational from the perspective of venture capital and mature international investors. As a result of that, we drew down our investment in extraneous businesses. Luck allowed Vanke to gain international funding in time, and it also enabled Vanke to reduce its own investing activity while still "blindly" expanding its real estate business. We continued massive expansion of our real estate projects. The macro adjustments of 1993 did not curtail our main projects. Only in 1995 did we find that our cross-regional expansion was too piecemeal for our available funds to deal with properly, and we cut back on them decisively. These included projects in Chengdu, Shenzhen, Wuhan, Tianjin, Shandong, and elsewhere. A number of investments were essentially abandoned, to be remodeled into different projects at a later time.

For Whom the Bell Tolls

Vanke deliberately went through a process of retrenchment in its real estate projects and its cross-regional development in general. We assessed our projects realistically and cut back on nonessential lines of business. This retrenchment was to continue for some years. We realized that we should concentrate our developments in economically advanced parts of the country, given the group's current resources and also human resource capacity. Shenzhen in particular had a high and also stable level of economic growth. The real estate development industry was fairly standardized and the market was fairly mature. The rate at which individuals purchased their own housing was far above that of other cities around the country. After the recession of 1993 and 1994, housing as an industry began to grow.

In the second half of 1995, the company adopted a Return to Shenzhen policy. One year and a half later, it successfully completed its strategic retrenchment. From 12 cities throughout the entire country, Vanke now focused on operations in Shenzhen, Shanghai, Beijing, and Tianjin. Among these, the main emphasis was placed on Shenzhen.

In June 1997, the company increased available funds by issuing shares and raised RMB 383 million (USD 46.26 million). Most of this was put to real estate projects in Shenzhen as well as to building up land reserves.

In October 1997, we continued a process that had begun in 1995, restructuring resources and institutions with respect to the trade-related business. The company sold the Shenzhen Yibao Food and Beverage Company, Ltd., in April 1996, and the group then came to an agreement to spin off two subsidiaries, one in manufacturing and one in power supply. We thereby basically completed the restructuring of noncore businesses, that is, businesses that were not in real estate, franchise chain stores, or film and television.

The sale of Vanguard, in 2001, signaled that Vanke had completed the transformation of its corporate structure and had entered a new round of growth.

In the mid-1990s, Vanke was not the only one going through such restructuring; many outstanding companies in Shenzhen were doing the same. In 1993, a man named Ren Kelei became CEO of the Overseas Chinese Town Group after being Secretary General of the Municipal Party Committee of Shenzhen. This group had adhered to a growth strategy that focused on manufacturing but was still comprehensive. In addition to making color televisions, it did tourism, had a department store, and was spread across more than 20 different industries. Ren Kelei put a decisive stop to this overexpansion. His approach was in line with the national policy of holding onto the big ones and letting the little ones go as he concentrated on core businesses.

In 1994, the group made the same decision that Vanke made in 1995. Its funding, resources, and human and material forces went into a concerted effort to support electronics, tourism, and real estate businesses. The singular purpose now was to grow big and strong. After the pruning of extraneous branches, the number of companies in the group went from 101 to around 60 by May 25, 1998. The number of industries the group was involved in went down from 20 to just a focus on several main lines: household electronics, with the company Konka as the primary entity; tourism, with several large theme parks; and real estate.

Looking back on it now, we can see the price that Vanke paid for wanting to go big. Only in 2001 did the Vanke Anshan Company, for instance, finally clear out its debts and move back into normal operating mode. The Wuhan office building got up as far as three stories and then stopped construction; in 2001 we tore down what had been done and started again. That building became a decade-long problem. The Haishen Building was turned into housing as the only way to deal with that fiasco and try to make a little profit.

The real estate development business is highly sensitive to government policy. Since the development time for any given project is fairly long, it is easy to be hit by macro policy changes. Because of this, a thorough understanding of policy trends and local political considerations in any given city is crucial. We did detailed research before selecting cities in which we planned to develop projects. We wanted to avoid investing in an arbitrary fashion, on the basis of scratching our heads or certainly just shaking hands. Long-term opportunities can exist only in the context of markets that operate in standard ways.

Real estate development is also a business with a strongly regional character. Real estate might look great from the perspective of the entire country but be a disaster in specific cities. One can easily face bottlenecks in normal supply and demand due to local conditions, local purchasing power, and local government officials. Vanke policies had to strike a balance between the benefits of being cross-regional and the benefits of in-depth investment in any given market. We also had to stay flexible in how we allocated resources. All of these things had to be taken into consideration by decision makers.

Faced with the hyperheated market, Vanke too could not avoid the temptation of trying to go big. I knew well that in order for the company to become more mature, we needed to study first and not just pay tuition in the school of life.

The price that Vanke eventually did have to pay in its first round of expansion was not fatal. This was Vanke's good fortune. But the losses that the company encountered in the process were, from start to finish, a warning bell. They reminded us that we had to be sober minded and calculating before taking action. An enterprise with the goal of long-term growth has to deal with reality as it is, keep a steady course, and manage accordingly.

Strategic Thinking and a Lesson in Tianjin

On January 23 and 24, 1995, the Vanke Group held another of its strategic meetings. People in charge of each of the business lines and people from the group headquarters gathered at the Xiaomeisha Hotel. Altogether, this meeting included around two dozen people.

After years of expansion, Vanke now had a business structure that included 29 wholly owned subsidiaries and 25 enterprises in which we held an interest, either as joint ventures or cooperatives. Real estate was by now the dominant line of business. Our operations were spread throughout the country, however, and management was trying to handle an increasingly broad span of issues. Our growth pattern was increasingly cross-regional as well as cross-industry—we faced the urgent need to create a management structure that could handle the businesses in an efficient and organic manner.

Vanke had defined the primary direction in which it intended to move its key forces. Property ownership in the group as a whole was divided into two main forms, however. One was joint ventures, with investment brought in from different parties. The other was wholly owned, with investment only from Vanke. Real estate, for example, under the leadership of Yao Mumin, was wholly owned. It was managed strictly according to Vanke's own value judgments, its methodology, and code of behavior. The other form, combined investment, was epitomized by such companies as Yindu, Tianjin Wanxing, and Wanzhong in Shenyang. Vanke's immediate situation made it hard for the joint venture–type companies to fit into Vanke's own style of management and growth, the so-called Vanke Model. What's more, the various companies were managed out of different geographic regions. The northeast was under the unified control of Wanzhong. Tianjin was controlled by Wanxing. Shijiazhuang, Qingdao, and Chengdu were all under the control of Yindu Investments. The other cities were managed out of the main headquarters in Shenzhen.

Vanke's business structure, management structure, and geographic distribution were, to varying degrees, interrelated and complex. In this regard, it was similar to many of China's private enterprises.

Clearly, the company had to shift from rampant diversification toward a more professional form of specialization. Second, it had to comb out its ownership structures. This meant straightening out and unifying management, and clarifying business goals.

Such restructuring was necessarily going to impact interest relationships in the group. For a long time, Vanke had adhered to the 0.4 policy, which meant investing no more than 40 percent in a given company. This created fairly dispersed ownership structures in the companies that Vanke was involved in around the country. Each different investor had his own interests and requirements, which led to different interest factions within the various companies. For example, at Wanzhong in the northeast, the inclination was to want to create a holding company and do real estate on the side. When the real estate market was slack, however, the inclination was again to be mainly a holding company. At Wanzhong's main shareholders' meeting, Vanke announced that Vanke had decided to focus on real estate as its primary business, which meant that it wanted to sell off the non–real estate divisions of joint ventures in which it was involved. From a strategic perspective, this was in Vanke's long-term interests. Other investors raised loud objections, however, since immediate returns were more important to them. What's more, other businesses had always been profitable, while real estate carried a degree of risk—why should they take that risk on behalf of Vanke? At the same time, people who had underwritten companies in various parts of the country put their own price tag on things, which increased problems for headquarters and for the management style of senior management.

One example is well worth remembering, namely the case of Tianjin's Wanxing Industrial Company, Ltd. This relates to events that started in 1995. In the course of the restructuring known as "closing down, temporary closure, merging, and transforming," Wanxing suddenly opened up another restaurant. Wanxing in Tianjin was like a microcosm of Vanke's business overall. Essentially all of the overly ambitious mistakes that Vanke made were also played out in Tianjin. The company invested in multiple lines of business by using the 0.4 investment method and, in the three years between 1992 and 1995, ran up an enormous debt-to-asset ratio. As the Chinese saying goes, "The sparrow may be small, but it has all the vital organs." This was particularly true of the Tianjin operation.

In 1993, housing constituted just 25 percent of Vanke's total real estate business. The other 75 percent was in office buildings. Similarly, in late 1992–early 1993, Wanxing in Tianjin was able to acquire a piece of land within the Tianjin municipality. The plan was to build two office buildings with a skirt area in between for a shopping mall. In 1995, however, macroeconomic policies tightened up and the project had to stop when it was halfway done. We were later able to get the Hong Kong branch of a Japanese company to cooperate with us and turn the original plan into a hotel. We were also able to have the Ministry of Economics and Trade qualify this hotel as one that catered to foreign investment and foreign guests. We mortgaged part of the building and received a loan from a Japanese financial group in order to resolve the issue of funding and complete the construction.

Tianjin Wanxing therefore turned a problematic building into a project that attracted foreign investment. From a tactical perspective, we had solved the problem in inadequate funding and transformed a building with no market into one that had a market. From a strategic perspective, however, we had created an even bigger problem as we resolved an existing problem.

Vanke was already moving more deeply into public housing as its primary business. It was streamlining and readjusting projects that were outside the scope of such housing. Yet here in Tianjin we had not only built a large hotel for foreigners, but we had taken on several tens of millions of U.S. dollars in debt. The result of this restructuring also revealed deeper issues: not only could Vanke not extricate itself, but it also had to continue to invest money as it sank further into the project. The hotel was one thing, but the other building now came into focus. After construction stopped for a while, we tried to promote it on the market by leasing it as a package to a buyer. This approach seemed innovative, but it too came with later problems. The long and short of it was that the last lawsuits were not resolved until 2005. Vanke bore a large portion of the costs on those lawsuits as well.

Ultimately, Vanke divested itself of this project and also other external assets. We were able to replace them for some bank loans and ownership of a project called the Dongli Lake. Through all those years, however, Vanke did indeed hold onto something that it described as "a loss," and then as "a massive loss," and as "an ongoing loss." Why did Tianjin become such a huge burden to Vanke for so long? There is no doubt in my mind at all that if we had stopped investing in time, cut our losses, and admitted our mistake, the Tianjin problem would long since have been resolved.

Not long after, Vanke began to reevaluate itself and take courageous steps to correct its mistakes. Vanke's frank approach to its own shortcomings was what helped it get through a difficult period. Biting the bullet was what enabled it to become one of the stronger participants in the market economy.

CHAPTER THREE

The Thorn Birds,
1995–1999

Fundamentals of Investing

The Vanke Group formally established its Financial Settlement Center on May 2, 1995. This center was set up in recognition of the importance that capital had played in Vanke's first decade. It was to play a key role in reorganizing the group's resources and improving the performance of its management.

In August 1995, the Shenzhen municipality held its first conference on investment and financial management. I spoke at this conference, on the topic of "Investment Strategies for Enterprises That Are Changing Direction and Transforming Their Mode of Operations." I divided Shenzhen enterprises into three different categories, depending on their stage of development: policy type, market policy type, and market innovator type.

Policy-type companies were those that had relied completely on the protective umbrella of preferential government policies for their development. They also could receive direct support from the government. They participated in a diversity of businesses to the point that there was essentially nothing they were not willing to do. Special Development (SD) was an example of this type of company.

In the mid-1980s, companies in the Shenzhen Special Economic Zone were mainly of the second category, market policy–type companies. Vanke, which began in trade, belonged to this category. Market policy–type companies also received preferential policy treatment, but at the same time they relied on their own forces to grow. They found market opportunities that had been formed by policy discrepancies. It was easy for their pattern of growth to become diversified—this allowed them to become powerful quickly, but, on the other hand, it spread their resources too thinly and prevented them from growing in a stable manner.

In the 1990s, newly formed companies in Shenzhen were forced to take the path of the third type: market innovator–type companies. They had to carve out a market-oriented path by relying on their own R&D.

Meanwhile, in the course of making investments, Vanke also followed four fundamental principles. I summarized those as follows.

The first was the "70 percent–70 percent principle." Real estate was the heart of Vanke's business structure. Profits from real estate therefore had to account for more than 70 percent of the group's profits—this was the first 70 percent that Vanke's investment managers had to keep firmly in mind. Real estate itself is a very broad industry. It involves housing, commercial buildings, office buildings, industrial buildings, and so on, each with different kinds of investment. The main thrust of Vanke's real estate business was urban housing. Because of this, urban housing projects had to account for more than 70 percent of the size of Vanke's real estate business overall.

The second was the "25% principle." This principle said that we do not do business that exceeds a 25 percent profit margin. In 1993, the saying in the real estate industry was, "We do not do business that has less than a 40 percent profit margin." This expressed the clear desire to make explosive profits. It was in that climate of opinion that Vanke brought forth its own saying: "No business over 25 percent profit." This was not because Vanke did not want to make money. On the contrary, it was looking at the situation from a long-term perspective. If the company wanted to continue to grow, it had to decide on a reasonable rate of return. In theory, as competition intensified and policies were adjusted, the market had to move toward balancing out rates of return in society. In practice, Vanke too had experienced the pleasure of making explosive profits. In its earliest period, when it was trading, profit margins might be 1,000 percent or more—that is, not just doubling money but making 10 or more times a return on investment. However, the company also found out that the market is fair in the end. When Vanke hit the depths of its trading business, it lost more money than it had made in the era of explosive profits. The principle that Vanke came up with was based on its evaluation of the average rate of return in society if we were to avoid high risk, cultivate competitiveness, and strengthen the company's ability to weather economic cycles.

The third principle was that Vanke was going to invest in mass public housing for urban residents. Professional management required that we be precise and accurate in our market positioning. Vanke believed that this particular market had long-term and stable potential. The company had established a business approach that focused on meticulous design, first-rate quality, and outstanding building management. It had divided real estate products into different categories. In 1994, urban residential housing held 73.5 percent of all completed construction area.

The fourth principle was that we would not invest in overseas properties. Until the market opportunities abroad were fully ready for such investment, Vanke would not put in one penny. People who had been posted abroad often wrote reports to Vanke describing in glowing terms how much money one could make overseas. The company's attitude was that if the business was so good, China's many thousands of firms could go after it. Not only would we ourselves not invest, but also we would not serve as guarantor either. The company was concentrating its forces on developing domestic markets. It was working toward the advantage of economies of scale. With respect to overseas, the bigger consideration was how to use foreign capital markets to raise funds for our efforts in China. In the meantime, Vanke would not use those funds to invest abroad.

As the government's macro adjustments were rolled out and began to take effect, economic relationships were straightened out and the business environment began to become more orderly and market-oriented. This provided a more beneficial space in which Vanke could develop real estate as its primary business and engage in more focused growth. With an investment strategy that was also specialized, Vanke was able to achieve more sound and stable growth. Meanwhile, the public was benefiting as well, and this provided a fundamental guarantee for Vanke's own future. As the company's internal reorganization gradually took hold, the aim was to complete the process by the end of 1997 in order to enable Vanke to move forward with a more mature framework.

Since 1995, Vanke has reaped substantial benefits from its restructuring of resources. The group streamlined administration in its dominant businesses, such as trading, manufacturing, and culture. It brought the main lines of each into clearer focus. One such effort deserves mention here. In order to clarify the business policy of becoming more specialized and professional, in August 1995, Vanke undertook institutional restructuring of its manufacturing companies. Subsidiary companies that manufactured luxury products were merged into the Vanke Luxury Manufacturing Company, Ltd. At the same time, the company sold off the profitable parts of the Shenzhen Yibao Food and Beverage Company, Ltd. that still existed under its banner. At the time this company was sold, it was the largest manufacturer of distilled water in the country, producing 100,000 tons per year.

After the reorganization, noncore parts of Vanke still made considerable contributions to the group. In addition to providing simple profits, they had the advantage of not being in real estate, so they were able to get bank financing. The Vanguard Department Store was one good example. Due to the nature of its business, it had substantial retained earnings in its bank account, some RMB 80 million (about USD 9.59 million). This was significant when it came to getting bank loans for the group's real estate business.

Issuing Shares for a Capital Infusion

Vanke set up its very first board of directors in early 1989. Among 11 members, eight were representatives of shareholders, with overseas investors and China-side investors each holding four seats. The other three seats were occupied by people from senior management.

Not six months after the company went public, its share price began to soften. Some shareholders could not hold their breath long enough, and they sold at a low price. One year later, when the stock exchange situation improved, our shares began a steady rise. In the early 1990s, only a few companies were traded on the Shenzhen Exchange. As they say, "When there are many monks and little porridge, the porridge rises in value." Our share price went from slightly over RMB 1 [USD 0.12] to RMB 38 [USD 4.56] in short order. People were able to make thousands of percent profit in those days.

Regulations with regard to trading at the time were primitive. Transactions were still done manually, with handwritten slips, but a more significant difference was that all shares were treated equally and all could be traded on the board, including individual shares, legal-person shares, and state-owned shares. This led to abuse. People responsible for shares of state-owned enterprises were sometimes found to have sold off shares, with only a portion of the money finding its way back to the state. Large amounts in funds were transferred to somewhere else. Starting up a system of state-owned shares without adequate supervision meant that state assets inevitably went astray. As a result, it became necessary for the country to restrict the circulation of state-owned shares. When this happened, the state-owned shares incapable of being circulated piled up and obstructed the healthy development of China's stock markets. This was something the government had not anticipated.

At the time, Vanke's largest investor owned eight million shares. This was SD, the Shenzhen Special Economic Zone Development Company. Figured at an average price of RMB 25 (USD 3), SD's holdings were worth RMB 200 million (USD 23.98 million). In his office, I encouraged the CEO of SD, Wang Xinmin, to grab this opportunity, sell the shares, and bring that capital back into their bank account.

This old soldier laughed bitterly. Even though SD needed the money, he said, "The company is owned by the government. The company's shares are also therefore state-owned assets. Selling them is equivalent to embezzling state-owned assets. Who dares do that?"

Another example ended up with diametrically opposite results, however. The Beijing Broadcasting Instruments Firm (a non-board member shareholder in Vanke) was also a state-owned enterprise. It, however, used marketized methods to deal with this problem. When the market price of our shares was RMB 30 (USD 3.60), the head of the company, Wang Dianfu, notified Shenzhen that he was selling 400,000 "original shares." His heart was pounding as he did so. The profit he made from this sale came to nearly RMB 12 million (about USD 1.44 million). He invested it in building dormitories for employees, and was applauded by everyone in the company, from top to bottom. Several years later, Manager Wang was transferred to Shenzhen to be chairman of the board of Shen Electronics Group. He was rather proud of this when he mentioned it to me. Both companies were subject to the same structural constraints, but they handled them in different ways and the results were radically different.

Then there was another shareholder, a state-operated enterprise that was also not a member of the board. It lost no time in selling off its original shares. However, only a small portion of the profits came back into the account of the original unit. Tens of millions were instead siphoned off into another account. Without any regulatory mechanisms that allowed for the release of state-owned shares in a monitored way, it was obvious that state-owned assets would be embezzled. There is no real alternative to having restrictions on the transfer of state-owned shares that belong to the public at large. The problem is that there are more and more state-owned legal-person shares that are not liquid.

The inability to sell state-owned shares in secondary markets also becomes a problem when a company is trying to figure out shareholding structures as it issues new shares. If the state does not want to lose control, then its percentage of shareholdings has to move forward in equal measure and it has to subscribe to new shares. If it is not concerned about this, it loses control, since state shares are diluted every time the company issues more shares.

As Vanke proceeded with its plans, it worried what the company one tier above it (its largest shareholder) would think of this share expansion. Would it participate? It would be in a dilemma—it would not want to lose the opportunity to issue shares when the market was high, but it also would not want to pay that high price in order to keep its percentage of control. It made for an awkward situation.

Ever since Vanke undertook reform to become a joint-stock company, people have been envious of the dispersed nature of Vanke's shareholders. They feel that the shareholding structure of the company has allowed it to avoid having one dominant shareholder, which in turn has allowed it to achieve a separation between management authority and ownership rights. Vanke feels differently about this matter, however. Before the company grew to any size, the support of its largest shareholder was extremely important. However, that largest shareholder held only 9 percent of shares. It therefore was not inclined to do much to support Vanke's business development. This was particularly the case when Vanke needed financial support. The actual situation was that every time Vanke had a new share offering, it was put in conflict with its largest shareholder. This happened four times since Vanke was listed on the market in 1989. The exception is when it issued B shares in 1993. The most intense struggles came when it expanded its shares in 1997.

In 1997, Yu Liang and I went together to the Special Development Building to encourage our largest shareholder to take a 20 to 25 percent share of our new issue. We hoped to gain the support of the parent company by doing this. The CEO of our parent company (our largest shareholder) was a man named Chen. He was an extremely charming and also a fairly autocratic gentleman.

The plans for this share expansion would mean that the parent company had to hand over RMB 150 million (USD 18.11 million) to keep its ownership percentage.

"Where are we supposed to get so much money?" Chen cut straight through to the heart of the matter.

"Umm, sell land." The parent company had a patch of land in its reserves that was 100 square kilometers (62 square miles) by Honey Lake. It owned this in a joint venture with another company. Just 20 of these square kilometers (12.5 square miles) could offset the amount owed to Vanke.

Chen's eyebrows rose and his eyes sparkled. "Excellent idea!," he said.

After another three days, however, his attitude had taken a 180-degree turn and he refused to accept the proposal to issue shares. He said, "Headquarters is focusing on three main businesses right now: telecom, tourism, and high tech. We can't spread our capital around by investing in real estate."

He had gone back on his word, but I also had a feeling that this was a golden opportunity for Vanke. We could now bring in a financial group with real clout.

One week later, Yu Liang and I made a second proposal to Chen: "Sell Vanke's shares. Put the money back in your account. Support telecom, tourism, and high tech, your three main lines of business. You will be able to bring in RMD 180 million [about USD 27 million] at the net asset price for legal-person shares."

Chen was persuaded. He said categorically, "This time I won't change my mind."

Not long after, Vanke introduced a buyer for SD's shares. This was Mr. Huang Tieying, chief executive officer and board member of Huachuang, a company under the banner of the China Resources Group.* He presented himself in person and the negotiations went forward with great fanfare. Chen displayed his tougher side as he insisted on full payment in cash on the day the contract was to be signed. He did not trust Hong Kong companies, and he would not take foreign exchange in payment, he wanted renminbi.

One week before the contract was to be signed, I called Chen. Is everything all right?," I asked. "No changes?"

"How could we change something we agreed on?"

"Nothing can go wrong?"

"No way."

Huang Tieying therefore asked the chairman of the board of Huayuan in Beijing to bring a check to Shenzhen for the entire amount in renminbi. The man carrying this check was Ren Zhiqiang. With just one day to go before the signing date, I still had the feeling something was not right and I asked Yu Liang to call Chen to make sure.

Chen happily responded, "See you tomorrow. I'll sign as soon as I see that check."

---

*China Resources was founded in 1948. For a long time after the People's Republic of China (PRC) was established, it became the major window to the outside world for the PRC. It played a decisive role in China's foreign trade. For years, it was considered to have the direct support from the central government, but after the start of China's opening and reform process, central-government control over China Resources changed. From being a company that was the window on the West for China's foreign trade, it became only one of 45 superlarge enterprises directly under the control of Central. China Resources was still large. It had more than RMB 50 billion (about USD 7.5 billion) gross assets, and more than RMB 40 billion (more than USD 6 billion) in net assets. It soon included five publicly traded companies under its banner. Superficially, China Resources was a 100 percent China-invested company, but the publicly traded companies under its umbrella constituted more than 70 percent of the total capitalization of the group. Control shares of these five were held by China Resources itself, but financing was internationalized.

The next day, in the morning, Ren Zhiqiang was on a flight down to Shenzhen when I got a call. It was from a deputy manager at SD. "Chen is not selling our Vanke shares," he said.

"The man with the check is on his way right now," I protested. "You had better ask Chen to explain this directly to Mr. Huang and Manager Ren."

"Chen asked me to invite you all to dinner. He's busy and won't be able to attend himself."

All I could do was curse him internally and carry on. He might be our major shareholder, but we were still going to go through with the share issue.

Two days later, I made an appointment with Chen to discuss the share issue. Without the slightest bit of embarrassment or apology, Chen said that he was not willing to give up his position as dominant shareholder, nor was he willing to allow the share issue.

"Are you deliberately making things hard for us?," I asked.

Driven beyond endurance, I stood up and brought my fist down hard on the glass table. In the most belligerent way possible, I shouted out a phrase used by Chengdu ballgame fans: "*Xiongqi!*" [meaning "cheer up" in Chinese].

I completely lost control. If I had not experienced that moment myself, I would never have known just how it tasted.

My action did not break the glass, but it firmly closed the door on any chances of getting approval for the share expansion.

According to proper procedures, listed companies that want to issue more shares have to have a resolution drawn up by the board of directors. This then has to be voted on at a shareholders' meeting. Only after it has passed can the company submit a request to the China Securities Regulatory Commission, and only after that is approved can the company issue new shares.

The first hurdle was therefore the board of directors. In 1997, our board was composed of 19 members. The parent company, SD, had three seats, but I was one of those three. I had to decide which way to go. As chairman of the board, representing the interests of the entire body of shareholders, I felt I had to vote in favor of expansion. The other representatives of SD opposed this. Even if all three votes of the parent company had been opposed, however, without seven other board members voting with them, they could not have blocked the proposal to put the issue before the shareholders' meeting.

The entity holding control shares over our parent company was, in turn, the municipal State-Owned Assets Management Company. It was possible this company had a trick up its sleeve and was involved. In 1991, when Vanke expanded its shares a second time, the parent company did not have the resources to buy in the new shares so they were purchased instead by the State-Owned Assets Management Company, which then got a seat on the board. In 1997, this entity owned 2 percent. This 2 percent should not be regarded as insignificant. In defining shareholding rights by their type the parent company's 9 percent was legal-person shares, while the 2 percent held by the State-Owned Assets Management Company belonged to state shares. If the report being sent to the Securities Regulatory Commission noted that the state-owned shares were opposed to the share expansion, then no matter how small the percentage of such shares, this would have a negative impact on the specialists evaluating the proposal.

The vote of the state-owned shares now became critical. Both those in favor and those opposed recognized the significance of this symbolic vote. In the eyes of Chen, his company, SD, was already a fully cooked goose that would not be able to fly away. The government had full shares in his company, after all; if they did not support it, who were they going to support? At the time, Mayor Li Zibin was promoting the idea of huge projects as a way to support the state-owned sector and deepen enterprise reform. At the time, Vanke's business was worth just RMB 1.178 billion (USD 142.27 million). It could not compare with a parent company that could mobilize projects worth RMB 10 billion (about USD 1.21 billion).

From offices that looked out over the greenbelt in southern Shenzhen, Yu Liang and I now explained the dilemma that Vanke had with our parent company to the head of Shenzhen's municipal investment management company. This was a man named Xia Deming. His attitude was kind and considerate. After hearing us out, however, he explained: "The central government's policy now is to create enterprises that can handle investments in the tens of billions. In line with this national policy, we [the investment management company] actually should hand over our 2 percent to Chen. It's just that we have not yet initiated the procedures."

It would take a miracle to turn our parent company into a billion-dollar enterprise—it could not even handle its own problems. Chen was currently the fifth person to be in charge—SD's predecessor had been the Special Economic Zone management committee. In the early 1980s, this was reformed and turned into a company. For a long time, SD held the number two stamp in the Shenzhen government—that is, it had the second-highest power in the land to grant permits for all imports into Shenzhen. (The authorizing stamp of the Shenzhen government itself was number one.) It was therefore a classic example of the union of government and enterprise.

To lose like this to Chen was not pleasant. I stiffened my spine and made an appointment with Li Zibin, the mayor of Shenzhen. After hearing the whole story, the mayor made his position clear straight off the bat: "How could you pound the table like that? A little more modesty, more caution . . ."

"I was beside myself. I lost it," I replied.

"It is the most natural thing in the world for a listed company to want to expand shares," he explained. "However, as mayor, it is not easy for me to interfere directly in the investment decisions of an enterprise."

This meant that the mayor was tilting his balance in favor of our parent company, Special Development.

The board of directors voted in favor of Vanke's plan to issue new shares. The parent company voted against it, but the member of the board representing the state-owned shares did not vote against it. He also did not vote in favor; he abstained. This was the same stance he had taken during the Jun-Van conflict. After one month, at a special shareholders' meeting, the investment management company representing state-owned shares again chose to abstain. I realized that this was done to smooth over relations and not offend the self-opinionated Chen. In the complexity of government relationships, not casting a negative vote was the equivalent of voting to support Vanke.

Four Lessons from a Real Estate Developer

In February 1997, the people of Shenzhen carried fresh flowers as they came slowly down the Shennan Road—tears streamed down cheeks as they said goodbye to Mr. Deng.

On July 1, 1997, China's government restored administrative authority over Hong Kong. In Shenzhen, 200,000 people spent all night in the rain as they sent off the troops that were to be stationed there.

In October 1997, the celebratory atmosphere of the return of Hong Kong had not yet dissipated when an Asia-wide financial crisis stormed across the country.

In 1997, Vanke's real estate business continued to pull back its troops and sum up lessons from the past.

By that point, the company could be said to have gone through three main stages in the thirteen years since it was founded. It went from having no money (the start-up period in the 1980s) to having money and spending it recklessly (investing in everything after issuing B shares in 1993), to being able to spend money once again (but recognizing the calamitous nature of irregular business dealings and now restraining itself). The more its project management matured, the clearer management thinking became. The group continued to reorganize resources. In October, Vanke agreed to spin off two industrial projects—the Shenzhen Vanke industrial manufacturing plant for amplification instruments and the Shenzhen Vanke electric power supply services company. At this point, the manufacturing plant was making 40 percent of all amplifiers put in telephones made for the domestic market. After those spinoffs were complete, the group basically completed the readjustment of its core businesses.

In this same year, at a forum held to discuss real estate from an academic perspective, I told the story of three particular buildings in Shenzhen as a way to sum up Vanke's "four main lessons."

By 1997, Shenzhen was already a modern city with a forest of skyscrapers. In the late 1980s, the building that caused the greatest commotion was the Shenzhen International Trade Center, which had captured two firsts in China. At 43 stories, it was number one in height. Put up at the rate of one story each week (and at times, one story in three days), it was number one in speed of construction. At the same time, three other buildings broke ground: the Development Center Building, the Asia Hotel, and the Overseas Chinese Hotel. Among these, the Development Center was designed to be tallest, even surpassing the Shenzhen International Trade Center. The fate of these three buildings diverged from their designs, however, as each became a thorn in the hand of the developers.

All three of these buildings stopped construction in midstream, due to wrong calculations about the market as well as inadequate financing. Although all were finally built, the results were different from what was originally planned. Ninety percent of shares in the Development Center were bought by a Hong Kong developer; the Asia Hotel was bought by Robert Kuok, who changed its name to the Shangrila Hotel. The Overseas Chinese Hotel changed its name to the Fulin Hotel, and the bank that had financed it was forced to become its major shareholder.

After 1992, the story of these three buildings was gradually forgotten by people who again caught the real estate fever. A craze for tall buildings swept through Shenzhen and also began to extend to other parts of the country.

People who have been to Singapore can get a clear sense of how the grid of the city developed. That is, the height of buildings gradually progressed along with the city's economic development. Buildings went from five or six stories, to eleven or twelve, then seventeen or eighteen, and then finally to thirty or forty. In contrast, Shenzhen remained mainly a city of five or six stories in its early period. After 1992, building heights suddenly shot up to thirty stories, without anything in between. According to data of the Shenzhen Land Bureau, in 1993, the ratio between high-rises and several-story buildings in Shenzhen was 6:1. For every short building, there were six skyscrapers. Clearly, this was because developers had exceeded the ability of the market to absorb this amount of space, as well as their own capacity to build it. This blind expansion of capacity led to massive increases not only in construction costs but also in management fees and ongoing costs. By June 1996, however, the ratio of skyscrapers to several-story buildings had changed to 1:1. Circumstances were more powerful than individuals. Macro adjustments played an indispensable role in putting the market on the path to sound, healthy growth.

Vanke's first lesson: do not toy lightly with the idea of putting up skyscrapers. If they are not eventually memorials or milestones marking progress, they are likely to be your tombstone.

Overcapacity in the real estate business is not unrelated to the desire of real estate developers to make higher profits. However, overstocked inventory is also related to putting too high a price on properties. After Vanke established its principle of not doing business that brought in more than 25 percent, the average profit margin in its real estate business in 1995 was 20.5 percent. That still was higher than the 15 percent average in the rest of the country. In comparison to the international average profit margin of 8 to 10 percent, real estate in China can still be considered a high-profit industry.

Real estate developers must recognize that the market is fair. Explosive profits will ultimately be returned to the market. High profits in real estate must therefore come from standardizing business practices that suit the market.

Vanke's second lesson: do not chase after windfall profits.

Newly founded companies in Shenzhen generally started up without any money at all or with very little funding. In the process of building up their initial capital, money was always tight. The problems came when they found that they could raise money. They had become accustomed to not having money—they were not familiar with how to use it once they had it in their hands. When one adds enough money to a fevered craze for development, eight or nine out of ten developers will make wrong judgments. In other industries, people went madly into production lines for color televisions and washing machines, and in real estate serious mistakes were made as well. When developers had inadequate funds, they had to move forward one battle at a time—they would take a step and still be able to look out five or ten steps ahead. Once they had the funds, they would only look one step ahead. At first, this was not a problem, since people had money. Once money was short, they were in trouble. They had spread money around as if they were sprinkling pepper on everything, and they often had misjudged the market.

After 1992, it was the normal thing for people to get hotheaded and go overboard on developing projects. If you had a small amount of money in hand, you would just lock up land. If you had a middling amount, you would start driving piles. If you had a lot, you would start building buildings.

Vanke's third lesson: decisions made with money in hand combined with a fever in the brain is a recipe for disaster.

For example, in 1991, Vanke developed a set of villas in Shanghai's western suburbs. The moment the blueprints came out, these were sold in advance, all 88 of them. The market reaction was intense. After the places were actually built, however, buyers discovered that they could not drive their cars into the garages. The reason was simple—the turning radius had been built too tightly for cars to make the turn. The designer was someone who rode a bicycle. He had never driven a car before.

Another example: I went down to Hainan to look over some villas that were being made there, and discovered that the model bathroom on display had two toilet seats, one right next to the other. I asked the developer about this curious feature. "These are villas for lovers," he said. It sounded like a novel idea, but on second thought, lovers may like to shower together, but sit on the toilet together? There are plenty of similar examples, but one gets the idea.

Since the founding of the People's Republic of China in 1949, people had only been building commodity-type housing for 15 years. Developers had to go through the process of becoming familiar with how to develop real estate. In 1996, the stock market was so hot that many real estate developers could not keep themselves from plowing money into it. In the short run, putting capital into the stock market made sense. After the bull market ended, however, those developers who were doing so well discovered that people in the same industry who stayed focused on becoming professional real estate developers had left them in the dust.

Vanke's fourth lesson: developers should not pay too much attention to policies and government factors. Instead, they should cultivate their own professional capabilities.

Real Estate Consultant to the Vice Premier

Time: 10 a.m. on a day in November 1997. Scene: The conference room of the Shenzhen Municipal Office.

Six bosses of local firms were there: Wang Dianfu from the Shen Electronics Group, Wang Shi from Vanke, Wang Zhirong from Shenzhen Science & Technology, Ma Gongyuan from Tianjian, and a couple of others. They were notified that at three o'clock that afternoon, Vice Premier Zhu Rongji was expecting to hear them report on their individual companies. This was to happen at a meeting at the Qilin Mountain Resort.

The person who had called us together explained that "Vice Premier Zhu is not specifically paying a visit to Shenzhen. He is coming down here to officiate at the ribbon cutting ceremony for the Jing-Jiu Railway [Beijing–Kowloon Railway]. He's taking advantage of being here to check into how companies are doing. The Asian financial crisis still isn't over. China has promised not to depreciate its currency. The question is, how much of an impact has this had on China's exports, and how can we begin to increase domestic demand? The State Council is very concerned about these things. The Municipal Commission has set up meetings with three exporters to explain their side of things, and it also wants to hear from you real estate developers."

Each representative of the companies was allotted 10 minutes in which to make a presentation. The order of presentation put Vanke just behind Shen Electronics Group. Two topics were suggested for Vanke: first, its scientific management; second, its brand development.

Vanke was already well known for its real estate business. Why not let the company talk about real estate?

Three months earlier, Li Zibin had led a delegation on a visit to Vanke, including the party commissioners of various departments and the heads of four large state-owned groups. I made a report that highlighted the growth in Vanke's figures and the unique nature of its management: standardized, professional, and transparent. This report was displayed on a large screen via computer, and we also provided a printed form for each visitor. After I finished, Mayor Li held my materials in the air and said, "You all see what real transparency is? All the wage scales are right here, from the chairman of the board down to regular employees. You can see the bonuses at a glance. Who among you can claim to be as open as this?"

I therefore guessed that it had been Mayor Li who recommended Vanke. However, what the mayor was interested in was not necessarily what the vice premier was interested in. This was a rare opportunity for Vanke; we would choose a topic that Zhu Rongji truly wanted to learn more about.

By the time I got back to Vanke's headquarters at Shuibei, it was already eleven-thirty. I immediately called in Yu Liang and others to put together the outline of the upcoming report.

"Vanke is just one of Shenzhen's medium-sized companies," I said. "The vice premier will have no interest at all in how we are developing our brand or our scientific management. There is one topic that will make him excited, however, and that is the division of tax system. He has pushed that reform as hard as he can push it, since 1993. Right! We are going to talk about taxes." I felt my adrenalin surging.*

The division-of-taxation system called for the following changes: Spending at each level of government was to be defined and confirmed in a budget, depending on what central and local governments determined were to be within their governing authority. In line with the principle of matching up governing responsibilities and public-finance budgets, tax categories were to be defined in a nationwide, unified way. There were central government taxes, local government [provincial] taxes, and taxes mutually enjoyed by both central and local governments. To implement this, tax-revenue systems were to be set up at central and local government levels. Two sets of tax institutions were to levy and manage taxes separately at the central and local level. This arrangement would allow the implementation of standardized procedures whereby the central government reimbursed local governments for certain tax revenues and carried out the transfer payment system.

Yu Liang expressed doubts in his usual tactful way: "Vanke is not the Tax Bureau. Is it appropriate for it to start talking about the tax system?"

"It's decided," I replied. "We'll talk about the division-of-taxation system. Naturally, we won't approach it from some theoretical standpoint. We'll talk about the direct impact it has had on changes in the amount an enterprise has to pay. In the macro adjustments of 1993, what Zhu Rongji was aiming at was the bubble in the stock market and the real estate market. He did not have a very good impression of our business. How can we turn his mind around in a 10-minute presentation? First, talk about something he is interested in. Second, talk about how much we handed over in tax before the reform, and then, how much after. He will begin to think we're not so bad. Ask our finance people to get materials together right away. We have never talked about Vanke from this angle before. Make some charts that show our operating revenues between 1992 and 1997, how much we made in profit, and how much we paid in taxes. Make it so that a person can take it in at a glance. Get ready. Fast!"

Two-thirty that afternoon. The computer-generated images were not yet finished. It took 40 minutes to get from Shuibei to the Qilin Mountain Resort.

---

*From the late 1980s to the early 1990s, central government revenue had been declining due to the fiscal system then in place. This weakened the ability of the central government to have any control over the macroeconomic situation. Against this backdrop, reform of the tax system was first pushed through in 1994, and was further refined in the "division-of-taxation system."

Even if we left immediately, we would be 10 minutes late. I was pacing around in circles.

The head of the computer room, Wu Yang, tried to calm me down: "Boss, you go first. As soon as the charts are printed out, we'll send them over in a car."

"Sure," I said. "Top security. Battalions of armed police. You won't get through. I must have those charts in hand." I had heard that charts and statistics spoke to Vice Premier Zhu more than words, and I was not going to risk not having them.

The printer slowly spit out the paper. The first showed our revenues, the second our profits, and the third the amount of taxes we paid. As I examined the curve of the third chart, I let out a delighted howl. "It's going to be great," I exclaimed.

There was also a fourth chart. I quickly scooped it up and charged out of the computer room.

Three-fifteen. The meeting had already begun as I arrived at the Qilin Mountain Resort.

I pushed open the door and went in as the eyes of some 30 people turned in my direction. I was quite a sight since I had shaved my head three days earlier. My starched white shirt set off my shiny pate.

"Ah. This is the chairman of the board of Vanke, Wang Shi," said the man chairing the meeting, Li Youwei. "Please take your seat; we've already begun." He indicated my chair, and I sat with Wang Dianfu on my left and Ma Gongyuan on my right. Directly across from me were Zhu Rongji and several dignitaries, including the governor of Guangdong Province, the party secretary of the Provincial Committee, and the party secretary of the Shenzhen Municipal Committee.

It was Wang Dianfu's turn, and he spoke with great assurance and gusto: "When Shen Electronics Group was established, the government only invested RMB 3,000 [USD 811]. After 10 years, we now have net assets of 300 million [USD 36.23 million] At the same time, through holding controlling shares in others, we are in control of companies that have assets in the range of 10.3 billion [1.54 billion]."

"Please say that again. I didn't understand," Vice Premier Zhu Rongji interrupted.

I glanced at Wang Dianfu, thinking: *bad news for you*. The vice premier has found a fly in the ointment.

The chairman of the board of Shen Electronics Group was unaware of his predicament. "We have 300 million in net assets, but we control 10.3 billion in total assets."

"That means debt!" said Zhu Rongji. "It means your debt ratio is huge! Why did we run into this Asian currency crisis in the first place? For one, because enterprises are overloaded with debt. South Korea's enterprises also operated on a high debt ratio. When the market changed, their chain of financing was stretched so tightly it obviously had to break."

The vice premier's tone softened a little. "Central is very concerned about the high debt ratio of our state-owned enterprises. We're wondering if it can be offloaded by switching from debt to shares."

He added, "You can't go on this way. When the financing chain gets too tight, the enterprise is done for."

Dianfu was stuck, and he had nothing further to say.

It was my turn. I cleared my throat. I had not yet pulled out my charts when the man in charge of the conference turned to Wang Zhirong and asked him to speak next.

I was being punished for arriving late. They were not going to let me speak. The only thing to do was look obedient and listen quietly to others.

Wang Zhirong forecast an increase in exports of his computer components in 1998. "This is mainly because of a decline in our costs, and the way we've made management more efficient," he said.

The vice premier cut into him with one knife thrust: "By how much are you lowering costs?"

"By 20 to 30 percent."

"Not good enough. Let's say you lower costs by 30 percent; that still won't do. In Thailand and Malaysia, the currency has depreciated 40 to 50 percent in value. You export something for one renminbi, all you get is 0.5 to 0.6 renminbi for it. We are holding our currency stable and not depreciating. If you lower costs by 30 percent you'll have to lower your pricing as well. So how exactly do you plan to double your exports?"

His questions were not easy to answer. The atmosphere in the room grew tense. In just a few words, the vice premier had punctured two of the most influential companies in Shenzhen.

Li Youwei's opposition to Wang Shi now shifted a little. He turned in my direction. "Wang, you say a few words."

I had already assumed I would not be speaking. Hearing myself called, I felt the energy rising.

I first noted the business that Vanke is in. The vice premier was instantly impatient. "So you're going to tell us how many buildings you've built, how many homes you've sold."

"My report will not talk about buildings. It will address the influence of taxation on our company, numbers before and after the division-of-taxation system."

The vice premier's eyes flashed at this mention of tax.

I pulled out my first chart. "This shows our business from 1992 to 1997. The macro adjustments began in June of 1993. In 1995, our revenues began to decline. By 1996 and 1997, the growth line turned upward again."

The vice premier was silent.

I showed the second chart. "This shows profits from 1992 to 1997," I continued. "The growth curve slips in 1995, then begins to go up again in 1996 and 1997. It moved in sync with changes in revenues."

The vice premier still made no sound.

I raised the third chart and said, "This shows the change in the taxes we paid from 1992 to 1997. As you see, it is a straight line slanting upward. In the years in which our operations contracted and our profits went down, the amount of taxes we paid continued to rise."

"Why?," the vice premier asked, curious.

"Because of the system of division of taxation."

"Ha ha!" He let out a happy laugh. "Our tax system has even cut back on the practice of evading taxes!"

"Vanke is a publicly traded company," I replied. "It operates according to the law. We do not allow tax evasion. Moreover, we have no need to evade taxes."

"Then why are you paying more when you make less?"

"It's very simple. As you know, before the division-of-taxation system, the central government in China used the *cheng-bao* system with local governments. This meant that the local government, a province or a city, guaranteed that it would pay a fixed amount to the central government. No matter what, it had to hand over that amount. Enterprises had the same arrangement with local governments: a baseline figure was guaranteed to the tax authorities. Vanke, for example, had a contract with Shanghai for a baseline figure every year. Plus there was a mandated annual increase of 20 percent. This 20 percent bore no relationship to real profits.

"Once the division-of-taxation system was launched, our old *cheng-bao* contract with Shanghai was now invalid. We now paid on the basis of how much we made, just as municipalities pay the central government on the basis of actual results. Our tax went up not because of a mandated 20 percent, but because the system had changed and we were taxed on a higher basis."

The vice premier smiled contentedly.

"Even though our taxes went up, I raise both hands in applauding this. First, the old practice in China was to go for 'first big, second public,' and 'first egalitarianism, second, administrative allocation of resources.' We never recognized the interests of local governments. Through tax-system reform, for the first time we are explicitly confirming that the central government and local governments are actually different entities when it comes to interests.* In other words, if central and local relationships are not clarified in very explicit terms, how can we clarify the relationship between enterprises and governments? The division-of-taxation system can be seen not just as a reform of the tax-revenue system, but as a reform of political structures."

Without waiting for the vice premier to open his mouth, I pulled out my fourth chart, "This chart shows our profit after taxes from 1992 to 1997," I said, "and it shows how much tax we paid every year. You can see that in 1992 we paid only 16 percent in taxes since the Special Zone enjoyed all kinds of

---

*It recognizes that localities have the right to enjoy the fruits of their own efforts: they are not required to hand everything over to the national pot.

favorable treatment. As we extended our investments outside the zone, our tax rate gradually increased. By 1997, it had increased to 56 percent."

This chart was in fact a little devious. I had included the business tax and value-added tax into the income tax, in order to make the line steeper and give my audience a more dramatic picture.

"How can you be paying so much?," the provincial party secretary now asked me in his Chaozhou accent. I was preparing to explain when Vice Premier Zhu cut in, "Wang has added in the business tax and the value-added tax."

I couldn't help but be pleased. It is nice to be understood by someone you appreciate.

The atmosphere of the meeting had lightened up considerably. My allotted 10 minutes were long since up. I glanced at Secretary Li, but he was not inclined to stop me.

I now mustered the courage to really plunge ahead: "I'd like to bring up a contrary opinion with regard to the future of the real estate industry. The main question for the economy is how to stimulate domestic demand next year. Economic theorists are saying that steel won't be enough, and cars won't be enough. They are saying that only housing will do it. They have suggested that the housing industry will be the mainstay in stimulating demand.

"I disagree. I feel that for the next two to three years, the housing industry will not be a pillar industry, holding up the economy. Four reasons: First, purchasable housing still only makes up 30 percent of the total. More than 60 percent of housing is still government supplied. Second, the housing industry is capital-intensive. Given current policies, it is hard to finance it. Third, any pillar industry needs a dominant company, but in China our industry is fragmented. It has no such large dominant enterprise. Fourth, consumer credit is a key consideration in stimulating the market in other countries. Our system severely restricts such credit."

The vice premier was silent.

"Vanke is a developer that abides by the law," I continued. "At the end of 1992, when real estate was so hot it was on fire, I stood on the sidelines. I kept to our principle: we do not do business that makes more than 25 percent in profit margin. In the first half of 1993, the prices of construction materials doubled, and Vanke faced considerable operating difficulties. Then the macro adjustments in June brought the prices of our three main materials down and Vanke was able to turn around. From 1993 to 1997, Vanke's housing development has, on average, grown at a rate of 70 percent per year. Vanke greatly appreciates the measures that were taken in 1993. Up to now, I have never heard another businessman in China say such a thing."

Vice Premier Zhu confirmed this: "You are indeed unique!"

"I wonder what Vice Premier Zhu thinks of the housing market?"

He was silent for a moment, and then asked in turn, "If we abolished the benefit-housing system, that is, housing distributed to government employees, could the housing industry become a mainstay of the economy?"

"No, it could not," I replied.

"If we opened up the financial markets to competition, could it?"

"No, it could not.'

"If consumer credit were allowed, could it still not?"

Realizing that the vice premier asked this in earnest, I responded honestly, "Not within the next two years."

"Within the next two years, it is my intent to stimulate the housing industry so that it becomes a mainstay industry," the vice premier said decisively.

"Since you say so, that will certainly happen!"

Everyone laughed.

"You are a professional. I want to ask you to be my real estate consultant. However, the job comes without pay."

I blushed with pleasure. I had done no "thought preparation" and could merely stammer, "I am honored to accept!"

Wang Dianfu glared at me as he said under his breath, "You're going to Zhongnanhai."

"We want to hear differences of opinion that are constructive," said the vice premier. "Does anyone else have anything to report?"

Presentations made after that were considerably less tense.

After two months, a number of people were called to Beijing for a small internal* forum. Attendees included people from the Ministry of Construction, the Housing Office of the State Council, the State Commission for Restructuring, the Land Bureau, and other ministries under the State Council.

After two months of working in Beijing, I had the sense that it is a political center and also a center for balancing out different interest groups. My views on the housing industry were not particularly new, but other experts had not had the opportunity to come before the vice premier and bravely state their case, particularly their contrary opinions. The moment you stepped into the political vortex, however, you were bound to offend somebody else, even if you did it unintentionally.

Realizing this, I decided it was far safer to be one's own boss, to be a simple entrepreneur.

In April 1998, the People's Bank of China published a declaration regarding "Increasing Credit for Housing," known as Document No. 169 of 1998. It indicated that "appropriate relaxation of monetary policies" was finally being extended to the housing industry. The document extended financial support for the building and the purchase of housing.

In July 1998, the State Council published a notice entitled "Regarding Further Reform of the Housing System in Cities and Towns, and Regarding the Speeding Up of Housing Construction." This notice defined the goal of urban

---

* Off-the-record

housing-system reform: "We are stopping the allocation of actual living space to employees and gradually monetizing existing housing allocations. We are setting up a multitiered system of supplying housing in cities and towns and will be gradually improving upon that system. We are developing financing for housing, and developing standardized procedures for buying and selling housing."

For 40 years, physical housing had been allocated to urban residents as a social benefit. Changing this system was the most extraordinary breakthrough achieved by China's housing reform.

After the implementation of a series of policies, the real estate business pulled out of its slump, the lowest point being 1993, and began to head for a new era of growth.*

Resigning as CEO: A Real Resignation, or a Fake One?

In February 1999, the Vanke board of directors passed a motion to accept my resignation as CEO and to appoint Yao Mumin in my stead. At the same time, the board appointed Yu Liang standing deputy CEO as well as head of finance. This was in recognition of the fact that a team of professional managers was now mature enough to take over, plus we had completed the restructuring of the group.

Before coming into Vanke, Yu Liang worked in the Shenzhen Foreign Trade Group. He joined Vanke in 1990. He served as general manager (CEO) of the Vanke Finance Consulting Company based in Shenzhen, as board member of Vanke and as deputy general manager of Vanke. He was outstanding in terms of professional capabilities, but he also had a profoundly solid way of approaching business, and these things had made a strong impression on me.†

I had thought of stepping away from the CEO position several years earlier.

In the 1980s, my goal in setting up the company was very clear: to form a new kind of company, to create wealth for society, to give young people a place to exercise their creativity, and to stand in the forefront of the great wave of reform. My head was full of ideas every day about how to do this. Although I was not trained in business management, I took every opportunity to change that. At the same time, I was never too worried about my capabilities. The old saying is that "when there is no tiger in the mountains, the monkeys become

---

*All urban housing used to be a social benefit in the People's Republic of China, allocated to citizens by the "units" to which they were assigned. This system prevailed for a period of 40 years and finally came to an end in July 1998. (It did not end abruptly, but was phased out over time.) The end of the system propelled further changes in the urbanization of China, the development of consumer credit, and the growth of a residential housing market. Six months before the decision to change the system, Vice Premier Zhu Rongji held the meeting near Shenzhen that is described in this chapter.

†In 2001, after Yao Mumin emigrated to Australia, Yu Liang was made CEO of the Vanke Group.

king." Those who "jumped into the ocean" in the 1980s often had a low level of education, but I for one did not feel that a lack of formal education held me back.

After 1992, the situation in China changed dramatically. The character of those entering business shifted and the market itself changed. People who were "jumping into the ocean of business" were more educated. I began to feel more concerned about my ability to meet the new conditions. As the 1990s progressed, I began to feel that my ideas were getting fewer and my effectiveness was declining. The cycle for my coming up with good management strategies was stretching out to half a year. I began to think that I should reevaluate myself.

The times had changed in China. In the early days, Shenzhen was a baby with regard to a market economy, and it was protected by government policies. It was still an "experiment," and whether or not this experiment would succeed was still unclear. By 1997, enterprises throughout China were being rolled into the great wave of globalized business. Challenges we all faced now included a knowledge economy and the fact of a globalized marketplace. Speaking for myself, a mere dozen or so years of experience was going to be inadequate to deal with the tremendous challenges before us. The Asian currency crisis in the second half of 1997 put our markets through dramatic changes. If one were not careful, one could lose the entire game in a throw. Vanke was going to have to put more time and energy into researching, thinking, communicating with others, and creating new models to implement new measures for resolving new kinds of problems. That was the only way it was going to come up with accurate judgments about the market at a higher level of operations.

Resigning from the post of CEO would allow me more time and energy to study as well. If Vanke was to have a wider space in which to operate, it had to do everything possible to avoid being complacent. There were many companies from whom we could learn things, and Vanke needed to learn quite a lot. I was made aware of this particularly by my exposure to the practices of two companies on whose boards I served as an independent board member. These were both under the Huachuang Group, one based in Hong Kong and one in Heilongjiang. The staff of these companies had received rigorous training in modern management practices and they operated according to international standards. Watching this inspired me. Behind these companies was a whole set of modern enterprise operating standards—I knew that, in comparison to them, Vanke was way behind the curve.

In newly founded companies in Shenzhen, the founder was generally both the chairman of the board and CEO at the same time. Since 1988, when Vanke undertook shareholding company reform, I myself had served in both these positions. It should be noted that this dual role within one person was a product of the times. As times changed, and as Vanke began to take a more standardized path of business, my continued efforts to cover both positions would be detrimental to the company's sound growth.

I also knew that authority could be useful at one stage in a company's growth but a hindrance in another. The early development of most new companies in China depended to a considerable degree on authority. Over the years I constantly pointed out that if new companies wanted to become major enterprises, they had to get out from under the shadow of authority and escape the confines of a system that relied on personal relations. Authority was of course necessary at a certain point, when an enterprise had figured out how to survive and wanted to grow more vigorously. Authority was in itself a kind of resource. However, the kind of domineering authority that was nurtured in the extremely unregulated business climate back then was also a kind that could easily turn into a personality cult. It went along with the exaggerated kind of authority that refused to take advice from professionals and that charged forward with decisions based on personal preference. It often went for big projects and it often led to temperamental leadership. Its defects were apparent.

After an enterprise passed the stage of just trying to stay alive, the founder had to get rid of any of the negative aspects noted previously. In particular, at the corporate level, the founder had to encourage professionalism. He had to develop a mature management style and gradually weaken the role that his own authority played in the company.

As chairman of the board, I would still be able to play a role in decision making. The CEO would, however, play the key role in implementing decisions of the board of directors. Not only would this reduce the degree to which senior management relied on one individual, it would also lessen the risk of having insufficient human resources down the road. It would help force the establishment of standardized human resource development, which would cultivate a new crop of professional managers. Right now, the Chinese mainland has no lack of bosses. What it lacks is producers—people who really know how to do the work. It lacks professional managers, lawyers, accountants, designers, planners. My resignation was not as important as the idea of raising management effectiveness by igniting the energy and ideas of a new team. As Vanke put its efforts to cultivating professional managers, I gave myself the title of professional manager.

CHAPTER FOUR

The Glory and the Dream, 2000–2004

Resigning as CEO

I was 48 years old when I resigned as CEO. A man is generally in his prime at that age, just hitting his stride. All these years later, people still ask me how I could have let go so casually back then, said I would do it, and then just went ahead and did it.

Everybody has to leave at some point—that is an irrefutable law of nature. It doesn't matter how resourceful one is or how inexhaustibly energetic. I also felt, however, that Vanke also should not be red-hot during Wang Shi's tenure and then begin to decline once he had gone—if that were the case, the company was not mature to begin with. I did not want to wait until I could no longer carry on, until I failed to see things I should have seen coming. An early departure would be good for me as well as for Vanke. If the company continued to carry on just fine without me, well, that would be the surest sign of my success.

Naturally, for a period of time after I had resigned, I felt a certain feeling of loss. It wasn't all that easy. Indeed, it was tough. On the evening I resigned, I felt terrific—calm and happy. I slept soundly that night. Since I was still chairman of the board, I went to work the next morning as usual. The minute I entered my office I felt something wasn't right. It was too quiet. I looked at my calendar and the notebook I keep to record things. It wasn't Sunday, and there wasn't any special event that day. I finally went over to ask my former secretary, "Where is everyone?"

"Gone to the CEO's office for a meeting."

My first reaction was: why hadn't anyone called me in yet? My next was the realization that I was no longer CEO.

I paced back and forth in my office, tweaking my ears and scratching my head in indecision. I desperately wanted to charge in and see what was going on. I could say to them all, "You go ahead and have your meeting. I'll just sit in the corner and listen. I won't say anything."

It then occurred to me that if the old boss, and still chairman of the board, attended the meeting, it would be hard for the new boss to officiate and do his job. The only thing to do was hold myself down. "I cannot go over there, " I told myself. "I simply cannot. I cannot."

A day ago I had been full of vim and vigor, giving instructions to everyone.

Today I was supposed to pick up a cane and go take a slow stroll through the park. Perhaps take along some old photos so that I could sit on a bench and remember days gone by, years that flowed like a proverbial stream. I might even philosophize a little about life.

Certainly I could look content on the outside, but inside I was like a caged wild animal. I was still young and strong! My predicament slowly came into focus. The first day passed in this way, and the second day was much the same. By the third day, I still found my new position unbearable. On the fourth day, the new CEO came into my office to give a report on what had happened at the meeting.

"There are seven key points," he began. I listened patiently. Number one . . . number two . . . number three . . ." After hearing out the first three points, I said, "There's no need to tell me the rest. I know the fourth, fifth, sixth, and seventh things you discussed." I then enumerated them, one by one. The CEO was both astonished and perplexed. "Someone told you in advance, slipped things to you?"

No. The people in that meeting were quite recently my own troops, old soldiers I had trained up myself. I naturally had a clear idea of what they would be discussing. After that, I went on to say that the approach they were taking to the fifth point was wrong. The sixth was also incorrect. I told him how these things should be handled. The CEO heard me out, with tremendous admiration in his eyes, thinking: *The chairman of the board didn't even attend the meeting, yet he could narrate all the points after I just told him the first three! And he could tell us where we went wrong!* This response made me quite proud. I again felt a sense of accomplishment.

The next week, when the CEO came in to report, the same thing happened. He got to the third point, and I could not help but interrupt with the fifth, sixth, and seventh points. In similar fashion, I pointed out the problems. By the third week, when the CEO came in to report, I discovered his eyes were no longer sparkling. His whole demeanor seemed to say, "Anyway, you can already guess what we are thinking, what we discussed, what we decided. Instead of making a report, I might as well just listen to your instructions."

The moment I saw his body language, I knew we had problems. What's more, the problems came from me. I had inadvertently begun to play the role of ruler from behind the curtain. I decided then not to speak. I would listen to him. In fact, when he reached the third point, the old inclination rose up in me and I particularly wanted to interrupt him, but I bit my tongue. He already seemed to have learned the new rules, though—at the third point, he paused to hear what I would have to say. I did not make a sound. I indicated that he should proceed. After he talked through points four and five, he went ahead and finished. I held myself in for quite a while, and then simply said, "I have no opinion."

I thought about that a long time afterward. Where did the real problems lie? First, had I truly intended to hand over authority? Examining my conscience, I knew that nobody was forcing me to do so. I had indeed intended to transfer power. Second, since this transfer was voluntary, why was I so worried? The reason, I figured out, was that I was afraid they would make mistakes. I again examined my conscience. Had I myself not made constant mistakes from the time I founded the company up to now? I made mistakes all along. Why then did I not allow young people also to make mistakes? Making mistakes was necessary if one was to grow. If I refused to allow people to think for themselves and instead pointed out the problems, the same old thing would happen—they would not waste any time thinking for themselves. They would not be aware of the serious consequences of policy decisions, and they would not improve. They had to experience things for themselves before they could move forward in a secure and stable way. Letting them do that was something I had to get used to.

After that, I forced myself to stick to a rule—so long as the mistakes that were being made were not fundamental and would not upset the applecart, I would play dumb. I would pretend not to know. Otherwise, resigning and not resigning would be all the same, and the new successor would never be forced to grow.

As someone accustomed to taking action and doing things for myself, however, it was going to be impossible for me to resist intervening, commanding the course of events. If I stayed on with little to do in the company, I would surely make trouble. How was I going to balance a very rational understanding with my habitual way of doing things? I chose to distance myself. I would leave the company and go into nature as a way to create a new space in which I could release my energies. I would prove myself in another way. I went to Tibet and climbed mountains. Soon I had been gone a couple of months.

In 2005, a number of entrepreneurs and I were invited to visit the Mengniu headquarters by the founder of that company, Niu Gensheng. In telling him about what I had learned from managing a company, Mr. Niu commented, "How did you train up a successor? I envy you. You have so much time to do what you want to do now." The answer was very simple: I did not train a successor. Mr. Niu, well trained in the ways of the world, was puzzled.

I explained. "You and I both went through the Cultural Revolution. Lin Biao was supposed to be successor to Chairman Mao—it was even written into the Party constitution. What happened? He scooped up his family, put them on a plane, and fled the country. Crashed in Öndörkhaan, Mongolia. That tells the whole story. Think of the risk you are running when you put the future of the entire operation in the hands of one person. I have greater faith in institutions than I do in individuals. That means setting up the structures of a modern corporation and cultivating a team of people."

In 1999, as I was retiring as CEO, I summed up things that I felt I had contributed to Vanke. I selected a particular industry. I set up structures, corporate systems. I cultivated a team. I established a brand. Creating a team and a set of institutions was far more important than cultivating one or two successors. Naturally, the number one person was important, but institutional safeguards could help correct the mistakes if that person were the wrong choice.

Meanwhile, it was far more important to cultivate a corporate culture than it was to cultivate a successor. Not only was that true for a company, it was also true for the country at large.

One time I entertained a group of young entrepreneurs from Taiwan, and they told me the situation there. Either the heads of companies did not pass over control to someone else or they did so only with great trepidation. They said this might be due to the influence of Wang Yongqing, who at the time was 83 years old and still going strong, running things himself.* These Taiwanese entrepreneurs were curious about Vanke. They had a strong sense of Yu Liang's self-confidence when they met with him—he was completely his own man, and answered everything on his own. When I told them I had not cultivated him as a successor, they noted how successful I had been in "not cultivating a successor." I had several reasons for choosing Yu Liang, once the second CEO, Yao Mumin, left for Australia.

First, Vanke was in a period of fast growth, yet it was still an unstructured company, with irregular systems. If I parachuted in someone to run it, for example, someone who had run a large standard corporation, he would not necessarily be able to accommodate himself to Vanke's environment. At the same time, his business concepts might not tally with a company that was growing so fast. The new CEO had to be drawn from within the ranks of younger people at Vanke, and he also had to be someone who had worked at Vanke for quite a long time.

Second, from the standpoint of the Vanke Group, it was important but not essential for the number one man to know the real estate business. More importantly, he had to embody a package of qualities that included understanding Vanke's corporate culture, being innovative and willing to learn, and being able to communicate well with people. The ability to assemble all social resources was critical. Yu Liang had all of these qualities. After joining Vanke, he had been secretary to the board, and he had been responsible for the process of issuing shares. He displayed acute skills in financial matters, but he had never been directly in charge of a real estate project. My solution to that was to make sure he had an assistant who was in fact well versed in such projects.

In 2008, when *Fortune* magazine came out with its list of the "Most Influential Entrepreneurs on the Chinese Mainland," Ren Zhengfei of Huawei was listed as number one, and Yu Liang of Vanke was number two.

Yu Liang and I had a division of labor. He was responsible for already settled things, and I was responsible for things that were still uncertain. In fact, however, Yu Liang and the senior management team were also involved in thinking about and handling many things that were uncertain. For Vanke to grow to its current stage, it had to go through many things that tested the professional management team. The backbone management, from midlevel

---

*Y. C. Wang, an influential entrepreneur who founded the business empire known as Formosa Plastics in Taiwan. Born 1917, died in 2008.

managers on up, were an absolute mainstay in keeping the company steady. I had ultimate respect for them.

People sometimes put another hypothetical to me: if something happens, and Vanke faces some kind of crisis, will you come forward again to take over the reins? The answer was no. The reason: if I did take personal charge again, there could be two consequences. The first was that I put things right. The second was that I myself could not turn around the situation. If the second were true, why should I want to do something that proved I was incapable? If the first were true, this would simply show that I had not been successful in creating a competent team. If I kept on running things till I was 78 or 88, so what? In the span of one person's life, working 40 years or even longer is just fine. For a corporation, however, rule by the boss means that that corporation has no future. No matter what happened, I would not reverse my decision.

Aren't You Afraid China Resources Will Fire You?

By 2000, the Jun-Van conflict had been over for years, yet the experience continued to exert a subtle pressure on me, a sense of insecurity. I knew how dangerous it was to have an overly dispersed ownership of shares. The company also had a fairly modest market capitalization, yet was growing fast, which made it a prime target for a takeover.

The degree to which Vanke's shares were not controlled by any major shareholder was unusual in China's stock markets. Between 1993 and 1997, no shareholder held more than 9 percent of shares. Prior to 1998, the top 10 shareholders held a total of 23.95 percent, which meant that Vanke was the classic example of a publicly held company. At the same time, the company was one of the very few *private* enterprises in China that had experienced stable fast growth over the continuous span of a decade. By 1998, profits from its real estate business had grown steadily to represent 89.8 percent of group profits. This unique feature also made Vanke susceptible to becoming the target of a hostile takeover.

Although Vanke was a blue chip on the stock market, speculators often regarded it as an asset that could be traded for short-term gain. Starting in 1997, Vanke's top shareholder, Special Development (SD), reorganized its businesses and decided to focus on tourism and high-tech. Vanke, with its real estate focus, was then naturally outside the state plan, so getting support from SD in the event of a raid on our shares was essentially impossible.

The germ of an idea began to gestate in my mind. We had to find a new backer to help out, not just to support our real estate orientation and help it grow, but also to assist in opening up funding channels both domestically and abroad.

From 1993 to 1999, in the context of macro adjustments in China, Vanke did not go under as so many other listed companies did, nor was it hung out to dry in the shade. Our management team, its risk awareness, and the capabilities of our operations had a lot to do with that. It cannot be denied, however, that since we lacked the support of one large shareholder, Vanke's business found it hard to get extra help. Companies that had long since received a permit to list on the market, and that enjoyed support from one major shareholder, such as Haier, were seeing revenues surpass RMB 10 billion (about USD 1.21 billion), while self-reliant Vanke was still playing around at the level of RMB 3 to 4 billion (approximately USD 362.76 million to 483.68 million).

I reevaluated the relationship between Vanke and SD.

Real estate development is a capital-intensive industry. Without one large investor's support, Vanke had only two possible sources of financing: one was bank loans; the other was issuing more shares. We were limited by debt/asset ratios, so the amount we could borrow from banks was far below what we needed to really grow. Issuing new shares became our only alternative. Vanke issued shares four times between 1991 and 2000, and took in financing of RMB 1.7 billion (USD 205.56 million).

Issuing shares became the engine by which Vanke drove its growth. SD was not willing to continue to allow this, however. It was caught in a bind—although it was our largest shareholder, its shares were diluted every time we went to market. Plus it held only a small percentage of total shares, and these shares were state owned. They could not be traded in the secondary market. SD was not willing to increase its investment, since its business focus was elsewhere, but neither did it want to lose its status as largest shareholder. It therefore opposed ongoing issuing of more shares. In point of fact, SD's financial circumstances were not that great. A portion of the company's shareholding in Vanke had already been frozen by the courts.

In the mid-1990s, large real estate developers in Hong Kong invested in the mainland without thinking much of opportunities in Shenzhen. After going through various ups and downs inside China, however, they began to have a new appreciation for the real estate market there. A number of large developers now began to come into Shenzhen in order to build up land reserves and start projects. Their financial clout was undeniably greater than local developers. They could easily hand over RMB 700 (USD 84.64 million) or 800 million (about USD 95.73 million) in one payment for a piece of land, whereas doing so was quite hard for someone like Vanke.

Our shareholding structure was affecting our ability to grow. Given this bottleneck, I began to think about restructuring our stock ownership, bringing in a strategic investor who could also help us access overseas financing channels. Such an investor would have to meet certain conditions. It would have to have substantial land reserves within China, as well as existing real estate projects. At the same time, it should have sufficient financial backing or the ability to get funding. It should also allow the professional team at Vanke to exhibit its ability to make a profit. If we could accomplish this within the year 2000, we would have achieved a milestone that was equal in significance to turning Vanke into a joint-stock company.

Once a major shareholder came in, would it not restructure Vanke's management team? I was not worried about that. Vanke's value lay precisely in that professional team and its ability to do the business. The company did not have great reserves of land that a potential investor could sell to realize a profit. If a large shareholder switched out Vanke's management team, it would be working against its own interests.

Seen from another perspective, the introduction of a large shareholder into Vanke's business would undeniably constrain Vanke's own decision making and operations. So long as such constraints were in Vanke's own long-term interests, however, losing some freedom would be worth it. For both a major shareholder and for Vanke, this would benefit both sides. In this regard, Vanke was different from most listed companies. Most hoped to get out from under the interference of a large shareholder by weakening its position. Instead, we hoped to find a large shareholder since our value lay in our professional team.

The specific shareholder I had in mind was China Resources.

Vanke had its first close contact with China Resources in the first half of 1996. We sold China Resources our Yibao distilled water company, the largest bottled water company in China at the time. The chief operating officer of this China Resources subsidiary, a person named Huang Tieying, was also responsible for procuring beer and beverage companies in China. The first time we met, we agreed on a price for Yibao within 10 minutes. After that, however, the process seemed to slow down. I called Huang Tieying and complained. The purchase agreement that China Resources Venture was proposing for Yibao seemed unnecessarily complex. China Resources' lawyers in Hong Kong were asking Vanke to sign an agreement whereby Vanke guaranteed its assets and business, and this agreement had more than 30 provisions! Huang Tieying explained, "There are various uncertainties that have come up in the process of purchasing this company. We therefore want the seller to commit to covering those uncertainties." I exploded. "If you don't trust Vanke, you obviously are not intending to purchase!" He too got upset and shot back, "Look at it from our side. If we find out that Yibao is not what we expected once we've got it, and we can't get back what we paid for it, we are up a creek. If you have so much faith in your company, why aren't you willing to give us the guarantee that we will get back 90 percent of our investment if things go wrong? If the factories and equipment are truly as described, that is, all legally owned and correct, why aren't you willing to put that down in black and white and commit to it?"

I accepted his reasoning. It made me realize that China Resources' ways were far more standardized and in line with the principles of a market than ours were. Three days later, I signed the version of the purchase agreement that their lawyers had drafted. After signing, in front of a number of Vanke colleagues, I said to Huang Tieying, "If possible, I would like to invite you to come give a lecture to Vanke, specifically on corporate mergers and acquisitions. Four years ago, when Vanke purchased this company, the contract was one and one-half pages long. Now, four years later, your purchase agreement is more than 30 pages long. In this whole process, you have made us realize the distinction between professional and non-professional M&A."

China Resources and Vanke began to have increasingly frequent contacts after that, and our relationship grew ever closer. In 1998, I was asked to be an independent director on the board of a China Resources subsidiary called CR Land (Beijing). In 1999, Vanke invited Huang Tieying to be an independent director on our own board.

China Resources is a market-oriented financial group in Hong Kong. As a conglomerate, it was no different in most respects from similar Hong Kong companies, with the exception that the chairman of the board of China Resources was always assigned by Beijing, and this person was always a ministerial-level appointment. There was little distinction between China Resources and such companies as Cheung Kong (Holdings) Limited* and Sun Hung Kai. While the chairman was from Beijing, the CEO was the product of a marketized economy. Ning Gaoning was a prime example. A seasoned professional manager, he was a man who understood business. The five listed companies of the China Resources Group also enjoyed seasoned professional management teams.

Vanke was moving into a period of high-speed growth, and it needed the support of precisely this kind of international capital and professional management. To be incorporated in this whole system of listed companies within China Resources would be quite advantageous. Among China Resources' five lines of business, one focused on "producing and distributing construction materials that are aimed at meeting the needs of housing construction, including real estate development, building, and refurbishing." This was in line with Vanke's hopes to become the leader in China's real estate development business—China Resources was an ideal candidate for Vanke. The question was whether or not China Resources wanted to be Vanke's strategic primary shareholder.

After several years of doing business together, Huang Tieying and I had become good friends. One day, I asked him, "Since you understand and appreciate Vanke, have you given any thought to simply buying it?"

Huang Tieying asked back, "Since Vanke is so well managed, why would you want a different boss?"

I replied, "We need to be aligned with the world's capital markets if we are going to be the leader in China's real estate industry."

"But once you become the leader and are a very large corporation, " he continued, "that corporation will belong to someone else. Right now, you are your own boss, chairman of the board. Aren't you afraid that one day China Resources will mess with you, even kick you out?"

My response: "If anyone can do the job better than I can, I should be kicked out."

---

*The successor of this is now CK Hutchison Holdings, Limited. The founder of this major conglomerate is Li Ka-shing, who is currently chairman. His son Victor Li is managing director. In Mandarin, the name of the company is Chang Jiang, which in English is "Yangtze River."

Huang Tieying did not respond to this idea right away. After a period of time, though, a formal proposal was made to have the China Resources Land (Beijing) company purchase a controlling share in Vanke. In this proposal, it was suggested that prior to approaching Vanke's largest shareholder, Special Development, it might be good to have a full audit of Vanke's business undertaken by an international accounting firm. It might also be good for someone to work inside Vanke for a while, to understand its business operations. Later, Huang Tieying told me the reasons for this request. By buying into Vanke, China Resources would be able to complete the full scope of its real estate dealings in China, and it could get access to Vanke's local management resources. However, since Wang Shi seemed so eager to sell to China Resources, it wondered if there might not be some hidden problems in the company, details that were not easy to talk about. I agreed with Huang Tieying's request. For the price of more than HKD 2 million (USD 256,000), China Resources paid to have the Peat Marwick carry out a full audit of Vanke. Once the results of this audit came out, a partner in this accounting firm said he had never seen a Chinese company with such clean accounts.

Old Boss, New Boss

On March 8, 2000, Vanke published a notice: its largest shareholder, the Special Development Company, was intending to transfer its 8.11 percent of Vanke's shares to the China Resources Land (Beijing) company. Application for permission to do this had been submitted to the relevant authorities, which had not yet granted such permission. Since the China Resources Land (Beijing) already owned 17 million of Vanke B shares, constituting 2.71 percent of Vanke's share capitalization, if this transfer was successful, the China Resources Land (Beijing) company would have a total of 10.82 percent of Vanke's shares.

On August 10, 2000, the Shenzhen Special Development Company signed the agreement to proceed with the transfer. SD sold its entire Vanke holdings, 51,155,599 shares. After this transfer, the China Resources Group and its affiliated companies became Vanke's largest shareholder. China Resources appointed three people to Vanke's board of directors: Song Lin, Jiang Wei, and Wang Yin. Several other state-held investment funds continued to hold around 10 percent of shares, including Charm Yield Investment Ltd., Tongsheng Securities Investment Fund, the Jun'an Agenting Company, Ltd., and the Shanxi Securities Company, Ltd. That left 82.49 percent of Vanke's shares that were liquid, or in circulation, including A shares and B shares.

I felt a great deal better, and I wrote of my feelings on the Internet: "A rough relationship over these past seventeen years is now behind us. A matter that has dragged on for three years has come to a conclusion. Frustration that was so all encompassing yesterday has suddenly evaporated today. When I think back on the trauma, I look up at the Special Development Building and say with silent thanks, "Goodbye Old Boss, Goodbye!"

I have been asked why the CEO of the China Resources Group, Ning Gao-ning, should want to own Vanke shares. My answer: "Vanke has mastered the complexities of being a real estate developer. We know how to whitewash a wall, but when all is said and done, when you put on more whitewash it is still just a white wall. Ultimately, competition in the real estate world is a matter of size and capital. If you are big enough, you can change not just urban planning but how people actually live their lives. This is where the business really becomes significant. It is not just a matter of building a few buildings and selling them to make money. At this stage, capital and scale of operations are going to become the main force driving Vanke, not just getting better at details."

On December 2, 2000, Vanke announced it would be holding an interim shareholders' meeting with the intent to originate an additional 450 million B shares with China Resources as the intended new owner. This would increase the percentage of shares that China Resources held in the company. The interim shareholders' meeting was intended to convene in one month's time.

If this plan passed, not only would China Resources control Vanke even more completely but Vanke would have plenty of financial support with which to upgrade its ability to transform itself and go beyond the details stage. China Resources would in turn hold a dominant share in China's domestic real estate market and the ability to decide on deployment of resources. After this notice came out, Vanke's institutional investors focused on two main issues. First, once China Resources had increased its shareholdings, would there be any negative impact on Vanke's business? Second, was the disparity between the price of A shares and B shares too great? (A shares were trading at around RMB 13 [USD 2.24] per share at the time, while B shares were HKD 4.2 [USD 0.54] a share.)

Investors who opposed the increase in shares felt that there was not that much difference between the issuing price of HKD 4.2 (USD 0.54) and the net asset value per share of RMB 4.9 (USD 0.59), so increased shares would not bring the benefit of cheaper capital. In addition, since this issue was contemplating the creation of 450 million new shares, which would mean some 70 percent of total capitalization, this increase was too fast. It would result in a dilution of year-end income, which would in turn affect the price of shares. Since Vanke's A shares were over RMB 10 (USD 1.21) per share at the time, yet B shares were hovering at around HKD 4.5 per share (USD 0.58), the impact on price would mainly affect the A-share market.

The standard-bearer for investors who opposed the move was a man named Wu Chong. He had previously worked at Vanke and was now an employee of an Internet portal run by Jun'an Securities. On this website, he carried the battle into the public arena—he issued a statement to the effect that "once the plan is implemented, it will clearly dilute the interests of A shareholders." As a result, a number of funds as well as public investors began to express reservations.

Inarguably, there was a divergence in interests between those who looked to the long-term growth of the company and those who wanted short-term gains. Vanke and its larger shareholders were on one side and small and medium-sized shareholders on the other. China Resources and Vanke were looking at the situation from the perspective of structuring the shareholding in ways that allowed for the next stage of major development. Small and medium-sized shareholders were looking at how the issue of more B shares would affect the immediate price of the stock. The two were not necessarily unreconcilable, but when the conflict erupted it was necessary to balance interests.

The main problem was the difference in price/earnings ratios of A- and B-share markets. This became China's first case of a direct conflict of interest between A shareholders and B shareholders. To a degree it revealed the underlying ailments of the Chinese stock market. The B-share market in Hong Kong is priced relative to P/E ratios, while the A-share market in Shenzhen is priced by supply and demand considerations. A shares of Vanke have been known to trade as high as a 60 P/E ratio. The investment understanding of people inside and outside of China is different, and their investing behavior reflects this.

In traditional Chinese companies,* theoretical issues involving corporate governance structures are contested by large and small shareholders, but management does not participate in the game. Instead, it loyally executes the end results, and the end results are generally dictated by the large shareholders since they hold the advantage. Under modern corporate systems, however, the idea is to separate out ownership rights from management rights, and this allows professional management to have a much greater say in what happens. In companies that have broadly dispersed shareholdings, senior management has a major voice in any decisions.

In this particular case, the "game" had turned into a form of three-sided chess.† The players were large shareholders, small and medium-sized shareholders, and professional management. In calculating the long-term interests of the company, senior management should treat the entire body of shareholders fairly and even try to make up for the vulnerabilities of the smaller shareholders. Within the constraints of the corporate structure, professional management had to balance out the conflict of interest between large and smaller shareholders.

In fact, in the various proposals and motions that Vanke had put to the board of directors over the years, senior management had indeed tried hard to protect the interests of smaller investors. Our various policies of stable dividends and other things have led to Vanke's being recognized as a company that treats its investors well.

December 24, Christmas Eve. Vanke's board of directors reevaluated the

---

* Meaning state-owned enterprises that have not been fully "reformed" with corporate governance structures.

† The reference is to Weiqi, or Go, a sophisticated game that requires strategic thinking many moves in advance.

plan to increase shares in light of issues raised by investors. In the end, all 16 board members, including those representing China Resources, made the rational decision. It would give up the plan to increase shares and would cancel the interim shareholders' meeting.

The next day, Vanke made a public announcement: "The board of directors feels that cancelling the proposal described above will not influence immediate operations. However, it will influence the company's rate of growth, specifically its plans for fast growth. In line with the principle of taking actions that benefit both investors and the company's growth, at the appropriate time in the future the board will submit an alternate proposal. The China Resources Group has expressed its ongoing support for Vanke, as always."

We were fortunate that China Resources maintained a reasonable and positive attitude despite the failure of the plan to issue more B shares. It not only understood the decision to give up the plan, but it continued to support Vanke's ongoing real estate development plans. Ning Gaoning was in charge at the time, and he won my tremendous respect for this, as well as the respect of others at Vanke. He made decisions based on market principles and did not simply issue administrative commands to get things done. Prior to testing this issue of B shares and taking a controlling interest in Vanke, Mr. Ning asked BNP Paribas Peregrine, the investment banking arm of BNP Paribas in Asia, to do an assessment of Vanke's share price. During this process, he quickly found out the differences between capital markets inside China and those in Hong Kong, as smaller investors opposed any effort to put pricing on a par with Hong Kong. Given their explosive opposition, he concluded that it had been the right thing to do to abandon the B-share plan. He acted rationally, as befits an outstanding business administrator.

Later, when Vanke issued convertible bonds, China Resources subscribed to its full allotment. This was yet another confirmation that Vanke had made a correct decision on its strategic primary investor.

The Piracy Plan

Spring 1998. Scene: a hotel room in the Kempinski Hotel in Beijing.

A yellow squash sat on the table beside the bed of Sun Wenjie, CEO of China Overseas Property. I wasn't sure if it was put there by hotel staff or by the guest himself.

I was there to talk to Mr. Sun about my big idea of merging Vanke and China Overseas Property.

China Overseas Property is a China-invested construction company based in Hong Kong. Founded by Sun Wenjie himself, it is under the jurisdiction of the headquarters office of the China Construction Company, the state-owned construction company. It quickly became the largest contractor for construction projects in Hong Kong. In the late 1980s it moved into China to do real estate development while at the same time joining hands with Xinhe Real Estate

Company in Hong Kong to invest in real estate projects. When Vanke entered the real estate business in 1988, it looked to China Overseas Property as a company it could learn from. As time went on and relations between the two companies deepened, Vanke sent employees to train at China Overseas Property for such things as quality control and cost control, while China Overseas Property sent people to Vanke to learn about marketing, sales, and human resource planning. The two people who were most closely involved with this process were Vanke's Xie Dong, head of human resources at the time, and China Overseas Property's Zhang Yiping, head of personnel.

China Overseas Property was at least three times as big as Vanke in terms of its operations. It guaranteed back to the Chinese government some HKD 10 billion (USD 1.28 billion) worth of business, so Vanke and China Overseas Property were really not comparable. In 1997, however, the Hong Kong market turned south. The Southeast Asian currency crisis strongly impacted the Hong Kong real estate market and stock market.

China Overseas Property was hit on two fronts. The price of land that it had jointly invested in with Xinhe declined precipitously. As Sun Wenjie said, "This taught us what capitalism really means. Money earned from ten years of hard work went back to nothing." Secondly, the stock market went into a nosedive and China Overseas Property's shares plunged painfully. China Overseas Property had been the golden egg of the China Construction Company—it now turned into a nettle in the hand.

This therefore became an opportunity for our two companies to merge. I felt we should strike while the iron was hot, for the chance might not come again. Sitting in Mr. Sun's hotel room, I bravely set forth my proposal: "Vanke is listed on the stock market inside China. China Overseas Property is listed on the Hong Kong market. Vanke builds housing developments, multistory buildings of a certain scale in the suburban interface. China Overseas Property's strength is in building skyscrapers in the middle of cities. Vanke is strong in sales; China Overseas Property is excellent at controlling costs and ensuring quality. Think of what it could mean if these two companies were merged."

Sun gave no indication of what he was thinking, but his eyes said, "Keep talking."

I kept talking. "If we adopt some form of merger, it might be more appropriate at this time in the share prices of our respective companies for Vanke to buy China Overseas Property's government-held shares. Naturally, after merging the company could be called either Vanke-China Overseas Property or China Overseas Property-Vanke, depending on what you think. I'm easy either way."

Sun still gave no indication of his thoughts, but from his eyes I could tell he was no longer encouraging me to go on.

I felt a need to express my sincerity: "You would be the chairman of the board of the newly merged company, and I would be CEO. I would abide by your policy and decisions."

Sun simply smiled. Was it a polite refusal, or was it a tacit approval of the idea that he was unwilling to express outright? As time went on, I found it was the former. My proposal sank like a stone to the bottom of the ocean.

I still felt, however, that merging the two companies would allow each to use the strengths of the other to make up for shortcomings. Since China Overseas Property did not respond to this suggestion, the only thing for me to do was to poach people. I did not intend to poach one or two—I decided to poach whole troops of China Overseas Property employees. The main pillars supporting China Overseas Property's business could be very useful to Vanke. By taking in talent I could absorb the portions of China Overseas Property that were what Vanke most needed. I could swiftly improve Vanke's quality and cost controls. Kept from merging via a share transfer, we would use human resources to achieve the same ends. In Chinese business parlance, the phrase for this was "first be polite, then bring in the troops."

Human talent was Vanke's capital. This was the main tenet of our core value statement, and the reasons were compelling. Our need for outstanding talent was not just to satisfy a one-day thirst—it was a long-term strategy for the company, a fundamental task for one hundred years.

In 2000, Vanke's declared to itself the mission of becoming "pirates" in poaching over this talent.

China Overseas Property became the object of our attack. The company had an intensive training program. Many of its most outstanding employees had started out at the company on the bottom and, through detailed training, come to have an extremely good understanding of costs and logistics. All of the midlevel and high-level employees of the company had been brought up through this process.

As China Overseas Property's personnel began to flow towards Vanke, particularly in the areas of budgeting, engineering, and project management, China Overseas Property began to take notice. Mr. Sun soon expressed his opinion through the intermediary of his human resource department: "We respectfully ask Vanke to stop poaching our people. Otherwise, it will be difficult for our two companies to maintain friendly relations."

People continued to flow over to Vanke, including senior personnel at the deputy general manager level. This now enraged Mr. Sun. He issued a red-headline document to Vanke: due to Vanke's unfriendly behavior, he was stopping all communications between the companies.

Vanke discovered that its own team had many things in common with China Overseas Property, including a high degree of idealism, team spirit, discipline, and perfectionism. But China Overseas Property also had characteristics that we did not share. Its employees practiced absolute obedience when it came to following orders, and they were as efficient as highly trained crack troops. Vanke employees were far more democratic. They expressed their own opinions. They were less concerned about rank. One company was centralized and disciplined. The other was democratic and sometimes appeared uncoordinated.

The poaching was successful. The group of backbone personnel that came over to Vanke not only played an active role in terms of technology but also enhanced the areas in which Vanke was weak. By 2004, personnel records indicated that 40 percent of front-line managers came from the group of people poached over from China Overseas Property.

As Vanke implemented its piracy plan, China Overseas Property did not recruit a single person from Vanke. Did it not want to bring in Vanke people, or was it not able to? I suspect it was the latter.

Creating the China Urban Realty Association

Toward the end of 1998, three of us were sitting cross-legged on the heated floor of a local home near the ski resort of Yabuli. Feng Lun, chairman of Vantone Holdings, Hu Baosen, chairman of Central China Real Estate, and I were having a very tasty meal of steamed chicken with mushrooms and some vegetables braised in soy sauce as we passed around a bottle of local wine.

Wine had been served three times before people began to talk about what was really on their minds. Feng and Hu said, "Once you retire from being CEO next year, we are thinking of organizing something to keep you busy. We're thinking of bringing together China's main developers from the major cities. The purpose is to learn from one another."

This was actually a great idea.

The central government of China decided to implement housing reform in 1998. Policy makers decided that residential housing was to become a "growth point in the economy." As a result, the number of private companies in the business increased dramatically. In 1999, private companies occupied 60 percent of the market, whether figured in terms of square footage sold or square footage developed. Meanwhile, the percentage of the market held by state-owned enterprises dropped from 80 percent to 40 percent.

I predicted that the market share of privately owned companies would expand even further while that of state-owned enterprises would continue to shrink. Private companies would meanwhile have various kinds of ownership structures. The extent to which housing had been commodified around the country was different in different places, however, and these percentages also varied considerably. For example, in Beijing state-owned groups held the dominant share of the market; however, in Guangdong, where the percentage of individually purchased housing was already over 90 percent, and in Shanghai, the dragon-head city of the Yangtze River delta area, 70 percent of the top 10 developers were privately held companies.

Developers run by people, as opposed to government structures, used market mechanisms and were already dominant in the market, but they also were inefficient, given their small size and dispersed resources. They were not well suited to the needs of this kind of business.

One way to make the business more professional would be to learn from one another, take advantage of mutual strengths. This was simply obvious, yet developers on China's mainland still put up walls when it came to sharing information. To get any kind of information, we were all reduced to visiting one another's sample rooms at exhibitions. As the saying goes, we were still at the stage of trying to copy each other blindly. Wouldn't it be great if a group of outstanding developers could get together to set up a kind of platform for cooperation, a way to encourage greater communication in the industry, even to move to deeper levels of cooperation such as joint procurement of materials and fundraising in joint developments? Not only could we share resources and enjoy greater economies of scale, but we could also make the industry grow in a healthier way.

"Do you have a name? The name has to be right for the thing to fly," I asked.

Feng Lun was the one to answer. "At first, we thought we should call it the China Urban Housing Development Association. Or the China Urban Housing Allied Procurement Association. That would distinguish it from the traditional kind of industry organization. People would be joining a kind of alliance that self-regulates the industry. Later, though, we felt it would be better to call it the National Alliance of Real Estate Planners."

Obviously these two had been thinking about this for some time. I agreed to their proposal.

On May 18 1999, Feng Lun, Hu Baosen, and I met again, this time in Beihai, in the province of Guangxi. This small coastal town was quiet and peaceful, with miles of fine sand and gentle waves lapping up on the beach. With nothing to bother us, we could quietly think about the feasibility of this new alliance.

Our three companies soon came to a consensus. We would promote the establishment of the National Alliance of Real Estate Planners, and this idea soon had a positive response from some 16 of China's main real estate developers. It also was applauded by Nie Meisheng, chairman of the Housing Office of the Ministry of Construction and by Yang Shen, head of the Association of Chinese Real Estate Developers. In addition to Beijing Huayuan and Hong Kong China Overseas Property, companies agreeing to participate included Shanghai Jinqiao, Guangzhou Pearl River Investment, Tianjin Shunchi, Chongqing Longhu, Chengdu Jiaoda, and Shenyang Huaxin.

One unfortunate consideration at the time was the use of the name Alliance, since the Falungong Alliance also used this term—it was politically sensitive due to Falungong activities in various places. We therefore changed the name to the China Urban Real Estate Cooperative Network. This name also took advantage of the fashionable implications of being up to date, like the Internet.

On December 2, the China Urban Real Estate Cooperative Network was formally registered in Beijing, and I became the first rotating chairman with a term of two years. After six months, we held our first major event, a forum in Shanghai on the "New Housing Movement."

A wide range of people participated in this seminal event, including architects,* economists,† people from the construction industry, and people from the cultural sphere. Officials were represented by senior people from the Ministry of Construction‡ and the Department of Housing.§ It was a remarkable combination of people from different walks of life, coming together to discuss a subject of paramount significance in China. Its impact went far beyond what we ever expected. More than 500 people were in actual attendance, but more than 100 journalists were also there, spreading the word.

During the preparation for this forum, many government officials and also journalists asked me about the purpose of the New Housing Movement. I responded, "We have made a tremendous number of mistakes, and we can no longer go on developing projects in this random and chaotic way. It is hard for developers to recognize their own faults, however. That is why we have asked architects to participate as well as sociologists and economists, to look at the industry from an overall perspective."

Opinions were varied on this approach. There was quite a positive response from people in the spheres of sociology, economics, and architecture, who applauded this as a nongovernment type of meeting with participation from the market-economy sector as well as the cultural sphere. Others, however, felt that it was highly dubious that "a group of developers from all over the country were getting together to talk about culture." There definitely had to be private interests at stake when developers pushed this kind of activity—they did not get up early in the morning just for nothing. Either this was some kind of commercial game or a major strategic merger in the industry was afoot.

There was nothing strange in this. After all, the China Urban Real Estate Cooperative Network, later to be called the China Urban Realty Association, was a totally new thing at the time. It naturally attracted doubts and controversy.

Seen from today's perspective, the New Housing Movement as we billed this event was the very first time the real estate industry had declared itself and shared its views. The industry as a whole declared its market orientation, its stance in favor of marketization. At the same time, it began to evaluate itself in a new light given the doubts and opinions expressed by those outside the industry.

Such doubts were in full evidence in a heated virtual dialogue between Feng Lun and Zhang Weiying.¶ Feng Lun sparked this by asking rhetorically in one speech, "Why is it that people in the IT industry can burn through money and everyone thinks it is noble, while real estate developers are regarded as unscrupulous profiteers when they make money?" In a separate speech, Zhang

---

*Well-known Chinese architects included Wu Guanzhang, Luo Xiaowei, Xu Anzhi, Cui Kai, and Zhang Yonghe.

†Economists included Wang Dingding, Huang Ping, Zhou Xiaozheng, Yang Dongping, Mao Yushi, Shao Binhong, Wu Yaodong, and Wang Mingxian.

‡Xie Jiajin, head of the Real Estate Department.

§Nie Meisheng, head of the Center for the Housing Industry in the Ministry of Construction.

¶Deputy Director of the Guanghua School of Management at Peking University at that time.

Weiying poured fuel on the flames: "Ninety percent of developers in China are swindlers. Among this figure, 30 percent are big-time swindlers, 30 percent are little guys, and the others are cheating people without knowing they are doing so."

This one stone stirred up a thousand ripples. Neither of these comments was said directly in front of the other person, but they were swiftly conflated and became the subject of heated discussion. Many years later, when you mentioned the New Housing Movement, people remembered Feng Lun's grievances and Zhang Weiying's attack on the entire industry.

Building Excellent Homes for Ordinary People

The China Urban Realty Association held its forum on the New Housing Movement in Shanghai in the year 2000.

Real estate developers are not any different from other businesses in that their goal is to maximize profits. However, in China, real estate developers also have another unique attribute: they are the ones putting together an entire urban culture in the country. Unfortunately, the public generally misunderstands the first of these things in China, while developers themselves do not give adequate attention to the second.

Real estate developers are in a business that has extreme ramifications for both upstream and downstream industries. They influence society, the economy, and peoples' lives on a huge scale. The high price of residential housing makes this a major purchasing decision for consumers in any country. When you add to that the fact that land is generally scarce and often monopolized, real estate development is equated with explosive profits and spoken of with veiled criticism around the world. The situation in China is no exception. In the 1990s, real estate developers blindly built more and more expensive housing. They aristocratized housing and went all-out for luxury, which only made people condemn the industry more.

Around the time of the New Housing Movement, Vanke invited a professor from Tongji University named Professor Luo Xiaowei, to come talk to Vanke personnel about the history of architecture in other parts of the world. She also gave her evaluation of the last decade or so of urban housing development in China: "For the moment, let's not even talk about the kind of shoddy construction that is so bad you have to tear it down and start over. Even average buildings have glaring defects."*

What exactly did Professor Luo think these glaring defects were? She gave examples: "The architecture is moving in the direction of 'aristocratization.' The design of rooms makes places look like hotels for high-class guests. Plus you have all kinds of 'faux styles' in single-unit housing, like the European style,

---

*The description uses a phrase meaning a misdrawn stroke in Chinese calligraphy. Unfortunately, the erudition of the presentation does not come through in translation.

the ancient style, the British style, the Viennese style, as well as simply made-up styles."

Some developers at first disagreed with this, but on closer examination all had to agree that new housing developments in urban areas were appalling. What she said was true. Commodified housing had moved in the direction of being over-the-top, with exaggerated design, arbitrary and unplanned sprawl, and anything western and ultra-new as a way to set it apart from others.

Throughout the 1980s, housing was still mainly supplied to urban residents as a welfare benefit of state employment. At the same time, however, commodified housing was starting up in such places as Shenzhen, the Pearl River delta, and Xiamen, coastal cities that had access to the outside world. Who made up the market for this early period of commodity housing? They were mainly that very small percentage of people who had disposable incomes and buying power that far surpassed the normal Chinese citizen. Such people included overseas Chinese, people from Hong Kong and Macao, and white-collar people working in joint ventures. These people were living beyond the bounds of the normal state-controlled housing system. They included the heads of privately run companies and the independently employed. Obviously, housing developers built with this highly select group of consumers in mind—they built luxury housing or housing that was medium-to-high on the luxury scale. Vanke's series of Urban Garden projects fit this mold precisely.

By the mid-1990s, the market turned upside down. The dominant position of housing as a welfare benefit had given way to commodified housing by now, as ordinary people began to be able to buy their own homes. By 1999, commodified housing held 85 percent of the market, while non-commodified housing was not even 15 percent.

As China's economy grew, more and more people separated themselves from the structure of the state-run economy. They began to find non-planned-economy solutions to their own living needs. Market-economy methods now began to apply to incomes, benefits, and also housing. Such people are currently the mainstream market for urban housing, and this will continue into the future. They are both white-collar and blue-collar, and they are both professionals who have found their own jobs and businesspeople who have founded their own small companies. These people constitute the great majority of urban residents by now, and their average level of income and consumption dictates the average level of housing for most Chinese cities.

Chinese real estate now headed in an irreversible direction as privately owned housing went from being a luxury for a minority to a mass consumer item for the ordinary man. Many residential developers did not take note of this, however. They continued to create high-class and medium-to-high-class homes, which led to the ongoing phenomenon of high vacancy rates. As the New Housing Movement gathered steam, the key topic that both new and older developers were going to have to face together became how to build urban residences for regular people.

Under the planned-economy system, in the 1960s and 1970s and even into the 1980s, a huge number of matchbox-type housing units were built in China's cities. As the economy changed, these were rejected by the market and replaced with residences that focused more on aesthetics, greenery, comfort, and spaciousness. From the vantage point of being economical and capable of conserving resources, however, these matchbox buildings were the more rational choice.

In contrast, residential communities built in the 1990s were irrational from every economic standpoint. They had multiple bathrooms, were luxuriously appointed, grossly too large, and generally had manicured gardens around them. Having your own bathroom in your own home, as opposed to having to go out to a public toilet, is one of the marks of modern civilization. The problem comes when each individual residence has two or three or four such bathrooms. Vanke did a survey of this subject in high-class Japanese residential districts and found to its surprise that upper-class Japanese homes rarely had more than two bathrooms. What is the GDP per capita of Japan versus that of China? Why should we squander resources on this kind of thing?*

Clearly, we had major problems just in terms of the economics of the way we were building our commodity-type residential housing. During the period in which developers built for the *nouveau riche*, irrational use of resources was done for vanity consumption. Now that the market had changed, it had to be replaced by a focus on what normal consumers could actually afford, and what public resources could sustain as well. Developers had to provide products that met the needs of the common citizen. The prerequisites were therefore comfort, economy, and functionality.

As China developed, a growing disparity between rich and poor was unavoidable. Two kinds of housing in cities began to be a stark expression of the two ends of this increasing polarity—on the one hand, villa neighborhoods and luxury communities, and on the other, older housing that had not been redeveloped. As urban planners tried to figure out how to reduce the social tensions that were resulting from this polarity, they felt that developers had a social responsibility to allow for harmonious coexistence between different income levels of urban residents. By providing goods and services, developers themselves should enable different kinds of people to enjoy the fruits of urban civilization.

---

*One example is the Duomuo neighborhood of Tokyo, which has been in existence now for more than 30 years, as well as some satellite cities that are planned with the intent of mixing together residences of high-income people and those of modest means. Through ingenious design, the developers have achieved an organic unity between different classes of housing. People live near one another amicably and respectfully.

The planning that went into the Duomuo community inspired Vanke. If developers are to focus on the "common" citizen, they must be aware of this whole subject, which also means becoming aware of their social responsibilities. In recent years, Vanke has been able to preserve the quality of housing while still lowering housing prices by using economies of scale. This has allowed a great many more "ordinary people" to buy their own homes.

In the New Housing Movement, Vanke therefore advanced the concept of "focusing on the common man as we face the new economic era." After 2001, we began to implement this idea very deliberately.

In the decade that was to follow, 88 percent of all of Vanke's sales was made up of housing that had a floor space of less than 144 square meters (472 square feet) per unit. Residences with a floor space of less than 90 square meters (295 square feet) came to 53 percent of all sales. Products for first homeowners or first upgraded homeowners constituted 64 percent of all sales. At the same time, we initiated research on extremely small-scale housing, of around 15 square meters (about 50 square feet). We tried this out in pilot projects in Beijing and Xi'an, as a way to meet the housing needs of a segment of the market that includes young people just starting out on their own. Over the past 20-some years, Vanke has been one of the more active proponents of the idea of focusing on the common citizen in housing developments.

The Zhongnan Bus Incident

The Wonderland Garden is a classic example of one of Vanke's early suburban developments. Vanke built an unimaginably beautiful community in an unimaginable place. The success of this development changed the very definition of suburbs. In the early years, it became a project that people in the industry had to visit to see the possibilities. This part of Shenzhen was incorporated into overall urban planning fairly late; as a result, when we began working there, public transportation was not as well developed there as it was in proper urban areas.

Since that was the case, how were tenants of the Wonderland Garden supposed to get about? The Shenzhen Vanke Real Estate Company decided to promote a for-pay specialized bus service for Wonderland Garden residents. Starting in March 2000, Vanke brought in large buses and minibuses that ran concurrently for the convenience of Vanke tenants.

In August of that same year, however, the Shenzhen Municipal Transportation Department sent down an order explicitly forbidding the operations of any private transport vehicles for tenants in residential neighborhoods. Vanke began to have to confront the problems of a society that had diversified needs and ways to meet the demand for public services.

At the end of 2000, Vanke hired the services of the Economic Research Institute of Shenzhen University and asked them to research the prospects for establishing a service type of bus network. In April 2001, the Zhongnan Bus system formally began service to Vanke's Wonderland Garden.

As soon as this service began, it ran into sporadic complaints. These mainly centered on such issues as scheduling times and intervals between buses and the way large buses were severely overcrowded, tickets were expensive, service was substandard, drivers changed routes arbitrarily, and so on. Vanke held meetings with the Zhongnan Bus Company, Limited to try to address the main points, but the situation did not get any better.

By July 2001, 831 new households lived in the Wonderland Garden. Complaints increased and discussions heated up. When companies were getting off work, people had to wait for five buses before they could even squeeze on.

With Vanke's mediation, the Zhongnan Bus Company met with representatives of the owners of enterprises along the bus route and got them to promise to adjust scheduling times and frequencies. Meanwhile, the bus company was to set up more standardized service as well as complaint-response mechanisms. It was to strengthen its coordination of all aspects of this problem.

On the evening of August 17, 2001, however, buses were late, many people could not get on, and many others refused to buy tickets since they saw many others not buying tickets. The problems escalated. One bus reached the Wonderland Garden gates and did not even stop; it simply went on to the final stop. People wanting to get off at Wonderland Garden began a confrontation with the staff on that bus.

On the evening of August 21, the Zhongnan bus again was so full that people could not get on. People who had waited several hours finally ran out of patience. They intercepted and blocked the movement of seven buses in succession, leading to a complete traffic jam in a certain place. Senior management from Vanke hurried to the scene, together with the vice president of the Zhongnan Bus Company. With the assistance of traffic police, things were straightened out and traffic started moving again. However, before the emergency meeting on site had concluded, six or seven bus drivers had charged toward a Wonderland Garden tenant, shouting, "That's him! That's the one who led the mob!" They began to beat up this person.

The tenants of Wonderland Garden were furious. The next day, several hundred of them spontaneously gathered at a shopping mall that was normally peaceful and quiet. "Bring out who is responsible! Vanke doesn't keep its promises!" they shouted. Management of both Vanke and the Zhongnan Bus Company spent all night discussing with tenants' representatives what to do in order to keep the incident from getting worse.

On August 23, at midday, I got on an express bus run by the Zhongnan Bus Company that went in the direction of the Wonderland Garden. There were only a few other passengers and there was plenty of air conditioning. After around 20 minutes, I reached the Wonderland Garden. I ate lunch in the neighborhood, got back on a bus at around 1 p.m., and returned to the city. At that point, 11 or 12 seats were available, and very few people got on at the intermediate stops along the way. It took me 36 minutes to get back. The peak times for riding the bus were in the morning, when people were going to work, and when they were coming home in the evening. This was when the problems were occurring. The solutions should have been simple.

After this experiment of taking the express bus, I called the CEO of Shenzhen Vanke and asked him, "Do you know about this affair of the Wonderland Garden bus?"

"Sure I do!," he replied.

"Have you actually ridden on one of the buses?"

"No, never!"

One has no right to an opinion without doing the research. If you do express an opinion, it should be after investigation. This problem of the scheduling of buses had come up long ago—residents had raised issues. I myself had neglected my duties since I had not looked into the issue until problems intensified. Vanke not only should express its apologies to the tenants, but it should take immediate action to improve transport issues.

We spent the next several days communicating with all sides. On August 24, Wonderland Garden called a meeting of 10 representatives of the tenants. Shenzhen Vanke and the Zhongnan Bus Company participated in the discussion and in the end reached a consensus that was made public and which included 10 specific measures that had to be taken to improve the situation. These included adjusting the bus schedules and keeping to the schedules. The bus company apologized to tenants who had been beaten up and at the same time punished those who were responsible. It set up a hotline for complaints.

On September 6, the Zhongnan Bus Company started implementing a self-service system in their buses. There were basically no complaints, and traffic was restored to normal.

If we had recognized the early-warning signals on time, this violent confrontation might not have occurred. Not paying attention to the early signals and misjudgements about the incident led to the ultimate eruption of a crisis. Lacking early-warning mechanisms and sensitivity to any sense of crisis is what made Vanke lose the opportunity to defuse the problems and find solutions.

"Customers are the sole reason Vanke exists." "Our most important standard involves satisfying customers." These things are key components of Vanke's value statement. "Zero complaints" is our ideal. First, however, costs are often a constraining factor in determining the quality of our products. Second, we will never achieve quality standards that bring complaints to zero, since customers are not always 100 percent rational. What we can do, however, is improve quality even in the midst of ongoing complaints and make sure that our management services are as good as they can be.

In this particular instance, we relied on the bus company to reassure us of adequate service. Senior management did not take the matter in hand and investigate on its own. That was a mistake. Vanke's reputation relies on meeting the constantly increasing expectations of tenants, and it relies on the extent to which customers trust the Vanke brand. We must constantly surpass expectations—not because this is the core part of our value concept but because this is the only way we will continue to grow. We learned a good lesson in this regard from the Zhongnan Bus incident.

Selling Vanguard

After issuing B shares, Vanke began changing its strategy. Having expanded, it now began to contract. By the end, only two business lines remained: real estate and the Vanguard retail chain stores.

Which is harder, soccer or basketball? For Argentinians, basketball is harder. For Americans, soccer is harder. For Spaniards, neither is hard, and for Chinese, both are. In applying this to corporate management, the point is that choosing what to do is relative. It depends on your advantages at any given time. What you must avoid is doing what you like most but in fact have no talent for doing.

In 2000, both of Vanke's businesses showed great promise for future growth. Many people in the industry envied our position. "You have profits coming in from real estate but also cash flow coming in from retail," they said. "You can make money off real estate and scale up with the retail chain stores." After all, wasn't Li Ka-shing using that same strategy? He had the Cheung Kong real estate business as well as the PARKnSHOP chain stores. Some people were even saying that Vanke was a mini Cheung Kong.

Was that true? Like Russians, was Vanke really able to play both soccer and basketball? Vanke people did not believe that it could. They wanted to spin off one or the other.

At that time, both of these industries had potential for growth. Retail had given birth to the world's largest company, Walmart, as figured by sales volume. Later, Huang Guangyu was to become the richest man in China three times in a row, based on his retail business.* I believed that if Vanke chose retail chain stores, it could in fact become the largest company in China. And real estate? That would be different. Not only would Vanke find it hard to grow to that kind of size, but international real estate companies also did not have an example similar to Walmart. Real estate is a dispersed kind of business—it doesn't lend itself to consolidation. Among the largest five names in real estate, none controls more than 20 percent of the market.

If we were really ambitious and simply wanted size, we would choose retail chain stores. We weighed the pros and cons, however. Some 85 percent of Vanke's resources were already in real estate, while only 15 percent were in retail. Ninety-five percent of its human resources were in real estate, and only 5 percent in retail. What's more, Vanke already ranked number one among more than 70 listed real estate companies in China, while in retail it was a mere number 13. The choice was actually quite simple. Not only should Vanke do real estate, but it should get rid of its retail business as soon as possible. Retail competition was extremely intense, and it demanded swift growth. If you stayed for long in a state of uneasy coexistence with your competition, each would check the other's growth and you would both be stymied. Meanwhile, trying to expand brought with it opportunities but also a tremendous number of hassles.

For Vanke, doing a retail business was much harder than doing real estate. Swiftly selling off Vanguard became the logical and rational decision.

Vanguard had been established in 1990. After gaining a good reputation in Shenzhen, it leveraged its brand to expand to Harbin, Urumqi, Wuhan,

---

*Huang Guangyu, chairman of GOME at the time, a consumer electronics retailer.

Chengdu, and other cities. As a listed company, Vanke needed to show profits every year. While real estate is still worth something even if you are not selling it, it also has the potential to depreciate in value. At the time, therefore, many investors were hoping that Vanke would not get rid of its chainstore business.

In February 2001, the board of directors considered and then passed a proposal to allow Yao Mumin to resign from the position of CEO of the company and to replace him with Yu Liang. In September, at a second interim board meeting held in the Donghu Hotel, Vanke's board passed a resolution to sell its shares in the Vanguard department store business. It was selling to China Resources, which fortunately at that time wanted to expand. Getting completely out of the retail business was the final step in the strategy of turning Vanke from a diversified entity into a company focused on real estate. To this day, some people regret this. They feel that if we had not sold Vanguard, we would have grown to unimaginable size. In fact, however, I drew a long sigh of relief when we sold Vanguard. Time has already proven, and continues to prove, that specialization is the necessary route to becoming strong and powerful. Our "golden fingers" were attractive, but we had to cut them off if we were to move forward.

In 2000, Vanke added 4.388 million square meters (14.4 million square feet) of land reserves to its portfolio. We continued to expand in 2001, signing agreements for projects in Shanghai, Shenzhen, Beijing, Chengdu, and Shenyang. We also went into four other cities: Nanjing, Wuhan, Changchun, and Nanchang. Our second round of expansion had begun.

It had taken Vanke roughly nine years to go from being diversified to being focused solely on real estate. By now, Vanke is well known inside China. Everyone is quite aware of who we are. In other countries, however, I am frequently asked, "What is Vanke?" It might be good to give a quick answer to that here.

It should generally take two seconds to describe a first-class, mature, great company. For example, with beverages, who is biggest? There's no need to guess—Coca-Cola. Who is the biggest housing developer in the world? Not only is this hard to say, but it is certainly not Vanke. Nevertheless, I can say in six seconds what Vanke is: it is an urban housing developer based in China and a highly respected listed blue-chip company.

Many companies emerged from the great wave of reform and opening up in China. They are mostly diversified, engaged in a multitude of businesses. Not only could you not describe them in six seconds, but you couldn't do it in several minutes. Ten years ago, it probably would have taken me 10 minutes to describe Vanke. If anyone wanted to know what Vanke's parent company, the Shenzhen Special Economic Zone Development Company, was involved in, that would have taken even more time since its businesses ranged from gas stations to feedstock factories to industrial development parks to graveyards.

Vanke is in real estate. Real estate has five main categories: office buildings, shopping malls, hotels, factory construction, and housing. Among those, Vanke is mainly in housing.

The reason Vanke chose this mode of growth is that the market for housing is extremely large. By going into this, Vanke had the potential to become largest in the world—that was apparent. Now, Vanke itself might not become the biggest housing developer in the world, but the biggest will definitely come out of China. One you have built housing, you can sell it. Malls and office buildings are different. The profit model is more suited to long-term leasing, which requires the ability to wield a massive amount of capital. A company must have enormous ability to raise money. In 1998, we compared ourselves to Sun Hung Kai. At the time, Vanke had assets on the order of RMB 5.4 billion (USD 652.96 million), while Sun Hung Kai's were RMB 180 billion (USD 26.94 billion). Vanke's net assets were RMB 4 billion (USD 598.6 million), while Sun Hung Kai's were RMB 130 billion (USD 21.76 billion). If we had chosen to take the model that Sun Hung Kai took, we would be forever trotting along behind that company. The assets required for holding onto and leasing just two offices would have crushed us; we would not have been able to do further development.

Vanke therefore buys land, builds buildings, and sells them. It then buys more land, builds more buildings, and sells them. It maintains a certain turnover of capital as it goes along. Although the size of Vanke's capital is much smaller than Sun Hung Kai, after 10 years, Sun Hung Kai has increased in size to far more than RMB 200 billion (USD 28.57 billion), but Vanke meanwhile has grown to over RMB 50 billion (USD 7.14 billion). It has narrowed the gap. By now, Vanke has become the largest housing developer in the world by carrying on this strategy for all these years.

Vanke has become ever more simplified, but not ever smaller. Instead, it has become the largest in its field. We therefore believe in the power of streamlining, in simplification.

In April 2008, I gave a course of lectures at the Harvard Business School during which I ran into the chairman of the board of the Fosun Group, Guo Guangchang. For a second time, the two of us debated the merits of diversification versus simplification. Fosun had taken the route of diversification. It was in four major areas: real estate, steel, pharmaceuticals, and retail. Its argument was that you do not put all your eggs in one basket—you diversify in order to counter market risk. Three years earlier, I had this same debate with Guangchang while attending lectures in Yabuli. At the time, Vanke's annual operating revenues from its focused approach were RMB 7.2 billion (USD 1.03 billion)—by now, they had jumped to RMB 52 billion (USD 7.43 billion). Diversified Fosun, however, had also grown enormously.

McKinsey has analyzed corporate models by dividing them into three groups. These are concentrated operations (67 percent of operating revenues come from one business unit), a certain degree of diversification (at least 67 percent of operating revenues come from two business units), and diversified operations (less than 67 percent of operating revenues come from any two business units.) McKinsey's conclusion: the total return on shares of concentrated operations is 22 percent. That of a certain degree of diversification: 18 percent. That of diversified operations: 16 percent. From the standpoint of return on investment, McKinsey supports a concentrated approach to business operations.

If that is the case, why is diversification so common in the China market?

As privately operated companies grew in China, most were competing in each industry with either state-owned enterprises or multinationals that were many times their size. *Private* companies were forced to opt for speed as a way to combat such strength. They needed to build up resources fast as a way to fight superior forces. In newly emerging markets, resources generally flow toward size. Diversification is a shortcut as a way to expand. Because of this, private companies with limited resources often diversified as a way to achieve scale and used that scale as a way to attract resources. They then used these resources to fight superior capabilities and thereby to survive.

As I saw it, however, this worked over the short term but not for the long term. Using short-term resources to combat the long-term capabilities of large enterprises was rational as a partial and short-term approach, but it could not be the best strategy for the long haul. Behind the debate on simplification versus diversification also lay the issue of how to handle governance structures of companies in the short term. This involved decisions on how to allocate resources over diversified entities in the most effective way.

In brief, it looks as though Vanke and Fosun are going to continue to argue this for some time to come.

Forcing Ourselves to Change

May 2002. Scene: the Grand Hyatt Hotel in Beijing. Vanke was holding a press conference to formally launch a nationwide promotion campaign. It was branding itself as a company that allowed people to taste the full richness of life.

Real estate has to be highly specific when it comes to geographic location. Different parts of the country are differentiated by a number of factors, including climate and customs but also consumer psychology, lifestyle, and social structure. Because of this, branding and corporate image that might work in some places are bound to be out of sync in other places. Projects within a company, and branding among companies, must be specifically targeted to the location.

In the mind of consumers, however, one developer is not much different from another. People's impression of a developer mainly comes from their experience in the building in which they currently reside. Although they might get as far as name recognition, they generally are in the dark about what is really behind a given brand. Although some companies put their name on every project, the great majority of consumers do not associate the name of the developer with the name of a given set of buildings.

Despite this fact, Vanke was determined to develop its own brand in an industry in which the brand effect is quite limited.

Vanke went into real estate development in 1988. Since that time, it was able to develop a certain reputation among people in the business as well as consumers with respect to its performance. It was well liked for such things as community planning, landscaping, product design, overall style, building management and maintenance, post-sales and after-sales service, as well as its corporate culture.

Based on this foundation, Vanke now decided to promote its very first slogan, or branding message: architecture that is built for living a boundless life. Several years later, it came out with a second message: architecture that celebrates beautiful lives.

Other developers later came out with branding messages. People noted that Vanke's message emphasized architectural aspects and extolled the way architecture is something people love and can relate to. I was quite surprised when I heard that, since I myself had no emotional response to architecture when I first started out.

Being an entrepreneur was also not my dream occupation when I started out. My ideal was to be a doctor, a detective, a seaman on an oceangoing vessel, or perhaps a war journalist. I certainly had not thought of becoming an entrepreneur, and becoming a real estate developer was even more out of the question. All of the things I tended to read, including classics but also daily news, talked about real estate in terms of greed, corruption, and explosive profits. Developers drove people out of where they had been living. They were said to destroy the memory of a city. These were far from my own image of myself. A person's reality is closely tied to the context of the times in which he lives, however. I grew up in an era that created entrepreneurs. I went with the flow, and became one myself. In 1988, Vanke went into real estate after completing a project to build the Weideng Villa. Going into real estate was a rational decision on my part: I recognized it had fairly low barriers to entry and enormous potential.

My major in college had been drainage, which is a part of civil engineering. As Vanke began to get bigger in the real estate arena, some friends naturally linked this to my college experience. In fact, however, we students, called "workers, farmers, and soldiers" at the time, gained very little from our education. What's more, I myself had not chosen this field of drainage, nor did I care for it. I delighted in literature. Now, even though Vanke's main business is real estate, I still have not been able to bring myself to love the industry. In public, I have even been known to express distaste for the industry in general. One time, Yu Liang took me to task for this. "The chairman of the board may have his own personal opinions," he said, "but it is inappropriate to say such things out loud. Otherwise, how will you get Vanke's managers and employees to like this business?" From then on, I stopped expressing my negative attitude in public.

It is possible to dislike something or fail to love it and still throw yourself into it. Indeed, you should throw yourself wholeheartedly into what you are doing until you are able to do what you truly love. People all want to do something they like and be successful at it. In most cases, however, they are not very clear on what they truly love and what their lifelong profession should be. While they are figuring this out, they focus on what they are doing, and they try to do it well. Their experience in life, and their ongoing accumulation of experience, then becomes a part of finding out what really interests them.

From top to bottom, everyone in Vanke has to go through the progression of being a novice to becoming an expert in the business. Even if Vanke people do not actually like the industry, they have to force themselves to undergo training, examinations, communicating, and learning. The company engages professors from Tsinghua, Tongji, and Dongnan universities to teach senior management and top management levels in systematic fashion. Groups of managers are sent abroad on survey trips. Most of these go to Japan, since that country's situation is similar to China's—its process of urbanization has been similar, and both have large populations on a limited amount of land. Urban density forces the building of large numbers of super-high residential buildings. In addition, Japan's residential housing industry is highly developed. It serves Vanke well as a model to follow. Starting in 1994, Vanke began annual investigation trips to Japan. After 2000, it began more extensive study of engineering techniques and the concept of turning housing into a manufacturing process. It began cooperating with various Japanese companies as well as Japanese associations.

One time, I happened to go by the headquarters of a gas company in Japan. It had an exhibition hall, offices, and R&D all in the same complex—a fascinating array of everything to do with natural gas, right there before my eyes. This in turn led me to think of having the first building that Vanke built and put to use for itself be an Architectural R&D Center that would allow the company to interact with urban citizens. This experience directly influenced the formation of what later became Vanke's headquarters at 63 Meilin Road.

One trip that some colleagues and I made to Japan came at the end of October 2002. The itinerary included a visit to the large construction company called Tadao Ando. This had been arranged by the Hitachi Elevator Company.

We arrived at the Hitachi Mizuto elevator plant in the morning. The testing facilities for elevators were striking, alternating columns of red and white. A reception committee lined both sides of the road to receive us, and we were familiar by now with the etiquette, bowing repeatedly as we moved forward into the plant. Our hosts opened up the "smart" R&D lab for our line of visitors and gave a highly detailed explanation of products. They answered the questions that their Chinese visitors posed with the same impeccable care. Hitachi is a company that makes almost everything from satellites to equipment for generating nuclear energy. It makes high-speed rail lines as well as regular electronics. It is independent from Japan's nine large comprehensive industry groups. It has made a name in high-tech and once ranked sixth among the top 500 in the world, although by 2001 it had slipped to being thirty-second. In terms of electronic appliances, it ranks third after Sony and Panasonic.

I first visited Japan on a study mission in the mid-1980s, and visits to factories were also part of my tour that time. I was curious and astonished at the gardenlike environment, the production lines controlled by robots, and the strict management and industrious employees. Everything was new and unusual. More than a decade later, we had begun to learn not just from Japan but also from corporations in Hong Kong, Singapore, Europe, and the United States.

We had unconsciously absorbed the influence of all of these and were no longer country mice come into the big city. Vanke colleagues generally felt familiar by now with the introductions of our Japanese friends. We no longer felt like such novices—Chinese companies were making progress.

As part of our visit to Hitachi, we also were taken to visit the Kobe industrial park area and its Hyogo Prefectural Art Museum. After the Kobe earthquake, the city was rebuilt. The architect Tadao Ando proposed to recover one of the most important aspects in the city's collective memory, namely its relationship with the sea, and this museum was designed by Tadao Ando as a result. A designer who was accompanying us introduced this architect to us: "Ando Tadao has the highest possible reputation among Japanese architects. He is originally from quite a poor family in Osaka. He is basically self-taught, since he could not afford a proper education. He fell in love with architecture at a young age and trained himself by reading books on the subject. In the 1960s, he made his way to Europe where he focused intensely on researching different buildings and styles. It may be that life has given him a more acute understanding of what goes into buildings than the average architect."

Our next stop was a place that had once been a quarry. The government had then intentionally turned it into a park, with facilities designed by the same architect. The use of light was a primary feature. What did Tadao Ando mean to express by this? My guess: modern people look at the changes going on in the reality around them, but they do not really see them. They are not observant. They do things too rashly, without sufficient thought. Ando is telling us to calm down and be more reflective. I was highly impressed by this architect, and eventually Vanke asked him to design the company's headquarters in Shenzhen.

After that, architecture and cities became the main focus of overseas study missions. In Greece, I was amazed to learn about the tiny cracks between stones in stone buildings, my understanding being that the stones had come to this state after eons of being ground away by earthquakes. No craftsman could have achieved that fit. In Marseille, I saw modern streamlined cars pulling through a beautifully ancient railway station, in a perfect dialogue between old and new. In Arles, I looked for the yellow buildings found in Vincent van Gogh's paintings. I came to realize that the cities I was seeing were far more than just a combination of steel, rebar, and concrete. Instead, they were organic entities in which people lived their lives.

In short, instead of being insensitive to architecture, I came to love it. As a professional manager, I had forced myself to change.

Life in High Places

May 22, 2003. Noon. Ascending Mount Everest and now at 8,700 meters (28,543 feet). Clouds are hanging low and snowflakes dance through the air. The peak is right before my eyes, but I am taking shorter and shorter steps. I begin to pause for longer rests, and suddenly I have trouble breathing and feel that my chest is about to split open. My oxygen tank is running low!

How much longer to the summit? At camp, the head of our guides had said it was "a little less than an hour" away, but we had already gone an hour and a half.

"Attention! Mr. Wang doesn't have enough oxygen!"

"Stop climbing and get back down immediately!" That was our guide, Zhaxi.

Zhaxi looked hard at me as I continued to move forward. I lifted my mitt and pointed in the direction of Everest's summit.

It was so very close! Was it putting me in some kind of trance? Of course it was. Many of those who died on its flanks were discovered after they had reached the top and were coming down again. With the thin air, hypoxia, and exhaustion, it is easy to have poor judgment up there and do things you should not do. When I climbed Mt. Bogda, and several times when I was hang gliding, I confidently and blindly made mistakes that should have been fatal. That they were not is due to sheer luck. Fate might not be so kind to me the next time. I knew the dangers of continuing to climb without oxygen, but I also knew that it would be dangerous to go back down from anything above 8,000 meters (about 26,250 feet). Since entering the main base camp, I had concentrated all my efforts, not allowed the slightest thing to interfere with my focus, nor did I make any extraneous movements. I had preserved an adequate amount of energy. Soldiers are trained a thousand days just for one brief battle. I was in the zone of "holding on a little longer."

May 22, 2003. 14:35 p.m. I reached the summit.

In May 1995, I suddenly had an intense pain in my left leg and an MRI discovered that I had an angioma* between my fourth and fifth vertebrae. Since it was pressing on nerves in the spinal cord, my left leg hurt.

"Can I still play tennis?" I asked the neurologist.

"You won't be able to play anything," he responded gravely. "From right now, you will be lying in bed getting ready for an operation. You may be paralyzed from the waist down if that angioma bursts."

Fear surged through me as I heard about the potential consequences, but the first thought that came into my head was, *I have to get to Tibet before the operation. It will be hard once I am in a wheelchair.*

The hospital put together a team of experts to evaluate me, and the authority on spinal columns had a different opinion. So long as the angioma did not get any bigger, he felt that I did not need to have the operation immediately. In the meantime, moderate exercise was all right. I took this to mean that overly advanced modern equipment had revealed something that might never make any difference in my life. I refused to have the operation, and I also did not stop being determined to get to Tibet.

In 1996, I began the physical preparation necessary for that trip. During

---

*An angioma is an abnormal growth produced by the dilation or new formation of blood vessels. It is a kind of benign tumor made up of blood vessels or lymph vessels. No further mention of this problem occurs in Wang Shi's book.

spring vacation, I climbed mountains in Zhangjiajie, Hunan province, for five days. I began the physical preparation necessary for taking a trip to Tibet.

On New Year's Day 1997, a friend named Xu Xiaodan and I agreed that we would set aside August as the time finally to go to Tibet, not to climb Everest but to do some climbing in general.

In order to acclimate myself to altitudes where oxygen was thinner, I carried extra weight as I trained. In June and July, I climbed four mountains over 1,000 meters (3,280 feet) in eastern Australia. On one of these trips, I met up with a young man named Zhou Xingkang, from Shenzhen, and he became my second climbing buddy. The two of us were passionate about mountain climbing. People who love to climb mountains call themselves "mountain friends." In order to connect with such friends on the Qinghai-Tibetan plateau, I asked the chairman of China's mountain climbing association, Zeng Shusheng, to write a letter of introduction for us to Tibetan and Qinghai mountain climbing associations.

In mid-August, we finally officially confirmed the dates for going to the Qinghai-Tibetan Plateau [Qing-Zang Plateau]. The evening prior to departure, Xu Xiaodan suddenly got a phone call asking him to go to New Zealand to negotiate a particular project. He could not accompany me along the way, but we could still keep to the original plan, with the two of us arriving in Tibet by different routes. We met up in Xining, flying from Beijing and from Guangdong. As dawn rose in Xining, we settled ourselves into a Mitsubishi jeep and hit the road.

On that trip, I was to spend a month on the Qing-Zang Plateau.*

On May 5, 2000, I joined the mountaineering group called the China Mountain-Climbing Team, led by Wang Yongfeng. We successfully ascended a mountain called Mount Zhangzi (in Chinese), 2,299 meters (7,542 feet) above sea level, located in the Himalayas. Mount Zhangzi is situated on the northern slopes of Everest. Standing on its summit, Everest rises before you to an awe-inspiring majestic height. I did not dare to think that one day I might be on top of that mighty mountain. It was too high and mystical to be something one climbed. Nevertheless, even at that moment, two teams of Chinese college students were climbing it, as well as two other Chinese individuals. One of these individuals was the Hong Kong resident Zhong Jianmin. This was his third attempt. Prior to this, he had already climbed the six other highest peaks on the seven continents. If he was successful, he would become the first Chinese person to climb all of the highest peaks on the seven continents. The other person was a man from Harbin named Yan Genghua. He was an avid marathon runner and had completed a run along the entire length of the Great Wall, but he had only been mountain climbing for two years. He organized his own team, and a crew from Harbin Television was following along, reporting his progress.

---

*Tibet in Chinese is Xizang [western zang]. Qinghai is part of the Tibetan plateau, and the name Qinghai (green or blue lake) is a direct Chinese translation of the old name in Mongolian and Turkic languages Hoh nuur or Karakul. The plateau is therefore called the Qing-Zang Plateau in Chinese.

As we descended to base camp on Mount Zhangzi, we learned that there had been an accident on Yuzhu Peak in Qinghai. Two had died and three others were missing. A search party immediately set off to try to find them.

Meanwhile, the curse of Everest had reappeared. Yan Genghua had disappeared after reaching the summit. The Ministry of Education now ordered the college team to stop its ascent. China's "civil* mountaineering movement" had taken a major hit.

Someone asked me, "Are you afraid, when someone dies on a mountain near you like that?"

"Not afraid, terrified," I replied. "But not just when an accident happens—the terror comes from the danger all around you, for example, crossing crevasses or an avalanche area. If you die from these things, you naturally are no longer afraid—the person who dies doesn't know what happened. But when other mountain friends get hit, you become extraordinarily quiet inside and saddened by it."

Someone asked me, "Well, why not give it up then?"

"I had not disciplined myself to think of giving up," I replied. "On the contrary, I had made myself decide not to give up. Mountain climbing is unusual in that way. It involves a mixture of vanity, self-satisfaction, curiosity, risk-taking, individual heroism, and also the ability to face your own terror. In the midst of this, you have the constant conflict between terror and controlling your terror. This makes you hyper-attentive. It brings on a kind of transcendental feeling of creative excitement. Once you have tasted that feeling, it is very hard to resist the temptation of the mountain."

Someone asked me, "Is there any connection between managing a company and climbing a mountain?"

I said, "No direct connection. Mountain climbing is the ultimate game for a minority of people. But if the one experiencing it is an entrepreneur, what he experiences affects the thinking behind how he runs his company. Business takes months or years to realize results. With mountain climbing, you are done in a few weeks or an even a shorter length of time. But in this condensed time frame, you have an extremely rare opportunity to experience things. As you go higher in elevation, your margin of error for making mistakes gets smaller. Meanwhile, the requirements placed on your abilities gets greater, such things as planning, communicating, and executing your plan. If you lose focus in the slightest way, you risk losing your life. Mountain climbing, and any kind of risk-taking activity, makes you think about how to run the company better. The process is fundamentally a kind of case study in management."

As a child, everyone experiences curiosity, the urge to find out about things. As a person becomes an adult, that urge declines and turns into the passion of idealism. By middle age, you begin to repress your passionate ideals as you

---

*People-sponsored as opposed to government-sponsored.

become more practical and realistic. Meanwhile, your curiosity is smothered by the trivialities of life and the weight of responsibilities. The wellsprings of passion lie in curiosity, individual awareness. Only if you possess that kind of curiosity, dare to experience things, observe things, study, and challenge yourself, can you go to unlimited heights as an entrepreneur and venture into unexplored territory.

The top of Everest has a cornice. It is larger than expected—a dozen or so people could stand on it.

People often ask me what you can see from a height of 8,844 meters (29,016 feet).* Actually, it was cloudy when we climbed Everest on May 22, 2003, and visibility was just 30 meters (98 feet). Other friends ask, "What did you feel the moment you got to the top?" I basically felt very little. High-altitude research estimates that a person's cognitive abilities are roughly those of a six-year-old at any altitude above 8,000 meters (about 26,250 feet), due to the lack of oxygen. Most people assume you feel an acute sense of danger up there. In fact, despite danger all around, you don't comprehend it. You could be taken down by an avalanche at any second, but your brain is so slow you don't register it. When you have metabolized all of your physical resources, you are already operating as a kind of automaton.

Once you are on top there are just two things you can do. First, you take a photo as evidence that you have been there—you strike the pose of having made the ascent. Two people go to the top so that each can photograph the other. You choose the right place for a second, and the right angle, then *click*, you're done. You have proof. Second, you wave the flag. Waving the national flag is obligatory. This is not so easy under the prevailing conditions. Down at sea level, it takes a few seconds. In extreme conditions, at more than 8,000 meters (about 26,250 feet), fumbling around, getting it out of your pack, it can take several minutes if you don't have the flag ready. As you hold it up with your team, your movements are mechanical and you are exhausted. You can't think—no passion, no thoughts, other than *will I get back down alive?*

I had also taken up a Vanke flag. It took quite an effort to pull it out, but just as I was managing this, Zhaxi ordered us off the mountain and I didn't have the chance to take a second photo.

The wind came up as we descended. As we were being buffeted by driving snow, the sky turned a leaden gray.

Our guide encouraged me onward. "Our A-team left a canister of oxygen at 8,700 meters [28,543 feet], yesterday, and a tent. We should be all right if we can make it to that location."

As I moved slowly downward, one foot, then another, I felt the back of my skull get hot. It was like being bathed in warm sunlight. *Strange*, I thought. *How can there be sunshine in the midst of this grayness and snow?* I turned to look

---

*The height is judged differently depending on "snow level" or "rock level," and some put it at 8,850 meters (29,035 feet).

around and the peak was already swathed in clouds. The sensation had been an illusion.

Moving on down, I now felt my cheeks warm up, as if they were getting sunburned. A feeling of extreme comfort came over me. My legs went soft and I felt how very wonderful it would be to sit down, right then and there, and think things over for a while. Not just a while—if only I could close my eyes and sit for a long time! Paradise seemed to be calling to me. Could this be heaven? I felt as though I had one foot in the pearly gates already. If I could sit down, close my eyes, I would be inside.

If there is indeed a heaven, people nevertheless seem to want to remain in the bitter dark world down here on earth. They still want to keep up the struggle in the reality they know. As I came to my senses, I warned myself to keep a clear head. The moment I sat down, I knew I would never get up again.

At 8,700 meters (28,543 feet), we did not find the canister of oxygen that the head of our team had mentioned. We kept going. Many empty canisters had been tossed out along our path. Zhaxi picked these up and found one that seemed slightly heavier—it still had some oxygen left. He switched out my oxygen and this lasted for the next 20 minutes. After that, he was able to find another. Our track went alongside a precipice. Our footsteps had to stay within a path that was around two fists wide—on one side was the sheer drop-off and on the other a crevasse.

I crawled this stretch. As one hand gripped the safety line, clipped into my harness with a carabiner, my other hand felt for the crevasse. If I had been able to see this in the early morning, as we ascended, I might well have given up going for the top. There was nothing to do now but force myself onward.

At 8,550 meters (28,050 feet), the ever-vigilant Zhaxi found a canister of oxygen that was still one-third full. What kind of carelessness was that? It still had three hours of air left in it! We estimated it would take two hours at the most to reach the base. At 8,460 meters (27,756 feet), however, when we could just make out the tents of that base below us, we met up with two high-altitude guides who were hauling up canisters of oxygen. I switched out my tank for one that was completely full, although I was not happy about this. The one we had already found had enough left in it, so that adding more oxygen was simply adding to the weight I had to carry.

In 2003, our team included seven amateur mountain climbers. Among them, several were regarded as most likely to make it. Nobody thought much of my ability to climb mountains, but I was one of those who actually did make it to the summit. Big Liu was an example of one who did not. He was 10 years younger than I and in superb physical condition. In 2001, the two of us received a prize in China for national-level mountaineering. He always carried heavier loads than the rest of us in training. and one would have assumed he would reach the top of Everest first. Thinking about it later, I attribute the fact that he did not to two main reasons. First, climbing the world's highest mountain is a daunting challenge, and from the start of our training, in March 2003, this man was consumed by the thrill of it all and highly motivated. He tackled the training enthusiastically and in fact went overboard. By the time we hit the real mountain, his motivation had peaked. I believe this influenced his performance.

Second, our ascent took place at the time of the severe acute respiratory syndrome (SARS) disaster. People were told by doctors to stay at home and stop outdoor activities, so it became a symbol of the will to defy SARS. Inappropriately, we were followed by a television crew and made into national heroes. Big Liu lacked experience in dealing with this kind of publicity. With the cameras rolling, he became the man of the hour. He enjoyed it immensely, and I think it sapped his energy. I had prepared for this by asking the cameramen not to film me. I knew it would make me nervous and take away my focus. This fellow, instead, agreed to interviews from reporters all the time and responded daily to Internet queries from all over China. China Mobile had made a website for this ascent, and even above 6,500 meters (21,325 feet) we could connect to the Internet via satellite.

By the time we reached 8,300 meters (20,669 feet), Big Liu's strength was gone. He himself knew that he would not be able to make the final push the next day. In the end, four out of the seven of us made it to the top. Of the entire group, I was the only one not to be injured—after reaching the top, I descended without incident. This was not because I had better mountain-climbing technique. It was because of my life experience. Throughout the process of climbing the mountain, my mind was open, and I did everything I could to conserve my physical strength.

My original plan had been to climb Everest in 2004. In 2003, I intended to climb the sixth highest of the Seven Peaks. In October 2002, however, CCTV decided to do a program on the fiftieth anniversary of mankind's ascents of this highest peak. They asked me to change my plans and climb Everest. The person making this request was a close friend, and CCTV said it would cover all expenses. As vice chairman of the China Mountaineering Association, I said yes. At the same time, I raised two conditions: first was that I would come back down once I reached 8,300 meters, for I felt that I had had not trained enough to climb to 8,800 meters. Second, I asked that the cameras not be pointed at me—I was not to be photographed. They were disappointed. After all, here was a famous entrepreneur and they were not allowed to photograph him. I held firm, and the director of the program finally respected these terms.

Before climbing a mountain, something I may have considered too hard to accomplish in one lifetime becomes easy. Managing Vanke, for example—when I come back from a mountain, I always have the feeling that I can handle several Vankes. Mountain climbing requires all of one's life experience, as applied to a very complex and yet very simple task: putting one foot in front of the next and getting to the top and back. This complex and yet simple act draws on a person's character, on his very wellsprings of life. For that reason, it is what I call an "extension of life as one has lived it" and also a pure expression of the way a human being intends to continue living his or her life.

The Garbage Dump Incident in Wuhan

In April 2001, Vanke signed an agreement with the city of Wuhan and obtained a piece of land for a development called the Wonderland Garden. This piece of land had a garbage dump nearby. By our agreement, it was to be no closer than 800 meters (2,625 feet) from the development. The agreement also specifically stated that the dump was to be closed and sealed within two to three years of Vanke's purchase of the land.

As construction proceeded on the project, flies and foul smells from the dump affected workers at the site. Nevertheless, the Wuhan offices of Vanke felt that everyone could put up with the problems since the dump was outside the red line and since flies and odors were a summer problem. What's more, the dump had been there a long time. All Wuhan residents knew about it and simply accepted it. "Not a big problem" was the attitude. In any event, the place would soon be shut down after Vanke's tenants moved in. It seemed best to suffer in silence.

In early 2002, Vanke began marketing to tenants. In June, some of these future tenants held a Vanke Forum to discuss the garbage problem. In the summer of 2003, Vanke formally finished the project and handed property over to tenants. The problem was that the city now illegally expanded the dump. What's more, prevailing winds from the southeast in the summer brought a particularly intense smell of burning garbage over Vanke's development. This was affecting people who had already moved in. Vanke staff repeatedly explained to tenants that the municipal government had promised to close the dump down and, after a round of confrontations, things quieted down. Tenants also assumed that there was hope the dump would be moved.

In April 2004, rumors spread among tenants that the government was in fact expanding the dump, not closing it. The city had not been able to find a new place to put the garbage. The government simply had no other option. What's more, the government planned to build a garbage transfer station here, where garbage trucked in from Wuhan would be compressed and then sent to another, more distant place. The lifespan of this transfer station was set at 30 years.

A mass protest erupted.

Just around this time, I agreed to give a lecture at Wuhan University. The tenants found out about this and planned to demonstrate at my lecture. Vanke's Wuhan offices recommended that I evade the problem and not go. I said that would be hard to do.

As I was on my way to the lecture, tenants from the Wonderland Garden blocked my car. I told them that I would be happy to meet with them separately, sometime after the lecture. They said they did not object to the chairman of the board giving a lecture, but as soon as it was finished they would begin a demonstration. What's more, they demanded that we carry on the discussion at the Wonderland Garden.

The general manager of Vanke in Wuhan accompanied me to Wuhan University. As we were approaching the lecture hall where I was to talk, I saw some young men standing nearby—in blue jeans and white shirts. "Security from Vanke?" I asked. The manager replied that he didn't know.

"That's fine if you truly don't know," I said. "But if these young men are members of our security, you have made two mistakes. First, you have told a lie. Second, our tenants want to put pressure on me, not capture me. The moment tenants find out we've sent guards to keep order, a physical conflict may well begin. At the very least, negative news will go out about us."

A few minutes later I noticed that the security guards had disappeared.

I was uneasy throughout the lecture. When students went out to the bathroom and reentered the hall I even thought it was tenants come in to demonstrate. I had been prepared for a confrontation right then and there, but that did not happen, for which I was very glad. I changed my flight and the next day went on my own initiative to the Wonderland Garden to meet with the tenants who were filing the complaint.

We met in the activities center on the second floor of the community building. Forty or fifty tenants were there to represent all the rest. Some were waving white flags; others had headbands made of white strips of cloth. The moment I arrived, they started shouting, "Down with the Vanke Wuhan manager!" This puzzled me, since by all rights it should have been, "Down with Wang Shi, head of Vanke!" Everyone now began shouting and calling out grievances, and I realized that the Vanke branch of the company had no experience whatsoever in dealing with mass complaints. All it had done was to hide from people.

Right about then, Taiwan was holding an election that had been in the news. Looking out over the white headbands, I joked, "Who are you for, the blue party or the green party?" People laughed at that, and the mood began to calm down.

As we began discussions, a pregnant woman, clearly about to give birth, stood up and made a very moving appeal. She said that not only was there a powerful stench of garbage in the air, but that scavengers were burning waste copper wiring to get off the outer peeling, and this was emitting a cancer-causing agent. She asked if we could call a recess and go to the garbage dump to see this for ourselves.

When we got there, the smell of the garbage was overpowering. I put myself in the position of a tenant. The emotions were quite convincing—I determined to get this problem resolved, no matter the cost. Back at the meeting, I told everyone, "Vanke takes full responsibility and will work with you to deal with it. It is going to take time. You will be compensated, and we will fix it. Right now, today, there can't be any conclusion, but if you will trust me, within one month I will come and meet with you all again. We will see if Vanke can get things put right. Is that okay?" The tenants agreed to let Vanke's chairman of the board depart. Before leaving, they all wanted to have their photographs taken with me.

How were we going to resolve this garbage dump problem? There was no easy situation. As I discussed it with our Vanke team, I came up with a last-ditch solution. If we truly could find no other way, we would allow tenants to move out and would compensate them in every way. We estimated that this would take a minimum of RMB 70 million (USD 8.46 million) and a rough maximum of RMB 130 million (about USD 15.72 million). One uncertainty was how much we would have to compensate tenants for the expense they had gone to in finishing their residences. Once our team realized that the chairman of the board was going to go to any lengths to resolve the issue, they were relieved to put down what had been a great psychological burden. They began to try to find solutions together with me. In May, our head of customer relations, Xie Dong, went to Wuhan as representative of headquarters. This was the front-line effort in the process, in which Vanke committed to supplying equipment for tenants at no cost as a temporary fix for the toxic emissions problem—air purifiers, screen windows, and so on. Xie Dong was also to meet with government officials to get a more proactive approach to dealing with the dump and to meet with members of the press in order to launch a more open and transparent process.

Xie Dong lost 5 kilograms (11 pounds) in his first week in Wuhan.

One month later, I traveled again to Wuhan to meet with the mayor. My intent was to get him to move the facility elsewhere. As soon as I sat down, Mayor Li got the jump on me. "Wuhan is a megacity," he pointed out. "Right now, we are having a hard time finding a place to put another crematorium. Do you have any idea how many people die in this city every day? We don't have enough crematoriums, but who wants one in his backyard? Nobody." This was effective in putting my problems in perspective.

How was I going to face the tenants? First, the deputy manager of the Wuhan office of Vanke, a man named Zhang Xu, together with the head of our customer relations center, Duan Shizhong, went to the site to gain firsthand experience.* This particular effort did in fact reveal the glimmers of a possible solution.

This dump had received financial assistance from the World Health Organization. Its initial design had been excellent, with precise rules and regulations on how to carry out operations. The moment a dump truck of garbage was unloaded, the trash was to be covered over immediately with a layer of dirt. Not only would this help cap the smell, but it would also create an anaerobic environment and stop the growth of microbes. What was in fact happening? In order to save on costs, proper procedures were being ignored. Once dump trucks unloaded garbage, nobody covered the trash, which then lay exposed to the open air. As days went by, garbage would begin to rot and attract flies and bacteria, exacerbating the pollution. Because the dump was large and exposed,

---

*The term used refers to a Party practice of having cadres stay at grassroots units to learn how to guide overall Party work.

the next problem was that scavengers came in to go through it for anything of value. As they rifled through trash, they exposed it even more, making the stench worse. The item of highest value was electric wiring. Once they found some, they burned it to get off the protective sheathing. The burning created dioxin, which wafted out to neighboring districts together with the smell of garbage.

One feasible solution: have Vanke take over the dump. We could buy dirt and be responsible for covering over the garbage. At the same time, we would of course have to compensate the scavengers. This was the first ray of light we had seen in some months as a way to solve this problem.

Vanke quickly did some work with the boss of the scavengers. We asked this chief to help us by dealing with the people below him. It turned out this chief had an older brother who insisted on continuing to glean. The two of them had a confrontation, and after that nobody scavenged any more. That particular problem at least was resolved.

Vanke customers did not stop demonstrating just because the toxic-dust problem was settled. "Wang Shi promised us that we would get five air conditioners and five air purifiers each. Also, he was going to meet with us again!"

The company's attorney, Yan Xueming, now drafted a letter. The gist of this said, "As the chairman of the board of a listed company, I am responsible for the interests of tenants, but I also cannot violate the interests of shareholders." What this implied was that now that the toxic-dust problem had been resolved, there was no longer a need for air purifiers. As for the issue of meeting again, naturally I had to meet with them.

It was noon when I arrived at the Tianhe Airport in Wuhan. The meeting was scheduled for 3 p.m., so there was time for lunch. The Vanke company car drove what seemed an interminable length of time to what was billed as a very special restaurant. It turned out to be a small secluded place, hidden from the street, facing an inside courtyard.

Once we were seated, I said, "So Wang Shi cannot appear on the streets in Wuhan? He can't even have lunch in public?"

My colleagues were stunned.

First, Wang Shi has not done anything wrong. Second, Vanke has not done anything that we should be ashamed of. If we run into problems in a project, we have to work together with our customers to resolve them. We don't hide. How did we let things get to this point?

"We'll switch to another place for lunch!" I said.

At 3 p.m., I was there promptly on time to meet with our customers. When it was nearly time to end the meeting, one of my colleagues reminded the audience, "Mr. Wang has another appointment and we had better draw things to a close . . ." I interrupted him. "I came here specifically to meet with everyone, to hear your opinions. I am now pretty clear on what you are thinking. I have appointed Xie Dong as my representative, with full authority to handle this matter. If you have anything to say beyond what has already been discussed, however, anything else you want to put in, please let me know. It is true that I have an appointment this evening, but if you feel you have not had your say, I will stay until you have finished. I can stay on."

The tenants said nothing more.

"Can I go to dinner?"

The next year, the government found a new site for its garbage dump. The dump near the Wonderland Garden was closed. On June 30, the day the second and third stages of the Four Seasons development were handed to new tenants, the dump was completely closed over and sealed. Colleagues from Vanke Wuhan and around 70 tenants planted the Vanke Woods on top of the previous site. People gradually forgot that this place had ever been a dump.

Meanwhile, the Wuhan Dump Incident brought a whole new set of systems and practices to Vanke. Notifications about any unfavorable factors outside the red line are posted. When apartments are being marketed, potential buyers are notified of unfavorable aspects inside the scope of the project, but they are also notified of any unfavorable aspects that are within 1 kilometer (0.62 miles) outside the project. Today, you will see such written notices on any Vanke site, and buyers are also verbally notified of all such information.

The primary driving force behind the growth of a company is the culture instilled in employees. I am firmly convinced that our employees understand that customer satisfaction must be the key standard by which we judge our success. After all, a corporate mistake can mean just a 1 percent difference to the company, but it can mean a 100 percent loss to customers.

CHAPTER FIVE

Great Expectations,
2005–2010

"Overturning, Looking into the Future, and Symbiosis"

Vanke has followed a corporate tradition since 1995: at the start of each year, it settles on a phrase that will represent the motto or theme for that year. In 1995, the motto was "Capital."

This practice was partly a reflection of management problems in the company, so the theme of the year was generally aimed at reversing those problems. We were to focus on this particular aspect throughout the year and make it better.

At the beginning of each year, corporate management and even the entire company would sit down and brainstorm on the appropriate motto for that year. Looking back on them, these phrases express Vanke's unique management style but they also provide a succinct history of the company.

Nineteen ninety-six was the year of quality management; 1997 was the year of the customer. After 1998, themes focused less on shortcomings in the company and more on innovations and improvements. We had years of professional management, team spirit, employee spirit, Internet alliance, customer smiles, boundless life, and so on. The year 2004 was the twentieth anniversary of founding the company, and the motto adopted to celebrate that fact was "Accomplishment, Life, Dreams."

As the industry as a whole moved into 2005, many firms put their energies into opening up new projects. Vanke already had plenty of projects in the pipeline—this was not its biggest problem. We also could see that we were moving into the fast track in terms of high-speed growth. The external environment was undergoing extreme changes. China's policy of raising interest rates was a matter of international concern. Listed companies earning profits was fine, but that did not seem to turn around a bear market. The enormous firm Delong Group had collapsed due to the rupture of its chain of financing. Lenovo purchased the personal computer division of IBM. As Vanke's own industry changed, it began to realize that it should take the initiative in order to break through bottlenecks to growth that might develop in the next three to five years. Two thousand five represented the first year in Vanke's third decade, so it was also the start of the company's third 10-year strategic plan. The question became: what motto could be significant and weighty enough to describe this year?

During discussions about the subject, I tried hard to get people to use at least one concept, which was "Overturning." I felt this motto suited the start of a 10-year strategic effort. It was weighty enough and calculating enough to wake people up. People in the company joked that they themselves could never have come up with such a phrase, turning the company upside down!

The path that Vanke now had to take involved not only turning itself upside down but also turning the industry in a new direction. Vanke had to drive the growth of the industry. In doing so, it had to crane its neck forward—look farther into the future. This phrase, "craning the neck and looking ahead," expressed our hope of being the frontrunner in China's real estate industry.

Any company is inseparable from its natural environment and also its social environment. A company that aspires to overturn and to see out over the future should be one that lives in a symbiotic relationship with its customers, its shareholders, its partners, its industry, and its overall environment. *Symbiotic* is the operative term here.

We therefore chose a three-part motto for this crucial year: "Overturning, Looking Out into the Future, and Symbiosis."

Forming an Alliance with Nandu

One prong of Vanke's three-pronged strategy for quality growth involved its intent to focus on metropolitan clusters. The Yangtze River delta area represents the largest such economic cluster in China. It is also generally regarded as the apex of economic growth in the country. In the future, the Yangtze River delta area will play the leading role in China's economy as Shanghai becomes the financial center of Asia and a major international metropolis. Few people would deny this. No Chinese real estate company that wants to play a leading role can overlook this enormous stage of operations.

In 2004, the prospects for the real estate market in China were booming but doubts were already beginning to be heard. Were Shanghai housing prices and land prices too high? Was a bubble forming? The controversy raged, but nobody can foresee the market. Accustomed to stable and conservative growth, Vanke did not want to neglect this market nor did it want to take too great a risk. It certainly did not want to go into hand-to-hand combat in the market for land. It had to be proactive in positioning itself in the delta, but it also had to prevent risk, and what this meant was overturning its customary thinking about investing in order to obtain land. It should instead cooperate with local firms that were already well endowed with land reserves. At least, this should be one option.

In March 2004, Vanke began a strategic cooperation with a company called Nandu. This was the biggest news to hit the industry that year.

Vanke had already explored the idea of cooperating with China Overseas Property in similar fashion back in 1998, but nothing had come of it—China Overseas Property was not responsive. In 2000, Vanke now again approached an outstanding firm, once it had issued B shares aimed at greater shareholding by China Resources. This was the Nandu Group, regarded as a major force in the east China region. Unfortunately, at that time, the chairman of the board of Nandu, Zhou Qingzhi, did not respond to my proposal.

Four years later, quite a few companies found themselves in a tight financial situation due to the macro adjustments being implemented by the central government. I happened to attend the groundbreaking ceremony for a project that the China Urban Realty Association had invested in, and at this event I was approached by Zhou Qingzhi. "Does that offer you made a while back still hold?," he asked.

This was the best news I had heard in years! "It does!" I replied.

Our two sides quickly came to a strategic cooperative agreement. Shortly after, Vanke began an audit of Nandu, as part of its due diligence. By September of the same year, however, market conditions improved and Nandu became much more equivocal in its discussions with us. The attitude seemed to be: since the market has improved, Nandu could either work with Vanke or not. It didn't have to. The main reason for moving forward would be that Nandu had voluntarily approached Vanke when it was hard up, so it owed us something. Therefore, it would simply carry on with the cooperation.

I was very clear about Vanke's attitude: "If the cooperation really can't work, that is all right—Nandu does not owe Vanke some psychological debt. I believe, however, that Vanke and Nandu could have a very positive effect on each other and achieve a significant growth trajectory. The unfortunate thing is that we missed a good opportunity to have a powerful alliance."

This attitude actually accelerated our cooperation. On March 3, 2005, companies under our respective banners signed an agreement. The signatories were Shanghai Vanke, Pudong Vanke, and Shenzhen Vanke on Vanke's side, and the Shanghai Zhongqiao Construction Company on the side of the Nandu Group. For a total of RMB 1,858,750,000 (USD 224,758,162), the Vanke Group bought the Nandu Group, via its Zhongqiao shareholding in Shanghai, 70 percent of its rights and interests in Jiangsu province and 20 percent of its rights and interests in Zhejiang Province. To that time, this was the largest cooperation among real estate firms since the trend toward consolidating resources in the real estate industry began.

Zhou Qingzhi introduced Nandu's situation to Vanke at the start of our cooperation. After the companies had already begun working together, Vanke's financial people explored Nandu's finances and balance sheet in more detail and found out that the results of their investigation were essentially the same as what Zhou Qingzhi had described. This gave Nandu and Zhou Qingzhi considerable credibility in the eyes of Vanke people.

One outcome of this cooperation was that Vanke increased its project area by close to 2.2 million square meters (7.22 million square feet), at a cost that was far lower than what the company would have had to pay for land on the open market. If, by any chance, the real estate market in the Yangtze River delta area went south, the first to face market risk would be those who had paid high prices to obtain land. Vanke would have greater chances of coming through the high-risk period unscathed. If, on the other hand, the market in the Yangtze River delta area continued to grow at a stable pace, this method of obtaining project resources would still enable a faster return and better cash flow. It would improve the efficiency of using assets. Nandu's standing in the Zhejiang area was one of the best, and it had a strong reputation among consumers. By cooperating with the firm, Vanke was able to enter into the market there at a much lower risk than if it had purchased land and done the development itself.

On January 1, 2006, Vanke purchased 60 percent of the state assets of the Beijing Chaokai Real Estate Company for RMB 389 million (USD 48.26 million). For this sum, it obtained land reserves totaling 547,000 square meters (1.8 million square feet).

In August 2006, for the sum of RMB 1.77 billion (USD 229.4 million), Vanke again was granted 60 percent of the rights and interests that the Nandu Group held in the Nandu Real Estate Company, as well as the rights and interests of the Nandu Group in Shanghai and the rest of the group's real estate interests in Jiangsu.

In March 2007, for the price of RMB 1.005 billion (about USD 130 million), Vanke won the bid for the Fuchun Oriental Package, including seven projects in the east of Shenzhen.

Since 2004, Vanke has been cooperating with a number of foreign investment institutions that have very substantial resources. These include GIC in Singapore, the HI Investment Bank in Germany, and a number of trust funds. Within China, the company has launched numerous cooperative efforts with such entities as China Merchants Real Estate, AVIC Real Estate, COFCO Property, and China Minmetals Corporation.

In 2010, the China Securities Regulatory Commission and the China Land Resources Department closed the door on getting further financing of real estate from the stock market. In fact, given the policy restrictions in recent years, after 2007 Vanke was already financing its growth in other ways. It no longer needed to go to the market for funding. Without this method of funding through issuing shares, where did its funds come from to drive growth? Vanke's method was to cooperate with others in a variety of open ways. The company was very happy to work with others, whether they were state owned, central-government entities, or privately run companies; whether they were shareholding firms or joint ventures; and whether Vanke's participation was one-half, or one-third, or even one-fourth. From the beginning, Vanke had enjoyed a good reputation in both the capital markets and monetary markets, so it had an excellent credit record. It was transparent, standardized, and reliable. Others were quite happy to work with Vanke as well.

In 2006, more than half of Vanke's projects were obtained through various forms of cooperation. By today, more than 70 percent are cooperative ventures.

Making Homes the Way You Make Cars

Does a real estate company in China really need to set up its own R&D facility?

Not only has Vanke been in the forefront of the real estate industry in China but also its R&D Center has made substantial contributions. Despite this, many firms in the industry are reluctant to accept this and follow the same practice.

Instead, the industry still focuses maniacally on location. What's more, from the beginning of real estate development in China, growth has been extensive as opposed to intensive. Instead of putting investment into R&D for better products, the industry has poured its efforts and its money into buying land, essentially eating up land. If products are poorly made, never mind—just hold on and growth in the overall market will eventually make you money.

In its early days, Vanke's strong suit was in marketing and also design. I hoped to upgrade product quality and shift our strength in the direction of technology and the caliber of products, however—that was my intention at the time we started the R&D Center. Vanke should be making products that won customer approval and not just selling tricks.

We therefore set up the Vanke Architecture Research Center in 1999. Its standing within the company was somewhat vague at the outset, and it only had around 20 people in it. It was under the jurisdiction of the Vanke Design Management Center, which implied that its mission was to provide technological support for this part of the company. At the end of 2000, Vanke headquarters set up a Design Engineering Department and consolidated various efforts that had previously been dispersed, including design, engineering, procurement, and technology R&D. The Architecture Research Center then became a second-tier department.

It was moved around in terms of jurisdiction over it, and it was carved up in various ways. Its name changed several times, and staff turnover was high. The reason was simple—nobody could quite figure out what role architectural R&D should play in the overall corporate structure. As a listed company, Vanke had to focus on sales and the bottom line. Architects, meanwhile, could make more money and also realize greater market value by being on the front lines. Prospects were not as clear when they were working in a research center, doing experiments.

For the first few years, frankly speaking, the Architecture Research Center had no systematic focus or direction. Its various projects basically came along as ways to resolve specific problems that might come up in construction or design. It served the purpose of supplementary technical support. One time, listening to a report on what the center was doing, I finally interrupted the presenters and said those things were extraneous to the main role the group should be playing. They were fine for people outside the industry, but they did not address such things as environmental protection, water conservation, walls made of materials that could "breathe," and so on.

The problems lay not in our colleagues at the center, but rather in the fact that I myself was unclear on how to apply R&D to our industry. I decided to take a team of people to other countries to see how they were handling this—to take a study trip to Japan, the United States, and Europe.

I had first gone to Japan in 1986 and been immediately taken by that country's technology, industries, and culture. How did a small island, barely the size of Yunnan Province, become one of the top-seven largest industrialized nations in the world? After participating in the later architectural study trip, I was now deeply impressed by the way Japan had "industrialized" its housing. I gradually came to the conclusion that China should promote a similar kind of manufacturing process in how it built housing.

Put simply, industrializing the process of building housing means making housing in the same way you make cars.

In Japan, this process can be traced back to the late 1960s. Home appliances and automobiles were already fairly mature industries in Japan at that time, in terms of their manufacturing processes. Economic growth was moving onto a fast track, and demand for housing was growing rapidly. At the time, two- and three-story housing constituted between 60 and 70 percent of all housing in the country. Turning housing technology into an industrial process was something that was feasible, and Japanese companies quickly recognized the limitless commercial possibilities. A number of companies began to invest in the manufacture of the various components that go into housing. As housing began to get taller in Japan's major cities, these companies quickly went into the production of prefabricated high-rise buildings. The development of technologies for such production ensured that manufactured housing would be a sustainable industry.

However, on a global basis, developers have not been the ones to take the initiative in promoting this kind of industrialized housing, nor have they funded it with investment in R&D. In Japan, the process was jointly pushed forward by construction companies and component suppliers. In Singapore and Hong Kong, it was led by the government and then actually implemented by construction companies; the experiences in Europe and the United States have been much the same. In China, real estate developers are not very consolidated as an industry—no single company is sufficiently large enough to be able to push forward the prefab factory manufacture of housing.

When I raised the idea of having Vanke industrialize its housing, people within the company were not enthusiastic. Even Fu Zhiqiang, who had organized several of the study trips to Japan, was not inclined to support this. He met me at the airport one time when I was returning from a business trip to Japan, and I told him of my ideas on the ride home. He just laughed. "Your idea makes it sound easy," he said, "but industrialized housing is not so simple. How can one single company try to do it all?" Logically, it should be cheaper to make high-rise housing in a manufactured process as real estate markets continue to grow at a fast pace. Given the extreme scarcity of available land in China's cities, industrializing is the way to go. Why is it, then, that China's construction companies and suppliers seem to have no interest in this at all? The reason is that they can make more money on other things, and the profits come more easily as well. Such things include public infrastructure projects, bridges, and highways, which are larger and simpler than housing.

Secondly, China's labor situation is different from that in other countries. After World War II, labor costs began to rise in western countries as well as Japan and it became cheaper and more cost effective to mechanize industrial processes. The situation in China was exactly the opposite. Labor was cheap and it didn't pay to replace it with machines. For a long time, China had such an abundance of human labor that everyone thought it would go on forever. The government focused instead on how to find jobs for all these people, on how enterprises could provide employment by using more people and fewer machines. Making processes more industrial implied reducing the demand for labor, and government was highly averse to this idea.

Given that construction companies were uninterested, developers had even less motivation to push in this direction. Gross margins were already high in the real estate industry, and the current model was making plenty of money.

What I was beginning to realize, however, was that China's traditional methods of construction could not ensure quantity and high-quality production at the same time. Meanwhile, the individual consumer market was developing to a point where there was a substantial need for higher-quality housing. By the end of 2013, Vanke was already engaged in housing projects in 15 cities around China. Trying to control workmanlike quality was a dilemma if we were going to continue to do on-site building. Defects in walls, windows, and exteriors were not necessarily a structural problem, but they bothered both customers and developers. If we were going to resolve these things in a systematic way, we had to standardize manufacturing processes. It was the only option.

The Founding Year of Vanke as a Corporate Citizen

The "under-the-table" dealings of various companies in China began to be exposed in the media in 2002, including such things as fake accounts. This brought on a credibility crisis among the business community as a whole. Because of this, CCTV and PricewaterhouseCoopers (PwC) conducted a joint survey to find out which companies people felt were in fact trustworthy. Among 1,000 listed companies in China, people were asked to select 10 that they felt were worthy of respect. The results were interesting. Of the 10, three were far behind the other seven. Among the top seven, Vanke was ranked third. CCTV then invited representatives of these seven companies to appear on a program. It asked its guests to write out the reasons they felt their company was worthy of respect. Most people wrote such things as honesty, credibility, and trustworthiness. I wrote the words *social responsibility*.

"You don't think trustworthiness is important?" Our host asked in surprise.

Of course it is. But as I see it, that is a minimum requirement. As a listed company, honesty and trustworthiness is essential—if you can't even get that far, you had better do something else. If a company hopes to come up to any kind of standards, and be considered worthy of respect, it has to take on social responsibility. If it is not socially responsible, it may be profitable over the short term, but over the long term it can do serious damage to society.

At the end of 2004, I was asked to go to Beijing to receive an award for being the Most Admirable Corporate Citizen. This idea of a corporate citizen was new to me, but I knew that Vanke's ability to get this award was inseparable from its corporate culture, its corporate governance, and its sense of ethics and values.

The company went through extremely hard times as it grew. During a tough period when it transitioned away from diversification and toward a focus on real estate, salaries were low and there were few benefits. How did the company maintain its hold on energetic young people, make them willing to keep fighting with us? I believe it was because we respected the individual. We gave people an equal opportunity to display their own capabilities and express their own opinions. We gave each employee space to operate freely.

In the past, Vanke did almost any business that would make money—it was highly *profit* oriented. After moving into housing development, we were in a seller's market, so we shifted into a mode of being *product* oriented. This meant we had to respect our own profession and our own choices, but it was not really a stance that respected the customer. Several years ago, we promoted the concept of providing housing that was *customer* oriented. We engaged in a finer segmentation of the market, and from this process we derived the concept of respecting the customer.

At the same time, we began to evaluate and improve our relationships with our partners, specifically our suppliers. Without doubt, we were in a buyers' market with respect to procurement of materials. Since there was an oversupply, we could be aggressive in forcing down prices, and we could indeed be brutal. We began to recognize, however, that common prosperity of the entire chain of the business, upstream as well as downstream, was beneficial to long-term growth in the future. Indeed, it was essential. It required respect for our partners.

As for public welfare activities, I am not a major participant, although I contribute a substantial portion of my personal income to public endeavors. I am paid to be in advertisements, for instance—I do not do them for free. The price is set at whatever the market price will bear, but 100 percent of the proceeds then goes to public welfare. In deciding how much of my income to contribute, I simply do as much as I can. A friend of mine has a slightly different approach. As an entrepreneur, he believes that his contributions to society come from creating a number of millionaires among his employees. Plus he willingly pays his taxes. Between these things, he feels he has contributed as much as he can to society.

In the great pulse of reform and opening up in China, Vanke and I adhered to the idea that we must stay pure and noble in how we conduct ourselves. We do not take or receive bribes, we do our own business without relying on connections, and we keep a clear conscience. Once we were chosen as a highly respectable corporate citizen, however, we began to be more aware of what being a corporate citizen really means. We began to reevaluate ourselves and to change. Vanke has grown to be quite a substantial company. We now realize that its social influence is not as small as it once was; as its capabilities have grown, so have its responsibilities. Merely staying pure and noble on our own account is no longer enough. We now need to change our former attitude and be more proactive in how we bear social responsibility.

Recognizing this represented a turning point for me. It meant going from just happening to do what we do to actively becoming an agent for change.

In October 2005, Vanke began participating in a government-sponsored program to resolve the housing problems of low- and middle-income people on a nationwide basis. This effort was supported by the Ministry of Construction. Our participation indicated that Vanke was not just taking the direct interests of shareholders, employees, and customers into consideration but was also considering the indirect interests of others. The company felt it was no longer possible to ignore issues of public security and social harmony in particular. Given the disparity between rich and poor, and the reality that "common people" are unable to buy housing, no housing developer can say in all good conscience that these things lie outside its sphere of concern.

Inside the company, this program was dubbed the "conch activity," which implied two different things. First, small conch shells are often used by hermit crabs as a dwelling, and what we were concerned with was dwellings. Second, a conch shell is sometimes used as a kind of horn, to call others. We wanted to call attention to the issues.

During our first conch activity, we received 263 proposals for solutions to low- and middle-income community housing in cities. We ultimately selected 13 of the most outstanding of these proposals and presented them to Ministry of Construction for execution by the Housing and Real Estate Department.

The public response to this activity was highly positive—indeed, I was astonished. We had simply meant to express a certain attitude on our part, but the public responded with overwhelming gratitude. We invested RMB 1 million (USD 123,700) in the conch activity—half of which went as prizes to the outstanding proposals and the other half to the costs of administering the project over 10 months. In evaluating the benefits of public acclaim for this effort, one should remember that placing an outdoor ad in Shenzhen for one year costs RMB 3 million (about USD 375,000).

If real estate developers can provide the public with housing that is reasonably priced and guaranteed at certain levels of quality and security, they should be applauded. That is already a contribution. I once held Vanke to this ideal as well—build excellent buildings and that should be enough. Now it is not enough. With housing prices spiraling upward and many people unable to come up with funds to buy a home, Vanke must face this problem head on. It must find better solutions. Yes, the issue of urban housing for low- and middle-income people is a problem for the government, but it is also an issue for developers. They must recognize that they bear a responsibility as well. They must do all they can to help resolve this pressing issue.

After the first conch shell project, I traveled to the remote mountain area of Fujian Province with some Vanke architects to study the traditional circular housing there. A traditional Hakka housing community is preserved there in its entirety.

A great number of immigrants flowed into Guangdong Province after the start of reform and opening up.* They came from elsewhere in China, but the earliest immigrants into Guangdong were the Hakka people, who have a unique form of communal housing. After studying their dwellings, we came up with a form of low-income housing that preserves the outer form of the Hakka-style round house but that also accommodates the space needs of cities. Depending on the location, such communal housing can be built in semicircles or quarter circles. Surrounding walls are made of earth in the originals, but modern construction methods can turn this into a double-layered wall with space in between for airflow as well as aesthetic appeal. Lower levels can become open-style sub-ground-level plazas or gathering places.

On November 27, 2006, we broke ground for the first such pilot project. It was a program specifically aimed at low- and middle-income groups and was given the name Vanhuilou. People moved into Vanhuilou in May 2008, and it was then also listed among the Guangdong provincial Construction Department projects as a pilot project for low-income rental housing.

Vanhuilou has 283 regular apartments as well as dormitories for group accommodation. Individual apartments are around 35 square meters (115 square feet) in size. The public housing is aimed at young people, those who get in contact through the Internet and who do not arrive in cars to sign their contracts. The target population is people who are just starting out in life. People mostly sign rental agreements for six months, and they are allowed to sign on for no more than one year. They cannot sublease to others, but they can colease with others. Each dormitory room cannot hold more than six people. The Vanhuilou contracts specify that people can play cards but they cannot play mah jong. They can only have pets if neighbors do not object. Only the most basic facilities are provided by the management company. Sweeping up and general care of the public space and surrounding areas must be done by residents themselves. Garbage must be divided into categories for recycling. Without doing any special promotion, Vanke has found that occupancy at this pilot project is generally 90 percent and at certain times reaches 100 percent.

Recently, I have begun to participate more in non-governmental organizations (NGOs) run by our industry and by entrepreneurs. In 2004, I joined the

---

*Reform and opening up started roughly in 1978, then picked up speed in the mid-1980s. Deng Xiaoping's 1992 trip to the south was decisive in confirming central-government support for the process.

group called SEE,* which is aimed at stopping desertification, and I joined an association composed of three different kinds of entrepreneurs: mainlanders, returned overseas students, and overseas Chinese. A tremendous controversy broke out in the course of writing the bylaws of this organization, and I became aware that China is highly unfamiliar with the organizational aspects of NGOs. Not only do we members of NGOs need to consider how funds are donated, but we need to understand how to set up projects and manage them properly. First, we need to understand how best to make use of philanthropic funds, and then we need to use such funds effectively. As I was involved in this effort, I became aware that it is much harder to spend money than it is to make it. In public welfare endeavors, you not only need to have your heart in the right place and pull out your wallet, you also need to put in lot of time and effort. You can get loaded down with details—coordination, use of funds, and consulting with everyone.

By now, the Alashan† SEE‡ is the largest NGO in the world focused on controlling desertification. It looks at botanical solutions in arid zones, in terms of both cultivating species and planting plants, and it supports local pastoral livelihoods by changing destructive modes of animal husbandry to more sustainable modes. It seeks to address the natural and social factors that lie at the root of sandstorms and desertification. At the same time, SEE seeks to find rational rules of procedure that can mediate among groups of people with different interests. In doing so, it seeks to use a form of democratic self-governance that utilizes civil organizations in Chinese society.

I arrived in Shenzhen in 1983. Only in 2005 did I begin to think I had been successful and was even fairly "high-minded." In 2006, Vanke announced its own corporate citizenship plan, and 2006 then became the founding year of Vanke as a corporate citizen. The theme for that year was "Cutting-Edge Reform and Corporate Citizen."

Following on that, the theme for 2007 went further in expressing Vanke's hopes and plans for being a corporate citizen. The company published a green paper detailing Vanke's social responsibilities. It summed up Vanke's efforts in the past; more importantly, it outlined a strategic blueprint for action in the future. Instead of focusing on its own moral rectitude, the company now intended to stride out along a broader path. From random projects, it intended

---

* Society of Entrepreneurs & Ecology. This is described in more detail in the text that follows.

† Or Alxa. This area, located in Inner Mongolia, is called a seedbed of sandstorms. Sandstorms have been endangering Beijing in recent years, but have also had an environmental impact on southeastern coastal areas as well as parts of Japan and Korea.

‡ This was the first nongovernmental public welfare organization in China, composed of 80 entrepreneurs who declared their social responsibility. They committed to a decade-long endeavor to slow down sandstorms and create a more harmonious relationship between humans and nature, humans and society, and humans and humans. Around 100 major private entrepreneurs came together to launch this initiative. It represented the starting line for displaying a new awareness of social responsibility among Chinese businesspeople.

to move toward more systematic practices and to monitor and evaluate how it benefits the interests of the public and relevant interest groups.

Vanke therefore now seeks to justify the title that the press gave it some years ago: corporate citizen. The company made a conscious decision to use this crowning accolade not just as a stage prop during coronation ceremonies, but as a habitual way of thinking. The idea of being a corporate citizen now has to be in the very marrow of Vanke's bones, as well as in my own.

Turning Point

At first, the idea of a turning point was just a reasoned judgment of a listed company about conditions in the real estate market. From that innocent start, however, it became a hot topic of discussion in the media. Rumors raced through every alley in China, and the idea of a turning point eventually stirred up a major national controversy.

It began in the second half of 2006. At that point, housing prices were beginning to rise steeply. You could almost see the tidal wave moving from Shenzhen northward, passing over the Pearl River delta area and then the Yangtze River delta, on up to the Bohai Gulf.

In 2004, Vanke's sales revenue came to RMB 9.16 billion (USD 1.11 billion). The number in 2005 rose by 52 percent over 2004. Sales rose again by 52 percent in 2006, and in 2007 they exploded upward by 146 percent to reach RMB 52.36 billion (USD 7.17 billion). This was 5.7 times the sales volume of just three years earlier. The unbelievable figures were already beyond what anyone could have predicted or imagined. Three years earlier, no Vanke employee would have thought that sales would break through RMB 50 billion (USD 6.85 billion) in 2007.

China's GDP had been growing by over 9 percent per year on average for a decade, while the floor space sold in the housing market was increasing by an average of 20 percent per year, and the sales volume by an average of 27 percent per year. Meanwhile, land sold at auctions hit new records every day. Housing was going up in price, but land was going up even more. It was as though the price of flour was even more than the price of bread!

Optimism oozed from between the lines in Vanke's 2006 annual report, as the year's accomplishments were described in glowing terms: "This has been an epoch-making year, not only for Vanke, and not only for the Chinese housing market, but for the housing industry worldwide. . . . Whether we recognize it or not, we are in the midst of an extraordinary era. We may already have witnessed the passing of miracles, but we are just beginning to write a new chapter in history."

This was typical of how real estate people felt in those years. The entire market was crazy. and Vanke as well as everyone else was swept up in the madness. In July 2007, Vanke participated in an auction for a piece of land in Guangdong. The bidding started at RMB 640 million (USD 82.55 million). It went up by an average of RMB 100 million (USD 13,205,000) every single minute after that. Vanke ultimately made the winning bid of RMB 2.68 billion (USD 345.67 million), and thereafter it became known as the Land King of Guangdong.

In September 2007, after 239 rounds of fierce bidding, Vanke again cast the winning bid for a piece of land, this time in Fuzhou. The price was RMB 2.72 billion (USD 362.18 million), and Vanke became known as the Land King of Fuzhou. The price per 1 square meter (3.28 square feet) of buildable space was RMB 7,096 (USD 944.87). This was nearly RMB 100 (USD 13.32) over the previous record per square meter in the neighboring area. What's more, given Vanke's reputation now as Land King, anyone selling buildings in Fuzhou refused to entertain any offers prior to this bidding, since they knew the price would go up. They prepared to raise the ante after the auction.

One has to remember that just four years earlier Vanke had bid just RMB 970 million (USD 117.29 million) for a piece of land in Shenzhen—and that itself had caused a furor. Looking back on it, one had a sense of suspended disbelief. We had entered a different universe.

From the outset, I already had a feeling of unease. By the end of 2007, prices had risen so fast that I felt I was experiencing a kind of heart attack. On November 10, 2007, Vanke held its regular meeting at Zhuhai. As usual, winter there was sunny and lovely, people enjoyed the hot springs, and laughter filled the air. The talk among senior management was all about how Vanke was king of this and king of that, and everyone was full of complacent good humor. Such an atmosphere and such behavior were common at the time.

There were those who felt concerned. Liu Rongxian, general manager at the time of the strategy and investment management department, was the first to sound the alarm with a market report. He noted that the market had already begun to change. Indications from the "golden September" in most cities were still good, but reports from the "silver October" was less promising. Clear signals of a market decline had already become apparent in such cities as Shenzhen, Shanghai, Beijing, Chengdu, and Wuhan. The volume of transactions was declining, in fact by 20 to 30 percent. His conclusion: the overall situation pointed unavoidably to a market correction.

The facts were there before our eyes. A change in the market was not just a guess but a reality. This report increased my sense of unease.

Faced with this market change, Vanke senior management now deliberately and firmly adjusted the company's plan for ongoing construction. We cut the plans for new construction by nearly 20 percent. Not long after that, based on the lower adjustment, management again reduced plans by another 23 percent. Plans now called for new construction of 5.23 million square meters (17.16 million square feet), which was a reduction of 38 percent from the original figure.

At the same time, management decided to go with the market trend and reduce prices. On December 9, sales began of a Vanke project in Guangzhou called the Golden Kangyuan—prices per square meter were set between RMB 3,000 (USD 410.75) and 4,000 (USD 547.65) lower than prices in surrounding buildings. Senior management had done a thorough study of market conditions and come to a consensus that the company should change its market strategy.

On December 13, 2007, I participated in a press conference at the International Center at Tsinghua University. The subject related to a comparison between housing solutions in China and in England with respect to low-income earners. A reporter asked me, "Since October, the volume of housing sales in the Pearl River delta area has been contracting to varying degrees. . . . Do you think the market has reached a turning point?" I said, "I concur with your term *turning point.*"

The moment I said this, the place erupted.

Nevertheless, during the early period of this "turning point," the mainstream of opinion within the industry felt that I was talking nonsense.

For example, Developer A told the media that a "cooling off" could not be described as a turning point. Those who were dreaming of a major falloff in the market were going to miss out on opportunities. Developer B said, "There are still great discrepancies between the level to which China's cities are developed and people's incomes—it is simply inaccurate to say we have any kind of turning point." Developer C said, "It clearly is an exaggeration to say that the real estate market is near collapse." Economist A said, "This so-called turning point of Wang Shi is mistaken. That's just his personal view." Real Estate Expert A then put in: "From the level of economics and of overall demand, at present we do not see any indication of overall decline in the real estate market." Meanwhile, the report put out by the Chinese Academy of Sciences, called "Report on the Growth of China's Real Estate Market," had stated that "the chances of a turning point in China's real estate market in 2008 are slim."

Gradually, voices began to say that I might have made a correct call. Nevertheless, people now also surmised that I had various personal motivations for making that turning-point judgment. Some said that my idea of a turning point was a plot—Vanke wanted to let steam out of the industry and then take the opportunity to merge with and acquire others. I was therefore a "traitor" to the industry. Others within the industry said, "No turning point is in sight—Vanke is just cleaning up its own portfolio by lowering prices. Anyway, Vanke's market penetration is just 2 percent, so it has limited influence on housing prices." I answered these things head on by saying, "Vanke is indeed making preparations for a colder spell, but we have been telling the industry to recognize this coming winter for some time now. Nobody takes us seriously." In March–April 2008, the talk about a plot by Vanke was particularly shrill.

The negative publicity and doubts in the industry put a great deal of pressure on us—they made that a hard period for me and for Vanke in general.

As an example, a young woman from Changsha asked me for advice on buying an apartment. I asked if she was getting married, and she said no, that she was just worried prices would go up and she would not be able to afford one in three or four years. I told her, "If you cannot buy an apartment in three or four years, there is something wrong with the market." By this, I meant that it was not possible for the price of housing to stay far above purchasing power for any length of time.

The next day, newspapers reported: "Wang Shi says we are at a turning point and we should buy apartments after three or four years."

Another time, I was being interviewed and the host asked me, as a personal matter, whether or not he should buy an apartment. I replied, "I won't comment on that." He then said, "Everyone, please turn off your cameras and any recording devices." Seeing he was sincere, I asked his situation, and he said he had come back from several years of working overseas and he had adequate income. I then asked, "Are you going to work for a long time at this current job?" He said, probably not. I told him not to be in such a hurry to buy in Beijing, since he might well have to go to Shanghai for his next job. Before one's long-term prospects are settled, why rush? I pointed to myself as an example—I did not buy an apartment until I was 40. The next day the news reported: "Wang Shi recommends not buying an apartment until after you are 40. "

I almost lost my temper over the issue of a turning point with the well-known television host Chai Jing. She repeatedly asked me on air what I thought about the issue. When I answered her conscientiously, she simply asked again and kept it up several times. I began to think that she was like a police officer interrogating a thief—she clearly did not believe me. Fortunately, prior to this interview some friends had warned me that she used this technique until the person she was interviewing lost control. I held myself in.

Later I found out that she had interviewed Ren Zhiqiang and Pan Shiyi in the same manner. She then took the footage and edited it so as to look as though all of us were sitting together, talking to one another. After I answered, Mr. Ren immediately asked, "How can there be a turning point?" as though he were debating me. In fact, the scenes were shot at different times in different places. Pan Shiyi was best—he simply said, "I'm going to look for a glass of water!"

During this period, I simply stopped saying anything at all once I learned that whatever I might say would be used against me.

It was natural that our industry should have different ideas on whether or not the market had reached a turning point. Since 2004, the central government put into effect a variety of macroeconomic measures to dampen down growth, but housing prices continued to rise after each one. People then took this as an indication that prices would continue to rise—they had learned from their previous experience. The results of government intervention were the opposite of what the results intended. What's more, the industry had become quite happily accustomed to a bull market.

Because of this, everyone was watching to see which side would win out during this current round of economic measures. Who carried the greater weight, government commands or the force of the market? It was easy to see why the industry could not understand why Vanke would lower prices. Either Wang Shi was trying to shuck off problems on the rest of us by being first or he was intentionally trying to make the market fall. In Shenzhen, some real estate bosses came to me to ask my real opinion, and I spent 40 minutes telling them my thoughts on the matter. I analyzed what was obvious, there before our eyes, and I encouraged them not to deceive themselves. I told them how Vanke itself was intending to deal with a market decline. At the end, one of these bosses said, "Mr. Wang, could you please say in a public forum that the market is going to continue to go up?"

Had he heard nothing that I just said?

He went on, "Last year, I sold 40 apartments in a day. Now, I can't sell one apartment in 40 days." This was quite candid. The other bosses seemed to concur with this man's understanding, however: the reason the market had cooled off was that Wang Shi said we had reached a turning point. If Wang Shi would just put in a word, the market would turn around and get better!

How can the laws of the market be subject to manipulation by Vanke?

In addition to pressure from people in the industry, we got even more pressure from local governments. The response of provincial governments to central-government mandates was subtle—naturally, they could not refuse to respond, but at the same time they did not want to see housing prices fall. The interests of local governments are intimately related to real estate prices.

In May 2008, a certain city held a conference for developers and did not invite Vanke. The gist of this meeting could be described in a few short words: we do not allow prices to fall, and we distance ourselves from Vanke.

I was not unhappy about the first part of this dictate. Under the cover of the main forces, Vanke could get out more smoothly. The second part, however, alarmed me. The real estate business involves land, regulations, building safety codes, and so on, and therefore is closely tied to the various departments in local governments. If local governments isolate you, you have no chance of doing business.

I could understand the suspicions and jealousies of others in the business, and I could understand the unhappiness of local governments when it came to falling prices, but this part about isolating Vanke was extremely troubling.

In Hangzhou, some purchasers who had already bought Vanke apartments were distressed at the falling prices. They charged into the Vanke sales office and not only tore the place up but detained and to an extent did harm to Vanke workers. Similar behavior was disrupting normal operations in other places—the government should have come forward to intervene and protect order. Instead, police officers arrived but then simply stood aside. The market was already going down. If rule of law went down too, Vanke would be facing a very real problem of survival.

Around this time, the government dispatched investigation teams to Vanke's operations in a number of key cities, ostensibly to check out Vanke's accounts and taxes. Vanke was already operating in more than 30 cities. How far was this kind of malicious intent going to go? I wasn't sure.

In September, as planned, I climbed the mountain in Tibet called Shisha-pangma. The controversy about the turning point went on without me as Vanke continued to be besieged by doubts and pressures. I had never gone into the mountains with such a weight of concern on my mind. I had no idea how far these actions would go, these curses, calling Vanke a "traitor" to the industry, deciding to isolate the company, and accusing it of plotting to acquire smaller developers. Meanwhile, China's real estate industry has long relied on what is called Golden Week for a spike in sales, which occurs around the time of National Day in October. By October 6, Golden Week was over when I came down the mountain and returned via Lhasa. In Lhasa, as soon as I went online I discovered what had happened. All of the major websites had the same news about the real estate market: developers had collectively "taken a dive." The market had contracted to an enormous degree. During the national holiday period, all developers lowered prices nationwide without getting any positive response from buyers.

The lack of any response meant there was no demand. It also meant that Vanke had made a rational decision in lowering prices—it had recognized market trends and taken the appropriate action.

By now, the global financial crisis was underway as well, further depressing housing prices in China. China's major developers saw their market valuations decline precipitously in the capital markets. Vanke's shares dropped by 78 percent between November 2007 and September 2008. In the same period, Poly shares dropped by 72 percent, Country Garden dropped by 82 percent, and China Overseas Property dropped by 56 percent.

On October 22, China's Ministry of Finance announced measures to boost the industry. These new policies of the Ministry of Finance and Central Bank had only a limited effect for the time being, but they served to indicate that the central government itself had recognized the arrival of "winter" and taken policy action to deal with this turning point.

A turning point had indeed appeared after the long period of controversy. Overall, the media now pivoted to a confirmation that Vanke had been correct in its initial views and the actions it took. *China Economic Journal* wrote that "Facts have yet again proved Vanke right. Vanke saw the crisis first while others in the industry were still immersed in savoring the crazy times."

Back in Shenzhen, I found that I was suddenly an oracle. This came after nearly a year of opprobrium, of seeing "the whites" of other people's eyes. The dust was settling on the turning-point controversy, but more importantly, Vanke had survived. It had come through.

The various crises it now had to face were not yet over, however.

Back in September, I had received a phone call from Yu Liang when I was still on the mountain. He told me that an article had appeared on the Internet several days after Vanke lowered its prices in Shanghai. This purported to be coming from senior management in Vanke, and it was given the title "Notes from a Vanke Meeting at Pine Mountain Lake." The article revealed that Vanke planned a campaign to undermine the land reserves that other real estate developers had been hoarding. It stated that local governments around China would be forced to start selling land at cheaper prices within half a year, given budgetary pressures. With only a few potential buyers in the market, Vanke planned to depress prices as much as possible and then buy hard and fast and quickly build very cheap housing. Real estate developers who were unwilling to lower prices would be left sitting on expensive hoardings.

This article further enflamed the negative feelings that other developers had toward Vanke. It put Vanke on the spot, and it put Vanke employees in a tough position since disparaging others in the industry was not in line with our corporate culture. Headquarters immediately held an emergency meeting to evaluate the truth of the claim. There had in fact been no such meeting at the Pine Mountain Lake. No Vanke employee had issued such a document. The company then held a press conference to refute the rumor, while at the same time making every effort to track down its source.

When Yu Liang called me, I told him that this rumor not only threatened Vanke's reputation but had the potential to disrupt society overall. I said that we had to report the case to the Public Security Bureau as soon as possible.

Rumors spread quickly on the Internet. Most major websites were soon carrying the news. Despite the company's formal denial, people were inclined to believe it. Their reasoning? Some said that the tone of the wording was very like Wang Shi, while others said it was very like Yu Liang. In fact, despite being younger, Yu Liang is cautious and guarded, while "old" Wang Shi has always been overly candid.

Colleagues inside the company quickly traced the path of the message. The person had planned things very carefully: after listing the notice on website A, he transmitted it to B and deleted it from A, then went from B to C, and so on. Not only did these manipulations serve to amplify the message but they made it hard to find the original source.

Nevertheless, our own internal analysis showed that the source pointed to a certain website in Shenzhen, and this was later corroborated by the Public Security Bureau. Several days later, feedback came from the police: they knew who had originally put up the article, but the person had fled shortly after Vanke reported the case. He expressed willingness to apologize to Vanke via police authorities. The police meanwhile asked Vanke to agree to settle the case.

This one rumor was followed by many others. As the economic situation deteriorated and the real estate market changed, Vanke faced numerous rumors about the turning-point issue and the lowering of real estate prices. In June, a rumor was put out that Vanke's chain of financing had been broken and the company was facing liquidity problems. In early August 2008, a rumor went out that Vanke had been denied the request for RMB 3 billion (USD 439.24 million) from the Minsheng Bank. All of these rumors soon spread to China's major websites.

In mid-October, a notice went up on the Internet that Vanke was facing bankruptcy. Its liabilities totaled RMB 11 billion (about USD 1.61 billion). Its bank accounts were being sealed in various parts of the country. Assets were being sold at low prices. This notice went so far as to say that Vanke would be having a press conference on October 26 to announce its bankruptcy proceedings.

This particular notice was quite explicit and was transferred 46 times from one site to another on the day it appeared. Since it seemed particularly shrill, it was actually less credible than others, and it also spread more slowly than the rumor about the Pine Mountain Lake meeting. Nevertheless, the international financial crisis was erupting at the time, taking the stock market down, as well as other economic indicators, and because of this situation, the notice came to the attention of the central government.

On October 23, the Ministry of Construction advised Vanke that the company was under investigation. The ministry dispatched five investigating teams to Vanke's branches to look into Vanke's operations and finances. The results of the investigation proved that Vanke's operations were stable and that its finances were sound. The rumor was shown to be a total fabrication.

On November 4, we learned that the person suspected of spreading the rumor about Vanke's bankruptcy had been apprehended by Public Security personnel and was being held for questioning.

A Horizontal Skyscraper

We arrived at the construction site of the Vanke Center as a sudden May rain was just ending. The project manager for the facility, Zhang Xuefeng, started talking about the engineering features of the structure, particularly the cable struts: "They are the largest within China, with load-bearing strength equivalent to those holding the Stonecutters Bridge in Hong Kong."

"How much of a load?"

"Three thousand three hundred and ninety-nine tons."

White hard hats on, we climbed to the top level of construction to look out over the surrounding countryside and the view of the ocean near Dameisha.

The building was to handle a variety of functions, including an office building for Shenzhen Vanke, the Vanke University, a recreation center, a library, a museum, a restaurant, and an international conference center. Not only did it have to encompass all that, but it had to do so in a highly unusual shape. Being near the ocean and built on reclaimed land, it was restricted by various municipal regulations and had to take multiple environmental factors into consideration. The architect was the renowned Steven Holl, always given an honorific by our Vanke colleagues: Master Holl. To deal with these issues, he found a simple and creative solution: instead of having it go up, make it go sideways. Make it in a long line and divide it into segments, extend it out like a branch on the ground. Allow each function to coexist within the building as natural and unrestricted components of the whole. Some people thought it was like an AK-47 assault rifle, while others described it as a dinosaur, and still others thought it was like a reclining person with his head propped up.

Most often, it is described as a horizontal skyscraper. It measures 380 meters (about 1,250 feet) from its easternmost section to the end of the western section, which is as long as the Empire State Building is tall.

If one simply put this long building on the ground, however, it would be like a great wall blocking the winds coming off the ocean. What's more, in the summertime it would become unbearably hot. It also would use a tremendous amount of space, and its footprint would replace greenery. How to handle the matter? Master Holl had the concept of not using any ground space at all, instead, elevating the structure and letting the ocean breezes flow right through it. The ground area would then become a park, open to the public. The building would enable a view of the undulating landscape.

The question was how to hold the building up. Vanke's Architecture Research Center at 63 Meilin Road had been built with a structural framework that allowed a span of some 20 meters (66 feet)—that was approaching the maximum that could be achieved. The Vanke Center, however, would require spans of nearly 60 meters (197 feet). Master Holl's solution: use suspension cables to tie the whole thing together. Make an office building that was like a bridge. As the head of the Design Department, Hu Jingsong, explained it, "The design used a combined system of cable struts that went crosswise as well as prestressed cast steel structures that held things up. This saved on space as well as materials, and allowed for a building that is low energy, allows for views from inside and outside, and is adapted for green specifications."

What kind of design, specifically?

"First, with spans of over 50 meters [165 feet], the building could be suspended in the air to a height of 25 meters [82 feet]. This allowed the first floor to use as small a footprint on the ground as possible—the only contact points are the entry hall and the elevators. Second, by using a suspension-cable structure, we estimate we saved around RMB 60 million [USD 8.80 million] on the cost of steel alone. Third, the weight of the building is much lighter, given the dimensions of structural components, yet the space that the building encompasses is much larger."

"Can you give me a figure for how much less the structural components weigh?," I asked.

"The usual building structure has steel girders that are 900 × 1200. The diameter of the suspension cables is 550 millimeters (21.7 inches) for some and 650 millimeters (25.6 inches) for others."

As we climbed back down the temporary staircase to the first floor, I asked, "Are you absolutely sure we will get LEED platinum* certification?"

"The design specifications are LEED platinum-level specs, which is the top rating," he replied. "From how things are going, I don't think there will be any problem."

---

*Leadership in Energy and Environmental Design (LEED) is one of the most popular green building certification programs used worldwide. "Platinum" is the highest LEED rating.

"Well, that's a relief!," I exclaimed.

Vanke's staff all felt that the highest green standards should apply to this Vanke Center. It should represent the apex of environmental protection. The building is sheathed in metallic louvers that are fine-tuned to the orientation of the sun. The designer also took into consideration the proximity to the ocean. A second layer of perforated aluminum louvers is suspended from the glass curtain wall to create a double-skinned façade—not only does this create convection currents for air, but it makes the building look like leaves with light showing through.

The setting of the building is part of the municipal storm water management system. It functions as a bioswale that filters, aerates, and irrigates the surrounding landscape. No processed municipal water is used for maintenance. Native ecosystems have been restored to the landscape under and around the building, while the roof is also planted in native species as well as vegetables. Staff can tend their own gardens and harvest their own meals!

The building uses renewable materials to the maximum extent. Instead of wood or metal, bamboo has been used for scaffolding. According to LEED standards, materials must be produced within a radius of 805 kilometers (500 miles), which made bamboo a natural material to use in southern China.

As for "smart" systems, the use of natural wind flows, natural light, convection currents for air conditioning, and natural permeability of flooring not only increased the comfortability of the building but also reduced energy consumption. The Vanke Center uses 75 percent of the energy used by a comparable building. It saves roughly RMB 500,000 (about USD 73,314) every year on air-conditioning costs alone. Natural daylight penetrates into nearly all interior spaces. Solar energy provides 12.5 percent of all electricity. Wastewater is completely used within the scope of the landscape/building, while water usage is cut by 30 percent through use of drought-resistant plants and water-conservation methods. One hundred percent of all garbage is divided into categories and recycled.

On the evening before China's National Day in 2009, CEO Yu Liang led a group of colleagues from Vanke's headquarters at 63 Meilin Road on a twisting route through Shenzhen to the new Vanke Center site. They walked through a light rain all night long. As dawn broke the next day, they arrived at the new headquarters and officially inaugurated the Vanke Center at Dameisha and put it into operation.

The Vanke Center is not a static building. As I had hoped, it will continue to change and incorporate all kinds of minor innovations, but major ones as well. One example is the artificial lake nearby. After we moved into the building, the municipal government asked Vanke to take over management of this lake, in order to improve its environmentally sound maintenance. We have carried out numerous experiments with wetland species for water purification, as well as putting some floating islands in the center for visiting wildfowl. We have seen the occasional migrating swan, and some have stayed for a fairly long time.

Experts say one of the reasons is that we use no pesticides or chemicals in treating the water or surrounding foliage. Unfortunately, no phoenixes have come to alight on the islands as yet!

We are constantly making adjustments to the plantings on and around the building. Not only are these attracting butterflies, but we have installed a number of beehives that now produce honey for employees. The World Wildlife Fund (WWF) has advised us on wildlife management for the area, including what species would be suited to an environment that also contains humans. We also have installed systems that monitor the microclimate in various ways. Information is provided on a regular basis to the regional authorities, but the practice also allows local schoolchildren to participate in monitoring their environment.

A walkway leads through the entire landscape of the Vanke Center, under and around the building. It extends for over one kilometer (0.62 mile) and is open to the public. Meanwhile, a 50-meter (164 feet) swimming pool has been built, as well as facilities for a variety of sports. Inside the building will be a museum and the Vanke University with library, classrooms, and so on. When you add all of this up, what does it come to? A university campus! This place is intended as a resource that changes and innovates constantly, that is connected to residents in the neighboring community, and that serves not only Vanke people but also people from all over the world.*

Corporate Citizenship and the Spirit of Entrepreneurship

In 2009, some friends and I responded to the call of the international NGO WildAid and launched an initiative to stop the practice of eating shark fins in China. We formed an alliance of entrepreneurs, one of whom then later told me that he couldn't sign on when he learned more about it: "If the Minister invites me to a banquet, how can I refuse to eat sharks fin soup? What do you think would happen to my business?" All the others signed. Three years went by. In those years, I never heard that any one of the signatories lost any business. Even the famous Chinese basketball player Yao Ming put out ads against eating shark fins, and yet he does not seem to have suffered in any way.

Any person who thinks that his eating behavior will upset government officials has diminished his own stature. That includes not just eating shark fins but also drinking alcohol. What's more, making the assumption that it will hurt business presumes that officials are overgrown children, petulant when their own preferences are not followed. Obviously, this is ludicrous and not in accord with reality.

---

*The facility has been used extensively for architectural conferences. One, in June 2012, included a number of internationally famous architects. Students, scholars, and the public at large have taken good advantage of this extraordinary resource.

From early on, Vanke set a rule for itself: we do not give or take bribes. Since then, people have constantly wondered how we can do any real estate business in China that way. The facts have proven that not only has our principle not hurt our real estate business, it has made us the largest residential housing developer in the world.

The social standing of businesspeople is a topic to which Chinese entrepreneurs as a group pay a lot of attention. Meanwhile, the social status of any given entrepreneur is connected to his or her own psychological self-regard. If a person wants to be acknowledged and respected by society, he must first believe that he is worthy of such respect. This applies not only to China but also to elsewhere in the world.

China began to modernize in the mid-nineteenth century, and a "commercial civilization," in today's sense, began at the same time. The first generation of Chinese entrepreneurs were people like Hu Xueyan and Lei Lutai, masters at business. Correspondingly, society regarded them as rural gentry who also engaged in commerce. By the late nineteenth and early twentieth century, however, a new generation of entrepreneurs emerged who were of a totally different stripe. They included such people as Rong Desheng.* Not only were these people businesspeople, they also considered themselves to be pillars of society. In addition to investing in business, they built roads, bridges, and public parks. They supported education and participated in urban planning and regional economic development. They even formulated social security plans. Everywhere they went, they espoused the ideas of saving the nation through education and saving the nation through industry and commerce.

The term that the Chinese language uses for the English word *entrepreneur* is far more limited in meaning than what is implied in English. In China, it simply means a person engaged in managing a business entity. It lacks the kind of vigor, drive, and innovative enthusiasm contained in the English word. All societies have traditions, standards, and models they follow. Entrepreneurs, in the true sense, are people who recognize the limitations of the models, who reorganize factors in new ways and thereby create value in society. This is what I think should in fact be meant by "entrepreneurial spirit."

The reason this entrepreneurial spirit is so important in modern societies is that the division of labor in society is ever more fine-grained and knowledge is ever more specialized. Innovation in any given field now requires the cooperation of a team. In any field of scientific research, or in any well-functioning lab, not only does there have to be extensive cooperation and communication internally but there has to be coordination of interests externally. People need to

---

*Rong Desheng (1875–1952) was a textile magnate from Wuxi, southern China. He was the father of Rong Yiren. Rong Yiren, who died in 2005, was known as the Red Capitalist in China since he navigated both capitalist and communist worlds. He was crucial in the process of starting the process of reform and opening up, and he created CITIC in 1978.

be able to recognize when a certain research orientation is producing real value and to persuade the team to go in that direction. When problems come up, they need to make time adjustments. At the same time, they need to deal with funding sources, including government and corporations, in order to ensure ongoing support. All of this effort requires the entrepreneurial spirit.

Innovations in the sphere of society are the same. Any public welfare type of endeavor that hopes to gain the support and participation of society must sell the idea, including handling public relations. That, too, is included in the entrepreneurial spirit.

Chinese private enterprises that are operated by people as opposed to the government started from zero just 30 years ago. They now provide 60 percent of the country's GDP and 80 percent of its employment. In doing this, they use just 40 percent of society's total resources. Entrepreneurs are the so-called weight on the balance in this process, the thing that has made the difference in terms of both social stability and economic growth. The processes of modernization and urbanization came to a halt in the first 30 years of the People's Republic of China. In the most recent 30 years, however, modernization and urbanization have been condensed into an extremely short period of time. It took two generations of entrepreneurs to complete a qualitative transformation in China's first round of modernization in the early twentieth century. The same kind of progress has now been compressed into the space of one lifetime. The question I therefore pose to Chinese entrepreneurs is this: Are you ready for this kind of change, and have you done the necessary preparation?

Previously, I mentioned a friend who refused to stop eating shark fins. The company that this man founded several decades ago is one of China's premier enterprises. With respect to eating shark fins, however, he did not display his customary entrepreneurial brilliance. Entrepreneurs not only need to believe that they are doing things that the public respects, but they need to demonstrate their contribution to the public in concrete ways. Seventy or eighty years ago, our older generation raised the call to "save the nation through industry and commerce." They persuaded people through their concrete actions, and they were indeed rewarded with immense respect. Now it is our turn to reflect on this issue. Our generation has a responsibility toward society—how can we express and actually realize that responsibility?

Entrepreneurs excel in having vision and being able to plan, manage, organize, coordinate, persuade, mobilize, and compromise. If we do not contribute these talents to society, however, we have not truly fulfilled our obligation to society. This is particularly true if we just pull a little money out of our pockets to show we are philanthropists. Entrepreneurs can wield their influence in ways that are quite different from scholars and celebrities. Our contributions do not and should not end at making speeches. The positive energy that we pour into society should relate to the skills of handling modern management systems, organizing institutions, and making connections.

I mention all this because China's reform is an endeavor that is desperately in need of the spirit of entrepreneurs. Reform not only needs to uncover the problems that lie before us but it also needs to realize a certain degree of consensus within a society that has very diverse values. It needs to coordinate the interests of many different conflicting interest groups, in order to push forward innovation and ongoing change. The greatest possible entrepreneurial spirit is expressed by Deng Xiaoping's advice to "feel for the rocks as we cross the river." Another expression, however, can be found at New York's Rockefeller Center, which has a statue of Atlas in front of it. This was put there in 1937, at a time when the concept of the spirit of entrepreneurs had recently been suggested in the West. The image of Atlas holding up the heavens displayed the sense of responsibility of New York's entrepreneurs at the time. It said to the world, "We are the giants responsible for carrying the weight of America's economy and society." The narrative of the entrepreneur as hero then began to permeate American society. It gave American entrepreneurs the courage to take on social responsibility, to pour themselves into public works, and, at the same time, win for themselves the respect of society.

Entrepreneurs not only provide society with employment and wealth. More importantly, they motivate society to move forward. The self-confidence of entrepreneurs and their desire to achieve self-realization are what push them to greater effort. Entrepreneurs try to change things in ways that they themselves feel have value. It takes a certain kind of ethics and a certain kind of courage to want to move into realms that are unfamiliar. To my way of thinking, it takes the entrepreneurial spirit.

Garbage Sorting

In 2004, the amount of garbage that China produces every year surpassed the amount that the United States produces every year. Since then, China's garbage problem has grown even worse.

Cities throughout China are facing a disastrous problem: they are utterly surrounded by garbage. The landfills that surround Beijing are already full. In Wuhan, Vanke's Wonderland Garden project had to be delayed because a nearby dump could not be closed on schedule, and local residents began a violent protest that turned into a major media incident. The question of how to deal with urban waste has become a major issue for municipal governments in China.

Under immense pressure, China has begun to design and build huge incinerators. Since 2000, a number of policies have been launched to promote growth of the incinerating industry, and many places are pushing ahead with generating electricity from such garbage incinerators.

Incineration might appear to be a better method of disposal than burying, given higher efficiencies and less use of space, plus garbage can be got rid of more quickly. Japan has built more than 6,000 incinerators and thereby leads the rest of the world in this mode of disposal. Other developed countries are copying Japan's example, and incineration seems to be on the rise.

The public has never willingly accepted this mode of garbage disposal, however. It uses a large amount of energy, wastes resources, and is hard to do right, but more importantly, it involves hidden pollution. Every ton of incinerated garbage produces 5,000 square meters (16,400 square feet) of waste gases, as well as roughly half the original volume in ash. Even the most advanced incinerating technologies, operating properly, release several dozen toxic substances that are extremely hard to filter out through high-tech filtering and adsorption processes.

Among these toxic substances, tetrachlorodibenzo-*p*-dioxin ("dioxin") is recognized internationally as a primary carcinogen. It has been called "the most potent toxin on earth." It is almost nonexistent in the natural world and is generated only through chemical processes. It is one hundred times more toxic than potassium cyanide and 900 times more toxic than white arsenic. Its half-life is between 14 and 273 years, and it accumulates in the tissues of humans.

In fact, the best way to deal with garbage has long been with us, namely reducing the amount of garbage that humans generate in the first place. This method includes reducing the amount of packaging and promoting recycling. Even if garbage is not recycled, just dividing it into categories makes it easier for incinerators to meet required standards for emissions. When furnaces are burning just one type of garbage, the temperature can be more accurately controlled.

We have to begin to handle garbage by respecting one cardinal principle: reduce the amount of it to begin with, reuse it, and recycle it. The most important part of this process comes at the beginning, with reduction in quantity and with separating garbage into different categories.

Statistics show that 30 percent of the total amount of urban garbage comes from construction waste. As a forerunner in the housing industry, Vanke began promoting industrialized processes of manufactured housing and the sale of completely fitted-out housing as its primary business in 2010. In so doing, it has been able to reduce construction waste by over 70 percent.

In 2009, I observed how Taipei handles its municipal garbage. I found out that the city's residents organized a movement on their own to improve garbage handling, including the separation of garbage into categories. In addition to improving the urban environment, this effort raised public awareness of the subject. Seeing that made me want to carry out similar projects in Vanke's communities. Back on the mainland, I discussed the matter with colleagues at our headquarters and learned that one of Vanke's communities in Beijing had already been carrying out a similar pilot project for three years. Among the equipment it uses for garbage disposal is a facility that handles kitchen waste.

I was astonished that this effort had been initiated by the community itself. It was not subject to corporate rules and regulations or the need to meet any standards, but had been a voluntary movement on the part of the local people.

The specifics of this particular effort are as follows. More than 1,800 people, totaling 644 households, live in a Vanke community in Beijing called the Xishan Courtyard. This community generates roughly 1.2 tons of garbage per day. In May 2006, the Beijing municipality awarded this community with the designation of Model Example of Green Living. The government told the community's management office that it could decide to take the award in the form of money or in the form of a microbial facility to compost kitchen waste.

The management office decided for the composting facility.

Once it arrived, however, they discovered that you do not just plug in electricity to make the thing work. Instead, you have to mobilize a whole social system, which is a complex undertaking. The facility therefore just sat there.

A new manager soon came on board, however, a person named Luo Yutian, with a one-track mind. She saw that the facility was there and ready, and she decided that it was a great shame not to be using it.

The Xishan Courtyard has one great advantage, which is that its tenants are generally well educated due to the proximity of institutes of higher education. Their high caliber still did not prepare them with the knowledge of how to separate garbage. The most common question management had to answer those days was how to do it properly. Luo Yutian knew that she had to raise awareness but also increase informed participation in the whole effort. She therefore divided people into categories—older people, children, household help, and young adults—and proposed using different methods for each. Older people and help tended to be the least aware of garbage issues, so she made small cards that described little ways daily life could be improved with respect to conserving water, efficiently using electricity, and greening up the environment. For young adults, she supplied more sophisticated articles on environmental issues. For heads of households, she made up magnetic notices to put on refrigerators about how to divide garbage into categories, so as to remind and improve the accuracy of garbage-disposal behavior.

On the fourth Saturday of every month, the management office of the Xishan Courtyard holds a promotion activity in the community with respect to garbage differentiation. Tenants can get recycled plastic bags that are divided into three categories and printed with the words *Recyclable, Kitchen Waste,* and *Other*. Each tenant receives 30 of each kind of bag.

At the beginning, the results were not all that great. Luo Yutian and her colleagues persisted for a year. When tenants did a poor job of dividing things up, the management itself did a secondary division. The municipal government took note of this effort. "These people have real stamina!" they said. It helped out by making connections for the community on the latter stages of the process. Plastic containers and newspaper had greater recycling value, so the municipal government introduced a company that was willing to pay RMB 6,000 (USD $870) per year for collecting this. It put up a retrieval station in the community. Trash that was not regarded as having much recycling value, such as one-time-use plastic bags and so on, were retrieved by the company for reuse. Garbage that could not be recycled, as well as construction and landscaping waste, was hauled off by the local environmental bureau.

The hardest thing to deal with in the community was kitchen waste. Over 50 percent of all garbage generated came from the kitchen, due to the eating habits of Chinese people. The composting system of the Xishan Courtyard works 24 hours a day. Each 300 kilograms (660 pounds) of waste is put through a high-temperature composting process that turns it into 35 to 40 kilograms (77 to 88 pounds) of organic fertilizer. In May and October of every year, that organic fertilizer is then spread around the landscaped areas of the community—it comes completely from composted waste material from local kitchens. As a reward to tenants who do a particularly good job of dividing up their garbage, the management office gives them some of the fertilizer for their own gardens.

The community has gradually been able to reduce the quantity of its garbage by an average of over 30 percent. Every day, the community processes around 120 kilograms (265 pounds) of kitchen waste and retrieves around 100 kilograms (220 pounds) of reusable paper, plastic, and metals. It has standardized the way garbage is disposed of and retrieved within the community. In 2007, the Xishan Courtyard became a Model Unit within the Beijing municipal area for how it handles the separation of different kinds of garbage. In April 2010, the community went further in becoming a pilot-program entity that is aiming for zero waste.

When I went to visit the Xishan Courtyard, I was amazed and very moved by the rigorous and energetic approach of Luo Yutian and her colleagues at the management services center. All of this was without the benefit of any orders from on high, without any demands to meet certain performance standards. What's more, they were at it for four years before becoming successful.

I asked Ms. Luo if the company could help them in any way. She in turn asked for new equipment. She said that the equipment awarded by the government some time ago was out of date and becoming less effective. Naturally, I agreed to this.

My understanding now is that Xishan Courtyard has reduced its total quantity of garbage by 46 percent by its efforts to separate garbage into different categories. At the same time, the local environment is far cleaner. Surveys of the local residents indicate that 95 percent of tenants are aware of the effort to separate out garbage and 88 percent actually do so. Ninety-five percent support the effort, and 60 percent do so accurately. To date, this puts this particular community at an "S rating" in terms of Vanke's community garbage separation efforts, which is the company's highest rating. As a result, the community has been listed as one that other communities should visit in order to learn the processes. The government has made this a priority in educating others on how to handle garbage. In 2011, the management office received as many daily visitors as Vanke's headquarters in Shenzhen.

I am increasingly confident that Vanke's communities will in fact be successful in handling the disposal of garbage, and my reason stems from the example of Xishan Courtyard. If they can do it, other Vanke communities should be able to as well.

Our next goal, therefore, is to see similar practices in the more than 100 communities that Vanke has in 29 cities nationwide.

CHAPTER SIX

Back to the Future, After 2010

After "Coming Home from the War," I Go Back to School

When I first moved from Guangzhou to Shenzhen in 1983 to start a business, the future of the Special Economic Zone was uncertain. My plan was to spend a couple of years there and then use that place as a springboard to study abroad. My goal was California, specifically Berkeley. As it happened, I did not budge from Shenzhen after going into business. The years flew by and I got older, but the dream of going to school remained in the back of my mind. Only as I approached 50 did I begin to think I had missed my opportunity, and I gave up the idea.

For the next 10 years, I focused on outdoor adventure and public welfare activities, apart from spending time on the company. I felt fulfilled by these things. Something unexpected happened to change the rhythm of my life, however. This gradually opened vistas to me that I could not have imagined.

I should explain it all by starting with a particular conference. In early 2010, I accepted the invitation of Mr. Gao Xijun to attend a forum in Taipei. During breaks in the meeting, the financial manager of the Alashan SEE, a person named Zhang Min, introduced me to Ms. Chen Huizhu, deputy director of the Business School of Hong Kong Polytechnic University. She was an authority on educational administration. I assumed that she too had been invited as a guest to the forum, but this was not the case. "I came specifically to meet you," she said. Why? Wasn't Shenzhen closer to Hong Kong and a much easier trip?

"I tried to reach you several times through the proper channels at Vanke, but was not successful."

This was something I could understand. What did she want to talk to me about?

"I would like to invite you to teach at our Executive MBA program in the business school. I have heard you speak and been extremely moved by what you have to say. Your personal experience and Vanke's business practices would make an excellent case study. They would be well received by our students. Did you know that our Executive MBA program has an international ranking?"

I no longer remember what else she told me. I just remember being excited and also moved by her enthusiasm and sincerity. This, however, was not most important. The most important consideration was that I had already been thinking of lecturing at a business school for several years. What's more, I had expressed this interest to various schools. They may have thought I was joking, or they may only have been interested in two-hour lectures from me. For whatever reason, nothing came of it. Here was someone who had specifically sought me out and made the effort to find me in Taipei. Not only was I interested, but there was a demand for me! The thing was soon decided. Hong Kong Polytechnic organized a reception for me, and Director Chen issued a formal invitation, with a one-year contract.

Teaching a case study was different from my previous lectures at universities in two main ways. First, one-off lectures generally lasted an hour and a half, with another hour added for questions and answers. At most, the whole would take no more than four hours. In teaching a course, however, I had to prepare a full syllabus. In addition, giving a speech gave considerable latitude for talking about a variety of things, and I could be more spontaneous, depending on what moved me. Teaching was different. Not only did lectures have to stand up to logical analysis, but they had to be supported by theory. I now saw that other schools might have had good reason not to take me on.

I soon found that I lost the confidence and breezy manner I could call on as an entrepreneur when I stood at a lectern. I could always charm people with stories of mountain climbing and starting a company, but organizing a case study was something else. In Chinese tradition, the teacher should be able to present in such a way that students can "pick up the other three corners themselves when you give them just one corner." Trying to cover over my inadequate knowledge with the personal aura of an entrepreneur was definitely not acceptable. Not only was it disrespectful to students and the school, but it hurt my own self-esteem. After teaching two sessions, I began to feel that I ought to go back to studying myself. As we say, I should "go back to school after returning from the battlefields."

In April of the same year, I attended a banquet organized by the Harvard China Fund. Three years earlier, Vanke had set up a cooperative program with Harvard—each year, we received Harvard students as summer interns. Other Chinese entities also cooperated with Harvard, including Taikang Insurance, TCL, and various government departments and NGOs. Talk at our particular table at this banquet ranged over a variety of subjects, including the differences between education in eastern and western institutions. The head of the China Foundation unexpectedly turned to me and said, "Would you be interested in studying at Harvard? Say, for three months or half a year, or even as long as a year?" Without giving it a second thought, I responded, "Yes. One year."

After this event, I began to wait for Harvard's invitation.

There was no news for a long time. I began to have doubts. Could that have been just small talk at the table? Did they think I wasn't in earnest? Later I learned that there had been quite a controversy in the school about inviting a Chinese businessperson to come in as a visiting scholar, and it took some time to get the matter resolved. In July, however, another meeting was arranged in

Hong Kong. On the Harvard side was Professor Kleinman, director of the Asian Center at Harvard, and his assistant, Mr. Meyer. Arthur Kleinman is professor of medical anthropology at Harvard Medical School as well as a sinologist. In the 1980s, he taught at the Xiangya Medical School in Changsha. Our conversation proceeded in Chinese. In the course of it, we discussed Vanke's business practices and its principle of not taking or giving bribes. This sparked a very positive response from Professor Kleinman, who then invited me to Harvard in no uncertain terms. Ah! I had passed the interview and was in.

I soon received a letter of invitation signed by Professor Kleinman. After going to Harvard, friends occasionally asked me what the kind of red tape I had to go through. My experience was that all you needed was a letter signed from a Harvard professor—that counted as a ticket to enter the place.

Once the letter of invitation arrived, my assistant began to make the necessary visa arrangements while I began to have a guilty conscience. How could I possibly pose as a Harvard student with my rudimentary level of English? I could read a little and comprehend what was said to me, but my spoken English was limited to making a toast at a banquet. Meanwhile, I had been attending an intensive English-language training course in Shenzhen, but the results so far were near zero. Classes were soon to begin. I should just go to Boston as a "short-seller," a kind of phony, and then see what happened. Language depends on the total environment, and I was hoping that the old Chinese phrase would ring true: once the cart gets to the mountain, it finds a way through. Later, due to insurmountable reasons, I was not in fact able to attend Harvard that fall. I was more jubilant than upset, since I now had more time to prepare. The fall semester slipped away.

The year 2011 arrived in the blink of an eye. The spring semester was to start on January 25, yet this year Chinese New Year was going to be in February. I asked my assistant to let the school know that I would be there as soon as Spring Festival was over. In other words, without yet even registering I was already skipping class!

The message came back from Mr. Meyer: "All the preparations are made. Are you coming or not? After all, this is Harvard." Hearing the tone in his voice, I immediately responded, "I'm coming! I'll spend Spring Festival in Boston!"

I gathered up the few volumes I had been advised to read and dashed off. Flying from Hong Kong to Boston, I had to change flights in San Francisco. Off with the shoes, the belt, through the security gate with the warning on it: "Security First!" Any doubt and travelers were put into a small glass room: lift the hands, hold while a puff of air blows around the body, posture something like surrendering as a prisoner of war. How odd to realize that the feeling of security in the United States is as thin as ice.

I landed at Boston Logan Airport. Professor Yang Xiaohui from Northeastern University and her husband, the designer Zheng Dong, were there to meet me, together with Chang Zheng, who had worked at Vanke and was now studying for a doctorate at Harvard. We entered the city of Boston as night came on.

As one of America's oldest cities, Boston not only represents the accumulation of wealth but also the nurturing of culture. In the past, it served as an important port as well as a manufacturing center. These days, it is the center of higher education and healthcare industries. We passed over a frozen Charles River and entered Cambridge. The apartment I would be renting belongs to the college and is only rented out to visiting scholars. It is said that the eminent Chinese author Eileen Chang once lived in the same red brick building.*

Harvard Yard was immersed in snowflakes the next morning. Well-wrapped students hurried by, stung by the cold, amid red brick buildings and church steeples, the sound of bells, squirrels chasing, a blanket of snow on a statue. Registering, getting settled in the apartment, buying things at a store, and getting familiar with the city subway (the "T") kept me busy.

Chang Zheng had arranged for me to attend the Spring Festival evening celebrations organized by the Overseas Chinese Association, in the Harvard memorial building. The 1,000-seat hall was filled to the brim. Professors associated with East Asian studies were also invited. The remarks of the director of the China Research Center made a particular impression—his initial words were spoken in ancient Manchu. Professor Mark Elliott was a scholar of Manchu documents of the Qing dynasty. As the leading authority at Harvard on Qing Dynasty history, he saw Qing history from the perspective of a Manchu.

Chinese students from overseas then performed various pieces. Chang Zheng, sitting near me, passed over a slip of paper that read, "Mr. Wang, in a bit they will be doing a magic trick. Are you willing to participate?" I nodded yes.

This turned out to be a magic show performed by a graduate student from Beijing, now studying at the Harvard Institute of Education. The master of ceremonies announced, "A mystery guest in the audience will be coming up to the stage to assist in this performance." When he announced my name, Chinese students in the audience loudly applauded. My role was to select a poker card and see if he could guess the suit and number of the card, a job that was fairly easy. After the trick, the host asked me to say a couple of words. I chose to speak in my role as executive chairman of the Harvard China Fund. I ended with an invitation. "This evening I have begun to appreciate the artistic talents of our Chinese overseas students. I wonder about their prowess in athletic sports, however. If anyone is interested in skiing, we could go together to a ski resort in New Hampshire. Anyone interested?"

Getting Through the Language Barrier

My office at the Asia Center had a bulletin board on which notices could be tacked. I tacked up the course schedule I had just received and noticed that in fact it was not a schedule for Harvard but for a language school. Every Monday through Friday, I was to study English while also auditing courses at Harvard.

---

*Eileen Chang, one of China's most influential modern writers. died in Los Angeles in 1995.

The school was located near campus in a dormitory building, six minutes walk away. Classes in English were divided into four levels: beginning, intermediate, high, and highest. I was placed in intermediate. Each level involved a 10-week course. After 10 weeks an exam was given, and if you passed it you went on to the next level. If you didn't, you stayed on at the same level for another 10 weeks. There were also nonelective courses that one could take without having to take the exam. The first day I arrived at the school, the other students thought I was the teacher.

Between 8:30 and 11:30 a.m. were formal English lessons, then between 11:40 a.m. and 1 p.m. were such electives as business English. Each class had 12 or 13 students in it, from all over the world, mostly between the ages of 15 and 23. Very few were over 30. It was a funny feeling, being among a bunch of such young people. Because courses focused on interaction, we were often teamed up, one on one. One student would mime a word and the other would try to guess it. My team generally lost. Exams were every weekend. Some students finished up in 30 minutes and briskly took off, while others took longer; eventually there would be just one lone student sitting there, head down, trying to figure things out—namely, me. The teacher would walk over to me, and say, "Peter [my English name], time's up." I felt a mixture of exhaustion and relief when I handed over the test and could go back to my room and sleep. From the time classes started on Monday, I looked forward to being able to sleep on Saturday.

The most exhausting thing was not going to classes or even the weekend exams, but doing the homework at night after dinner. Dinner would be over at 7:30, and from 8 p.m. I would do English grammar, work on sentence construction, and compose a short piece. Writing was particularly hard, but I generally finished the work by 10 p.m. The hard part was still to come, however. At that point I generally made myself some coffee. Boston in February is cold, and the building was not well heated, so I used the hot cup of coffee to bolster me. I then would begin to go through the notes from that afternoon's lectures at Harvard. How did I choose which lectures to attend? I chose professors who used PowerPoint presentations. At the same time, I had an assistant sitting next to me at these lectures who wrote English notes about the lectures so that I could study them every evening. This was a Chinese student who had just graduated and been selected for the work by Professor Yang. I generally studied well into the night—the material was new to me, even in Chinese.

Around dawn one day, I heard the snowplow coming along the streets with its clanking and beeping. Cold by now, I subconsciously got up and went into the kitchen to fix another hot cup of coffee and discovered I had left the kettle on to boil. It had burned dry. The bottom was glowing red, and the top knob had melted. Once I let it cool down, however, it could still boil water! German brand, excellent quality. By now it was 4 a.m.—time to stop, no matter how much was still left to finish.

I often found that I couldn't sleep no matter how late it was—I was in such a state of excitement that I simply couldn't force myself to rest. During the years that I started Vanke, pressures were intense, but I always slept well. What's more, the tougher things were, the better I slept. The sun was always going to come up the next day. When I climbed mountains, I was physically exhausted and mentally terrified, but even Everest was just a matter of two months. I was going to be at Harvard a whole 12 months! In climbing Everest there was a summit, while at Harvard there seemed to be no end to it. Maybe I should just hire an interpreter, choose things I liked, and spend time at the library. This also would be better for the teachers, since I wouldn't bother them so much. On the other hand, wasn't that giving up? Had I really tried my hardest? I was only going to have this one chance to come to Harvard, and later I might regret not having done more. As a philosopher once said: existence may have no meaning, but people live marvelous lives anyway, creating their own meaning.

People must constantly recreate who they are, constantly grow. They can't just allow fate to decide things for them. Hadn't my last 20 years of founding a company been a matter of rejecting what was preordained? Hadn't it been done by taking chances, pushing beyond limitations? No matter what, I would continue to struggle onward. As always, the sun would come up in the east.

Early the next morning I took a cold shower, had a cup of hot coffee, and ate two pieces of toast and half a pomelo—a three-minute breakfast. I slung my book bag over my shoulder and headed off to school, with spirits high.

The original plan had been to ski every weekend. That did not happen. I went once to New Hampshire, but after that my weekends were devoted to studying English. Depending on the English level of a visiting scholar, the Asia Center provided a tutor to help out. Mine was a retired editor from a publishing company, a woman with impeccable English and literary accomplishments. We met three times a week, for an hour and a half each time. Since my schedule was packed from Monday to Sunday, I avoided any socializing and especially getting together with Chinese students. I had two reasons for that. First, going out to dinner took at least an hour and a half. Second, Chinese students were prone to communicating in Chinese, which would be no help at all to my English. Harvard's student organizations were extremely active, and I was often asked to speak to the Chinese overseas association. With one exception, I refused. The exception was if I could talk on environmental protection and a green economy—in those cases, I insisted on speaking in English. That way I could kill two birds with one stone: promote conservation and also improve my English.

Boston in March is both rainy and sleety, and an umbrella and boots become a necessity. Magnolias finally began to bud and soft tendrils appeared on the maples in Harvard Yard. Busy as I was, I often had to stop to watch the squirrels play.

Giving a Speech in English

After my first speaking appearance at Harvard, all kinds of people began inviting me to speak elsewhere, including Chinese student associations. I refused all those I could, out of concern for my studies, but I was delighted to accept one from the World Wildlife Fund (WWF) in the United States. I had first visited their offices in Washington, D.C., in the summer of 2008 and had been deeply impressed. Vanke then launched a cooperative effort with the organization to protect forests and stop illicit traffic in endangered species. The WWF knew about my speech at Harvard and now asked me to speak at the celebrations surrounding their fiftieth anniversary. I myself proposed the idea of speaking in English.

English is written phonetically using an alphabet—since the pronunciation is right there, how hard could it be to read a speech? The problem is cadence and putting emphasis on the right words so that it doesn't sound stilted. I hoped to be able to last for 30 minutes. I was already sleep deprived from my studies. This impending speech was like adding another final exam.

On February 24, I flew from Boston to Washington, D.C. A woman from the WWF offices was there to greet me: Ms. Niu Hongwei, in charge of China affairs for the organization. She was so enthusiastic and meticulous about everything that I began to relax. The speech was to be given in the third-floor conference room of the WWF headquarters. I had prepared a PowerPoint presentation, so that if the audience could not understand me, at least they could read the slides.

I began: "Ladies and Gentlemen, good afternoon!" A strange sort of sound barked into the room. It didn't seem to be coming from my own throat—it was much too low. My mind went blank, and for a moment I discovered that my mouth was open but nothing was coming out of it. The audience was down below, looking at me. Should I just forget it and speak in Chinese? Ms. Niu had said she would serve as interpreter if I needed one. No—I calmed my nerves and plunged ahead. In my strange new voice, I began to read the English. Although I was just reading the words, at least I was talking about three things I had personally experienced.

Story one: In 2002, I climbed the highest peak in Africa: Kilimanjaro. Records show that this was once snow-covered year round, but I saw no snow at all when I climbed the mountain. Due to global warming, snow now falls on Kilimanjaro only in Africa's winter season. Scientists forecast that Kilimanjaro's glaciers will be completely melted within 30 years, which will be the makings of an ecological disaster. My conclusion: the closer one is to nature, the more one has a visceral feel for global warming.

Story two: This was about the destruction of tropical rainforests, which truly are the lungs of the globe, necessary for replenishing oxygen. However, 70 percent of the wood that is cut from these forests is exported to China. Once in China, the great majority is used for construction, and 70 percent of that construction is for residential housing. Vanke is currently China's largest residential housing developer. What can Vanke do about this? To look for answers, I paid a call on the Greenpeace offices in Beijing. They were utterly shocked, since no major Chinese corporation had ever come to them before—most Chinese companies were actually attacking them.

Story three: Vanke imported made-in-factory construction techniques from

Japan that reduced the use of lumber by 85 percent, of water by 60 percent, and of construction waste by 90 percent. By this time, reading away, I was already drenched in sweat, but my audience was fully supportive. They were unaccustomed to a Chinese businessperson who had any awareness of the need for environmental protection.

My nerves had calmed down, but that was no help to my pronunciation. I had to repeat some words two or three times before I got them right, but the audience now stepped in to help. Those in the front row began to whisper words to me as I came to them, since they could read them in the PowerPoint slides.

The end of the story: In 2007, China's Ministry of Construction published a system of standards that is similar to LEED in the United States. In China, it is called the Three Star green standard system. In 2009, only one project met the three-star standards, which was a Vanke project. In 2010, more enterprises applied for the Three Star rating. Vanke's projects constituted 60 percent of the more than 30 projects that met the standards. In 2011, we predicted that Vanke projects will make up more than half of the Three Star ratings as well. Vanke holds only 2 percent of the market share of all residential housing in China. That is insignificant when it comes to the total need to reach a target quota for carbon emissions. However, Vanke is not only doing green building itself but is actively promoting such building within the industry. This is the reason Vanke is cooperating with WWF, from beginning to reduce the amount of lumber it uses to protecting tropical rainforests.

This speech turned out to be a success, but more importantly I had made a psychological breakthrough—I now knew I could speak English in public.

Back in Boston, I threw myself into studying. In April, yet another invitation came from the WWF—another request to participate in their fiftieth anniversary.

"Hey! Didn't I just do that?"

That was the celebration in the United States, I was told. The celebration to which I was invited was in Switzerland, in the organization's headquarters in Geneva. The actual event was to be held in the ancient city of St. Gallen. The WWF had representatives in many countries, and people would be gathering not just for the annual meeting but for the celebration of the fiftieth anniversary. Ten honored guests would be speaking during a one-day forum, and among these, they were asking two businesspeople to speak. One was the CEO of Unilever, Mr. Paul Polman,* and the other was Wang Shi, from Vanke. This time, however, the speaker was also to answer questions in a question-and-answer session after the talk. "Am I to speak in English again?," I asked. "Of course." "And during the question-and-answer session too?" I knew I could answer in English, but I was not sure I could understand the questions, nor was I sure

---

*Paul Polman has been CEO of Unilever since January 2009. He is recognized for championing the Unilever Sustainable Living Plan.

the audience could understand my English! We agreed that I would have an interpreter for this part.

In early May, I flew from Boston to Zurich, and from Zurich drove around one hour toward the east, to the town of St. Gallen on the shores of Lake Bodensee (Lake Constance). This town was once the religious center of eastern Switzerland and contained a great Carolingian monastery. It was highly prosperous during the eighth century and became a center of scholarship during the Middle Ages. The buildings are no longer used for their previous purposes, but the massive cathedral in its baroque style and the abbey library of Saint Gall are listed as UNESCO world heritage sites.

The next day, I got up at 5 a.m. and drove half an hour into the mountains to do some hiking. The U.S. offices of WWF had organized this outing on my behalf, knowing my love of outdoor activity. I was accompanied by the president and CEO of the U.S. organization, Mr. Carter Roberts. The hike was simply beautiful. As day broke, we traversed green hillsides, heard the lowing of cattle in the fields, took in the fragrance of freshly deposited manure, and listened to the church bells chime below. The golden light of sunrise came across the lake that marks the border with Germany. Mr. Roberts is also an avid outdoorsman. He has been involved in environmental conservation for many years and has even been one of the few people to see a snow leopard in the wild, not just in a zoo. The U.S. division of WWF is currently undertaking an exciting project to protect this wildcat, which is near extinction. We climbed for two hours and took an hour getting back down. By the time I appeared at the conference hall, I was totally refreshed.

The World Wildlife Fund was set up in 1961, so has been going already for more than 55 years. It is the largest independent non-governmental organization that undertakes environmental protection in the world. It has an active network of close to 5.2 million supporters in more than 100 countries. It has launched more than 12,000 environmental protection projects, which include such things as protecting tigers in the wild, marine animals, and tropical rainforests, and stopping the trade in ivory and rhinoceros horn. After many years of mountain climbing, I have found the endearing WWF panda logo in every country I have visited, and it is known throughout China's cities as well. In 1996, WWF set up an office in Beijing, and it then gradually expanded to eight more cities in China as it extended financial support for more than 100 projects.

The speaker just before me was CEO of Unilever, Mr. Paul Polman. A tall man with a ruddy complexion, Mr. Polman held his audience in thrall as he spoke of Unilever plans. This company was formed in 1929 when two companies merged, Lever in England and Margarine United in Holland. It then became one of the world's largest providers of consumer goods. With 170,000 employees in more than 100 countries, it provides a broad range of goods for some two billion consumers on a daily basis. Unilever's determination to achieve sustainable growth has been broadly applauded. For 10 years in a row, the company has ranked first in the Dow Jones index of sustainability in the food industry. In 2010, Unilever set up a "Sustainable Living Plan." By 2020, it intends to realize three main objectives: to cut its environmental impact in half, to achieve 100 percent sustainable procurement of agricultural raw materials, and to improve the health conditions of one billion people.

It was now the turn of the entrepreneur from China to speak. Having had that experience in Washington, D.C., I approached the lectern with more confidence than I had before. I again narrated my three stories, but this time I added some images of how I personally had come to be aware of global warming. In 2004 and 2005, I saw what was happening at the North and South Poles. In 2007, I experienced temperatures of 52 degrees Celsius (125 degrees Fahrenheit) as I traversed Lop Nur in Xinjiang in May. "As a lover of nature," I began, "the closer I get to nature, the more I have a visceral understanding of how it is heating up."

I described why I believed that China's commitment to a 40 to 45 percent reduction in carbon emissions by the year 2020, agreed to at a meeting in Copenhagen in 2009, was a major turning point. I noted that China's construction and housing industry is going to have to play an instrumental role in that process. Energy consumption in China's construction industry accounts for between 30 and 35 percent of all energy consumption in the country (that includes such things as lighting, heating, and air conditioning). Vanke has set green-construction goals for the year 2020 that will enable the country to reduce emissions, but this contribution will still just account for 1.2 thousandths of a percent of all of China's target for total emissions reduction. If the entire construction and housing industry in the country could match Vanke's level, however, that would contribute 12.5 percent to China's total reduction in emissions.

My stories were vivid enough and my numbers were persuasive enough that I earned applause. The problem now came with the question-and-answer session. I discovered that my responses were being mistranslated into English—what was coming out was not what I had just said. I couldn't help but interrupt the interpreter and begin to answer myself, in English. Who knows where I found the courage to do this? I sounded fairly incoherent, but I got the message across. Somehow, English phrases I had never used before came to mind.

During the breaks between meetings, I had the opportunity to talk to representatives from other WWF offices. One of those conversations was with the head of WWF in Nepal. I had stopped into this office in May 2010, after I climbed Everest from the south side and stayed briefly to recuperate in Katmandu. I wanted to explore ways in which the two countries might conserve wildlife on the Sino-Nepalese border. This head of the office had been absent during my visit, yet at the meeting in Switzerland, fortuitously, we met up thousands of miles away from Nepal.

Not long after I returned to Boston, the headquarters of WWF in Switzerland asked me to join their board of directors. I was honored by their faith in me, but I also wondered which part of WWF I might serve better. It was logical to want to be on the board of the headquarters in Geneva, but at the same time

I was close to people in headquarters in the United States. We had worked on a number of cooperative projects together, so on the human relations side, we had a certain bond. In the end, I chose the United States.

I was encouraged by the success of these two speeches for WWF. I seemed to have found an excellent way to practice my English, and I did not mind creating further opportunities for myself. In September, I spoke at the Guggenheim Museum in New York at a forum on the subject of "The City of the Future." In October, I spoke to the Chinese Student and Scholar Association of MIT at a forum on innovation. In November, I spoke at the London School of Economics on mega-metropolises in the age of the Internet. I used English for all of these speeches, but I still needed the help of an interpreter in answering questions.

Water, the Elixir of Life, and an Urban Mine

Learning is not confined to a lecture hall. During summer vacation of 2011, I took advantage of a short return to China to visit Singapore and learn about its water conservancy and to Japan to learn about its recycling. These visits were brief, but they made a strong impression.

In Singapore, I was shown around by Mao Daqing, who has worked there many years. He introduced me to specialists in water conservation at the National University of Singapore. Singapore has a land mass of around 700 square kilometers (435 square miles), yet this area has to support a population of 4.5 million people. Water is perhaps the scarcest of Singapore's resources. Lee Kuan Yew, former prime minister of Singapore, once described the situation vividly: "All of Singapore's policies pay homage to the importance of life-giving water." Singapore relies on neighboring Malaysia for its water supply. When the country was founded, it signed a 100-year agreement with Malaysia for water, so one could say that the country's fate hangs on the consideration of just one water pipe. Whenever there is a dispute between the two countries, Malaysia has a stranglehold on Singapore because of this ability to cut off the water supply. Lee Kuan Yew swore to make Singapore self-reliant in water in order to prevent the potential paralysis of the city state.

The government has therefore set out a triumvirate of policies for rainwater collection, recycling technology, and water conservation.

I stood before a body of water that meandered into the distance, not wide but quite extensive. This was in fact a reservoir, built to collect rainwater. There are 15 such water-collecting points in Singapore, which take up over half of the land area. Each part of the city is connected to wastewater treatment systems so that all used water is collected and recycled. It undergoes various kinds of treatment to make it reusable, including superfine filtration, reverse osmosis, and ultraviolet radiation for sterilization.

The Public Works Department of Singapore has launched a plan to make the city even more livable within the next 10 to 15 years. It is building 150 waterways that originally were simply functional water facilities but that now will become part of the beautification of Singapore. The reservoir I visited had a number of small islets on it—on closer examination, these moved slightly on the surface of the water. It turned out they are artificial floating islands, with highly aesthetic plantings of grasses and flowers. Not only does this help improve water quality, but it attracts birdlife. I immediately started planning a project with colleagues—Vanke has a lake on the southeast side of its main center. On occasion, we have had a visiting white swan, and once we even had a flock of these birds stay for a few weeks. We do not have sufficient marshland to allow for real habitat, however. I wondered if we could not create floating islands that provided more of a mini-environment for birds?*

By 2065, Singapore plans to be 100 percent self-reliant in water supply, which coincides with the end of the agreement with Malaysia. At the same time, Singapore plans to become an international communications center for information on how to recycle water. This is both remarkable and admirable. A small island state with limited resources, hemmed in on all sides, still has managed to lead the way in this vital direction.

More than 60 percent of China's cities have a water shortage. We need to take a lesson from Singapore and adopt a few new methods!

After visiting Singapore, I flew to Japan. The architect Tadao Ando had strongly recommended that I visit a place in Akita prefecture, on the main island of Honshu, which has a facility that is known as the Koba Refinery.

This place was originally an integrated steel-smelting operation, in operation for over 100 years. In the 1990s, it ran out of iron ore and could no longer smelt steel. Twenty years went by in which it was abandoned, but now Koba is in operation again. What it "mines" now is recycled household appliances.

The plant is situated on a leveled-off area on a low hill. It is surrounded by luxuriant greenery and is quite attractive. Visitors don hard hats and protective gloves before going into the area. They first pass through a section of warehouses that holds abandoned refrigerators, televisions, and air conditioners, among other things. Forklift trucks bring items to dismantling lines. The trucks shuttle back and forth, but in a very organized fashion. Visitors move into a viewing area with one long wall of glass from which they can observe the separation of materials in a separating room.

The head of this separating room explained the procedure to us. The return value from the metal in refrigerators is lowest, while that from air conditioners is highest, with a particularly high percentage of copper. As items are being dismantled, the process retrieves the Freon in their components, since this is the prime culprit in destroying the ozone layer. Electronics are the most difficult things from which to retrieve metals, but they also have the highest value in terms of their gold and rare metals. Once materials are dismantled, they are divided into categories and then sent along a conveyor belt for treatment. On

---

* As noted elsewhere in the text, this plan was later realized.

a screen, visitors can see the plastic covers of electronics being pulverized into powder for reuse.

Once metals are retrieved from items, they are put into high-temperature furnaces. The temperatures in these furnaces range from 800 to 1,300 degrees Celsius (1,472 to 2,372 degrees Fahrenheit), at which metals can be separated into different pure metal types. One can see steam puffing out of the wide mouths of these furnaces. Our guide explained, "Those smokestacks are actually emitting high-temperature water vapor. They do not contain any harmful elements."

We drove to the place where finished products are warehoused and were astonished to see a piece of 99.99 percent pure gold weighing 15 kilograms (33 pounds). At present, the annual output of the Koba Refinery includes roughly 6 tons of gold, 200 tons of bismuth, 500 tons of silver, 12,000 tons of copper, and 25,000 tons of lead. Looking at the lead ingots and the copper, one has to admire Japan for turning scarcity into an opportunity. Japan's need stimulated the country's ability to recycle resources, and that has operated very much to the country's competitive advantage.

Research indicates that by now Japan's ability to recycle allows it to stand up favorably to many countries that are well endowed with resources. This recycling effort has been called "urban mining." This process has been successful in retrieving gold, silver, and such rare metals as indium. Japan's gold reserves from urban mining total around 6,800 tons; silver, 60,000 tons; indium, 1,700 tons; and tantalum, 4,400 tons. These equate roughly to 16 percent of the world's gold reserves, 22 percent of its silver reserves, 61 percent of its Indium, and 10 percent of its tantalum. Garbage that is not used becomes a public hazard, but garbage that is used can be a source of real wealth.

After the start of reform and opening up, the swift growth of China's economy made it a major player in the world, but in terms of mode of growth, efficiency of growth, and innovative abilities, China lags far behind. Not only is the United States, a country with the largest economy in the world, much more efficient in how it uses materials, but even Japan is. (Note that many people have been thinking of Japan as already exhausted or depleted.) Meanwhile, tiny Singapore, on a mere patch of land, is doing things far more efficiently than China.

Technological innovations in all these places are ongoing. Chinese entrepreneurs can and should learn from their examples.

How Can You Manage Vanke While in the United States?

My roommate at the Harvard Asia Center was a retired general from the Japan's Ministry of Defense, attending Harvard as a visiting scholar for one year. It became clear from our conversations that he assumed I was retired. I soon discovered that nobody at Harvard could believe I was still chairman of the board of the largest real estate company in China. How could that be? How did I find time, and how did I handle such things as board meetings, shareholders' meeting, and business meetings from the United States?

After I resigned from the position of CEO in 1999, I no longer was active in daily affairs, but as chairman of the board, I still had to attend board meetings and shareholders' meetings. (There were rare exceptions, such as the April 2003 shareholders' meeting when I was climbing Mt. Everest.) As a listed company, Vanke held board meetings every quarter, at the very least. As it turned out, attending those meetings was easy thanks to the Internet and video-teleconferencing. Vanke set up systems to do this quite early. I had all the necessary software on my computer, but there was some question as to how appropriate it was to participate from a college dorm room, with its student-like backdrop. Our IT department said that that didn't matter, but the office of the board of directors indicated that that arrangement would not do. The atmosphere of a dorm was different from that of a boardroom, and they suggested that I find someplace in Boston that was more suitable for conducting business. I found a business center in a hotel, and the director was delighted—the equipment had been there for three years without once being used. I was the first user, and I was to become a constant presence after that.

Since coming to study on my own in the United States, I have had numerous occasions to hold board meetings simultaneously with other members in several different cities, for example, Boston, Shenzhen, Beijing, and Hong Kong. With modern telecommunications technology, you need not sit face to face in order to chair a meeting—long-distance meetings have become quite common.

Since I no longer handled day-to-day matters at the company, what in fact did I do as chairman of the board?

As Vanke's chairman, I personally felt I should focus on three things: strategy, personnel, and being the person who is ultimately responsible.

With respect to strategy, Vanke had chosen to be in the real estate business and become highly professional in that field. The decision to specialize in this way made things relatively easy. If we had diversified, decisions would have covered a much broader range of topics and things would have been more complicated. The cost of reaching decisions would also have been greater. I once said that if China's urbanization ended, and cities no longer needed housing, I would hope that Vanke would be building the very last community and providing it with services. What I meant was that deciding upon a strategy is one thing, but carrying it through to the very end is another. We could not equivocate once we had set our course.

With respect to human resources, there is that old saying, "Don't doubt the people you have hired, and don't hire people whom you have doubts about." My view is a little different. From the standpoint of management theory, everyone has potential problems and is questionable, including myself. It is necessary to be clear-minded in recognizing that everyone is a common person, has virtues and faults, good inclinations and bad inclinations, and broad-minded aspects and petty jealousies. One should in fact doubt these things but limit their negative potential through systems, through the use of corporate institutions. Such things as human resource systems, management systems, financial systems, contractual audits, audits when people leave, and so on are done precisely to make sure problems are discovered in time and can be corrected.

All people are different. Among the multitude of common people, one finds some super-able people. However, my principle is that we should use such able people as little as possible. Such people are terrific as inventors or as the founders of start-ups. They are not suited to being corporate managers. Able people like to break out of conventions. They do not like to abide by rules and systems. They can play a role in companies at certain times, but they can also do great harm. The goal is to have systems that simplify human relations as much as possible, that do not allow for hiring relatives, for example, and that do uphold principles of equal opportunity. Ultimately, the goal is to understand that employees are the greatest treasure an enterprise has. An enterprise must cultivate them and protect them. Constant job training and education is an indispensable part of this.

Finally, take responsibility. When a company does well, all the kudos and glory naturally go to the founder and to the chairman of the board. When things go badly, however, who takes responsibility? The blame also should be placed on the chairman of the board. Many corporate leaders do not agree. They shove off the blame on their underlings. They berate their staff for damaging the credibility of the chairman. When a company has problems, however, it is imperative for the number one boss to take responsibility. First, there may have been policy mistakes or misjudgments. That certainly comes down to corporate leadership. Second, policies may be correct but the wrong people may have been hired to do the job. That oversight is also the responsibility of corporate leaders. Meanwhile, if problems mount up, the chairman needs to consider taking the blame fully by resigning.

In fact, prior to going to Harvard, I spent a lot of the previous decade climbing mountains. I might have been away two months at a time. That absence did not affect Vanke's normal operations. By going to Harvard, all I did was swap a campus and studying for mountain climbing. At least at school it is a lot easier to connect with people back at the business than it is at the mountains. I am still climbing mountains, just not physical peaks. I am trying to scale different heights, namely those of greater knowledge.

The Force of an Alliance: Joint Procurement of Construction Materials

In September 2002, a real estate investment group was established known as the China Urban Housing Network. Its 12 original members agreed that each member would put in RMB 10 million (USD 1.5 million) to set up a fund in which no single company had control shares; it was one of the earliest real estate investment funds in China. Over the course of a decade, investments went from being mainly a way to help one another out, a mutual aid type of investment, to more of a corporate type of investment. It then changed further into being an investment management shareholding company that mainly managed funds. Within 10 years, it grew from 12 to 51 members, and its capital grew to RMB 500 million (USD 79.24 million). Dividends for the shareholders and investors in the fund came to a combined RMB 750 million (USD 118.86 million). The size of the fund reached RMB 7 billion (USD 1.11 billion), with cumulative sum of investments of RMB 11 billion (USD 1.74 billion).

What surprised and pleased people most about this fund was that there was a zero rate of defaults on loans, given the high degree of trust that members had in one another.

In 2003, the China Urban Housing Network finally changed its name to the China Urban Realty Association. In 2006, Dai Dawei took over as secretary general, and his energy and enthusiasm brought new life to the endeavor. Under his leadership, membership in the association has increased to 64 members, all of whom have much more frequent communication with one another. The meetings, activities, and surveys of the organization are highly disciplined as well as practical, and close friendships have grown up among members. Within business alliances in China, the association has a high reputation.

Four broad objectives were defined when the association was first established: mutual sharing of information, joint training, joint procurement, and joint raising and investing of funds. Among these, all except the goal of joint procurement were promoted and developed as per plans. I am pleased that the last goal lately has begun to be realized more effectively in recent years.

In the past decade, the association has been active in the sphere of corporate responsibility. After the large earthquake in Sichuan Province on May 12, 2008, it participated in a project called "Extend a Hand to a Child." Among all the institutions that participated in this, the association had faster reaction time, and more money actually reached its goal than with any of the others. At the same time, many members set up public welfare funds themselves, such as Vanke, Vantone, Nandu, Jianye, Tiantai, Zhongda, Ronghua, and Junfa, among others. Corporate responsibility in the social arena gradually became one of the main themes of association activities.

More importantly, the association has been active in promoting joint procurement. As China has urbanized, its housing industry has generated a large number of private companies. For example, between 2001 and 2005, the number of people living in cities increased by over 60 million. Clearly, China has the largest residential property market in the world. To meet this market, many companies were set up and were listed on exchanges as a way to raise funds. By 1999, close to 40 real estate companies were listed on the Shanghai and Shenzhen exchanges. Vanke is the largest among them, the industry leader, but in global terms Vanke too is a very small company. I believe that this industry fragmentation is detrimental to rational use of resources. It will eventually have to change. As a key industry, housing uses large amounts of scarce resources, including land. We all know that society's resources must be allocated rationally, given China's population. How to do that and still not return to state planning in this industry is the challenge. We set up the association to try to deal with that concern—to educate and coordinate the industry. It uses the Internet to break through traditional barriers to communication. We encourage information exchange among members, training initiatives, and common use of resources. The association tries to have a breakthrough influence on educating the public as well, in order to avoid repeating the same old mistakes. It promotes standardization of various aspects of the industry, such as documentation. It aims at developing a solid foundation of scientific management.

Each year, the association has two regular meetings for the heads of the boards of member companies. In January 2010, the members of the association held their annual spring meeting. This time, in addition to having a banquet, the organization held a forum to discuss strategy.

What could I do to help the association upgrade its overall strategy? For many years, I had felt that green housing should be the primary focus of Vanke's efforts. I intended to introduce Vanke's Green Strategy to the other members at this forum. At the same time, I knew that making a presentation at a meeting would have limited effect. I needed more leverage if I was going to inspire members to undertake new things and raise the overall green capacity of the association.

In recent years, three other companies in China have enjoyed a high reputation for undertaking green building, namely Fengshang, Modernland, and Landsea. These three new sharp-minded companies are courageously using such things as geothermal energy, radiant floor technology, and more airtight building methods. They put out the slogan, "Say goodbye to the age of air conditioning and heating," which has been having quite an impact on the market. I intended to ask members at the association forum to learn from Fengshang, Modernland, and Landsea. If I could get those organizations to join the association, that would be even better. These three were more similar to the great majority of members in terms of size and methodologies than we were—the other members would have more opportunity to use them as a model.

In January, I invited the heads of the three companies to come to Vanke's headquarters at Dameisha in order to participate in the spring banquet and the strategic forum of the association. The three board chairmen were Zhang Zaidong of Fengshang, Zhang Lei of Modernland, and Tian Ming of Landsea. When I met with Tian Ming, we exchanged the usual pleasantries, and I then made a suggestion: "What would you think of having Vanke invest in Landsea, take us in as a strategic partner?"

Tian Ming was taken by surprise: "Mr. Wang, this is quite sudden! I'm delighted at the idea, but I can't answer you right away."

"That is understandable," I said. "Naturally, you'll need time to think it over."

"What made you think of this?"

"We did some basic due diligence. Landsea is similar to Vanke in terms of its conceptual framework. It is a leader in technology; its management is systematic. It pursues ideals and is also highly transparent as a corporation."

My suggestion of a strategic investment did not in fact happen, but our discussion, which lasted an hour, gave me a very good impression of Tian Ming. He comes from a government background, but he has the refreshing qualities of entrepreneurs who were born in 1960s: well educated, meticulous, deliberate in his dealings, and favoring technological solutions to problems.

Prior to the forum, Zhang Zaidong, Zhang Lei, and Tian Ming visited the Vanke Center. They were excited by our Platinum LEED certification. Each of these three entrepreneurs had his own ideas about green architecture. As they went along, they asked the volunteer who was taking them around all kinds of technical questions, to the extent that he could barely deal with them all. Like all outstanding entrepreneurs, they were highly curious and wanted to know more.

The next day at the association meeting, I warmly introduced the three men as "The Three Swordmasters of Green Building." Soon after, their three companies did in fact formally join the China Urban Realty Association.

In the same year, a number of companies in the association set up a committee to deal specifically with green building in order to speed up understanding and adoption of green practices. The companies Vanke, Fengshang, Modernland, Landsea, and Vantone were leaders in this effort. In 2011, members of the association represented the majority of projects certified under the Three Star green certification of the Ministry of Construction. Vanke completed 2.74 million square meters (8.99 million square feet) of green construction, which represented 41 percent of all Three Star certified projects, and Landsea completed 740,000 square meters (2.43 million square feet), representing 11 percent of all Three Star certified projects.

The Three Swordmasters of Green Building had definitely injected new vitality into the association. Having this new energy was precisely what I had intended as a way to push it in the direction of green strategies. Another change that later occurred was unanticipated, however, and highly welcome: the move to start combined procurement in order to lower costs and improve efficiencies.

September 2011. Xi'an.

This was the very first joint procurement meeting to be held by the China Urban Realty Association. On the association side were around nine member companies, including Jianye, Vantone, Huayuan, and Landsea. Around 13 suppliers participated, including TOTO, Robam, and Kone. Together, we signed RMB 220 million worth (USD 34.65 million) of procurement agreements, which is not in itself a small number. In terms of efficiencies, however, it also lowered average procurement costs by 5 to 10 percent.

The significance of this joint procurement effort went far beyond the numbers. This was the very first joint procurement in the China real estate industry, which signified that the China Urban Realty Association was taking a major step forward. At the time, I was far away in the United States. I got the news from the Dai Dawei. It turned out Tian Ming was the one to have carried the ball in making this initiative a success.

Real estate developers play a critical role in assembling and organizing the resources of society. The quantity of things they buy is enormous. To a large extent, the costs and quality of their purchases determine the ultimate cost and quality of the housing they are building. Joint procurement had been one of the primary objectives when the association was first set up. It had been our number one goal, but was hard to make happen. When I was rotating chair of the organization, I put major effort into it, but I saw little success. The reason: when the association was first set up, member companies not only distrusted one another but had very different procedures in how they purchased supplies. Standards for products were also different, so it was hard to achieve unified action.

When Feng Lun was rotating chair, he too worked hard on this and even set up a company specifically for promoting joint procurement. He was extremely creative, but he too saw few results.

By the time Ren Zhiqiang was rotating chair, the company Landsea, under Tian Ming, had become the entity responsible for heading the joint procurement committee. Under Tian Ming's command, a number of vice presidents for procurement and various managers also now joined the project team. Landsea's leadership in green building was intimately related to the powerful purchasing power of these people. After one year of exploratory efforts, Tian Ming and his team were able to lead the entire brotherhood of the association along the same path. This led to the signing ceremony that took place in September 2011, in Xi'an.

Tian Ming then quickly decided to strike while the iron was hot. He began preparations for a second joint procurement. This time, instead of being led just by Landsea, a number of other companies championed joint procurement of various categories of products. Vantone spearheaded the effort with elevator lighting, Jianye led the charge with coatings, paints, and hardware, Huayuan was in charge of kitchen appliances, while Xindi led the way with flooring and floor and wall tiles.

Starting on January 6, 2012, the joint procurement committee held around 500 procurement meetings in six cities, spread out over 95 days. More than 300 suppliers participated. A signing ceremony was held in April, with 17 association members joining in this time, signing purchasing contracts with 24 suppliers. The total sum of procurements was double what it had been the first time, and came to RMB 550 million (USD 87.16 million)

The cost savings on these procurements was considerable, which in turn resulted in higher efficiencies and higher quality. In specific categories, elevator costs saved 4 percent on average; lighting, in general, 5.5 percent; paints, 11.8 percent; hardware, 8.2 percent; kitchen appliances, 12.6 percent; flooring, 8.1 percent; floor and wall tiles, 22.3 percent; front doors, 7 percent; and air conditioning, 4.4 percent. The overall average savings for all categories came to 8.4 percent.

In addition, when suppliers bid for contracts, they increased the transparency of their dealings. One reason is that they were interested not just in the items for which the procurement meetings were organized but also in bidding on other goods in the projects. Via the association, many members found outstanding suppliers they would not otherwise have known about.

In April 2012, Tian Ming announced at the annual meeting of the association that 26 members were expected to participate in the third joint procurement. This was nearly 50 percent of all members, plus the categories of goods being bought had greatly increased. The total amount in financial terms was also expected to double again.

Amid applause, Tian Ming stepped down from his successful tenure as chair of the procurement committee. By this time, the joint procurement practices of the China Urban Realty Association were moving in the right direction. Looking back on it, the success of this joint purchasing was due to the way the association served as an intermediate platform, not just to increased trust among members and the standardization of procedures. The association allowed for procurement that was more public, more transparent, and more effective in lowering costs. Meanwhile, the capable individual efforts of Tian Ming were the most critical link in this whole chain of events.

Among the three labels that people generally hang on me—*entrepreneur, mountain climber*, and *a person who does not give or take bribes*—I like the last one the best.

People always place unlimited expectations on themselves; they are always trying to create meaning out of what they are doing. As material wants are satisfied, they want to do more unconventional things, achieve greater success, and thereby have a greater impact on society. This amplifies their need to define their own hopes and wishes in life. All these things applied to the entrepreneurs we brought together for a conference on corporate ethics.

The key elements of Vanke's corporate culture have been boiled down to simplicity, transparency, standardization, and responsibility. Achieving these things is not easy, given China's traditional culture and given the realities of the country right now and a society in the midst of transition. The difficulty of achieving such things, however, is part of why we have to do them. This is, after all, part of the Vanke spirit.

In early 2012, Vanke and the Asia Center at Harvard jointly sponsored a forum in Shenzhen on the topic of "The Morality [*lunli*] of Asian Business." The title of this forum incorporated the word *lunli*, a Confucian term that encompasses more than simply morality. It refers to a world view of ethical principles by which to harmonize the way people interact with society. At this forum, businesspeople came together from all over Asia* to explore the mechanisms by which each company forms its own ethical principles. In addition to

---

*Attendees came from Japan, South Korea, India, East Asia, and China's Taiwan and Hong Kong.

scholars from the Harvard Business School and Harvard's Asia Center, attendees included the well-known Confucian scholar from both sides of the Straits, Professor Tu Weiming.* Holding this forum was an important part of my relationship with Harvard.

The chairman of Harvard's Asia Center, Arthur Kleinman, attended the proceedings via teleconferencing, since he was not well enough to travel to China. Professor Kleinman spoke about the influence that traditional concepts of morality in eastern and western philosophies have on modern enterprises. Ethics come into play particularly when individuals and groups of people have to figure out how to deal with crises or abnormalities in their lives. In the narrow sense, ethical norms are generally defined by local conditions, but local standpoints must also be judged by more universal norms. An ethical life is closely connected to ethical values that transcend local conditions and serve as a guide in our daily lives. Those who seek to live an ethical life may become aware that they are being placed in unethical situations, as based on the broader sense of ethics. Some therefore stand up to criticize and oppose, no matter how unfavorable doing so might be for them personally. The dangers involved also mean, however, that many others are willing to express opinions in private but go with the flow in public.

Those who attended the conference sat in the midst of large display screens showing Professor Kleinman as though he was with us right there in the room. Modern technology can reduce the distance among people, but in some ways it can also increase that distance. In some ways, it has accelerated a decline in morality. Ancient societies generally expressed a common sense of ethics through such institutions as the household, the nation, and religion. That has now changed, and corporations have become one of the primary vehicles by which ethical concepts are carried forward. Since the rise of the modern corporation, enterprises have become a critical social organism. They have a profound impact on the formation and evolution of ethics. This then forces those who run companies, entrepreneurs, to take stock of their own significance in that process.

The forum was not that large but it challenged Vanke's Center at Dameisha, since this was the first time we had held an international meeting like this. It was our first test of both hardware and software. Since then, we have held many similar activities, including a Sino-U.S. real estate investment summit, and various ad hoc public discussions by ambassadors. We hope this place will become more of a platform for international interaction in the future.

The deputy director of the Harvard Business School, Ms. Lynn S. Paine, also participated in the forum on business ethics. She was the first person with

---

*The name in *pinyin* spelling is Du Weiming. Born in Kunming in 1940, he studied in China before taking a doctorate at Harvard in 1968. He taught at Princeton and the University of California, Berkeley, before starting a long tenure at Harvard in 1981. He is generally regarded as the world's leading Confucian scholar and leading advocate for Confucian thought.

whom Vanke had any contact at the Harvard Business School. She approved of Vanke's ethical approach to business and later invited me to speak three times at the school. She also hoped to use Vanke as a Harvard case study, to be incorporated in the library of case studies that are used in courses. In August 2012 and August 2013, she personally led a team to Vanke to carry out the research and make that happen.

We provided a special beverage for attendees at the 2012 forum, a drink made out of honey produced from hives at the Vanke Center. I explained to our guests that my visit to the WWF headquarters in the United States had made a deep impression on me.*

Companies can fine-tune the environment surrounding their buildings. They can create microenvironments that are conducive to harmonious relations, extending even to bees, but they can also destroy their environments. The same is true of their social environment. The question for all of us is: what kind of ethical environment are we creating right now? Are we driving society in the direction of the good or toward unbridled greed?

That evening's banquet was also held at the Vanke Center. Guests continued to debate the day's topics, wine glasses in hand, as the forum continued over dinner. Professor Tu Weiming comes from Taiwan where he is regarded as the central figure in neo-Confucianism. Modest and self-reserved, he is someone I had always heard about and wanted to meet, but this was my first opportunity. As we looked out over the beautiful sight of Dameisha at night, this elegant gentleman congratulated Vanke on creating the Vanke Center. "Unbelievable," he kept saying. Then, looking at me, he added, "This must be the most beautiful community in all of China. I hope that we can have next year's forum here again. If so, I will attend."

How Big Is the Real Estate Bubble?

It was a wet, rainy day. I spent all night working on my speech, then hurried across campus the next morning to the Harvard Business School. My professor at the school had put together a series of lectures on the Chinese real estate market and had asked me to talk about the subject of Chinese real estate and real estate bubbles.

At class, he first described his belief that the real estate bubble in China would burst in 2013. His reasoning was as follows. Given the severe macro economic adjustments that the central government was putting in place, housing prices would stop rising. The idea that land prices would continue to rise indefinitely was a myth. Instead, prices would fall, leading to the bankruptcy

---

*Located at 1250 24th Street, NW, Washington, D.C., this building has Platinum LEED certification. It is regarded as green for numerous activities that achieve energy efficiency, water use reduction, and so on. Most impressively, the building has a green roof with state-of-the-art living system of locally grown plant life.

of local governments that depended on land sales to cover their budgets. This would lead to a crisis in nonperforming loans. A financial crisis would then appear in China that was similar to the financial crisis in America.

It was not unreasonable to come up with this conclusion if one used analytical models. However, as an "honored guest" at the discussion, I presented a different point of view. My reasons were simple. China's financial system was vastly different from that in the West. The financial system in China had not in fact been marketized. Even if it were to run up against a large number of nonperforming loans, that would not swiftly lead to the bankruptcy of large numbers of companies and a restructuring of the market. The situation would not force the bankruptcy of local governments. Second, the real estate bubble that does indeed exist in China is not comparable to the credit crisis in the United States, which involved overdrafts on credit. The two things were occurring at fundamentally different stages of economic development. The bubble in China is indeed spurred on by the idea that land can only go up in value, not down, during the process of industrialization and urbanization. The one in the United States was a bubble spurred on by the financial derivatives of a post-industrialized era. If you wanted to make a comparison, it was more realistic to contrast China's situation with the real estate bubble in Japan in the 1990s. While the situations were different, that thought was not a comforting one.

Since 2004, the central government of China has constantly put forth policies that try to curb overly fast increases in housing prices. The result has been a kind of retaliatory response—after a short period of holding prices down, they surge even more. By the second half of 2007, strict monetary measures had been taken to control the market. Many real estate developers did as they had always done. They were reluctant to sell and tried to hold onto the status quo. Vanke instead took a different point of view. It felt that the macro adjustments were having an effect and that prices had indeed reached a turning point. It therefore lowered its prices, while the great majority of the industry adopted a wait-and-see attitude. Moving into 2008, consumers too adopted the same wait-and-see attitude, and the market began to shrink. Most developers still refused to lower prices. The market then entered a period of treacherous stalemate. By October, those developers that could no longer hold on lowered their prices. Macro policies were seen to be effective. At this point, the industry realized that Vanke had been right to take the first step in lowering prices. The reason Vanke lowered prices, however, related as much to its unwillingness to condone greed as its ability to read the future.

The financial tsunami that started in the United States in 2008 led to enormous changes in the international environment. Trying to contain inflation quickly turned into trying to stop deflation. The central government of China adopted a new stimulus policy, putting RMD 4 trillion (USD 585.7 billion) into trying to stimulate the economy. China's housing prices went through a period of correction, but ultimately they rose again. By 2009, prices rebounded in a retaliatory way. They reached unprecedented levels in 12 of 20 key cities. In the other eight, prices were nearly at their historic highs. The situation in Beijing was particularly severe, where average housing prices rose by more than 60 percent. Shenzhen followed suit shortly thereafter. The madness spread from first-line cities to housing in second- and third-line cities. The most ironic thing is that developers who had refused to lower prices in 2008 found that they were making one-and-a-half times their previous profits in 2009. Vanke, which had lowered its prices, made far less. The press now said that Wang Shi could generally see the trends—so why did he drop prices so early? I did not regret the decision. Instead, I continued to be extremely fearful about this crazy rise in prices. The memory of what happened when Japan's bubble burst was fresh in my mind.

In the 1970s, the Japanese government began a program of building highways, the Shinkansen,* and other projects as part of a substantial effort to build up basic infrastructure. Given this, a large amount of "hot money" flowed into the country after the Plaza Accord, which led to an explosive rise in real estate prices. That increase began in the Tokyo area but soon spread to Osaka, Nagoya, and other large cities. Seduced by the promise of rising real estate prices, many Japanese people spent their hard-earned savings on property, and they also began to play the stock market. By 1989, the land value of all of Japan, an area roughly the size of California, was worth four times the value of all land in the United States. By 1990, land values in Tokyo alone were roughly equivalent to the total land value of the United States. This was an unprecedented real estate bubble.

Faced with this bubble, the Japanese government did not take timely action to control things. It only started to intervene in 1987. In 1988, prices in Tokyo began to fall; however, prices in Osaka, Nagoya, and other large metropolitan areas continued to rise. In 1991, prices finally began to fall on a nationwide basis. By 1993, real estate prices had completely collapsed. Unpayable loans now reached USD 600 billion (RMB 3.438 trillion). Japan now faced what has become the longest depression known in economic history. To this day, it has not yet completely emerged from the shadow of the disaster. Meanwhile, looking back at China, there are many similarities. We too have a real estate fever formed through a long period of investment in basic infrastructure and urbanization. The crazy rise in prices of 2009 was enough to make one fear for the future.

In 2010, the central government in China began a new round of measures aimed at limiting credit, limiting purchasing, and tightening up on administrative permits. These three channels were intended to restrict speculative demand, and in fact they successfully controlled the situation. According to data on new housing prices in 70 large and medium-sized cities, in 2011 housing prices rose slightly, by 1.6 percent, while the real increase in per capita incomes was 14

---

*The bullet train, a high-speed rail line.

percent. By the third quarter of 2012, housing prices over the same period the previous year had fallen by 1.1 percent, while per capital disposable income had increased by 13 percent. In other words, in terms of purchasing power, housing prices have fallen by an annual real rate of 12 percent.

Turning now to Vanke's situation, despite tightening because of central government policies, the company held to its main business of selling to the consumer market. Its revenues were RMB 120 billion (USD 18.6 billion) in 2011 and maintained the momentum in 2012. At the same time, the company continued to look to the future. It pushed forward the industrialization of housing, the sale of housing that was already fully equipped and ready to live in, green housing, and a general upgrading of both quality and product features. At present, it is transitioning from being a sales-type developer toward being a technology-type company with R&D as its main thrust. If the economy continues to grow and macro policies are maintained, in another two to three years, the housing market should achieve a soft landing. In that process, the industry as a whole should be moving from growth that depends on quantity to growth that depends on higher quality.

One year after I presented this summary of my thoughts to Harvard, the TV news program *60 Minutes* interviewed me about the Chinese real estate market.

HOST: *So Vanke is the world's largest builder of housing, is that true?*
WANG SHI: *I guess it probably is.*
HOST: *That means, maybe?*
WANG SHI: *Correct. That is true only with respect to quantity. Not to quality.*
HOST: *Are housing prices too high right now?*
WANG SHI: *Absolutely.*
HOST: *Is there a bubble?*
WANG SHI: *Of course there is.*
HOST: *If a bubble exists, the key question is whether or not it will burst?*
WANG SHI: *If it bursts, that will be a disaster.*
HOST: *Many economists are saying that the bubble is so big that this government cannot control it.*
WANG SHI: *I believe that the highest leadership in the country possesses enough intelligence to handle this matter. My own feeling is that the Chinese economy in 2013 will not have a hard landing because of a real estate bubble. However, we must stay vigilant and not let down our guard.*

Flooringgate

At noon on February 16, 2012, I was in an airplane making my way from New York back to Beijing. What should have been a tranquil and uneventful day back in China was suddenly disrupted by a notice put up on the Internet.

At 11:50 a.m. Beijing time, an article appeared on the Kaidi website under the pseudonym of Li Xiaoyan. The author said that the formaldehyde levels in flooring being sold by the A&W Flooring Company had exceeded the levels required by State standards. What's more, it pointed to improper dealings between the procurement system of Vanke and its supplier A&W. As a result of these improper dealings,* unacceptable flooring was being installed in many of Vanke's buildings.

This so-called Li Xiaoyan purported to be the deputy editor of a magazine focusing on domestic building materials. This magazine informed against and exposed violations of building code that were believed to be damaging to human health. The notice said, "Two months ago, I received irrefutable evidence from a friend and I followed this up with my own investigations. They confirmed that the leading real estate company Vanke has been installing large quantities of inferior flooring in as many as ten thousand units in more than a dozen cities in the country. This flooring, sold under the A&W brand, emits seriously dangerous levels of formaldehyde that grossly exceed standards. Some batches of this flooring emit as much as five times what is acceptable. This has become a lethal problem to the extent that people are calling it 'killer flooring.' What's more, this inferior flooring is too thin, which gives it just twenty percent the life of standard products."

The term "killer flooring" used in this notice was then picked up on by other media and had the potential to do great damage, despite the fact that no actual circumstances had been properly confirmed.

Vanke's senior management team learned the news within an hour of the posting. If the accusations were true, not only would the reputation of China's entire flooring industry collapse, but the quality of Vanke's products in general would be hard to guarantee and the whole strategy of providing fully equipped housing would come under question.† Without question, this was the most severe crisis that Vanke had faced to date. Even if the notice was a fabrication, it was highly likely that Vanke's reputation would take a hit, the greatest since the year 2008. I was in the plane flying back to China, while CEO Yu Liang was at the Dongguan R&D base participating in a conference on commercial systems. There was no time to wait for orders—the fire had to be put out! The executive vice president mobilized emergency measures by calling a meeting of key parts of the company to analyze the situation. He brought together the heads of such departments as project management, procurement, public relations, legal office, as well as the office of the CEO, to evaluate countermeasures. Once Yu Liang finished his meeting, he too hurried back to headquarters and reached the conference room at 4 p.m.

---

*In my opinion, this article was implying that bribes were being paid by A&W to Vanke procurement people (which they most certainly weren't) in order to sell off inferior low-cost goods.

†Housing is sold "unfinished" in many developments, and the buyer himself is responsible for "furbishing."

Using a speakerphone, the group in the room called the cellphone of the chairman of the board of A&W, a man named Lu Weiguang. His phone had been turned off. Some people began to have grave suspicions—was Lu Weiguang on the run? Could something even worse have happened?

Headquarters now came up with a list of the names of all first-line companies that had used A&W flooring. It asked these companies to form emergency groups themselves in order to understand exactly what the situation was. At the same time, those in the conference room analyzed the message of Li Xiaoyan. It gave the impression of having verifiable evidence and it showed photos.

By now, news of A&W's quality problems was becoming quite strident. One website sent out a mass questionnaire asking people, "Do you believe this?" Sixty-nine percent of those who responded said, "Still air doesn't stir up waves—there is something behind this. Yes, I believe that A&W is selling killer flooring." Another 17.4 percent said, "Vanke has no conscience whatsoever. It is poisoning its customers." Only 14 percent were willing to be impartial, pending the results of an investigation.

Even the emergency team huddled in Vanke's conference room was inclined to believe the substance of this so-called Li Xiaoyan's message.

It was impossible at that immediate moment to verify how much truth there was behind the Internet exposé. It was highly unlikely that Vanke had systemic problems overall in terms of its project control systems and procurement. People inside the company were confident of Vanke's procedures. It was always possible, however, that there were lacunae here and there.

A&W flooring ranked third overall in Vanke's procurement of flooring materials. This came to a substantial amount. If there were indeed loopholes in Vanke's procurement systems and quality control systems, this would indeed have a serious impact on the health of Vanke's tenants. Vanke's reputation would suffer a mortal blow.

The team in the conference room continued to call the cellphone of Lu Weiguang—and they got through! His voice came on the line. He had just got off an airplane. He seemed not to have a full grasp of the implications of the matter—there were many considerations. He had to look into it. This made the emergency group even more suspicious—was A&W implicated, or was it inexperienced?

Whichever the case, the group decided to make a public announcement. First, Vanke was treating the matter seriously and had launched an emergency investigation. It also had required a full explanation from A&W. Second, prior to results of this investigation, it was temporarily halting all purchase of flooring from A&W. It was also impounding all flooring it had purchased from A&W that was not yet installed. Third, it was reinspecting A&W flooring that had already been installed. It was asking official certification bodies to participate in this inspection. Fourth, it was carrying out an internal investigation of its own management procedures.

The final two sentences of this public announcement were: "If the investigation shows there is indeed a problem with the quality of our products, Vanke will bear full responsibility and take all necessary measures. That includes protecting the legal rights and interests of its customers."

This last sentence implied that Vanke would not be standing on the side of A&W in this matter.

Meanwhile, we continued to dial the telephone number of Li Xiaoyan as it was given on the Internet message. That number continued to be unavailable. Several days later, Vanke was able to find out through various channels that this person did not in fact exist. By that time, however, the media had stirred up so much attention about the quality of A&W flooring that nobody paid any attention to this detail.

As soon as my flight landed in Beijing, I turned on my cellphone and learned about this whole incident. A call from the CEO's office reported all that had happened and steps that were already underway to address the situation. I felt that the management team had responded swiftly and appropriately. What's more, their highly responsible attitude put me at ease.

On February 17, the head of Vanke's auditing and investigation department, Zhou Qingping, and the head of its project management office, Wang Weifeng, flew to Shanghai to begin an investigation of the A&W company. They met with Lu Weiguang and asked that A&W take full responsibility for its products, that it be proactive and transparent in its dealings with the public on this matter, and that it undertake its own investigation and carry out responsible countermeasures.

Meanwhile, Vanke held meetings of the emergency group twice a day at scheduled times, 9 a.m. and 5 p.m. If any new information surfaced, the group called ad hoc meetings as well to discuss how to deal with it. On every aspect, the team first came up with its own conclusions. Yu Liang then had the final say. By noon on February 17, Vanke's announcement had already gone to the 29 projects using A&W flooring in 16 cities around the country. Vanke had already applied to the state institutions that inspect and certify quality for reinspection, and some investigations were already underway.

The first batch of results was obtained within around 10 days. The final batch of results took around 20 days to one month to come in (that is, by around the middle of March.) As soon as each testing report came in, it was revealed to the public and to Vanke customers immediately.

Vanke took the initiative in reaching out to customers. Once public notices went out, however, customers who had A&W flooring in their apartments were extremely worried. They expressed their concern either through the Internet or directly to Vanke, which suddenly increased the pressure on the company. Vanke had put itself under a microscope with respect to the public, and it had no idea how inspections would turn out. As we all made phone calls, held meetings, collected data, and tried to evaluate what to do, we worried.

Dealing with the A&W incident became the number one concern of the entire Vanke Group during this period.

One problem now presented itself to the team working on the issue. We found out that Vanke was just the third-largest customer for A&W flooring. The first and second largest were our major competitors. One hundred percent of the flooring of the larger of these two was provided by A&W.

Some colleagues in the team made a suggestion. What if we surreptitiously let this fact become known? Right now, all media attention was focused on Vanke and Vanke alone. It was as though we were the only bad apple in the group. If we implicated others in the industry—"pulled them into the water too," as the saying goes—that would relieve the pressure on us. What's more, our competitor was fully endowed with the resources to manipulate public opinion, which would facilitate the process of calming down this crisis. Anyway, there was always the possibility that Vanke's competitors themselves had put us in this beleaguered position.

It would be a tricky move. Once everyone had discussed the matter, however, they came to a consensus of opinion: we would not make evil conjectures about our own industry. We also would not pull others in the industry into the water with us. Vanke was the leader in the housing industry—whether good or bad, most things that happened in the industry happened to Vanke first. When something bad happened, we, as the industry leader, had to take responsibility. Later, this idea of pulling others into the water came up several times in discussions among the group. Yu Liang rejected the suggestion every time.

I was reminded of what a colleague said when he joined our team around the time of a separate incident in 2008. He said that Vanke people were highly intelligent, which meant they would think of every possible crooked way to get things done. My take on that was that Vanke people are indeed highly intelligent, so they ultimately reject such crooked ways and means.

On the afternoon of the February 17, A&W held a press conference. The format was simple and direct, and the spokesperson for the company was candid and self-confident. He explained things clearly down to the last detail, and he also put in a bit of humor. People got the impression that this person represented a company that was honest and mature.

February 18 was a Saturday. The results of our internal investigation came out: procurement procedures were in accord with regulations. All documentation on inspections was complete, and there had been no irregular dealings between personnel in the procurement department and A&W. At the same time, Zhou Qingping and Wang Weifeng returned from Shanghai with the same conclusion. They had completed an investigation of the possibility of kickbacks, and there was no evidence at all to support the existence of any systemic risk.

We convened a meeting of the team and summed up the latest information. Everyone now began to think that there was a considerable chance that Li Xiaoyan's message was fraudulent. We all drew a deep breath and thought we might be able to calm down over the weekend. We hoped that this incident would gradually disappear on its own. I, however, took a different slant on it. The fact that the A&W flooring incident had developed to this degree meant that it was already having a major impact on A&W, on Vanke, and on the flooring industry in general. It was particularly damaging to the prospects for our developing the refurbishing industry. If we took a conservative approach and just let this matter blow over, we could weather this immediate crisis but we would not eliminate the greater damage done to the industry. I recommended the following course of action: be proactive instead of conservative, take the initiative instead of being forced into a passive position. Hold a press conference and state the facts clearly—go on the counteroffensive. Shortly afterward, I expressed this recommendation in the form of a Weibo message on the Sina website. The moment any customer discovered problems with a Vanke product, Vanke would take full responsibility. It would protect the rights and interests of consumers. Even if there was a 1 percent discrepancy, that was the same as a 100 percent loss to the consumer! By February 20, the incident was into its fifth day and Vanke held a press conference. It described its situation. In 2010–2011, the largest supplier of flooring to Vanke was a company called Shengxiang, with a 40 percent share of Vanke's flooring needs. The second-largest was Sino-Maple. The third largest was A&W. In its entire history of cooperation with A&W, Vanke had never discovered levels of formaldehyde that exceeded regulatory standards, nor had it discovered other substandard problems.

After this press conference, Vanke took the high road in responding to the flooring issue in other forms of media and on the Internet. Some of its Net "friends" were supportive of this responsible attitude, and others expressed doubts. Why should Vanke take the risk of standing on the side of A&W?

It was true that at this point Vanke itself was confident of A&W flooring, but the results of the testing had not yet come in. What's more, there were bound to be human error factors and accidents in the process of testing—if bad news came out, could we deal with it? The principle of crisis management calls for sticking to what is simplest. Less is more. One has to take the high road and have ultimate confidence in one's colleagues, one's systems, and one's corporate culture. At the same time, one must be courageous and decisive.

On February 22, the first batch of results came in. The Wuhan quality-control inspection bureau confirmed that the A&W composite flooring used in Vanke's buildings, made up of reconstituted wood particles, complied with national standards for the emission of formaldehyde. The allowable limit of formaldehyde was 1.5 milligrams per liter, whereas A&W's flooring was far below that, at 0.2 milligrams per liter. What's more, the flooring met other required national standards for such things as durability and tensile strength.

This positive report did not put everyone at ease. On the contrary, it made us even more nervous, since each report that would be coming in would be promptly reported to the public. In the following days, inspection reports came in from various places around the country. Wuhan had passed, Qindao passed, Guangzhou passed, Chongqing passed, Beijing passed, Hangzhou passed, and so on.

On the afternoon of March 1, a report came in from the city of Foshan that did not pass. Instead of being below 1.5 milligrams per liters, the formaldehyde emissions came to 1.9 milligrams per liter. We now faced a decision. The procedures for national testing allowed a company three separate evaluations. If the first passed, the company was fine. If it did not, then the company still had two chances to see if the first was valid. The ultimate result was the average of all three. That is, Vanke still had a chance to get a better result. What should we do? A meeting of the crisis team decided to go ahead with two more tests but to make the results of this first test known to the public and to regard it as the final result. That is, Vanke accepted the conclusion that this location used substandard materials.

We relayed this information to A&W. A&W felt we had done them a grave disservice. The chairman of the board, Lu Weiguang, said, "We have faith in our own products, and we would hope that Vanke would allow a second chance before jumping to conclusions." Vanke explained its rationale: "In complex situations, the simpler the better. The more transparency, the more credibility you have with the public. If you talk about overly complex testing procedures and get ambivalent about things, rumors begin to fly. The public gets suspicious." Ultimately, A&W accepted our decision.

We quickly began emergency procedures in Foshan. We discussed how to provide compensation to customers and how to change out the flooring with suppliers. At the same time, we asked A&W for an explanation of the excessive emissions on this batch of flooring. We organized materials from companies that included A&W, as a way to express our confidence in and support for that company. We allowed other brands to be included, and asked customers themselves to make the choice.

On March 2, Vanke held another press conference in Foshan. It announced the results of the tests in Foshan and explained all details while also apologizing to customers. As per its promise, it confirmed that Vanke would switch out the old flooring for new flooring, as well as pay compensation to customers if just one test was not up to standards. The amount of flooring space involved came to 3,012 square meters (9,882 square feet). Of that, 104 apartments in the number 7 building at the development had been finished. The building had been readied for occupancy at the end of September 2011, although at present only 25 families had actually moved in.

As it replaced flooring and provided compensation, Vanke committed to fulfilling its responsibilities to the letter. It would resolve any issues that customers had as fast as possible and as completely as possible. If any other issues arose from using this batch of flooring, the company would bear 100 percent of the responsibility.

By now, all 17 reports had come in from around the country.* They were made public one by one as they came in. Of the 72 groups of results, 71 showed formaldehyde emission levels that were below the nationally required standard. One sample exceeded the standard.

---

*The places tested were in Wuhan, Qingdao, Guangzhou, Chongqing, Beijing, Hangzhou, Kunming, Xiamen, Nanjing, Zhenjiang, Hefei, Shanghai, Tianjin, Foshan, Xi'an, and Zhongshan.

Among all the sampled test sites, 41 were taken from places where the tenant had already assumed occupancy. Twenty-two were from warehouses that stored the materials to be installed, and three came from locations where the material had been delivered but not yet installed. Six came from exhibit rooms at various projects.

During this period, the inspection bureaus of the Wujiang district in Suzhou and of Shanghai also did law-enforcement sampling of A&W flooring materials. On February 21, samples were taken from four projects in Shanghai that Vanke and A&W had worked on together. This was done under the scrutiny of a host of people, including representatives of Vanke's tenants, people in the media, the construction commission of the Shanghai Party organization, the Housing Management Bureau, and Vanke itself. On March 1, the Shanghai Inspection Bureau publicly announced the results: formaldehyde emissions were in compliance with national standards.

Several days later, the results arrived from the second two tests of the Foshan samples. The formaldehyde emissions were within national requirements. I was not happy that the unfavorable results of the first test had affected people's lives. At the same time, however, I felt that the negative results had positive consequences. It was logical that an industrial process should have occasional hiccups. If all tests had passed muster, senior management might become arrogant and self-satisfied. They might well become careless. You could compare such occasional hiccups to the kind of colds that a healthy person gets—they help regulate and strengthen the immune system.

When negative news comes out, some companies try to resolve the problems by covering them up. By doing that, by developing the ability to cover things up, they unfortunately lose other abilities. Vanke does not operate that way. It needs to have the ability to deal with its own problems. By being upfront and candid with media and with itself, it helps create clearly defined standards and values.

After the A&W flooring incident, some people within Vanke began to question our goal of going into the refurbishing business. Outsiders had doubts about it—why should we even do it?

My answer to this was as follows. Refurbishing apartments did indeed pose problems. If Vanke did not do it, however, customers would be forced to do it on their own, and they were even less prepared to face the issue of quality control than we were. We had far more resources than our customers and much greater capacity. At the same time, undertaking refurbishing ourselves helped build our competitive advantage. I also believed that pushing forward this side of the business would have real significance in terms of our goals vis-à-vis environmental protection and energy savings. We were not going to abandon our ideals.

Hello, Milan!

Vanke participated in Expo 2010 Shanghai by setting up its own separate pavilion with an environmental theme that it called "The Possibility of Respect."

This introduced the company's concepts and activities with respect to environmental protection. It described the possibilities for mutual respect among people, nature, and urban environments. As soon as that expo finished, a small team from the company traveled to Milan to begin the process of planning the next expo, to be held in 2015.

During June to September 2013, I led a delegation to Milan twice. The first time had been to evaluate the location and confirm that the pavilion would be designed by Daniel Libeskind. This second time was to carry out formal discussions with the management of the event.

We met Mr. Libeskind and his wife at eight-thirty in the morning at the SDL (Studio Daniel Libeskind) offices in Milan, and then we went together to the management office to pay a call on Mr. Sala, chief operating officer of the Milan Expo 2015. We quickly came to the point of our meeting, and the Vanke team demonstrated our concept.

At big world events like expos and the Olympics, China has been somewhat self-aggrandizing in that the country uses these opportunities to display its own power. It has kept to the age-old custom of allowing visitors to pay court to the Middle Kingdom. This has been true of other countries as well, since the start of world's fairs. London's Great Exhibition in 1851 demonstrated the reach of the Industrial Revolution and the power of imperialism, with its idea that "the sun never sets on the empire." Queen Victoria herself sent out the invitations. The Chicago World's Fair in 1933 was entitled "A Century of Progress." It demonstrated the great accomplishments of the United States as well as world industry; such things as aviation technology, neon lighting, and air-conditioned buildings made their first public appearance there. The Expo in Osaka highlighted Japan's achievements since the Tokyo 1964 Summer Olympics. After that fair in 1970, Japan's economy took off.

As technological advances have become more widespread around the world, and as globalization has increased, a subtle change has occurred in the way countries approach big world events like expos and Olympics. This nationalistic attitude, extolling one's own system, has become more muted. The London Olympics was the clearest expression of this different way of thinking. It provided a stark contrast with the grand show put on at the Beijing Olympics.

I attended the London 2012 Summer Olympics. No expense was spared to build the facilities at the Beijing 2008 Summer Olympics, but the London facilities focused on efficiency and practicality. Many of the new buildings were in fact temporary structures, and the main hall was then sold to serve as the building for the next Olympics. Meanwhile, the opening ceremony emphasized the rural aspects of England. China cannot fully appreciate such nostalgia for the past in the midst of its own hyperfast urbanization, but to English people, quiet living in a country village is the ultimate in pure, aesthetic pleasure. The precious legacy of such a past is worth preserving in the midst of modernity.

An even more classic contrast between the London and Beijing Olympics was the way Londoners, as hosts, were unenthusiastic about having people from all parts of the globe converge on their city. Quite the contrary—many

Londoners complained about how the Olympics would clog up traffic. The demonstrations calmed down after the opening ceremony, partly due to inclement weather, but they did not stop altogether. Customs workers even threatened to go out on strike. Londoners made fun of themselves, saying that the sole reason the workers were going to go on strike was to keep foreign athletes outside so that English people could win some gold medals.

In sum, the trend of such massive world events as Olympics and expos is toward allowing life to go on as usual, to restore a measure of functionality and pleasure to the events as opposed to national aggrandizement.

What, then, was Vanke's theme for the Milan expo?

Libeskind designed a "Canteen." It was a traditional dining hall, called a *shi-tang*. Italians and Chinese both love their cuisines, and the Chinese even have a saying that "people live to eat." China experienced canteens at people's communes in the days of the planned economy, then canteens at college campuses, at Vanke's urban communities—all of these express living patterns and life situations.

After Vanke presented its idea to the Milan expo management, there was a brief question-and-answer session. As representative of the Expo Committee, Mr. Sala then praised the idea and welcomed Vanke to participate in Milan Expo 2015 as the first corporate participant.* Photos were taken to commemorate the occasion, and everyone symbolically lifted a glass of champagne.

A Member of the American Board of the World Wildlife Fund

The sounds of a choir and pipe organ issued from the cathedral not too far from the White House in Washington, D.C., on October 18, 2012. I was in the city to attend the annual board meeting of the World Wildlife Fund in the United States. One of the items on the agenda was the funeral of Russell Train, the founder of this organization in the United States. The ceremony was in a style very different from China, with no leaders giving speeches and no representatives of this or that entity holding forth. The proceedings were modest and respectful, just people presenting their remembrance of this man's life and his work, and an appreciation of the sound of his laughter. After the commemoration, a board member of WWF noted that that prior to his own funeral, he intended to remember to make a final contribution to environmental protection!

I have been involved with WWF for a number of years and I deeply respect the organization's activities and concepts. During this annual meeting, I was formally brought onto the board as the first foreign board member in the U.S. organization. For me personally, as well as for Vanke, this was both a great honor and a responsibility.

---

*The theme of Milan Expo 2015 was "Feeding the Planet, Energy for Life." The design of the Vanke pavilion incorporated three ideas drawn from Chinese culture related to food: the *shitang*, a traditional Chinese dining hall; the landscape, the fundamental element to life; and the dragon, metaphorically related to farming and sustenance.

Vanke has been working with the WWF in a variety of ways. In 2009, we responded to the organization's call to respect the globe for one hour by turning out the lights. Together with people from 135 countries, we turned out the lights for one hour in the last weekend of March as a way to raise awareness of global warming and environmental problems. I was fortunate to be one of the "image spokespeople" for the project in China. Based on the success of this activity, we then launched the garbage recycling program—we transitioned from an activity that involved one hour a day to one that involved one *day* in the lifestyle of people. The slogan was "Immediate Action Day," with the Chinese character for *immediate* making use of a different component that is also used in the term for *garbage*. The slogan therefore used a double entendre to signify that people should get that garbage divided into categories and recycled right away.

We expanded this effort in 2010 to a transnational program that focused on environmental protection in the Everest region. Forestry and sustainable use of wood products is particularly significant for Vanke, since housing construction uses an enormous amount of wood. We went on to promote "sustainable forestry certifications," a form of green certification for lumber, in order to reduce illegal timber felling and protect tropical rainforests.

China's rapid economic growth has astonished the world, but it has also caused considerable alarm about use of resources and resulting carbon emissions. At the 2012 WWF meeting in Washington, D.C., experts presented the data on the percentages of global resources that China consumes: 38.2 percent of the world's lead, 41.3 percent of its zinc, 45.5 percent of its steel, 46.6 percent of its coal, and 52.2 percent of its concrete. China's mode of economic growth is unsustainable, given its high consumption of energy per unit produced and its low efficiencies. Since the 2009 United Nations Climate Change Conference in Copenhagen, China's government has put greater priority on energy conservation and has implemented measures to reduce carbon emissions, which WWF experts have commended in positive terms. In contrast, some experts feel that the Obama administration has not done enough.

Meanwhile, what should a Chinese company do, particularly one that consumes large quantities of wood materials? What in fact did we do? Vanke's answer was to assume social responsibility, to take the path of using green products in its construction.

We agree wholeheartedly with the message of a speech given by WWF president Carter Roberts at this meeting. Ten years earlier, his wife gave birth to a daughter who was diagnosed with leukemia. Chances that she would live were 7 percent. Through the efforts of both parents and medical experts, the child did in fact survive. Mr. Roberts used this analogy to describe the situation of the planet today, whose inhabitants face the challenges of global warming, environmental pollution, and mass extinction of species, among others. We all must take aggressive steps to master and actually achieve environmental protection if we are to continue to enjoy the only planet that humanity relies on for its existence. His message was clear: chances do not look good, but we have to do all we can.

In 2012, after this annual WWF meeting, Vanke took a further step in cooperating with WWF by using WWF technology and monitoring mechanisms to push Vanke further in the direction of being a responsible corporate citizen. For its part, by cooperating with Vanke, WWF hopes to promote a sustainable wood certification program, particularly in rapidly growing economies. This is similar to the way the organization cooperated with the Coca-Cola Company for many years in promoting the conservation of water resources. At the end of 2012, Vanke joined the newest WWF project, aimed at protecting snow leopards in the Himalayas. Not only are snow leopards an endangered species in the cat family, but they are also a symbol of animals that live in the world's highest elevations. They are prey to hunters for several reasons, including people want their bones and their pelts, which is causing a dramatic decline is remaining numbers. Human activities are a threat to the existence of this large cat, which now is estimated to number just a few thousand individuals.

A four-year sustainable development project that is Asia-wide has been launched by the WWF and the United States Agency for International Development (USAID) that is also highly significant with respect to protecting snow leopards. This project is being implemented in a number of countries, including Bhutan, India, Kirgizstan, Mongolia, Nepal, and Pakistan. It is forming a snow-leopard alliance among countries that contain snow-leopard range. The project is aimed at raising awareness and action at all levels of snow-leopard range—local, national, and regional—in order to protect this endangered species. Vanke's welfare foundation has committed to investing funds in the project in order to support snow-leopard conservation in the northern Himalayan mountain range. In 2014, it organized a scientific survey of the number of snow leopards in snow-leopard protected areas along the border of China and Nepal.

Half a year after this idea was first proposed, I was in Washington, D.C., to attend a board meeting of WWF US and was delighted to learn that the action plan is moving forward. Since I began studying at Harvard in 2011, I have not been able to do more mountain climbing. I definitely hope to use this project as an opportunity to get back up into the Himalayas!

Rowing and the Spirit of Cooperation

The Charles River winds through Boston on its way to the ocean. By the twentieth century, this river was dyed various shades of pink and orange as untreated waste was poured into it from factories and a growing population. Fish died, and it gave off a toxic stench. In 1972, the United States passed the Clean Water Act and gradually began to use modern treatment technologies to process the waste. Boston began to improve hydrology systems and to move factories to more outlying areas. The measures were effective. The fish came back. By now, this stretch of the Charles has become one of the world's most famous sites for water sports. In the spring of 2011 and 2012, Vanke's rowing teams participated in international rowing competitions on the Charles—the five-starred red flag of China floated among the flags of other nations.

Once a given sport becomes a "state of being" in your life, you find you cannot give it up. I first started rowing 12 years ago, and it has been a state of being for me for the past six years. By my calculations, I hope to be able to keep rowing for another decade.

Rowing is one of the most traditional sports in the Olympics. It calls for a highly coordinated team, which is in line with Vanke's corporate spirit. Dragon-boat racing has a solid foundation in China, but the sport of racing this kind of racing shell has been virtually unknown in the country—it is far more scientific and requires much greater athletic skill than other kinds of boat racing. This lack of familiarity has put China at a disadvantage when it comes to competing at the Olympic level. In 2008, a team made up of Vanke's Shanghai employees participated in the Hutian International Rowing Invitational in Shanghai. The next year, the teams included one from Vanke's Hangzhou company. Starting in 2010, we participated in the international invitational at Shatin in Hong Kong. We were the only team active in rowing from all of mainland China. As time went on, Vanke finally entered the apex of the racing competition, on the Charles River in Boston. In 2012, I was one of the oarsmen in the "coxed eight" race, and we did not do badly—at least we beat our own record in 2011 by 28 seconds. In the "coxless four" we were docked for touching another boat with an oar and did not perform well. Nevertheless, our cheering squad on the bank, overseas Chinese students, roared as if we had won.

After this race, some of the team members from the Shanghai Vanke company paid their own way to go to Hong Kong to participate in the thirty-fourth international rowing competition there. They came in first among the four teams competing in the "fours," against teams from the MTR Corporation, the Standard Chartered Bank, and Lee Kum Kee. I hope that rowing will become more popular on China's mainland, at the very least on the many lakes in the south. Vanke's employees are active in a number of sports, including soccer, which has the longest tradition. Mountain climbing has the highest reputation, but is still an activity for a minority of people. Golf has long been beloved by many. Badminton stands up well, particularly among young women. Cycling and marathon running are the new fashion these days, but I still think that rowing can be the dark horse that comes up from the rear.

In May 2013, not only did Vanke compete again at Hutian, but this time there was a women's team competing in the "quad" race, which has two people each rowing with two oars.* Among the different categories of rowing, rowing an eight is the skill that requires the greatest degree of team coordination. Four years ago, Vanke could only assemble enough people to row one eight in races.

---

*In contrast, a "pair" has two people each rowing with a single oar. A "four" is four people each rowing with one oar, while a "quad" is four people each rowing with four oars. Your humble translator is a former sculling afficionado, having sculled on the Potomac in Washington (one of the first women to break the all-male Potomac Boat Club) and the waters around Seattle (Lake Union Boat Club).

By this year, it already has enough for two. Clearly, the sport is attracting more attention and Vanke's force is getting stronger!

The coxswain for the Vanke team, Fu Sang, started out in 2008 at a weight of 65 kilograms (143 pounds). Six years later, he was still serving as coxswain, but he had reduced his weight down to 60 kilograms (132 pounds). The ideal weight for a cox is roughly 55 kilograms (121 pounds), however—which is why many teams choose to have a woman take that position. If Fu Sang intends to continue, he had better lose more weight!

As the stroke in an eight,* I finally was able to win a bronze medal. The four from Shanghai Vanke won a gold, beating out a four from the Royal Yacht Club in Hong Kong, as well as breaking their own record. People from Vanke's Hangzhou company won a gold in the quad as well as a single scull. For the first time, a women's double participated in the race and unexpectedly took first place! Wow!

In the second half of 2013, when I moved from Harvard to Cambridge, I lived in a place not too far from the River Cam. Opposite me were rows of boathouses. One day, the head of the academy asked me, "Would you like to visit the boat club? I've heard you like rowing." When I responded positively, he organized a visit and someone to coach me. I showed up on time, but instead of being allowed on the water was first put through drills on land. I was kept at this activity for an hour and a half to the point that my legs felt like jelly. I was more tired than if I had competed in a competition. After training, I rode my bicycle home to the dormitory, swaying from side to side and singing all the way. At the next training session, I asked the coach, "How many times a week does the team train?"

"Ten times."

"Surely not." I thought I had misheard.

"Monday to Friday, twice a day. On the water at 6 a.m."

Several days later, I was chatting about this with some English friends, and they laughed. "Don't you know about Cambridge rowing?," they asked. "All of those guys are in the Olympics! How can you possibly expect to keep up with them?" I was sure that could not be true. "Cambridge has lots of teams," I replied. "Not all compete in the Olympics. I'm sure they wouldn't put me in a club of that caliber." Still, I wondered about that myself. When I got home, I checked it out on the Internet. My team was called the "Cambridge University Boat Club." It has been going for more than one hundred years† and competes at the highest level of rowing in the world. This was indeed the team that had competed in the Olympics and won.

I must be dreaming!

---

*The stroke sits in first place, with his back to the other players, who watch his oars and follow his rhythm. He is the key to coordinated performance.

†Founded in 1828.

Journalist from the Front Lines, Wang Shi

In April 2013, Harvard's Asia Center organized a roundtable discussion for businesspeople from China and the United States. Ninety-year-old former secretary of state Kissinger spoke with great vigor.

Soon after sending off the Chinese participants at this event, I welcomed a 15-person team from Vanke, in Boston to run the Boston Marathon. Nine of these people were Vanke employees, while two were business owners and another four were cooperative partners. The head of the team was our executive vice president, Wang Wenjin, a specialist in finance. The whole team looked lean and bronzed and full of vigor since taking up long-distance running. This was to be the first time a corporate team from China ever ran in the Boston Marathon. Some others joined in with our team, making the total 31 people. In 2012, a total of 47 Chinese people had run in the Boston Marathon. In 2013, the total came to 87, the greatest number of Chinese ever to have run in the event.

The Boston Marathon began in 1897, which was the year after the beginning of the Olympics in its modern incarnation. In 1897 there were only 15 participants, but this early date makes it the oldest urban marathon in the world. Since that time, the race has gone on annually without interruption. It is always held on the third Monday of April, which is Patriots' Day in the United States. Prior to 1986, the event followed the tradition of ancient Greece, which was to bestow a garland of olive leaves on the winner but no other prize. Due to the hilly inclines of Boston's route, this race has not produced the world's greatest marathon records, but that has not influenced its popularity. Nowadays, more than 30,000 participants run every year, and more than 500,000 spectators cheer along the way. Running in the Boston Marathon is the crowning glory for anyone who loves long-distance running. Unfortunately, many can only "gaze at the sight of the ocean" from a distance, as there are strict limits to the number of people allowed to run. The qualifying times are almost at a professional level.

The marathon leaves open one window of opportunity, however, namely participation by companies that help sponsor the event. Could Vanke possibly become such a sponsor? In July 2012, I decided to find out. I made an appointment to visit the Boston Athletic Association (BAA), which organizes the marathon.

A housing developer from China? You have got to be kidding! The person receiving me at the BAA was somewhat surprised. As he took me around the "Honorable Mention" exhibition room of the Boston Marathon, he hinted politely that the standards for taking in sponsorship were high. The committee was picky about the status and reputation of sponsors.

The visitor from Vanke patiently described the company: the largest housing developer in the world, and so on. Eyebrows went up; semidisbelief was now mingled with respect.

"We do all we can to be a green developer," the visitor from Vanke said. "In China, one out of every three certified Three Star buildings is a Vanke building."

The visitor from Vanke went on to introduce Vanke's merits. The American host seemed mollified. "Oh! We'll see what we can do, and we will be in touch," he said. Three months later, the committee told Vanke that it had been selected as a sponsor of the Boston Marathon for the coming three years. Vanke would have the right to let 15 participants run the race every year.

Noon on April 15, 2013, Eastern Standard Time, in the United States. One of Vanke's team charged across the finish line, waving a Chinese flag. This was Wei Zhigang, owner of the Wonderland Garden in Beijing. Running time: three hours and seven minutes, a personal record. Twenty minutes later, Xia Haiyin charged across the finish line, a member of the Vanke running association. Then came the first Vanke employee to cross the line, Xiao Min from the Fuzhou company. Zhong Cunhuang came next, from Zhongcheng Investments, and Wang Wenjin of Vanke headquarters at roughly the same time.

Chen Weiwen, Wang Bin, Zhu Wenming . . . as others reached the finish line, I suddenly heard a blast from the righthand side of my position on the viewing platform, then saw some smoke. Subconsciously, I thought a car tire had burst, but the sound seemed too loud. People around me expressed surprise, but nobody seemed alarmed. Around 10 seconds later, I heard another explosion from my left, just around 20 meters (66 feet) away. Objects spattered out from the explosion, and smoke again erupted. This time I thought, *something's wrong*! As I took in what was now pandemonium on the platform, I instinctively thought that this place was safer and I shouted, "Crouch, don't run!" Only when I had come to my senses did I realize I was shouting Chinese in the midst of Americans.

As I evaluated the danger, I drew out my cellphone and took a photo of the scene.

Immediately after these explosions, there was a brief moment of chaos when even the guards ran away from the direction of the blasts. Soon, however, without anyone giving orders but as though someone was guiding the action, security personnel made a cordon around the scene and began giving assistance to those who had been hurt. Some bystanders calmly walked away, not panicking, while others helped out with the rescue effort. Everyone maintained good order. Then there was the sound of sirens coming through the air. Children were shaking. Ambulances arrived on the scene. Residents from the neighborhood began bringing in clothes and hot water for those who had been hurt. It was astonishing: the response time of American society in general as well as American emergency services is fast.

Away from the scene of action, I called together our Vanke team and friends, and we all confirmed that everyone was safe. Together, we went back to the hotel and turned on the television which was already confirming the terrorist attack. Telephone calls began pouring in from people concerned about the safety of the Vanke team.

The photo that I had put up on the Internet got around quickly. A journalist from CCTV was soon in touch, asking me questions about "the front lines." As

I took the call, I could hear the alarm in his voice. On air, he referred to me as "Journalist Wang Shi from the front lines." I was now a journalist! The new title surprised me at first, but I realized that we have all become journalists in this age of new media. I therefore became the reporter from the front lines of the terrorist attack at the Boston Marathon. "I was standing in the VIP area of the viewing platform at the time," I said. "Eight of our Vanke team had already completed the run when I heard an explosion from the direction of the finish line . . ."

As time went on, people gradually calmed down and were able to talk. My assistant, Feng Nan, had been the closest to the explosion. That day happened to be his birthday, and he noted that this day of celebration had almost turned into the day on which he would be remembered. Chen Weiwen, from the Guangzhou company, had a family member who had waited for him near the finish line and whose pants had been ripped by the explosion. Jia Xiaomeng, from the Beijing company, had come to within 500 meters (1,640 feet) of the finish when the explosions occurred. An American handed him a banana as he left the scene, and a Chinese child handed him some clothing. Wang Wenjin, who finished, said that he fortunately had stopped to go to the toilet as he ran by Wellesley. Otherwise, he would have been right on time for the blast.

That evening, several Chinese students approached us and said they had been trying to locate the whereabouts of a fellow student. They wondered if we could help. Feng Nan immediately contacted the police and tried various other channels, and we found out that she had indeed been killed in the terrorist attack. Her name was Lu Lingzi.*

Several days later, I used the occasion of a luncheon at the Harvard Faculty Club to express appreciation for our Vanke team. In talking about the race, some members said they had reached the 41-kilometer (25-mile) mark and were already feeling the thrill of finishing when they heard the explosions and stopped. It was a shame. Another member said that he had not felt the thrill of victory, but he experienced something even greater—the concern of Bostonians for the runners in the race. If the objective of the terrorists had been to create terror, the result was the opposite—they had made us feel the warmth of people who cared.

Boston, you are a very great city.

A Tale of Three Bronze Bulls

Early June 2013. Shanghai at dusk. The multicolored lights of the Shanghai-side Bund put a sheen of variegated lacquer on Pudong.

The renowned artwork known as the Bund Bull lifted its spiraling tail in the rainbow lights of Lujiazui, looking as though it was about to charge. With uplifted head, its bullness challenged the very heavens. I suddenly wondered

---

*Twenty-three years old, Lu Lingzi was a graduate student at Boston University. She came from Shenyang, in Liaoning Province.

why this bull seemed so similar to the one we always think about, on Wall Street. A quick search on my cellphone informed me of the reason. This was by the same artist as the Wall Street Bull, and the two bulls were not that different in age. The one in Wall Street was born in 1989, while the Bund Bull was born in 2010. Both were designed by Arturo Di Modica, an American citizen of Italian descent.

These two bulls led me to think of yet another bull, one created in 1984 by Professor Pan He to commemorate the start of the Shenzhen Special Economic Zone. This bull was actually made five years before the Wall Street Bull. The year 1984 was the second year of the founding of Vanke in Shenzhen. The zone had recently been established, and young dreamers from all over the country were converging on this place, driving bulldozers and dump trucks, operating cranes, doing anything to get a start on a new life. The air was full of dust, and the entire landscape was a construction site. The Bund Bull created by Pan He symbolized the spirit of the place.

He has described his recollection of how he came up with the idea of this bull. One day, he happened to see two ancient trees with interlocking roots and branches, which sparked the inspiration. "I thought of how the Xinhai Revolution* was meant to do away with feudalism, to cut at the mighty trunk of China's dynastic tradition," he said. "In fact, however, the roots of that feudal way of thinking stayed behind and are still with us. I created this Pioneering Bull, this emblem of breaking into new territory, to depict the idea of breaking up the feudal vestiges that bind us. The idea was to pull out the very roots of bureaucracy and a petty farming way of thinking. The original concept was meant to be fairly profound. However, once central-government leaders saw the plan, they praised the sculpture in terms that made it into the Willing Ox. This implied approval for the way the people are industrious in tilling the land. From that time onward, the original intent of the bull, as a pioneering spirit that pulled out the roots of a feudal way of thinking, was set aside. Instead, images of the Shenzhen Pioneering Bull, and all the souvenirs that were later produced, were associated with something quite different."

In the Chinese language, a Willing Ox and a Pioneering Bull are both terms of praise, but they have totally different meanings. The former implies the love and concern of parents for their child. Lu Xun used this meaning when he used the term to describe a willingness to serve the people. In this sense, however, the original intent of the sculptor is altered and indeed eradicated. The two terms in fact express two different concepts. One destroys current reality, innovates, and creates something new. The other is content to stay within the current reality, to work hard, head down, contributing in a selfless way that does not demand compensation.

In the early 1980s, a major controversy erupted about the proper "line" to take as the Special Economic Zone was being set up. "Time is money; efficiency

---

*A revolution in 1911, when the Manchu-ruled Qing Dynasty was overturned.

is life" was the motto of the China Merchants Bureau in Shekou. It expressed the passionate desire to create value through hard work, as well as the desire to generate wealth. It therefore epitomized the purest, most simple motivating force behind founding a company. In traditional Chinese ways of thinking, however, "wealth" is equivalent to original sin. It is given only to those who are unethical and have destroyed the very idea of proper behavior. The evolution of the term "Pioneering Bull" into "Willing Ox" was not accidental.

Modern civilization derives from a Renaissance philosophy that believes that wealth stems from the creative work of humankind. People create value by throwing their whole beings into active exchange. The idea that they should receive wealth in return is only natural and is something to be desired and protected. In a society that is moving rapidly toward modernization, as is China, if this approach to wealth is not set up as the mainstream way of thinking, it will be impossible to create wealth in a way that is sustainable. Right now, *private* companies are the main force driving the economy of Shenzhen. While private companies hold less than half the total assets that state-owned enterprises hold in China, not only do they generate more production value but they also generate more jobs. Nevertheless, state-owned capital monopolizes the industries that earn the highest profit margins. State-owned enterprises are favored by discriminatory policies, and private companies are deprived of any right to compete on an equal basis. They are treated unfairly in every respect, from market-entry provisions to price setting to financial channels to market competition. If this existing situation cannot be changed, private companies will inevitably move elsewhere. They will invest their capital in markets that are more transparent and fair.

If you trace back the genealogy of the Bund Bull, you see that it refers implicitly to the former glory of Shanghai while also explicitly calling for a re-creation of that glory. Shanghai's former glory was derived from its specific geographic position in the Far East, but its vitality came from its market principles—transparency, efficiency, and free competition. If we are to reestablish Shanghai as an international financial center, it will be necessary to confirm those principles and set up financial systems that incorporate fair and transparent competition. Retrieving the glory of Shanghai will require allowing private capital to enter into financial markets. It will require understanding that the relationship between state-owned financial institutions and privately owned financial institutions is not one of substituting one for the other or having one supplement the other. Instead, the relationship must be one of fair competition. If financial markets can indeed be completely open, such that state-owned capital, overseas capital, and Chinese private capital can compete on a fair and equal basis, China's financial markets and its entire economy will be infused with new vitality. Only if that happens, however, will the financial industry enable China's economy to prosper on a sustainable basis. Only then will Shanghai be able to relive its days of glory as an international financial center.

It is amusing to reflect that the story of the Wall Street Bull stems from an unruly and courageous incident. Di Modica is a Sicilian artist who had been in

America for a number of years without much success. One day he thought of a way to make people notice him. Wall Street is the very heart of the financial world—if his work could be set up there, it would definitely attract attention. On the night of December 15, 1989, he hauled a bronze bull he had created over to a place in front of the New York Stock Exchange. It weighed 3,200 kilograms (7,055 pounds), and he used a large truck. The next morning, journalists and police were ringing the statue, and people were coming in droves to see it. The New York City authorities ordered him to remove it at once. The New York City Department of Parks & Recreation asked him to move it to a nearby location, and it currently resides in Bowling Green Park. In 2004, the artist offered it up for sale on condition that it remains in its current location. By that time, however, the fame of this bull had spread far and wide, and citizens already regarded it as their own public property.

Vanke's International Strategy

June 26, 2013. San Francisco.

I was in San Francisco to attend the groundbreaking ceremony for Vanke's first project in the United States. This was at 201 Folsom Street and was a cooperative effort with the U.S. company Tishman Speyer. It was a beautiful clear day, one of the few in this city of mists and changeable weather. People joked that we would soon look like lobsters from the sunburns. This first project overseas was aimed at getting up a steep learning curve. Vanke's team had looked into markets in many countries including Italy, Japan, and England, as well as the United States, and been made aware of just what a gap there is between us and mature markets. This applies to project management, including project financing and capital markets, and is particularly evident in how we compare to Tishman Speyer.

I firmly believe that project development inside China will also make more stringent demands on us in the future, after we pass the stage of not having to worry about selling whatever we build. We will have to be more adept at using all kinds of financial tools, and we should be able to gain this knowledge by working in more mature markets. This project was therefore an opportunity not only for us but also for Tishman Speyer. They put in a smaller percentage of the investment and reaped generous rewards on a major project.

The minute word got out that Vanke was going to invest abroad, media within China began speculating that Vanke felt the market in China was no longer promising. Actually, as we were preparing to enter the U.S. market, Tishman Speyer had just come into the China market. In 2012, a Tishman Speyer delegation paid a visit to Vanke in Shenzhen. Before we even mentioned wanting to invest in the States, they asked us to help them develop a project in Tianjin. Tishman Speyer had already invested in Europe, Asia, and Latin America—a first-rate company has to be international. Our going abroad was done with the similar intent to become a world-class company and to become competitive with other world-class companies. We wanted to learn from such companies. We did not go abroad because we felt the China market was bad.

It was not until the end of 2012 that we first received the formal materials on the San Francisco project. The person in charge of our investments at the time was Executive Vice President Zhang Xu. He said that this was the best prospect Vanke had come across to date, in terms of the choice of city, neighborhood, and access to transportation. He intended to go for it, and I approved. I thought it would take some time to get everything ready, but within a month Zhang Xu came to ask me to attend the signing ceremony. The date for breaking ground had even been decided upon: Valentine's Day, February 14, 2013. On that day, Vanke and its first American partner, Tishman Speyer, formally signed the agreement.

The day we broke ground was the first time I had actually been to the site. Our partner Jerry Speyer, CEO of the company, explained that this site had originally held the warehouse of the U.S. Postal Service in San Francisco. As the city grew, warehouses were moved to the suburbs and this site came up for redevelopment. This gave me more confidence in the project. The U.S. Postal Service system was set up in the late nineteenth century. Like today's Internet, it caused a revolution in business practices. The system allowed for "daily news." This meant that prices on the Chicago Board of Exchange could be established one day and known the very next day at the breakfast table of farmers in Minnesota, affecting their planting decisions. The postal system enabled what had been several dozen allied states to truly become "one nation under God." Because of this, post offices in cities built before the World War II were built in prime locations. It is no surprise that the high-speed rail line that California's government is building between San Francisco and Los Angeles will have its terminus near this spot.

As news circulated about this project, Vanke's staff received hundreds of telephone calls from friends within China asking if they could buy condominiums in the LUMINA project at 201 Folsom Street.* This was a logical development—many Chinese people were setting up businesses overseas but were not familiar with international real estate markets. They had faith in Vanke's brand, however, and they knew that its management had a good eye for investments. Many were already Vanke tenants. Since one had to buy from someone, why not buy from a well-known developer? In fact, we were far from being ready to sell space at that point.

"If we run into problems in the United States, we wouldn't know where to look for help. With Vanke, at least we know full well that you are right here in Shenzhen at Dameisha!" This was the attitude of many customers and was therefore a second reason we decided to invest in the United States—to follow

---

*The Chinese name for the street and the project is propitious. The Chinese transliteration of *Folsom* uses characters that mean "rising wealth."

our customers.* After 30 years of reform and opening up, a class with considerable wealth has grown up in China, and these people all want to set up businesses abroad. Considerations include the ability to allocate resources globally, children's education, and a better living environment. Naturally, the United States has become the first choice.

Officiating at the groundbreaking ceremony on June 26 was the mayor of San Francisco, Ed Lee, or in Chinese, Li Mengxian.† As a second-generation Chinese American, with roots in the Toishan part of Guangdong,‡ he is the first Chinese American to become mayor of San Francisco in the city's 160 years. Mayor Lee told me that the municipal government had authorized Tishman Speyer to redevelop this particular site back in 2003, but due to the subprime crisis in 2008, work had not started until now. Since the developer was Tishman Speyer, the government had continued to have confidence that the site would be developed, and it had not retrieved the rights. Now that Tishman Speyer had brought Vanke into the project, and it involved the leading developers of both China and the United States, Mayor Lee was confident the work would be finished during his tenure in office.§

San Francisco has a long history of being a port of entry for Chinese people. It was the first place immigrants landed during the Gold Rush and the building of the American railroads. A vast number of Chinese people surged into the country from this portal, which also then made San Francisco the epicenter of the exclusionary policies of the early twentieth century.

Once this Vanke project in San Francisco was finished, it would have more than 600 residential units. That figure is modest inside China, but in San Francisco it was already the largest development in the city's history. The election of Mayor Lee and the development of 201 Folsom Street confirm in no uncertain terms that the world has truly entered an age of globalization.

One more reason Vanke was investing abroad was the same as Tishman Speyer's—it wanted to allocate assets on a global basis and thereby disperse risk. In the past, Vanke viewed the process of internationalization as a way to take advantage of international assets to develop its China business. That meant drawing in international funds, human resources, architectural design, international suppliers, and so on. This San Francisco project now signaled that Vanke was moving outward. It was taking its internationalization to a new stage of actually going into international markets.

---

*The condominiums of LUMINA were priced at around USD 2,000 (RMB 13,325) per square foot. The penthouse of one of the towers was priced at USD 49 million (RMB 326.5 million).

†Mayor Lee assumed office in 2011 after serving as city administrator for a number of years. He was appointed when the post became vacant but was reelected mayor in 2015 for a term of five years. He is the first Chinese American mayor in San Francisco's history, as well as being the first Asian American elected to the office.

‡In Mandarin, Taishan; in Cantonese, Toishan. This is the part of southern China from which the majority of early Chinese immigrants came to California.

§The Sales Center opened in the summer of 2014, and the two towers were completed in 2015–2016. One is 42 stories high, the other 37 stories high.

In July 2012, Vanke purchased 75 percent of the shares of a company listed in Hong Kong called Winsor Properties Holdings Limited. It changed the name to the Vanke Property (Overseas) Limited. It now had an overseas listed platform. Meanwhile, the general movement in B shares is to transform them into H shares. As this happens, Vanke will have two listed platforms overseas.

There are clear benefits to having a listed platform. As the saying goes, water forms a channel wherever it begins to flow. Such listing is helpful in getting funding for projects we launch in Hong Kong, but there is another reason as well. Around this time, a Hong Kong company called New World Development had expressed an interest in working with Vanke as a strategic partner in projects in both the Hong Kong and mainland markets. The company felt there were synergies between our two companies. At the end of January 2013, Vanke and New World joined hands in winning the bid for a major project in Chai Wan's western district of Hong Kong. It beat out eight other Hong Kong financial groups including Cheung Kong, Sun Hung Kai, and Henderson Land Development with a winning bid of HKD 3.4 billion (USD 436 million).

In April 2013, Vanke signed a strategic agreement with the Singapore company Keppel Land. By cooperating in the development of the Gladers project, we entered the Singapore market. Our cooperation with Tishman Speyer, New World Development, and Keppel Land followed the same reasoning. First, we chose to work with industry leaders. Tishman Speyer was a global force in real estate, New World Development was a substantial financial force in Hong Kong, and Keppel Land was under the Temasek banner in Singapore. Second, we each contributed our own strengths to the partnership, making up for what the other lacked. Third, we simultaneously partnered on projects inside and outside China.

In an age of globalization, I believe that the competitiveness of any company depends on its ability to compete internationally. I am delighted that Vanke has taken this step. I am even more delighted that the eyes of Vanke people begin to shine when they realize how innovative their international partners are and what they can learn from their new models.

The Spirit of Contract

As Vanke has expanded internationally, I have been astonished at how fast our projects move forward. The San Francisco project with Tishman Speyer is a good example. We began talking at the end of 2012, signed an agreement in February 2013, and broke ground in June of that same year. What's more, my colleagues told me that the process of working with Tishman Speyer was extremely congenial. The relationship was smooth and easy, easier than working with many partners in China.

I believe that has partly to do with Vanke's experience of working with the Franklin Mint in the early days. That was back at the end of 1980, when the Franklin Mint approached us to see if we would work together in setting up a joint venture factory in value-added processing. The first time people from

Franklin Mint came to Shenzhen, they brought along with them a book-length contract. It specified every detail, down to the windows. I was not pleased about it, since this contract seemed to talk about how to split things up before we even began the business. At the time, Vanke's contracts were just a few pages long.

This contract taught us a good lesson, however, and Vanke's contracts also began to be book length after that. They covered every detail and every possible contingency. Several years later, we began to focus exclusively on the real estate business. We became the first real estate company to declare publicly in the prospectus for buildings and on-site display rooms that "we were not liable for unfavorable elements that went beyond the bounds of the red line." This all came from that lesson we had learned much earlier, about how to respect and abide by contracts. The ease with which Vanke was able to work with international partners may well be due to the extent to which Vanke believes in transparency and corporate institutions. These are in accord with abiding by contracts, and I believe that this whole concept is of ultimate importance in modern society.

In traditional societies, relationships among people depend on the moral imperative of respecting promises among a community of people who know one another well. As mobility increases, however, communities of people who are familiar with one another rapidly become communities of strangers. A society that respects the letter of the law, or the letter of a contract, then has the advantage. Strangers can rely on this new form of mutual trust. When adherents of this new approach come to the Chinese mainland and decide whom they want to work with, they generally choose partners that believe in their own set of principles.

This idea of abiding by the spirit of a contract can be traced back to the Bible. In the Bible, Esau and Jacob are the grandsons of Abraham. Esau is the elder, with a greater birthright than Jacob. One day, Esau comes home from hunting, tired and hungry, and Jacob says he will trade him his bowl of red bean soup for the authority of being the elder. By agreement between the two of them, Jacob now owns the birthright. Later, when Abraham wants to pass on the divine birthright to his sons, he can only transfer it to Jacob but not to Esau. Divine authority no longer trumps an agreement made in the secular sphere. In this ancient story, God is the sole judge, with decisive authority, but when two parties on earth conclude an agreement, that agreement takes precedence and must be followed.

After the religious reformation, new Christian beliefs further promoted the idea that all are equal under the eyes of the law. This became one of the great abiding principles of modernity. In the nineteenth century, the English scholar of jurisprudence, Henry Sumner Maine, noted that as advanced societies develop, they rely less on the authority of the clan and more on respect for the rights and duties of the individual person. That is, as societies advance, they move from reliance on status alone to respect for contracts.

Signing contracts as a way to agree on business is as ancient as humankind itself. Both ancient Rome and ancient China used law to govern the implementation of agreements, deeds, and contracts. However, in China these agreements, deeds, and contracts were based on social standing, on one's status. In ancient China, the Household Statute stated that "preferential rights go to relatives and neighbors in the canon of ownership." If a person wanted to sell a piece of land, he first had to consider the wishes of higher authority. Then he had to see if anyone within the family clan was willing to buy. Only then could he sell that land on the market. This respected the Confucian ideals of human relations, as incorporated into the legislation set forth by government. The state itself ultimately played the role of head of the family. It was appointed by heaven and so ruled by divine right, and in turn it decreed that its "children," the people, must be in their rightful place. The order of authority proceeded from the sovereign ruler to ministers to fathers to sons. When contracts were made among members of the people, the head of the family, the state, was involved. Such participation was to ensure that ethical principles as expressed by Confucian ideals were incorporated. This was how the will of the state realized the aim of taking care of the "family" and its more vulnerable members.

It is not uncommon to see similar examples in ancient Roman law. The Law of Twelve Tables, inscribed on bronze,* determined the authority of the patriarchal head of the family. The elder in a family or clan had a variety of special rights. For example, he was authorized to decide on the disposition of assets that belonged to others in the clan. The civil law of ancient Rome basically legislated only down to the level of clans and the male elders of clans, however. It adjudicated on the relationships among clan groupings. Status and familial relationships governed after that.

This approach was effective in traditional societies. In ancient Rome or in Song Dynasty China, a farmer might spend his entire life in one village. The scope of his life was determined the moment he was born. Sunrise and sunset were in their accustomed place. Naturally, this arrangement allowed for relationships of trust and mutual reliance that could endure on a long-term basis. So long as everyone played his proper role in life, society remained stable. In modern days, however, achieving trust by this method is not only inefficient but impossible. A modern society can only function through a different mechanism. It must enable people who are total strangers to cooperate with one another quickly and easily through the means of social contracts.

The psychological influence of traditional societies, however, is not something that goes away in just one or two generations. This is particularly true in later-to-develop countries that are being forced to modernize, not taking that initiative themselves. Concepts that operate according to the letter of contracts are not keeping pace with the speed at which social mobility is changing. Many people therefore attempt to use traditional means to cope with the challenges of modernization. That is the case in China.

---

*The *duodecim Tabulae* was the legislation that served as the foundation of Roman law by consolidating earlier traditions into a set of rules. It established procedural rights for all Roman citizens as against one another. The formation of this set of rules occurred around 450 B.C.E.

When Chinese people do business, they first focus on establishing a good rapport. For example, since you and I are strangers, we first have to get together to eat and drink, maybe sing karaoke and set up some personal bond. We have to recognize each other's personal caliber, value judgments, even family background—only then can we begin to cooperate. This was particularly true when reform and opening up had just begun in China. The situation is by now somewhat better in coastal areas of the southeast. In general, the traditional approach is more prevalent the closer one is to an agrarian society in which everyone knows one another.

Given that the beat of modern society is accelerating, how many close relationships can anyone set up and try to maintain? Even now, businesspeople are exhausted with all the entertaining they have to do. They scarcely have time to handle managing their internal corporate affairs, let alone focus on strategic matters. They already have to keep up too many relationships. For many smaller companies, the extent to which the company can grow still depends on how many social connections the boss can manage to maintain.

By now, any fairly large enterprises in China that are not state owned have in fact grown by getting away from this reliance on personal relationships. Instead of depending on their standing with individuals, they have set up modern corporate institutions and corporate governance structures. Such modern corporate systems are centered on the idea of contracts, on mechanisms that authorize agents to serve on the behalf of others. They do not rely on individuals or a web of personal relationships. This situation is unlike the old days in Shanxi, when the forerunners of Chinese banks, called *piao hao*, or note companies, would be required to resign en masse if the head of the bank departed. Back then, companies could only survive on the basis of personal relationships. Now, companies that operate on that basis alone cannot survive.

In order for there to be cooperation among strangers, the spirit of contracts must be respected at all levels, whether that be national, social, corporate, or individual. Such contracts are arrived at by informed consent, among entities that operate at their own will, with sufficient information and without intent to deceive. They are not subject to coercion by outside forces. They are signed voluntarily, and each signatory is then obliged to abide by the sacred obligations of the contract. Agreements so made are arrived at between equals. They do not rely on the standing or status of the parties and cannot be "discounted" in implementation due to the nearness or distance of relationships. Meanwhile, the state's responsibility is not to try to organize relationships among entities such that the weak and vulnerable are protected or such that close relationships are protected. Instead, it is to safeguard an environment in which contracts are implemented and respected.

China's Role in Warsaw

On November 19, 2013, the United Nations held a conference on climate change in Warsaw, Poland.

The conference was held in the sports stadium of the city, a building shaped somewhat like a crown. Lit up at night, it looked like a large transparent cake. Since public transport is convenient in the center of Warsaw, we could take the light rail to get back and forth between our hotel and the conference. Our way ran along the banks of the Vistula River, which reflected the evening lights back from an oily black surface. The river is no less polluted than those in China's interior. In the distance, we could see huge smokestacks pumping out thick smoke from a coal-fired hydroelectric plant. Historically, Poland has concentrated on developing heavy industry, and the country now has severe environmental problems.

When I first attended one of the meetings of the Copenhagen Agreement in 2009, several of us businesspeople from China took advantage of breaks during the meeting to look around. Companies and NGO organizations from various countries had set up their own pavilions to let other parts of the world know how their own country had progressed in protecting the environment. The European Union and American pavilions were the most strident. This time, in Warsaw, China too had a pavilion.

Indeed, this was the third occasion on which China had a "China Corner" in a global climate conference. On the first occasion, it was set up by the central-government state-owned enterprise, China Petroleum, and on the second by China Energy Conservation and Environmental Protection Group. This third time, Vanke ran the China Corner and organized two forums at the conference. Vanke began to be active in environmental protection in 2008, when it set up a cooperative relationship with the United Nations Environmental Programme (UNEP). This launched it onto the international stage.

When you walked in to the China Corner, there were no sofas to sit on and no coffee machine from which you could help yourself to coffee. Cardboard-type conceptual chairs expressed a desire to economize and preserve the environment. The top of the entryway was designed in the shape of smile. There were a few lines of calligraphy at the entrance but nothing more—no Vanke logo, no standard Vanke colors. The design just sketched out the contours of what could have been a minimalist gallery. This was a classic expression of Vanke's sense of aesthetics.

Vanke's style could be seen most expressively in a three-dimensional concrete sign that was put front and center: CHINA CORNER—WARSAW. The English caption next to this exhibit read: "China uses one-third of the concrete in the world. Concrete is the primary material used in construction—since it is so common, people often overlook it. It might be good to have more of a dialogue with this material. It should also be recognized that one-third of all energy consumed in China is consumed by construction."

This clearly was the work of Vanke's Architecture Research Center.

I was asked to speak at the corporate event, and I titled my presentation "Environmental Protection Is Far Harder Than Climbing Everest." My reason: climbing a mountain is an individual passion and an individual's contest with himself. Environmental protection cannot be done by one person alone.

It involves governments, corporations, and society at large. Once I started traveling abroad to study, I put aside the idea of climbing Everest a third time—scaling knowledge was far harder than scaling physical mountains and therefore more challenging. This was like the relationship between growing the economy and protecting the environment. Given scarce resources and scarce time, we collectively must make a choice. One of the choices is to try to grow the economy while putting more investment of time and energy into protecting the environment.

Four years earlier, I paid a call on the Greenpeace office in Beijing. I asked them how we might calculate the carbon footprint of Vanke's activities. They were astonished. Typically, Chinese corporations have avoided any contact with this organization. The person responsible for Greenpeace in China asked me why I had come. I said, "Vanke is the largest developer of residential housing in the world. It was inevitable that you and I should meet one day. It was better that I should come to you than that you should finally have to come looking for me."

After arriving in Warsaw, many foreign friends and members of the press asked me what role Vanke intended to play in this United Nations conference. In fact, we had already been playing a role. I first organized a meeting between the UNEP and some of China's privately run enterprises in 2008. I knew at that time that environmental protection was not just a matter for the United Nations, nor was it a matter just for governments. It was a matter that enterprises had to deal with. The matter was quite simple. Environmental protection is something we all must undertake. In coming to Warsaw, I told these people, I would just like others to know what Chinese entrepreneurs are thinking and what they are doing.

I continue to believe that the Copenhagen Agreement was a turning point. After this meeting, public opinion was disappointed in the United States as well as in China, but my take on things was different. I felt that the performance of China's government was worthy of applause. For Premier Wen Jiabao, as representative of the Chinese government, to announce a carbon emission reduction target by 2020 was an extremely high-minded move. Prior to this, China had protected itself by declaring itself to be a developing country so that it could be excluded from the constraints of the Kyoto Protocol, the international treaty that commits state parties to reduce greenhouse gas emissions. That China should now indicate it was willing to take on the responsibility of reducing emissions meant that it was setting forth a whole new role for itself. This role was dramatically different from before.

In Warsaw, I observed that the American pavilion had various kinds of advanced technologies on display. Technology is one thing, and it may well be that in this regard China is not as advanced as western industrialized nations. However, many of China's traditional values are in fact in line with modern notions of sustainability in western countries. Such traditional values are the wellsprings of ideas about sustainability that can be both low-cost and low-tech. Bamboo is one example. In traditional Chinese culture, bamboo has always represented aesthetic values and also ethical ideals. There is, for example, that line of the famous literati scholar, Su Shi: "I would rather live without meat than live without bamboo." As a rapidly renewable resource, bamboo is well documented as being an excellent construction material. Vanke has been promoting its use in green construction for some time.

Energy conservation in construction must look at two aspects. One is how to carry out construction, how to conserve energy in the course of building buildings. The other is deciding on what kind of buildings to build in the first place. In this latter regard, each country has its own standards. England, France, Germany, and the United States all have their own standards. China too has Three Star green building standards, which were published by the Ministry of Construction in 2007. These Three Star standards are not mandatory. One can choose whether or not to adopt them, but Vanke does adopt them.

Right now, Vanke is developing roughly 15 million square meters (almost 50 million square feet) of space every year. The government is adjusting, or holding down, real estate development in China. Against this overall backdrop, however, Vanke has not slowed the pace of its Three Star developments. Vanke holds just 2 percent of market share in all of China, but its share is critical. It enables us to recognize what the potential is for promoting green building in China.

As a country, China's green strategy remains focused on the limited areas of energy, automobiles, and oceans. In fact, however, energy consumed by construction accounts for one-third of all energy consumed in the country, and perhaps even more. The issue of whether or not construction can conserve energy is highly significant when it comes to environmental protection. China's traditional modes of building require enormous consumption of energy and resources—right now, therefore, Vanke's full efforts can only help China realize a 0.1 percent decrease in carbon emissions. In 2012, the Chinese government announced a goal of having 30 percent of new development projects incorporate green construction by 2020 and stated that subsidies would be available to meet that goal. This target will require the concerted efforts of all parties involved. If the entire industry can join us in the ranks of those developing through green construction methods, this will help China achieve a 12 percent decline in emissions by the year 2020.

Even with government subsidies, however, green building costs more than normal-type building, so there is opposition to it in the market. It takes time for environmental protection concepts to be absorbed and supported. Vanke's willingness to undertake the China Corner at Warsaw was an expression of its hope to be able to reach a broader range of people in promoting sustainable economic and social development, via the platform of the United Nations Climate Conference.

The Last Three Decades at Vanke—Past and Future Transformations

I was something of an anomaly when I studied at Harvard. As a Chinese entrepreneur, I was thinking about problems that were different from those of the normal student. The experience of studying at Harvard also exerted a subtle influence on my thinking about Vanke's future. I went there for my own self-cultivation, but at the same time I went not just as an individual but as a businessperson. The question I wanted to answer related to that second role, and it was "Where is Chinese business headed?" Through study, I hoped to be able to find some answers. In the past, my main concern had been to make the company a success. Now, I was more preoccupied with issues that lay behind success. Before, I sought to become, without thinking much about why has it been possible for us to become what we are, and what is next.

After founding Vanke, my management of the company owed a lot to the management of Japanese companies after World War II, companies such as Sony, Panasonic, and Toyota. Not only were they successful internationally but their culture had a profound impact on social development. I hoped that Vanke could become such a company, not just a supplier of goods and services. Could cultural factors be enough to answer such questions? My previous explorations of such issues had been inadequate. Given China's reform and opening-up policies, its market economy, and the fact that Vanke is a private company, was it going to be possible for Vanke to influence events in ways that Sony and Toyota were able to do? In the past, I had thought this might be possible. Now, I felt that these factors did not add up to an answer.

In the past, my management approach was utilitarian. Modern industry, and modernization itself, was the product of western civilization, so my natural response was to study western ways. Indeed, I distanced myself from traditional Chinese culture. What's more, the Cultural Revolution erupted just as I was being educated, and I failed to learn much of anything. In contrast, nothing blocked my way when I later studied western concepts and tried to apply them to Vanke. I felt that such things as operating under the light of day and not taking bribes were patently obvious. If I could not undertake them in China, then I would simply internationalize. By developing international business I would be able to avoid the limitations of the Chinese market.

When Vanke invested in the joint venture in San Francisco, everything about that project went smoothly. In fact, I was astonished by how easy it was. The reason is not hard to imagine. Inside China, we found it extremely difficult when we tried to adhere to the values of a modern commercial society yet still had to operate within a less-than-perfect and less-than-modern society. Nevertheless, we did it. Once I started operating in a market environment that was mature and institutionalized, it was a piece of cake. Things that I managed to accomplish in a tough environment were simple in an environment that was standardized, transparent, and predictable. This was a comfortable change.

If I kept on doing this kind of project, would that resolve all problems for Vanke? No, not at all. I had always admired Nokia, for example, yet this company suddenly had problems. A number of creative American companies had sprung up, taking a dominant position. It seemed that corporate brands in other countries might flourish for a while, but real leadership and innovative drive still resided in America. Just because you were ahead for a short time did not guarantee that you would always be the leader. Reform and opening up in China were a major dividend for companies like us, and the Chinese market was huge. It was due to these advantages that Vanke had become the largest residential developer in the world.

Right now, Chinese companies rank among the top 10 in many industries. Does our competitive ability really justify being in the top 10? Does Vanke really merit the rank of number one in the world? No, it does not. The question Vanke needs to reflect upon now is: how can it go from being number one in mere quantity to being better in quality? Vanke must participate in China's urbanization in ways that reflect a quality contribution.

Prior to 2013, Vanke was in the position of being able to sell everything it wanted to sell. It put all its efforts into selling more, and bringing in revenues. In 2010, Vanke's sales volume reached RMB 100 billion (USD 14.79 billion). In 2011, we wanted to control that figure, and we settled on a plan not to exceed RMB 140 billion (USD 21.77 billion). In fact, the sales figure we actually achieved was just RMB 120 billion (USD 18.66 billion). This was not intentional, however—we had to work as hard as we could just to sell that much. Essential changes had already occurred in the market.

Senior management in the company and I are united in thinking that Vanke's main aim should not be to increase quantity but rather to improve quality. Vanke must achieve a transformation in its growth mode, from quantitative change to qualitative change. This is very much in line with the national policy of upgrading China's overall mode of economic growth, as the country modernizes. Second, we believe that Vanke should give concerted attention to the uncertainties of the market. We are in the midst of the intensification of a market bubble. I am extremely worried that China may take the same path that Japan took in the latter part of the 1980s. At that time, Japan's middle class represented a large percentage of the population, however, while the same is not true in China. In China, the disparity between rich and poor is already large. If the bubble bursts, the consequences will be far more severe in China than they were in Japan.

Enormous opportunities exist in China's process of urbanization. In addition to just building excellent residential housing, Vanke can and should plan its own future in ways that allow it to participate in the building of public infrastructure and urban services. It should become a supplier of auxiliary urban services. For example, as the company builds commercial districts within communities, it should consider how these add value to the community and how they make the lives of residents more comfortable. Such things as water treatment and garbage treatment should be opportunities for company growth.

Around the year 2000, Vanke successfully transformed itself from being a diversified company to one focused on the real estate industry. Now, it must achieve a similar transformation as it goes from being a quantity-oriented to a quality-oriented company. In terms of employee structure, Vanke focused on sales in the past—the great majority of people in its real estate business were salespeople. We gradually have been transferring that function to outside agents and will in fact no longer have a sales team. Engineers have already become the largest single category of employees. Among more than 6,000 employees, more than 40 percent are engineers. Vanke in fact has more engineers than some very large construction companies.

The Vanke that I have in mind, the kind of company that I am hoping for, is oriented around technology. We aim to make Vanke into a research-driven company.

At Cambridge

I arrived at Cambridge University in October 2013 to start a new adventure in learning. Prior to then, I already had a feel for a certain constraint that characterizes English people, and was somewhat prepared for a different culture in England. Once I arrived and saw people in long robes, impeccably courteous to one another, however, I was apprehensive. Americans are so open and enthusiastic, so unconcerned about manners. I had grown accustomed to that. Chinese are not punctilious about table manners and not too familiar with how to use a knife and fork—this was not a problem in the United States. Americans can be quite casual even at a banquet. They will pick things up with their fingers and nobody notices. The skill with which English people use a knife and fork is altogether different, since it must be done in just such a way. Dressing is the same. Americans are casual, even professors on campus sometimes, while this does not happen at Cambridge University. Ancient customs are highly entrenched, including such rituals as the donning of long gowns. People even use the term "town and gown" to differentiate people in academia from regular citizens. Harvard had been unrestrained compared to Cambridge University, which has over 800 years of history behind it, all kinds of "regulations, taboos, and commandments."* It also is quite class conscious. Would I fit in?

To my surprise, I acclimated to Cambridge very quickly. After my experience at Harvard, I was an old hand at setting up my courses, getting into the discipline of studying, getting in touch with professors and tutors on my own, and living a solitary but highly fulfilled life. I quickly took to the rhythm. Since I had

---

*The term is generally used in the context of Taoist and Buddhist monasteries.

started from near zero at Harvard, I had an initial period of stage fright there and, despite a native ability to take the initiative, I simply didn't. At Cambridge, I already had a good foundation. Not only could I take action, but I did, which opened new horizons in studies and life in general.

I had decided to study Judaism, in both religious and cultural aspects, and therefore wanted to choose the right college for the subject. The demands of Pembroke College of Cambridge University were extremely rigorous. Professor Simon Learmount provided me with a list of the reading requirements and a glance at it seemed to have nothing to do with Judaism. On closer examination, however, I realized that these books were more about the methodology of how to study and how to write essays, for someone who had not ever been systematically trained in such things. One month later, the school advised me on which courses and professors would be best for learning about various aspects of Judaism. The guidance was extremely beneficial. Cambridge placed high demands on a visiting scholar but provided a clear path for learning, which left a deep impression on me.

The assistance made me think back to my time at Harvard and the way things had worked there. Harvard has a tradition of setting a new student up with an older mentor, also a student but one who provides guidance in course selection and how to get along in every way. Since I was neither an undergraduate nor a graduate student, I did not have such a person to help me. After coming to Harvard, I had a great deal of contact with Chang Zheng. As a previous Vanke employee, he would often come over to see his old boss, and he was happy and willing to help me out. Given these frequent contacts, we unconsciously settled into the pattern of young novice, me, and old hand, him.

I encountered many wonderful professors at Cambridge. Pembroke College introduced a particular tutor to help improve my English. His manner of teaching was unique and extremely effective, something like that film about how King George VI learned to get over his stutter. I had never been trained this way nor had I ever learned so quickly. At the outset, I told this professor that I had studied American English and was unfamiliar with British English. He responded, "There is no such thing as American English. There are only two kinds of English: one is British English, and the other is incorrect English!"

Dress was a major problem at Cambridge. One example was the event just before the Christmas holidays, a gathering of professors and students to which I was invited. The invitation specified "black tie." I confirmed this with my secretary—yes, black tie. Not sure about this, I assumed it had to mean formal evening attire, which I wore to the dinner. I also, however, took a bag with casual clothes along with me, just in case I was wrong. Before going into the hall, I peeked and saw that my first guess had been right—formal attire. In almost everything, Cambridge was very class conscious. Only fellows of a given college could park their cars outside the gates of that college, or could park their bicycles near the gates, or indeed could even walk on the grass of that college. At formal occasions, people lined up in order of rank, as shown by the type of gown they wore. Every evening at dinner, the head of the college would ring a bell and then stand and say a prayer in Latin. If he happened to be absent, the next in line of seniority would give the invocation. When people stood in line, they stood in order, and a glance at the robes showed that everyone was in his proper place. Theoretically, if all the professors and students had been absent and I were the only one left, that would have been a major problem. Not only do I not pray, but I certainly do not understand Latin!

Some of these traditions at Cambridge were part of a formal system, but others were established through common usage. I gradually came to realize that they did not define an administrative or personal ranking so much as they defined levels of scholarship. They were actually an expression of an extreme respect for knowledge. They paid homage to the contribution that knowledge makes to the world. They created an environment in which one felt the strong power of culture.

"I think, therefore I am." Rational reflection is a fundamental attribute that makes humans what they are. When people are irrational, they cease to be human. The result of rational reflection is expressed through discovering knowledge and also creating knowledge. The discovery and creation of knowledge are what make people human, and they enable humanity to advance civilization in ways that the animal world cannot.

The ongoing accumulation of specialized knowledge and skill represents civilization's greatest wealth. In China, the critical impasse the country now faces is transitioning from development that is essentially "extensive" to growth that proceeds through the application of specialized knowledge. The level of a society's civilization can be seen in the way people answer the question "What does this society most highly respect?" When the answer is "officials," you have a society that regards officials as the gold standard. The highest praise that a parent can hear in such a society is that their child has the look of an official and will grow up to be one.

Such a society puts administrative officials in charge in any institute of higher learning. Such a society accords officials with power, resources, and the envy of the people. However, officials can only allocate wealth and safeguard public order. They do not create wealth or knowledge. A society that takes officials as the gold standard is one that cannot make sustained breakthroughs in knowledge. It is a society that cannot achieve sustainable growth. Only when those who bring forth new knowledge and new forms of wealth are most highly respected in a society will people's energies flow in the direction of innovations in knowledge as well as business. China's most fundamental institutional reform in the future will have to involve this kind of restructuring of society's values, what society respects and what it rejects. These things are what in fact will guide the allocation of resources.

Only two of all the professors and visiting scholars at Cambridge University were Chinese, and I was one of them. The other was a Chinese academician, and indeed the first Chinese academician at Cambridge. He had graduated there and then gone on to be successful in business. He returned to Cambridge to set up a private college. This college has 800 students and is mainly oriented toward taking in students from third-world countries. After he and I got to know each another, he expressed surprise that everyone at Cambridge seemed to know me. As an academician, he had his own parking space at college yet had few dealings with Cambridge professors, despite his many years there. I quickly understood why: he ate at home, while I ate at school. I threw myself into the local lifestyle, because I loved it and I also felt that the food at Cambridge was much better than at Harvard. I always ate western food, while this academician preferred Chinese food at home. I had mingled with English people over the past three months, and they would always greet me when we saw one another, whereas this highly successful old-school Chinese person had no way of penetrating these circles. Behind this lay his inability to eat western food. In fact, eating with professors was a wonderful way to get to know one another—a small glass of red wine is always an opportunity to connect, and often a meal would stretch on till 10 in the evening as ideas and good humor kept flowing. Unfortunately, the Chinese academician missed out on the pleasure of making friends, and he missed the chance to establish mutual connections.

Interacting with people in this way often provided surprising glimpses of new things. One time I sat next to a 91-year-old former professor, a renowned expert on cuckoos. I was amazed. I had heard of experts in ornithology, but I did not know that the specialization went down to cuckoos. I noted that the bird was rare in China, but was still taken as a harbinger of spring. When people heard a cuckoo, they began to prepare the fields for planting. He told me that quite the contrary was true in Europe, where the bird was regarded as an ill omen and was something to avoid. If two people heard a cuckoo, the one who ran faster could get to safety. The one who ran slower would be struck with disaster. We spent many happy times at table sharing such amusing bits of information.

Vanke used to have a saying: if you want to punish someone, send him overseas with the chairman of the board! I always immerse myself in new things as I go along—I always eat the local food in particular, which many colleagues find difficult to do. In fact, I found out once that some colleagues would force themselves to eat western food with me, then sneak back to have their own Chinese meal. I myself found that eating western food is an extremely important part of learning western culture. If you are not willing to accommodate yourself to that, how are you going to adapt? If you want to be able to embrace the world out there, you must first embrace its appetite. Embracing the appetites of others allowed me smooth entry into inner circles at Cambridge.

If you insist on maintaining your own singular customs, you shut the door to the outside world. Opening yourself, absorbing new things, allows entry into a whole new universe. From the time I founded a company in Shenzhen, to my studies in the United States and England, I maintained a strong sense of curiosity about the world. I delighted in communicating, sharing, connecting, trying to understand, and absorbing. As the saying goes, "The ocean can accommodate one hundred rivers." New knowledge and new emotions gave me new resources and also new strength.

When I was 52 and came back down from climbing Mount Everest, I told a reporter, "Fifty is just the start of the splendid years in a person's life." Now I feel that 60 is just the start.

My advice, to others and myself, is to open yourself up. Transform yourself. Recognize that the search for perfection also allows for imperfections, but keep going.

Vanke came through a major crisis around the time of the company's tenth anniversary, namely the "Jun-Van conflict." By the time of Vanke's twentieth anniversary, I had come to the conclusion that the company would no longer have to experience such thrilling events. Instead, it would be like Coca-Cola or GE, companies that were not subject to rumor-mongering and takeovers. From now on, Vanke would grow in deliberate steps and according to its own internal logic. Four years before Vanke's thirtieth anniversary, it achieved the target of RMB 100 billion (USD 14.86 billion) in sales. The company then smoothly surpassed the milestone of RMB 200 billion (USD 20.73 billion). By that time, it was no longer aiming for purely quantitative goals. Instead, Vanke people were beginning to think of how to position the company in the coming decade, how to take on greater social responsibility, and how to internationalize in a strong and stable way.

On June 25, 2014, after a year and a half of hard work, Vanke finally completed the transition from B shares to Hong Kong H shares. It became the third China mainland company to achieve this. It began trading on the Hong Kong Stock Exchange with a code of 02202.HK.

Vanke first issued B shares back in 1993. Back then, this special kind of RMB-denominated stock was being promoted by the Chinese government as a new innovation, and nobody knew how things would develop in the future. Once controls over the issuing of H shares were relaxed, B shares quickly withered as a way to finance a company. The last new B shares were issued in 1999, and since that time B shares have remained dormant. They basically lost the function of helping a company raise funds as well as restructure through mergers and acquisitions. They became less meaningful as a way to help companies grow.

Vanke's B shares were therefore no longer able to support Vanke's growth. This was particularly true with respect to the company's new internationalization strategy. In addition to that consideration was the fact that Hong Kong's capital markets could provide Vanke with a vast platform for growing its business. Implementing the plan to turn B shares into H shares would raise the name-recognition value of the company and would strengthen the company's international business. The use of external funding sources and the stimulation of external markets would help strengthen Vanke's core competitiveness. At the shareholder's meeting in February of 2013, a resolution to turn B shares into H shares therefore passed, with more than 99 percent of shareholders voting in favor.

Naturally, the process was not all smooth sailing. As the saying goes, all good things require a certain amount of refining and polishing before they come to fruition. It took a year for the China Securities Regulatory Commission to grant official approval for Vanke's plan. It took another three months for the Listing Department in the Hong Kong Stock Exchange to pass. For a year and a half, Vanke lived with the risk of failure at any time. Among the risks was the lack of effective cooperation from external parties. The company had to push forward the process very patiently while protecting investors' interests as well as respecting their right to know what was going on.

Most dealers had a good opinion of the investment value of Vanke's H shares. The four main investment banks rated them a "buy." On the day Vanke's B shares were turned into H shares, Vanke's H shares rose by 7 percent and continued to rise the following day. On August 4, 2014, the closing price was 12.4 percent higher than the opening price had been on June 25. This steady rise in value made it clear that the shift from one stock exchange to another had been successful.

Meanwhile, far away in Milan, Italy, Vanke was just beginning the construction phase of the Vanke pavilion at Milan Expo 2015. In the 164 years of world expos, Vanke was the first Chinese company to participate by building its own pavilion. Vanke had been a co-investor in other overseas construction projects before in order to develop its international business, including projects in New York, San Francisco, and Singapore. This was the first project that Vanke was undertaking on its own and the first in which it was handling the entire process.

In undertaking this project, Vanke was attempting to find its own form of expression, one that could be understood easily by people who come from both Chinese and western cultures. For this reason, the company did not put any restrictions on the designers working on the project, other than the general idea that this was to be a "canteen," a place to eat. Designers were to use their own imagination to express this overall theme.

Since the design team came from diverse cultural backgrounds, many of its members did not understand Vanke's concept of a canteen until the very end. But this lifestyle concept did not faze architect Daniel Libeskind. He was able to derive raw material from China's agricultural heritage as well as from his own experience of collective life on an Israeli kibbutz and come up with the form of a coiled dragon for the building. The concept also did not hold back the exhibition design team at Ralph Appelbaum Associates (RAA). Based on the concept of a canteen, they aimed at interpreting and realizing the atmosphere of China's traditional approach to gathering together to enjoy a meal. The results were well received by the western audience. The concept was transmitted effectively. It merged various levels of abstract and concrete expression. As Vanke offered up this new kind of meal to its guests, it also continued to test its own abilities.

In this age of globalization, we often have the impression that we already fully understand one another. In fact, this understanding is both marvelously familiar and refreshingly new. An example might be the young child who visited the pavilion and saw the Chinese noodles on display. "Look, spaghetti!" he said to his mother.

During the 184 days that the Vanke pavilion was open to the public, it hosted 10 events that centered on the theme of urbanization, it held 48 events that brought together Chinese and foreign companies, and it hosted some 440,000 visitors.

Naturally commerce must obey its own laws, and Vanke did not intend for this activity to serve merely as a platform for enabling interaction with others, a way for it to be a cultural ambassador. Instead, the motivation related to honing the most fundamental driving force behind the company's growth and development. Vanke needed to explore a new path for itself as it faced the Internet economy and the megatrends of a changing real estate business. My aim for the Vanke pavilion was very simple: I wanted it to be a vehicle for training our troops. Despite being a temporary structure that encompassed less than 1,000 square meters (3,280 square feet) of space, the pavilion involved all aspects of a real-life project. In building it, Vanke had to respect all the laws of international markets. It had to come in on budget and on time. It had to develop the ability to pull together global resources.

In the summer of 2015, even as Vanke's pavilion shone under Milan's splendid sunshine, however, dark clouds were gathering elsewhere. Unexpectedly, they drew ever closer to the Vanke headquarters at Dameisha in Shenzhen.

On July 10, 2015, a company controlled by the Baoneng Group announced that it had purchased a 5 percent interest in Vanke. It did this by purchasing 553 million A shares on the secondary market. That company was the Foresea Life Insurance, which thereby reached the 5 percent "red line" that must make its stake public as mandated by the China Securities Regulatory Commission.

At the time, the Chinese stock market was at a low ebb after going through a stock market crisis. Two weeks after this announcement, even as people were absorbing the news and trying to figure out what it meant, another company controlled by the Baoneng Group announced that it too had purchased a 5 percent interest in Vanke. This mysterious company, called Jushenghua, then linked up with Foresea Life to control a 10 percent interest in Vanke shares.

What was Baoneng up to? Vanke tried to communicate with the company, but it was unable to get any clear answer to this question. It analyzed funding sources for these purchases. In its early years, Baoneng had also been in the real estate business, but it had a scale of operations, name recognition, and credibility that were considerably less than those of Vanke. The company only later went into insurance and became a player on capital markets. The funds of Foresea Life came mainly from universal life insurance, which had grown tremendously in recent years in China. Meanwhile, the capital from Jushenghua had come from asset management products of brokers and wealth investment products from banks. According to the estimate of J.P. Morgan, Baoneng leveraged these funds by 4.2 times in order to purchase Vanke shares.

Given the unclear intentions of Baoneng, Vanke's senior management flew to Hong Kong to solicit the support of its major shareholder, China Resources. Baoneng acted quickly, however, raising its holdings to 15 percent. This made it the largest shareholder in Vanke, with holdings that now surpassed those of

China Resources. Five days later, China Resources in turn made a move and increased its holdings to 15.29 percent, slightly more than Baoneng's 15.04 percent. It thereby briefly returned to the position of being Vanke's largest shareholder. After that, however, it did not continue to increase its holdings.

As Vanke was carrying on talks with China Resources, evaluating such options as issuing more shares and restructuring its capital, Baoneng intensified the voltage of its attacks. In early December, it increased its ownership of Vanke shares to more than 20 percent and swiftly began to approach 25 percent. This left China Resources behind and unable to catch up, given that Vanke's shares had now appreciated by close to 70 percent within half a month's time. During this time, another insurance company in China, the Anbang Group, had also purchased 6.18 percent of Vanke's shares.

Given the extraordinary circumstances, which made it impossible for China Resources to carry out a restructuring plan, Vanke applied for a temporary halt to trading. It also began talks with another large company in Shenzhen, the Shenzhen Metro Group, in an attempt to find an alternative solution.

Shenzhen Metro had an abundance of land supply in the center of Shenzhen, while Vanke had more than two decades of experience in developing real estate. The basis for cooperation was obvious, but specific details on how to cooperate had to take interests of all sides into account. After half a year of planning and preparation, the preliminary proposal put forth by Vanke was passed by Vanke's board of directors. The proposal involves having Vanke issue more shares in order to acquire part of the land resource of Shenzhen Metro. Although the formal proposal still requires the approval of the board of directors and the shareholders' meeting, Vanke is confident that it has found a window of opportunity through which it can resolve this incident.

Vanke shares resumed trading on July 4, 2016, at which time Baoneng increased its holdings to 25 percent. This means that it could not sell its Vanke shares within a year, according to China's stock market regulations. Everyone assumed that this was prelude to a major turning point in the action. In early August, however, another Chinese company named Evergrande suddenly increased its holdings in Vanke to 6.82 percent. Evergrande has not yet revealed its intentions, and the entry of this new actor onto the stage has introduced yet another variable into the state of play.

As the English version of this book goes to press, Vanke has for the first time joined the ranks of the Fortune 500. It ranks 356 of corporations around the globe in terms of revenue. Although the situation with respect to its shareholding is still an ongoing issue and the company's future holds many uncertainties, one thing is certain. Since its founding in 1984, Vanke has served as a miniature of the course of reform and opening up in contemporary China. It has weathered all the turbulence. As the song goes, "You see rainbows after a storm." We can all hope that there is indeed a bright tomorrow on the horizon.

China Merchants Bureau, Yuan Geng, and Shekou

The first large enterprise set up by the Qing-dynasty government in the nineteenth century was called the China Merchants Bureau. It was established in 1872 by the great minister Li Hongzhang. Together with two other enterprises, this was one of the three large commercial institutions of late-Qing-dynasty China.

The company continued to exist through the vicissitudes of Minguo China (1911 to 1949) and the People's Republic of China (1949 to today). Its business was modest but the name continued, and in 1979 its twenty-ninth chairman of the board became a man named Yuan Geng.

Yuan Geng came from a military background. He participated in the liberation of the Pearl River delta area and in 1949 was part of the liberating force in Shenzhen. In 1955 he served in China's foreign service in Jakarta. During the Cultural Revolution (1966–1976), due to his "crime of being an international spy," he was put in jail in Beijing for seven years. He was released after the fall of the Gang of Four and appointed as head of China Merchants. Shortly afterward he presented a courageous report to the government.

This was handed to the Politburo and to the State Council on October 9, 1978. It recommended opening to the outside and allowing people to do trade. On January 31, 1979, Yuan Geng met with officials in Zhongnanhai. He brought a map. "The China Merchants Bureau has next to nothing to show for it after being established for 106 years," he said. "What I need is a piece of land. It will be made into an industrial zone that combines the benefits of China's cheap land and labor with overseas capital and technical expertise. It should be in the area of Hong Kong."

A pen summarily drew a large circle in the southern coastal area, and Yuan Geng said it was too big. The line was then narrowed down to the peninsula of Shekou. "We give this to you," they said.

This land was accompanied by certain privileges: Yuan Geng had authority to approve projects under the amount of USD 5 million by himself. He was allowed to borrow money from foreign banks. None of this was written into the standard government plan.

Due to Yuan Geng's efforts, Shekou was already up and running when Shenzhen was set up as a Special Economic Zone six months later. One man, of relatively low rank, was successful in pushing China into setting up its first "open zone" as a model for what was to come later. It was as if he picked up the stitches, the knits and the purls, where they had stopped so many years earlier. He did not start from scratch: he had the patterns already in mind.

Credit: by the Chinese author Wu Xiaobo, an unpublished excerpt translated by M. Avery

INDEX